Public–Private Partnerships for Infrastructure Development

Public–Private Partnerships for Infrastructure Development

Finance, Stakeholder Alignment, Governance

Edited by

Raymond E. Levitt

Operating Partner at Blackthorn Ventures, LLC and formerly Kumagai Professor of Engineering Emeritus, Stanford University, USA

W. Richard Scott

Professor Emeritus of Sociology, recalled to active duty in the Department of Civil and Environmental Engineering, Stanford University, USA

Michael J. Garvin

Professor, Via Department of Civil and Environmental Engineering, Virginia Tech, USA

Cheltenham, UK • Northampton, MA, USA

© Raymond E. Levitt, W. Richard Scott and Michael J. Garvin 2019

All rights reserved. No part of this publication may be reproduced, stored in a retrieval system or transmitted in any form or by any means, electronic, mechanical or photocopying, recording, or otherwise without the prior permission of the publisher.

Published by
Edward Elgar Publishing Limited
The Lypiatts
15 Lansdown Road
Cheltenham
Glos GL50 2JA
UK

Edward Elgar Publishing, Inc.
William Pratt House
9 Dewey Court
Northampton
Massachusetts 01060
USA

Paperback edition 2020

A catalogue record for this book
is available from the British Library

Library of Congress Control Number: 2018967815

This book is available electronically in the Elgaronline
Social and Political Science subject collection
DOI 10.4337/9781788973182

ISBN 978 1 78897 317 5 (cased)
ISBN 978 1 78897 318 2 (eBook)
ISBN 978 1 80037 732 5 (paperback)

Typeset by Servis Filmsetting Ltd, Stockport, Cheshire
Printed and bound by CPI Group (UK) Ltd, Croydon, CR0 4YY

Contents

List of contributors	vii
Preface	ix

Introduction: PPPs – theoretical challenges and directions forward   1
W. Richard Scott, Raymond E. Levitt and Michael J. Garvin

PART I   PUBLIC–PRIVATE PARTNERSHIPS: DEFINITIONS, MYTHS AND INSTITUTIONAL CHALLENGES

1. Public–private partnerships for infrastructure delivery   19
   Ashby H.B. Monk, Raymond E. Levitt, Michael J. Garvin, Andrew J. South and George Carollo

2. Stakeholder network dynamics in public–private partnerships   35
   Andrew J. South, Raymond E. Levitt and Geert P.M.R. Dewulf

3. Toward a unified theory of project governance: economic, sociological and psychological supports for relational contracting   60
   Witold J. Henisz, Raymond E. Levitt and W. Richard Scott

4. Stakeholders, issues and the shaping of large engineering projects   87
   Wen Feng, Donald R. Lessard, Bruce G. Cameron and Edward F. Crawley

PART II   GOVERNANCE MECHANISMS IN PPP PLANNING, DELIVERY, CONTRACTING AND MANAGEMENT

5. Mitigating PPP governance challenges: lessons from eastern Australia   104
   Raymond E. Levitt and Kent Eriksson

6. Contractual risk sharing mechanisms in US highway PPP projects   121
   Duc A. Nguyen and Michael J. Garvin

PART III LEVERAGING INSTITUTIONAL CAPITAL AND GOVERNMENTAL FISCAL SUPPORT FOR PPPs TO ENABLE THE "GOLDEN HANDSHAKE"

7 The role of institutional investors in financing PPP infrastructure 142
   Ashby H.B. Monk and Rajiv Sharma

8 Framework to assess fiscal support mechanisms for mitigating revenue risk in transportation public–private partnerships 170
   Ting Liu and Michael J. Garvin

PART IV THE EVOLUTION OF MATURE PPP INSTITUTIONAL FIELDS

9 (Re)assessing public–private partnership governance challenges: an institutional maturity perspective 188
   Carter B. Casady, Kent Eriksson, Raymond E. Levitt and W. Richard Scott

10 Transportation public–private partnership market in the United States: moving beyond its current state 205
    Michael J. Garvin

11 Private participation in US infrastructure: the role of regional PPP units 224
    Carter B. Casady and R. Richard Geddes

PART V EMERGING TOOLS FOR INFRASTRUCTURE PROJECT FINANCE AND DELIVERY

12 The financier state: infrastructure planning and asset recycling in New South Wales, Australia 246
    Caroline Nowacki

13 Community investment and crowdfunding as partnership strategies for local infrastructure delivery 265
    Kate E. Gasparro

Bibliography 282
Index 327

Contributors

Bruce G. Cameron, Lecturer, System Design and Management, Massachusetts Institute of Technology, Cambridge, MA, USA.

George Carollo, Co-Founder, TopFunnel, Inc., San Francisco, CA, USA.

Carter B. Casady, PhD Candidate, Department of Civil and Environmental Engineering, Stanford University, Stanford, CA, USA.

Edward F. Crawley, Ford Professor of Engineering, Department of Aeronautics and Astronautics, Massachusetts Institute of Technology, Cambridge, MA, USA.

Geert P.M.R. Dewulf, Dean of Engineering and Professor of Civil Engineering, University of Twente, Enschede, Netherlands.

Kent Eriksson, Professor, School of Architecture and the Built Environment, KTH Royal Institute of Technology, Stockholm, Sweden.

Wen Feng, Assistant Mayor, Chaoyang District People's Government of Beijing Municipality, P.R. China.

Michael J. Garvin, Associate Professor, Department of Civil and Environmental Engineering, Virginia Tech, Blacksburg, VA, USA.

Kate E. Gasparro, PhD Candidate, Civil and Environmental Engineering Department, Stanford University, Stanford, CA, USA.

R. Richard Geddes, Professor and Director of the Cornell Program in Infrastructure Policy, Cornell University, Ithaca, NY, USA.

Witold J. Henisz, Deloitte & Touche Professor of Management, The Wharton School, University of Pennsylvania, Philadelphia, PA, USA.

Donald R. Lessard, Epoch Foundation Professor of International Management, Emeritus, Sloan School of Management, Massachusetts Institute of Technology, Cambridge, MA, USA.

Raymond E. Levitt, Kumagai Professor of Engineering Emeritus and Academic Director, Global Projects Center, Stanford University, Stanford, CA, USA and Operating Partner, Blackhorn Ventures, LLC since 2017.

Ting Liu, Investment Manager, China Communications Construction Company, Beijing, China.

Ashby H.B. Monk, Executive Director, Global Projects Center, Stanford University, Stanford, CA, USA.

Duc A. Nguyen, Faculty, Dept. of Civil & Industrial Construction, University of Civil Engineering, Ha Noi, Viet Nam.

Caroline Nowacki, PhD Candidate, Civil and Environmental Engineering Department, Stanford University, Stanford, CA, USA.

W. Richard Scott, Professor Emeritus, Department of Sociology, Stanford University, Stanford, CA, USA.

Rajiv Sharma, Research Director, Global Projects Center, Stanford University, Stanford, CA, USA.

Andrew J. South, PhD Candidate, Civil and Environmental Engineering Department, Stanford University, Stanford, CA, USA.

Preface

A decade after the global financial crisis of 2008, most governments worldwide are still facing severe fiscal and financial constraints. At the same time, burgeoning populations in emerging economies and rapid urbanization everywhere are putting huge strains on old and obsolete infrastructure in mature market economies and on already stressed infrastructure in emerging market economies. Large institutional investors such as pension funds and sovereign funds that collectively control as much as $100 trillion in investable assets are struggling to find prudent investments that can yield the roughly 8 percent per annum overall return on investments that their actuarial calculations require them to achieve, when fixed income investments are yielding zero or negative real returns. Privately developed and operated infrastructure, with its relatively high, long-term, risk-adjusted returns and its steady and inflation-adjusted cash flows, is an almost perfect match with their obligations.

Privately financed, developed and operated toll roads, toll bridges, ferries and other infrastructure were commonly employed in the United States (US) during colonial times, and in Europe as early as the 1200s; the Old Stone Bridge across the Danube in Regensberg that the Crusaders paid to cross is one example. However, since the 1800s, infrastructure became regarded as a natural monopoly that needed to be owned and operated – or at least heavily regulated – by governments. Thus many countries' governments have taken over the roles of planning, financing and operating infrastructure, outsourcing primarily their design and construction. Given governments' constraints, the public–private partnership (PPP) model, in which private consortia are granted concessions to finance, design, build, operate and maintain infrastructure that the government owns and regulates, has emerged as a new way to deliver and govern infrastructure assets. But delivering public infrastructure services via this kind of cross-sectoral partnerships raises many governance challenges that require new levels of knowledge, skill and capacity for the governments to procure them wisely, for the investors to deploy their capital prudently and efficiently, and for the consortia that deliver them to balance private economic interests against public benefits prudently.

Over the decade from 2008 to 2018 scholars associated with Stanford University's Global Projects Center (GPC) have been studying ways to enhance the governance of PPP projects for infrastructure service delivery at three levels: (1) enhancing governments' decision-making processes to prioritize needs for infrastructure assets rationally rather than based on local politics, and governmental agency capacity building to procure PPP infrastructure effectively; (2) capacity building and governance of institutional investors to allow them to invest prudently and effectively in infrastructure assets directly, rather than investing passively through intermediaries such as investment banks; and (3) governance of the special purpose vehicles to address conflicts of interest between debt and equity investors, and between pure financial investors and the industrial partners who design, build, operate and maintain the infrastructure so that private benefits can be equitably balanced against the public interest.

THE GLOBAL PROJECTS CENTER AT STANFORD UNIVERSITY

With start-up support from the Dean of Humanities and Sciences and Dean of Engineering, the GPC was able to bring together Stanford faculty, research associates, visiting scholars, postdocs and doctoral students from multiple departments in five of its schools who were interested in studying the complex phenomena and governance challenges associated with PPP delivery of global infrastructure projects. Beyond pulling together a multi-disciplinary research collaboration of almost unprecedented breadth from Stanford, the GPC – originally called the Collaboratory for Research on Global Projects – was fortunate to be able to engage scholars from multiple universities in the US, Europe, Asia, Africa and Australia in our program of research who had similar interests and who were able to provide us with access to study global projects in their regions; hence the initial name "Collaboratory." We changed the Center's name to the Global Projects Center in 2008 after a journalist from the *New York Times* suggested that our Center's original name was way too long, and told us that, in any case, he was unsure how to spell "Collaboratory."

At the same time, the GPC was extremely fortunate to find strong encouragement, support and guidance from senior managers in some of the world's largest engineering and construction companies, international law firms, financial and management consultants, multilateral banks, investment banks, sovereign wealth funds and pension funds. They verified that the problems we were interested to study were real and important to them, helped to guide and focus our research directions, and provided us with unparalleled access to their employees and projects across the globe. The tremendous intellectual, financial and in-kind support that these real-world players have continuously provided to the GPC since its founding significantly grounded and hugely leveraged the worldwide academic resources that the GPC could bring to bear on this program of research.

Work conducted under the umbrella of the Global Projects Center has evolved through several phases over its nearly 20 years of existence. During the early 2000s, research focused on the specific challenges posed for management when workers were engaged in projects requiring the collaboration of multiple specialists, as opposed to workers in a departmental structure who were engaged in similar or identical functional tasks. Building on the work of previous management theorists such as Galbraith (1973) and Stinchcombe (Stinchcombe and Heimer, 1985), Ray Levitt, in founding the Center, concentrated early attention on the information processing demands confronting project participants and, necessarily, managers who had to design work arrangements. Information processing approaches were themselves grounded in the then-dominant "contingency" theory holding that organizational structures, under "norms of rationality," were designed to be sufficiently complex to cope with the complexity posed by the tasks confronted (Thompson, 1967). Levitt's prior work (Jin and Levitt, 1997; Levitt et al., 1999), had employed agent-based simulation techniques to model information flows in project organizations, exploring the effects of various task and team configurations on team performance. Some early global projects research associated with the GPC pursued similar modeling techniques and was focused on issues of information processing (e.g., Horii et al., 2004); subsequent work in the Center has broadened to include the effects of broader cultural, institutional and political factors on the execution and governance of projects.

Early in the life of the Center, Levitt invited Dick Scott, a leading organizational sociologist and institutional theorist, and Doug North, Nobel Prize-winning institutional economist, to join the GPC faculty. In this second phase of work, the research focus of the GPC began to examine the special challenges posed for projects by the involvement of multinational teams engaged in projects across national boundaries. The salience of this emphasis was reinforced by developing collaboration with a growing collection of research partners scattered throughout Europe, Asia, Africa and South America; a series of roundtable discussions involving senior-level management, legal and investment officials to consider the legacy and lessons of distressed and failed global projects; and by the recruitment of firms and agencies such as Bechtel, Parsons Brinckerhoff, Coudert Brothers, Baker and McKenzie, Finnish Global Project Strategies Consortium, Japanese Marine Sciences and the Asian Development Bank as industry affiliates.

Dissatisfied by the then-dominant reliance on the "cultural values" scales developed by Hofstede (1984, 1991) to depict transnational differences, the Center embraced the more inclusive "institutional pillars" framework devised by Scott (1995, 2014). This approach distinguished among three interrelated but distinctive elements making up an institutional complex: (1) the "regulative," which singled out the legal and rule-based frameworks backed by surveillance and sanctions – elements emphasized by economists; (2) the "normative," which centered on the prescriptive, evaluative and obligational dimension of social life – stressed by sociologists; and (3) the "cultural-cognitive," highlighting the shared beliefs and assumptions which underpin all social life – elements favored by cultural anthropologists and cognitive psychologists. This broader conceptual framework allowed a more comprehensive set of theoretical lenses for our research and provided a richer and more varied toolkit for examining institutional and cultural differences.

This institutional focus was further expanded to include power and political factors affecting project design, performance and outcomes. In particular, the addition of Doug McAdam (McAdam et al., 1988; McAdam, 2011) to the Center's faculty introduced social movement theory, which articulated the ways in which projects, as they unfold, generate both opposition and support from communities previously uninvolved. In these and related ways, the agenda of the Center was broadened to include not simply the built physical environment (for example, buildings and bridges) but the "built social environment" (for example, various institutions and public, private and third sector political and power systems).

As the work proceeded, our research team began to become increasingly aware of the limitations of single-case methodology. While helpful in identifying important problems and processes and in suggesting connections and arguments, it is severely limited in sorting among or testing them. Hence, we were among the first research groups in this area to embrace the innovative qualitative comparative analysis (QCA) approach developed by Ragin (1987, 2000), who pioneered a comparative method allowing researchers to numerically employ categorical distinctions allowing them to combine data from across a modest number of cases (10–20 in our case) to test and refine arguments.

Thus, the first decade of the Center's research was grounded in efforts to examine a variety of cases describing projects employing multinational participants coping with varying levels of task complexity and operating under a variety of social and political conditions. The work was guided by a combination of contingency, institutional, political and social movement theory. A fair sampling of this work is reported and summarized in *Global Projects: Institutional and Political Challenges* (Scott et al., 2011).

Phase three of the research program of the Center was guided by the same theoretical approaches, but this more recent work began to shift primary attention away from cross-national societal differences to cross-sectoral differences affecting projects. Because of initiatives in the United Kingdom, Canada, Australia, Chile and other jurisdictions and political realignments in the US, increasing attention was being devoted to public–private partnerships as a mode of harnessing governmental (public) legitimacy with private expertise and financing. Our work has concentrated on exploring the governance challenges arising from institutional differences between political bodies and public agencies on the one hand, and market-based private firms on the other. The organization fields in which the two partners operate impose quite different standards and expectation on them; their internal organizational structures are significantly different, and the norms and logics controlling and guiding their actions are divergent (Lindblom, 1977).

In addition to emphasizing the significance of the sectoral differences characterizing the two types of partners in PPPs, this recent work has also attended to the multi-stage nature of project structures. Viewed longitudinally, projects are observed to move through several stages: from conception and shaping as locations, participants and financing are brought together; through design and construction; to operation, maintenance and, finally, dissolution (Miller and Lessard, 2000). Development processes are common to every type of organizational form, but what are distinctive about the evolution through time of large-scale projects are the changing types and combinations of participants involved. Participants who are leading members in early phases may be marginal players in later stages, and participants who are strongly affected by an earlier decision may not have been party to that decision. Such issues pose singular problems for those attempting to design and participate in governance structures.

Another aspect of PPPs that has attracted attention is the problem posed in securing adequate financing. While infrastructure projects would appear at first glance to be ideal vehicles for attracting patient institutional investors such as pension funds that require long-term, steady, inflation-adjusted returns on invested capital, the failure or disappointing performance of many recent projects has dampened interest among many capital managers. The challenge of allocating cash flows and risks among various shifting coalitions of participants adds to the governance burden of project management. This line of work has been led by Ashby Monk, Executive Director of GPC.

As the GPC's interest in PPPs grew, the GPC was fortunate to engage Michael J. Garvin of Virginia Tech to collaborate on private involvement in infrastructure development. In particular, Garvin's research group at

Virginia Tech had examined regulative and financial aspects of PPPs in the United States since the early 2000s through both theoretical and case-based research (Garvin and Cheah, 2004; Garvin and Bosso, 2008; Gross and Garvin, 2011), and it had established a reputation for applications of real options theory (Myers, 1977; Trigeorgis, 1999) to infrastructure projects and PPPs. It also had a strong track record of placing graduates with some of the largest infrastructure consultants and developers in the world, such as Arup, ACS Infrastructure Development, Cintra, KPMG and Skanska Infrastructure Development. With the GPC's growing interest in PPP shaping, management and financing, Stanford and Virginia Tech began collaborative research funded by the US National Science Foundation to bring various views about governing complex arrangements such as PPPs together in a common framework.

These are among the principal theoretical frameworks utilized and techniques employed to address the problems and issues described in the present volume. The diverse perspectives on PPP governance represented by the various chapters in this book are the outcomes of this collaboration.

ACKNOWLEDGMENTS

The Global Projects Center and the editors and authors of this book have all benefited enormously from the contributions of many researchers, and our research has been financed, guided and assisted by dozens of governmental and corporate leaders. We express our very sincere appreciation to all of them for their inspiration, passion and efforts in support of our work. We want to single out some of the key contributors, while thanking all of the others whom we do not name explicitly.

The GPC's first two Executive Directors, Dr Julie Kim and Dr Ryan Orr, worked heroically to bring together the initial industry and government affiliates and shape the research agenda of the Center from its beginning. They have continued to support the center as it has evolved. Dr Ashby Monk, a co-author of two chapters in this book, is the third Executive Director of the GPC. Ashby added the investor perspective on PPP governance to our research agenda, along with a new set of highly engaged industry affiliates from global pension and sovereign funds.

To our past and present industry and government affiliates we express our heartfelt thanks for their farsighted vision in providing financial support, access and guidance for GPC's basic and applied research program. Their support provided the critical early funding and guidance for us to lay the groundwork for larger, externally funded projects aimed at understanding and enhancing PPP and investor governance.

To our "collaboratory" partners in other academic institutions we express our sincere appreciation and enormous respect for their openness to share information, contacts and ideas with us. At different times, we have benefited from deep collaborations with colleagues at: Aalto and Åbo Akademi Universities in Finland; UCL, Imperial College and Manchester Business School in the United Kingdom; QUT and Monash University in Australia; Stellenbosch University in South Africa; and Tsinghua and Tongji Universities in China.

Australia's three eastern states – Queensland, New South Wales and Victoria – all have long histories of PPP delivery and have evolved mature PPP governance regimes and innovative new PPP delivery models. Ross Israel and his colleagues at Queensland Investment Corporation, a long-term GPC affiliate, generously organized access for the GPC to a tremendous set of contacts from all sectors of the PPP institutional field, and provided rich in-kind support for Dr Levitt's interviews during 2016 to learn about Australia's history with, and current governance of, PPPs.

The GPC's Advisory Board – Duncan Sinclair, Ed Schafer, Elliott Donnelley II, Joe Lonsdale, Mei Ye, Paul Rosenstiel and Peter Pereira Gray – have provided valuable review and input to many of our initiatives over the years. We thank them for their service.

As in most university research, the real heroes behind the book are the many students, postdoctoral scholars, research associates and visiting scholars who did the 7 x 24 "heavy lifting" in developing the data, understandings, insights and theories laid out in the chapters of the book. We thank all of them for their passion, curiosity, energy and integrity, and wish them well in their careers.

Pouya Rezazadeh Kalehbasti, a Stanford graduate student, provided valuable copy-editing and organization of the chapters and figures in preparing the final manuscript. We thank Pouya for his careful assistance in organizing a coherent submission package of this manuscript to the publishers under tight deadlines.

We gratefully acknowledge financial support from the US National Science Foundation's Grant #1334292 for a four-year Stanford–Virginia Tech collaborative research program on PPP governance, and the ongoing support of the Global Projects Center for many of the research efforts reported in this book.

All conclusions and opinions expressed in the book are exclusively those of the editors and authors. We sincerely regret any errors or omissions in our reporting of the research and take full responsibility for them.

Introduction: PPPs – theoretical challenges and directions forward
W. Richard Scott, Raymond E. Levitt and Michael J. Garvin

We do not subscribe to a goal of unconstrained development for its own sake; but assuring an adequate supply of civic infrastructure (including housing, roads and public transport, power, water supply and sanitation) is essential to meet the needs of developing countries where populations are growing and becoming more urbanized, as well as those of developed countries where infrastructure is aging and in need of repair and/or replacement. Important as it is, however, providing the necessary infrastructure confronts severe difficulties. Governments of emerging market countries face enormous shortfalls in financial and governance capacity in delivering sorely needed new infrastructure for their growing populations. At the same time, financially strapped governments of mature market economies are struggling to upgrade and retrofit their aging and obsolete infrastructure. Societies at both ends of the development spectrum need more robust project governance structures that can enable new forms of financing coupled with improved systems of managerial oversight and control.

Infrastructure is central to societal welfare, and the high cost of replicating the "last mile of pipe or wire" often requires a monopolistic state provision or regulated private provision strategy. We would thus ordinarily expect that the state would play a major role in its prioritization, funding, development and operation. However, historically this has not always been the case. Specific countries vary in their experience, but the United States (US) is not atypical. As Miller and Floricel (2000) point out, during much of the nineteenth century US transportation systems and power networks were built by private entrepreneurs, with minimal public involvement. Toward the end of the century, large corporate groups replaced the entrepreneurs but still experienced only modest public oversight. However, during the Progressive era of the early twentieth century, private initiatives were increasingly regulated and, over time, nationalized as public enterprises. For the greater part of the century, federal, state and local authorities planned, funded, built and operated the bulk of infrastructure. However, during the 1980s, buoyed by a more conservative political wave, calls intensified for the privatization of these enterprises. From that period to the present, varying combinations of private and public entities have partnered to provide these facilities and services.

In liberal democracies, the public presence typically takes the form of leadership and continuing participation by elected officials, public agencies and varying types of civic associations in the planning and oversight of projects. Private, for-profit firms are viewed as essential to supply private resources and technical know-how in the service of creating, maintaining and operating public facilities. Hence, over roughly the past four decades, governments worldwide have been experimenting with varying types of public–private partnerships (PPPs) which are expected to shape and oversee long-term – for example, 25- to 50-year – concession contracts to finance, design, construct and operate infrastructure projects. Countries and regions vary substantially in their capacity to mount and manage these complex arrangements successfully. Compared to other developed societies that have led the way in constructing supportive national or regional frameworks for PPPs, the US has been relatively slow to adopt these approaches and so stands to benefit from the experience of other countries.

THE NEED FOR INFRASTRUCTURE

The term "infrastructure" is a broad one, encompassing multiple and diverse elements of the built and natural environment. It is used to encompass such varied features as roads, railroads, rapid transit, ports, airports, power generation and transmission, telecommunications, water supply and waste treatment, dams, and public buildings such as courthouses, schools and hospitals. Each of these sectors poses its own special technical and business challenges. In order to simplify our task, we have chosen to focus our empirical attention on the transportation sector, even though much of our theoretical framework is applicable to a much wider range of infrastructure projects. Even with a more limited set of empirical cases, we will have more than enough complexity with which to contend.

In transportation, as is the case for most infrastructure projects, the demand for new roads and bridges, together with the need to maintain and restore existing systems, greatly exceeds the supply. Among ongoing and recent projects, the record of cost overruns, failure to meet schedules and shortfalls in user demand leading to financial restructuring is not encouraging.

In mature market economies, much of the infrastructure is several decades old and reaching the end of its useful life. In contrast, in emerging market economies with burgeoning populations, much of the economy is informal and tax collection regimes are often very weak even in the more formal part of the economy, so that the ability of governments to finance and fund infrastructure is severely constrained. Moreover, rapidly increasing urbanization in the twenty-first century is generating huge demands for expanding water, sewer, power and transportation infrastructure, along with social infrastructure services such as housing, schools and hospitals, in cities worldwide. The unmet need for civil and social infrastructure has been estimated by multiple sources as being in the tens of trillions of dollars per year.

At the same time, sovereign funds and pension funds worldwide control as much as $100 trillion in assets (Clark et al., 2011), a portion of which could be productively invested in infrastructure. Since the financial crisis of 2007, the real (after inflation) returns that pensions have been able to earn from fixed income securities have been essentially zero or negative, requiring them to seek out higher risk–return investments to meet their actuarially required returns of around 8 percent per year. Investing in infrastructure in their countries has both the direct benefit to the pensions of offering moderate-risk, long-term, inflation-adjusted returns above 8 percent, as well as strengthening the economies of their countries through the direct and indirect economic and social benefits that well-designed, built and maintained infrastructure can provide.

The goal of creating the right kinds of governance both within the pension funds and the infrastructure projects to enable the "golden handshake" between these vast pools of currently underperforming, discretionary capital and the proliferation of sorely needed infrastructure projects worldwide has been a major focus of the Global Projects Center at Stanford University over the past decade and was the impetus for much of the research presented in this book.

GOVERNANCE CHALLENGES

PPP projects are typically complex, uncertain, one-off, long-lived, multi-phased, expensive transactions involving a large and shifting number of internal and external stakeholders operating within ever-changing contexts. Let us unpack this dense description.

Project complexity begins with the number and types of tasks that must be performed to accomplish the objective. Campbell (1988, 43) proposes that "any objective task characteristic that implies an increase in information load, information diversity, or rate of information change can be considered a contributor to complexity." Complexity is increased by the presence of: (1) multiple desired goals; (2) diverse potential ways or paths to arrive at the objective; (3) conflicting interdependence among paths; and (4) uncertain links among paths and outcomes (Campbell, 1988). Focusing attention more on the problems of task coordination, Thompson (1967) emphasized attending to the different degrees and types of interdependence in the project workflows. They might reflect simple pooled interdependence, when each task or subtask independently contributes to the desired outcome. More complexity is imposed by sequentially interdependent tasks, in which one task cannot be undertaken until another has been completed. Even higher levels of complexity attend the presence of reciprocally interdependent tasks, which require mutual adjustment among actors who must align or reconcile their subgoals and activities with those of others as the work proceeds.

Levitt (2015) points out that reciprocal interdependence may assume two guises: compatible and contentious. In the former case, workers find that the subgoals governing their performance are aligned, whereas in the latter case they are conflicting. In general, increased complexity of the tasks being undertaken and increased interdependence of the project workflows – particularly, reciprocal contentious interdependence – creates increased demands on the managerial systems required to coordinate the workflows. Contentious interdependence is more likely when multinational firms are involved, when multiple jurisdictions are affected (for example, cross-county, cross-state), and when competing civic interests become activated. Highway projects also vary substantially in their technical complexity, depending on the nature of the terrain to be traversed, their elevation, the number of barriers (for example, rivers, mountains, other infrastructure) to be crossed, and the types and volume of traffic to be accommodated.

Technical uncertainty relates primarily to the inexact or unknown means–ends connections linking activities to their consequences (March and Simon, 1958). That is, projects vary in the extent to which the technologies are routine, familiar and time-tested or are more experimental and variable in their outcomes. The use of experimental or untested technical processes is not common on transportation projects but may occur on selected components such as bridges or tunnels. Uncertainty is far more likely to be associated with some aspects of the project organization, such as stakeholder composition and/or behavior, and the project's context, such as uncertain political and institutional conditions, as discussed below.

PPP projects are one-offs, in the sense that most project organizations are constructed *de novo* to construct a particular link in the transportation system; for example, a road from point A to point B. The developers, or some other agency with the proper authority, selects a lead company which then creates a special purpose vehicle (SPV) that serves as the focal organization of a unique network of participating organizations, including the public sponsor, financial backers, contractors, operators, clients, regulators, and affected parties such as users and broader publics. The fact that each project begins anew, often with different combinations of participants, means that projects are importantly "learning disabled": unable to carry forward the "lessons learned" from one project to the next. This liability is one reason why the existence of broader, "enabling" support structures at the state or regional level is often critical to the success of PPPs.

Infrastructure projects are relatively long-lived, their development and construction period typically extending over several years and their operation and maintenance over several decades. Because of their associated complexity and uncertainty, Miller and Olleros (2000) argue that the more successful projects are preceded by a long "shaping" period. Even if the technical problems are modest and the outcomes sought are known, it is important for the SPV to consider possible future problems, including how to set up governance arrangements to insure flexibility among team members and anticipate potential changes in key contextual elements, and how to build coalitions that create "buy-ins" among stakeholders.

Projects, of necessity, are multi-phased, passing from a period of exploration and project conception through project financing and shaping, followed by a combined period of design and construction, leading into one of maintenance and operation. It is obvious that these phases require differing talents and activities, so that it should not be a surprise that a project involves a changing collection of stakeholders as it proceeds from earlier to later stages. The coming and going of a varied set of participants also entails changes over time in the relative power of project participants. As might be expected, this condition poses severe challenges to project governance as when, for example, earlier participants' parties make binding decisions that negatively affect later, not yet represented, parties.

Financing of infrastructure projects poses yet another type of challenge. Through the period of public monopoly, the financing of projects was via some type of taxation regime at one or more levels: municipalities, counties, special taxing entities such as school districts or port authorities, states or the federal government. Monies were raised by general taxes but also by the sale of tax-exempt bonds, allowing the financing of public works projects at reduced interest rates. Their tax-exempt nature, however, costs public agencies because of the foregone taxes they would normally collect. The increasing resistance of taxpayers to any increase in taxes together with the international financial crisis of 2007–2008 has encouraged more and more government entities to explore the availability of private financing: partnering with private entities that control or can leverage private resources. Promising sources of private capital being cultivated are institutional investors (for example, pension funds and sovereign wealth funds) that control "patient capital" which would seem to be ideal for investing in long-term infrastructure projects. However, to mobilize these resources, institutional investors must acquire new capacities and devise new governance arrangements if they are to fully engage in and benefit from these collaborations.

Stakeholders include all those who are involved in and affected by the organization and operation of the project group. The stakeholders involved in infrastructure projects are likely to be a very large and diverse collection of interested parties. They range from "internal" stakeholders, for example, financial agents, stockholders, managers, other employees and contractual partners, to "external" stakeholders including "all of those groups and individuals that can affect, or are affected by, the accomplishment of [the firm's] organizational purpose" (Freeman, 1984, 25). Included would be such groups as the project's exchange partners, government regulators, consumers, affected communities and interested associations.

Infrastructure projects are also likely to entail efforts of long-term duration, with the completed objects – for example, bridges, rail and highway systems – being expected to be capable of use extending over many decades. Such longevity in itself, however, is not unusual. Government agencies and corporations are also likely to operate for many years. What is unusual is the extent to which the types of stakeholders associated with a project shift over time. Some stakeholders, such as developers, are heavily engaged during early phases and are highly influential, but their centrality wanes over time. Later stakeholders, such as project operators, user groups and various civic movements, become much more active and involved over time. The diverse and shifting nature of stakeholders poses daunting challenges to those designing governance systems.

"Context" is a general, non-specific term referring vaguely to "everything outside the specific unit or system being studied." The problem is, as many project managers have learned to their sorrow, many seemingly benign conditions formally outside of the system being managed can suddenly and unexpectedly change, substantially affecting the performance of the system for which they are responsible. Many types of contextual factors can affect infrastructure projects, ranging from physical and natural forces to market and economic, political, and the social and institutional. Because infrastructure projects are, by their nature, grounded in the physical environment, they are highly susceptible to such forces as earthquakes, fires, floods and severe storms. Tunnels or bridges may encounter unexpected geophysical conditions or hazards (Lessard and Miller, 2000).

Economic factors include more localized events such as miscalculation or fluctuation in the demand for the facility, to more macro incidents such as economic turndowns or financial crises. Political considerations are particularly salient to PPP projects, because one of the core parties is a government entity. Hence, such projects may become hostage to election cycles, political currents or social protests. Unexpected shortcomings or delays, or the outbreak of real or apparent conflicts of interest, may occasion intense media scrutiny. Social and institutional risks are substantial and can vary over the project phase. Among these are the many legal and regulatory provisions affecting infrastructure; normative elements, which include the varied types of professional standards that govern the work of lawyers, engineers and the various craft occupations engaged in the project; and the cultural assumptions and belief systems associated with private firms, public agencies and/or those associated with varying regions and participant groups (Scott et al., 2011).

In sum, the challenges and risks faced by PPP projects are substantial, varying by nature and location of project as well as by phase of development. Effectively confronting their technical, financial, political and institutional complexity calls for robust and resilient governance structures. The diversity and range of challenges posed have forced parties tasked with addressing them to seek help from an ever-widening range of scholarly fields. In the following section, we provide a brief overview of the major sets of ideas upon which project participants and scholars draw.

RELEVANT THEORETICAL FRAMEWORKS

We begin with a review of related concepts from organization theory and design.

Organization Theory and Design

Scholars studying organizations have long emphasized the ways in which the nature of the work performed – its complexity, uncertainty and interdependence – shapes the kinds of structures designed to cope with it. Different kinds of workflows for tasks that span the boundaries of individuals, teams or firms responsible for their execution require different types of coordination mechanisms. Thompson (1967) usefully identifies three types of workflows:

- The work can be such that workers carry out the work independently but, in aggregate, contribute to an overall outcome. This type of

work creates pooled interdependence, which managers can coordinate by specifying the types of work required and the necessary skills for workers.
- The work can be divided into various tasks to be performed independently by work units, but to be successful the tasks must be performed in a specific order. Such sequential interdependence is coordinated by schedules and by the use of some "buffering" mechanisms to smooth out the workflow.
- The work may require separate work units to take into account the work of others, because the work of each unit serves as both input and output for that of another. Such reciprocal independence requires mutual adjustment among the work units as the work proceeds and, hence, more delegation of discretion to the work units.

As noted earlier, Levitt (2015) suggests that reciprocal interdependence arises in two forms, requiring different mechanisms of coordination. He proposes that we distinguish "compatible" reciprocal interdependence, when conflicting subgoals do not appear during work exchanges, from "contentious" interdependence, when such conflicts do emerge. Contentious interdependence can sometimes be resolved by negotiation between the participants, but often end in deadlocks that require escalation and managerial intervention.

The larger message of this stream of work is that organizational complexity is a response to the complexity of the work involved: managerial frameworks reflect the nature of the work being controlled. This "contingency" framework to organizational structure developed over several decades of productive research (see Galbraith, 1973; Lawrence, 1993; Lawrence and Lorsch, 1967; Thompson, 1967; Burton and Obel, 2004), and has gradually been extended to incorporate the demands associated with managing non-technical aspects of work, including political and cultural factors (Scott and Davis, 2007).

Transaction Cost Economics

In an early seminal paper, Coase (1937) asked his fellow economists how they were to explain the existence of firms if market forces were thought to be the most effective way to insure the efficiency of exchanges. Nearly a half century later, Williamson (1975, 1985) proposed that firms exist because many types of exchange are difficult to negotiate: the processes involved in producing the good or service are complex or uncertain, or the parties involved may be untrustworthy and prone to "opportunism." He argued that firms emerged that served to erect boundaries to contain that subset of exchanges which exhibit high levels of complexity, uncertainty or opportunism. Within these boundaries, firms create hierarchical controls over exchange contracts which allow managers to: (1) provide appropriate information and resources to targeted employees; (2) create auditing and authority systems to exercise necessary controls; and (3) design incentive systems to encourage cooperation.

In general, then, the contracting negotiations which occur within "free" markets are not costless. There are always the questions of: Who can deliver? Who can predict? Who can you trust? The costs of managing exchanges are labeled "transaction costs." When they become sufficiently large, they justify the costs entailed in creating a hierarchy (organization) to oversee them; a hierarchy which itself is costly.

Some recurring transactions have high "asset specificity" – where one or both parties to the transaction can incur expenses that have no value outside of the given transaction if it fails, making them especially prone to opportunistic "hold-up" by the counterparty. For such transactions Williamson proposes that "relational contracting" approaches (versus classical, transactional contracting) supported by third-party mediators will be the optimal governance structure. PPP transactions fit this situation with their long durations, vulnerability to outside forces beyond either parties' control, and dynamic sets of stakeholders.

Of course, there is not one but many types of hierarchy or organization structure (Williamson, 1985). Analysts are encouraged to compare and contrast the varying modes of organizing within contemporary economies, from the simple unitary structure to the more complex multi-divisional and matrix structures to the decentralized network, such as the project-based form, within which the network of contracts can be used to recreate key elements of hierarchy (Stinchcombe, 1985). From the transaction cost perspective, the relational project form of governance is one mode of centralized control that has arisen to police and protect certain classes of complex contracts; and the PPP form is one variant of this structural design (Henisz et al., 2012).

Public Administration

The examination of public organizations and institutions emerged from the work of historical institutional scholars who compared various instances of governmental forms over time and space. One of the most imaginative was De Tocqueville (1835/2004; 1856/1998, 2001), who compared French and American political systems during pre- and post-revolutionary periods; and others such as Burgess (1902), who focused on differences among Western nations as reflected in their constitutional systems. Indeed, most of this early comparative work concentrated on "configurative descriptions" of formal institutions including "constitutions, cabinets, parliaments, courts and bureaucracies" (Bill and Hardgrave, 1981).

During the middle of the twentieth century, this early focus on institutionalized structures was largely supplanted by a behavioral approach, which diverted attention from political systems to political behavior; for example, voting, lobbying, decision-making. While much of this work has been informative and instructive, over time the pendulum has begun to swing back to incorporate structural elements, in part because they have been shown to effect behavior. Thus, Simon (1945/1997) and March and Simon (1958) examined the ways in which administrative structures affected – supported and constrained – the decisions made by their individual participants. Even social movement organizations, such as the women's suffrage struggle, have been shown to rely heavily on pre-existing political forms and recurring repertoires of routines (Clemens, 1997).

More recently, investigators have given more attention to the distinctive features of public organizations; to the ways in which they differ from private, market-driven organizations. Scholars from Downs (1967) to Wilson (1989) to Rainey (1991) have pointed out that the goals pursued by public organizations are more diffuse, ambiguous and conflicting then those of private organizations. Whereas private organizations are engaged in making a profit, public systems are expected to serve the public interest, where controversy surrounds the relative importance to be placed on equity and distributional fairness versus independence and freedom of choice. They also are expected to oversee and regulate private organizations, dealing with issues of information asymmetries between firms and clients and externalities, costs created by firms but borne by publics; again, complex, diffuse matters concerning which it is difficult to evaluate outcomes. Because of the ambiguity of goals pursued, government agencies are more likely to be governed by their adherence to processes rather than by assessment of outcomes. They are expected to focus on following established rules, procedures, norms and expectations (Downs, 1967; Wilson, 1989). Most lack profit-maximization incentives, are less attuned to concerns regarding appropriate resource allocation, and lack internal organizational goal alignment.

As explicated by Hult and Walcott (1990), the process values emphasized by public organizations include: (1) structured rationality – processes intended to insure that relevant expertise and information are incorporated into decision-making routines; (2) accountability – procedures to insure that governing officials are held responsible for their decisions and actions; (3) representativeness – procedures to allow those affected by the policies pursued to participate in the shaping of those policies; and

(4) legitimacy – the belief among the relevant publics that a given policy decision has been formulated in acceptable ways and implemented without undue favoritism. Largely because of the work of institutional scholars (DiMaggio and Powell, 1983; Meyer and Rowan, 1977) there is increased recognition of the importance of legitimacy in insuring the stability and support for all organizations, but especially public organizations.

The principal lesson to be learned from this body of work for those interested in PPPs is a heightened awareness of the differences obtaining between public agencies and private firms. These two organizational forms operate in decidedly different institutional contexts: they are subject to different modes of rationality, different "logics" of action and, for this reason, pose severe governance challenges to those who try to combine them into a single, meta-organizational entity.

Stakeholder Approaches

Attention to "stakeholders" began to take hold in the late 1970s and 1980s in reaction to the focus by some economists on shareholders as the central players in a rational theory of the firm. Economists such as Friedman (1970), argued that "rational" managers were those who adopted the maximization of return-on-value for shareholders as the touchstone of their decision criteria. To focus on other interests, such as those of workers or the general public, was "to preach pure and unadulterated socialism." The only "social responsibility" of business was "to use its resources and engage in activities designed to increase its profits" within the "rules of the game."

In reaction, other scholars adopted a more inclusive view of the varied groups having a legitimate interest – a "stake" – in the activities of private corporations. Such groups included, but were not limited to, employees, customers, suppliers and members of the community within which the organization was located. Arguments developed ranged from the empirical – corporations do respond to the interests of these groups; to the normative – corporations should respond to the interests of these groups (Freeman, 1984; Laplume et al., 2008; Mitchell et al., 1997). The empirical arguments were bolstered by reigning views within the organizational studies community that organizations were, by their nature, "open" systems, affected by and dependent on interactions with a variety of external groups (Scott and Davis, 2007, Ch. 4). And they were strengthened and informed by developments within network circles that created multiple measures of degrees and types of connectedness – for example, centrality, clustering, equivalence and density – between individuals and/or organizations (see Burt, 1980; Barnes, 1972; Smith-Doerr and Powell, 2005). Such measures allowed researchers to assess the extent and strength of connections between varying types of actors, both those formally included within the boundaries of firms or projects, and others technically outside.

Some researchers (see, e.g., Freeman, 1984) propose a simpler, "ego network" approach that focuses on those groups having a direct tie to the organizational unit of interest. More complex approaches attempt to map the overall network, which include all actors and relationships within a given domain or, given this broader topography, examine the network position or location of the various players (Burt, 1980; Kilduff and Tsai, 2003). Measures such as distance – the length of the shortest path between two actors; centrality – how many direct contacts a given actor has with others; or clustering – which examines how connected or cohesive neighbors are within a network, have been usefully deployed.

As noted above, because PPP infrastructure projects are likely to extend over several decades, the numbers and types of stakeholders involved change dramatically over time. So also does their degree of power or centrality in the network (Smith-Doerr and Powell, 2005). For example, design and development teams having great influence in stage one may no longer be active participants in the operational stage; and social movement groups that may not have existed when the project began may become prominent players in defending the interests of client or community groups when the project is up and running. Designing a governance system which will incorporate and accommodate such changes is clearly a challenging task.

Finance Theory

While economists such as Samuelson (1948), Friedman (1953) and Schumpeter (1954) had explored aspects of finance within economic systems, foundations of contemporary finance theory, in many respects, were established by Markowitz (1952) and Modigliani and Miller (1958). Markowitz's ideas about portfolios and risk versus return mobilized a series of studies that are the basis of theory and practice about investments and portfolio management to the present day. Alternatively, the theorems of Modigliani and Miller are at the heart of contemporary analyses of capital structure. In particular, their "irrelevance" proposition, that financing decisions do not affect firm value under specific conditions, has fueled contemplation of circumstances where financial structure does matter.

Nowhere are such considerations given more attention than in the financing of large infrastructure projects, such as PPPs, which has become fertile ground for studying the implications of financial architectures. Brealey et al. (2000) explained that reallocating project cash flows and risks among various participants in well-functioning markets does not typically create value or lower the cost of capital; however, financing choices can influence value and the cost of capital particularly when they enhance project performance and management through improving incentives. Indeed, the discipline and practice of project finance are largely premised on identifying those aspects of project structure that impact managerial incentives to generate value and manage risk (Esty, 2004). Not surprisingly, it is the dominant financing strategy for PPPs, since project finance can transfer risks to debt holders and contractors who can bear the risks at a lower cost or manage specific activities more expertly and efficiently.

Hence, realizing such advantages in PPPs – to the potential dismay of governments simply seeking a convenient avenue to move assets off their balance sheet – means far more than assembling private sources of money. It entails careful consideration of the network of stakeholders involved to allocate risks to those holding a comparative advantage, and to configure incentives for each to respond productively to diverse events over time (Brealey et al., 2000). Put more simply, the legitimacy of the prevailing PPP financial structure depends on good project governance.

STRUCTURE OF THIS VOLUME

Although this is an edited volume, the following chapters reflect a common perspective in the sense that all contributors draw on a broadly shared conceptual framework. More specifically, all of the contributors have ties to the Global Project Center (GPC) at Stanford University. The GPC has served as the focus of a broad "collaboratory" which, over its more than 16-year history, has attracted scholars from around the world to pursue research reflecting a broadly similar agenda. While there exists general agreement within the GPC community on the need to improve infrastructure project finance and governance, our contributors vary in their disciplinary background, on the specific focus of their scholarship, and in their choice of context for gathering data. Some of the assembled chapters have not previously been published, while others have appeared in a variety of venues. Most of them have been extensively edited for the purposes of this volume.

The chapters included in Part I describe the defining features of PPPs, consider their development and variants, and depict some of the common misconceptions or myths which have confounded them over the years. Also, they examine the continuing fundamental differences between public and private organizations; differences which underpin the difficulties that arise in combining them. The chapters of Part II deal with the multiple types of challenges confronting the design of governance structures for

PPPs as they progress through planning, design, construction, operations and maintenance phases of their life cycle. Part III focuses on the varied sources of private and public financing for PPPs, the difficulties associated with aligning the goals of private investors and public agencies, and mechanisms employed to distribute financial risk among the various parties and to govern them in the public interest. Part IV explores the potential for fostering the development of regional and national systems that have demonstrated, in some contexts, the potential for strengthening and enabling the performance of PPP projects, and their current levels of institutional maturity in different countries. And Part V describes two innovative project delivery approaches that are evolving for financing and delivering large versus small infrastructure projects: one top-down, and the other bottom-up.

PART I

Public–private partnerships: definitions, myths and institutional challenges

From the earliest days of organized society, there has been a need for goods and services intended for the use of all, rather than just of individuals or private groups. Arrangements for building and maintaining these assets to be used in common – public infrastructure – always pose difficult and often contentious challenges. It is difficult to construct and protect a "commons" benefiting all (Ostrom, 1990). Multiple and diverse interests need to be considered and accounted for if such projects are to succeed. Some participants will be lightly affected, others greatly; some are adversely affected, others receive benefits; some are already organized, others must mobilize. Public interests will be concentrated in and represented by specific agencies, elected officials and, perhaps, non-profits and social movement organizations. Private interests will be distributed across diverse types of players: financial interests, provider organizations and beneficiaries. And, when large-scale infrastructures are involved, large numbers of interests will be affected, since the resulting structures are likely to exist and operate over many years and even decades.

The four chapters contained in Part I provide an introduction to and overview of the complex and multiple challenges posed by the construction, operation and maintenance of large-scale infrastructure projects in modern and developing societies. To simplify the discussion, most of the chapters in this and succeeding parts of the book concentrate on large-scale transportation projects. While each type of project – water, energy, waste disposal, port and airport construction – poses its own unique challenges, all share important similarities in the coordination and control problems posed for project governance systems. A further simplification is that most of the chapters of this volume concern United States (US) projects or, if the focus is broader, consider the implications for projects in the US. The 50 states encompassed by this country provide more than enough variety of politics and culture to provide ample diversity for analytic purposes.

Chapter 1 begins with a brief overview of the evolution of governance arrangements for public infrastructure projects in the US. The distinctive characteristics of private–public partnerships (PPPs) are described, and some of the major subtypes identified. As a technique for delineating the major features of PPPs, the authors list and discuss some of the major misconceptions – both their strengths and their limitations – that have arisen in the discussion of these forms. The chapter concludes with a collection of recommendations to guide the appropriate design and application of this governance form to public projects.

Given that there are multiple and shifting interests associated with infrastructure construction and operation, how are we to assess them and their changing involvement and influence? Chapter 2 addresses this important question by proposing a dynamic stakeholder approach that suggests ways to identify these actors and processes empirically over time. As already noted, the concept of "stakeholder" was crafted to call attention to the reality that a sole focus on the interests of "stockholders" as financial beneficiaries of a private firm's operation is insufficient for dealing with the realities posed by corporations whose work affects the interests of many parties: employees, suppliers and buyers, customers and members of the broader public (Freeman, 1984). This is especially so in the case of public works projects, whose construction and operation are likely to affect not only all of the various types of direct participants, but also the broader public and civic groups.

The authors emphasize that the identity and potential involvement of these stakeholders is likely to change over the duration of the project's life cycle, as the project moves through identification, environmental impact review and development, through design and construction, to operation and maintenance. They employ the useful concept of "organization field" to identify the full range of individual and collective actors who are caught up in the project's vortex. Moreover, they suggest not simply the operation through time of a dynamic process of shifting stakeholders, but one in which the composition of the dominant partner – the "anchor-tenant" – undergoes change. The challenge of crafting a governance structure sufficiently resilient to accommodate such basic changes in interests and influence is great indeed. These processes are empirically illustrated by data drawn from a study of a California PPP highway project in which express lanes were added to the median of an existing freeway.

Chapter 3 proposes and illustrates the use of a broader theoretical framework drawn from organizational institutional theory (Greenwood et al., 2008; Scott, 2014) that can prove useful in describing the elements comprising institutional structures such as those employed in project governance. In their examination of governance structures created to manage complex contracts, institutional economists such as Williamson (1975), focus attention almost exclusively on financial and hierarchical controls to motivate conformity and curb opportunism. Drawing on Scott's (2014) "pillars" formulation, the authors urge attention be broadened from these "regulatory" systems to include the roles played by the "normative" and "cultural-cognitive" elements present in projects and their participants. For example, all projects involve varying combinations of banking and financial experts, multiple varieties of engineers and technicians, lawyers and other types of professional consultants, public and political officials from varying agencies and parties, and diverse groups of consumers and affected publics. Each of these groups is socialized into and oriented to the existence of various occupation, professional, and agency norms which prescribe how they are to conduct themselves under varying circumstances. The background presence of such norms can create misunderstanding, confusion, and conflicts that require managerial expertise and attention to resolve. In addition, the participants may be drawn from differing nationalities, regions, or cultural backgrounds each associated with varying assumptions and beliefs. Such "cultural" assumptions provide varying "cognitive" frames that guide the decisions and actions of their carriers.

The authors of Chapter 3 point out that the dynamic stakeholder processes identified in Chapter 2 often give rise to "displaced agency": situations in which some stakeholders are adversely affected by decisions made by others at a time when their own interests were not represented. Successful project managers account for the likelihood of such occurrences and accommodate them. Such managers also are able to successfully craft wider frames or cultural templates to identify encompassing project objectives to which the diverse participants can subscribe.

The stakeholders in a large infrastructure project are drawn from public, private and civic sectors and, as Chapter 2 describes, the stakeholders in PPP projects become more or less salient at different times during the life cycle of a decades-long public–private partnership concession. Chapter 4 introduces a novel theoretical approach to assessing the relative power of stakeholders among the participants in large projects such as PPPs. Social network analysis (SNA), supported by multiple software tools, has become an accepted methodology to document, visualize and interpret relationships among participants in an organization, community or other social network (Burt, 1982). Participants are represented as nodes in the network, with various kinds of social interactions – for example, advice seeking, or knowledge sharing – represented by unidirectional or bidirectional arcs or "edges" connecting the nodes. This chapter explains how social network analysis can be significantly extended to consider both direct and indirect, open or closed, social exchanges as well as economic value flows, and to aggregate the effects of these social and economic exchanges on the relative stakeholder power of the focal stakeholders in terms of the utility that each exchange relationship provides to them. This allows a given stakeholder – for example, a public agency, concessionaire or civic organization – to assess its power relative to other project stakeholders, and to identify possible value exchanges with other project participants that could better align their goals.

1. Public–private partnerships for infrastructure delivery

Ashby H.B. Monk, Raymond E. Levitt, Michael J. Garvin, Andrew J. South and George Carollo

INTRODUCTION

Given the current state of infrastructure needs in both developed and developing economies worldwide, does it not make sense for the public sector to draw on all potential project delivery systems, including public–private partnerships? Together, the public and private sectors can provide the best services to meet the growing needs of United States (US) infrastructure, with the private sector often tapped for its potential to deliver value and innovation. This does not suggest that alternative delivery systems or public–private partnerships are the sole solution for resolving the challenges involved. The art for policy-makers is to determine when and where public–private partnerships make sense, to develop procurement and other systems that balance the transfer of risk and reward to the private sector and, most importantly, to deliver maximum value for the public's money (paid as taxes and/or user fees) in the form of enhanced infrastructure services.

Developing and upgrading core infrastructure assets is a touchstone of a successful global economy. Research has demonstrated convincing links between the level of infrastructure investment, and social and economic development. Indeed, infrastructure assets have been shown to influence economic growth. Income inequalities decline with higher infrastructure quantity and quality. As the world economy struggles to regain its luster after the 2007 global financial crisis, investments in infrastructure can spark a new cycle of growth.

However, infrastructure investment has been waning in recent years and decades. The United States alone, by some estimates, will require at least $1.5 trillion to $2 trillion just to bring existing infrastructure assets up to a reasonable state of repair. This raises important questions for public authorities. How will they garner the resources to finance this infrastructure? Are there viable alternatives to traditional public delivery and operation of infrastructure? Can and should alternative financing and delivery mechanisms be nurtured so as to begin making up the infrastructure funding gap? These questions require serious and credible answers. They are the starting point of this chapter.

From Publicly Owned Natural Monopolies to Public–Private Hybrids

Some kinds of infrastructure constitute "natural monopolies" for which duplication of services imposes exceptionally high costs. Examples of natural monopolies are major roads between urban centers; large dams that provide flood control, irrigation and sometimes power generation; landline telephones, for which the last mile of copper wire to each home is prohibitively expensive to duplicate; and piped water supply and waterborne sewer collection systems, which must provide the last mile of water or sewer pipe to each home.

Natural monopolies have historically – but not always – been financed, owned and operated by governments (or by heavily regulated, monopoly private providers). Other kinds of civil and social infrastructure, even if not natural monopolies, have been widely perceived as public goods that should be financed, owned and operated by governments, although their design and construction have frequently been contracted out to private firms.

Technological and societal trends have changed this calculus in the last several decades. Technologies such as cellular telephones and power generation have unbundled the creation of goods and services from distribution. Telecom and power providers no longer need to build the last mile of wire or pipe, so they are no longer natural monopolies. This has led to a hybrid of publicly and privately financed, owned and operated wireless telecommunications and power generation facilities worldwide. Similar trends are rapidly advancing in the water treatment and waste treatment sectors. The politics and economics of government financing, delivery and operation of infrastructure have often made it increasingly attractive to supplement public involvement with the private sector's financing capacity, global expertise, and best practices for sustainable design, delivery and operations.

The private sector has played a role in US infrastructure development since the era of explorers and pioneers. However, private entities' inherent demand for infrastructure comes coupled with a mandate from investors to generate profits, and these cannot come at too great an expense to the public. Moreover, private entities – both domestic and international – tend to develop expertise in partnering with the public sector, but public policy-makers often lack the institutional and technical capacity to engage as effectively, or have only recently begun to develop it. This perceived imbalance has generated controversy throughout US history.

From Design–Bid–Build to Custom-Designed Public–Private Partnerships

The conventional American approach to infrastructure development is known as design–bid–build (DBB). It employs separate contractors for design and construction and typically uses public budgetary or borrowed funds from general obligation or revenue bonds to pay for design and construction services. It requires the public sector to obtain necessary financing and procure design and construction services via competitive qualifications-based and low-bid processes, respectively.

This approach has evolved dramatically over the last three decades. The newer approaches may place the responsibility for design, construction, operations and maintenance under a single contractor. It may use public budgets, borrowed funds and/or user fees to pay for capital costs (or to repay capital lent or invested). It may require the contractor to raise the necessary financing; typically through structured project finance from both equity and debt sources. And it may be procured through a multi-stage competitive proposals process.

In this changing environment, four key decisions form the basis of most infrastructure programs:

- What life cycle activities should the project's contractor(s) undertake?
- What revenue mechanism (user fees or other revenue sources) will be used to pay for capital costs and operating services, or to repay capital lent or invested?
- Which entity has responsibility for raising any necessary capital financing?
- What procurement or acquisition approach should the public sector adopt for service acquisition?

The answers to these questions determine participants' respective roles throughout the useful life of the infrastructure assets. These roles, taken together, will define a public–private partnership.

PUBLIC–PRIVATE PARTNERSHIPS

A public–private partnership (PPP) is created when a government agency enters into a long-term (typically 25- to 50-year) concession agreement with a project-based legal entity called a special purpose vehicle (SPV), under which the SPV has the right and obligation to finance, design, build, operate and maintain a facility (or some subset of these roles) in accordance with contractually specified performance standards. The government generally retains ownership of the infrastructure asset and the land on which it is built, conceding only the rights associated with the asset to the SPV for a defined term. General characteristics of PPPs include:

- a long-term contract(s) between the public sponsor and the private sector participant(s);
- a private, or joint private and public, commitment to provide "bundled" development and operational services;
- funding derived from user charges and/or governmental budgetary or borrowed resources over the lifetime of the asset.

Different types of PPPs provide project sponsors with different options for transferring risks and responsibilities to the private sector:

- A design–build (DB) PPP transfers the engineering and construction risks and responsibilities to an external consortium, firm or joint venture assembled for the project. The project sponsor pays a fixed fee and manages the financing, operations and maintenance of the asset.
- A design–build–operate–maintain (DBOM) PPP transfers the engineering, construction, operation and maintenance responsibilities and risks to the consortium, firm or joint venture. The financing and revenue risk of DBOM projects remain with the sponsoring authority.
- A design–build–finance–operate–maintain (DBFOM) PPP transfers to the consortium, firm or joint venture the engineering, construction, financing, operations and maintenance risks and responsibilities. For financing, the future stream of revenues from the infrastructure asset is leveraged to issue debt (which is underpinned by some private equity). This is what provides the funds for capital and project development. Within the DBFOM PPP, there exist two standard forms of project delivery:
  - a "patronage" concession, in which the private developer will collect revenues and bear all or much of the revenue risk; and
  - direct (or "availability") payments, in which the public owner makes periodic payments to the consortium, firm or joint venture from government revenues, for delivering the infrastructure service based on a set of defined operation and maintenance performance standards.

MYTHS AND MISCONCEPTIONS ABOUT PUBLIC–PRIVATE PARTNERSHIPS

A variety of misconceptions – indeed, myths – about the costs and benefits of PPPs warrant clarification before we press on to more substantive matters.

Myth 1: PPPs Provide New Private Funds to Pay for Public Infrastructure

Public infrastructure is never a "free lunch." Whether the investment required to pay for the capital costs of an infrastructure asset is financed by the government or by a private concessionaire, the investment cost and operating costs must ultimately be repaid from taxes assessed on citizens at various levels, from tolls or other user fees paid for by the users of the asset, or from some combination of these two sources. In recent years, governments worldwide have been very reluctant to raise taxes, especially in the wake of the global financial crisis of 2007. PPPs have often been presented as a way to fund infrastructure without imposing new taxes on the public. It is factually accurate to state that a PPP which will be entirely paid for by user fees does not require new taxes to be levied, but this is misleading. Users will now have to pay new or higher tolls or other usage fees for an asset that might otherwise have been fully or partly paid for by taxes, and then provided to users free or with lower, more-subsidized user fees: lower tolls in the case of a highway or bridge, and free or with lower passenger fares in the case of a transit project.

Myth 2: Public Financing in the US is Less Costly than Private Financing

Legislation and tax policy at multiple levels in the US have created a fiscal and taxation regime in which municipalities, counties, special tax entities (for example, school districts), states and the federal government can issue tax-exempt bonds that allow them to raise financing for public works projects at reduced interest rates. Being tax-exempt at one or more levels reduces the coupon rate of these bonds to reflect the fact that the buyers of the bonds do not pay taxes on the interest paid to them by the issuer. Thus, public financing is often argued to provide a lower-cost alternative to private financing.

However, the cities, counties, states and federal government agencies that issue these bonds are collectively subsidizing this difference in cost by foregoing the taxes they would normally collect on bond interest payments. The allegedly less costly tax exempt bonds result from a massive and costly cross-subsidization by governments of each other's projects through reduced tax receipts all around. And since this cross-subsidy scheme reduces tax revenues, governments at all levels faced with fiscal crunches have periodically considered removing this tax loophole. For example, in the post-2007 governmental fiscal crisis, certain representatives and senators in the US House and Senate were once again proposing the removal of this tax loophole.

Moreover, many of these bonds are not general obligation bonds of the government entity issuing them that are backed by the full faith, credit and taxing ability of the government entity involved. Rather, they are "revenue bonds," typically backed only by the revenues derived from the portfolio of revenue-generating assets operated by the public owner of the project for which the funds are being raised, and sometimes limited to the revenues from that specific project. So, the risk of a default borne by the purchaser of the bonds is essentially the same whether the bonds are issued by a government or a private issuer (unless the revenue bonds are guaranteed by revenue from a portfolio of infrastructure assets). Thus, the real risk-adjusted interest rate on a given public owner's portfolio of projects, net of tax subsidies, should be comparable. If proponents argue that government-issued bonds will be less expensive even after adjusting for these tax subsidies, because the local, state or federal government is likely to bail out government-issued revenue bonds with general taxpayer funds in the event of a default, then the cost savings from this perceived reduced risk of default are simply being transferred to taxpayers in the form of increased bail-out risks (Chapman, 2009).

Since other local or state jurisdictions continue to issue these tax-exempt bonds and impose the associated tax revenue reductions on their peer and higher-level government entities, a given jurisdiction can rightfully conclude that it would be foolish not to take advantage of the interest cost savings. So, as long as this cross-subsidization scheme persists, the reduced cost of public tax-exempt bond financing for a specific infrastructure project must be more than offset by a combination of risk transfer and other public benefits to make PPP delivery with private financing a preferred alternative to traditional public delivery with tax-exempt public financing.

Recent developments in the US such the Transportation Infrastructure Finance and Innovation Act (TIFIA) loan enhancement program and Public Activity Bonds (PABS) have made it possible for private developers to access partial project financing from enhanced and tax-exempt loans, reducing the difference in financing costs between traditional publicly financed delivery versus privately financed PPP infrastructure delivery.

Myth 3: The Only Benefit of a PPP is Privately Arranged Financing

It is true that private financing can help to augment or replace government financing, but we argue that it delivers four additional benefits:

1. Alternative sources of financing. Sometimes public agencies are able to generate funding from taxes or user fees to pay off the capital and operating costs of a given project but are unable to finance the otherwise viable and beneficial project for various reasons, including their own fiscal plight (as in the post-2007 financial meltdown), legal restrictions such as laws requiring legislative supermajorities or public referenda to authorize bond sales, or current capital market conditions. To the extent that public financing capacity becomes a constraint on the development of infrastructure, PPPs can dramatically increase the available sources of financing to build needed infrastructure.
2. Risk transfer. Transferring some or all of the project risks to the PPP concessionaire protects the state from mishaps and cost overruns. This, in turn, creates a level of profit-driven discipline that is often lacking in publicly funded projects (Flyvbjerg et al., 2005a). For resource-starved governments, this efficiency boost and transfer of risk is often welcome.
3. Sustainability. When a concessionaire assumes the life cycle costs of building, operating and maintaining an infrastructure asset to specified performance standards, the decisions that are made tend to focus on optimizing life cycle sustainability rather than simply on minimizing first cost or operating cost (Henisz et al., 2012).
4. Time savings. Designing and building an asset using innovative construction methods has been demonstrated to reduce design and construction time by up to two years (Chasey et al., 2012) when compared to a traditional design–bid–build public procurement approach. This time saving can often also help offset the higher cost of PPP financing.
5. Contractually guaranteed maintenance. When governments face fiscal shortfalls, the first thing to be cut is typically the maintenance of existing infrastructure assets. Deferring needed maintenance incurs the need for increasingly more costly compensating downstream maintenance. Many large infrastructure projects in the US that were funded by 90 percent federal funds with a requirement that local funds be used to maintain the project have rapidly fallen into disrepair for this reason. PPP contracts typically impose stringent performance standards for maintenance which, if not met, impose financial penalties on the concessionaire. Thus, PPP projects tend to be reliably well maintained as long as the concession remains viable.

In short, a variety of factors could make PPP an attractive project delivery option. And yet, a project's specific circumstances largely determine whether or not a PPP makes sense. The decision as to whether a project is best done through traditional public procurement or a PPP relies on a "value for money" analysis that compares the relative financing costs, administrative and legal costs, risk transfers, and the expected value to the public of transferring those risks to the private sector.

Myth 4: PPPs Mean Imposing Tolls, and Voters Dislike Tolls

Since many of the roads in the US – in particular, the Interstate Highway System – were primarily paid for with federal funds, citizens in the Western US, who developed their intercity road networks later than those in the East, have grown accustomed to driving in and between cities on "freeways" rather than paying by the mile for the use of tolled "turnpikes," which are much more common among the more densely populated and older intercity and urban roads in the Eastern US. Western drivers' resistance can create significant political challenges to any attempts to fund roads partially or fully through tolls. And in spite of a long history of tolling in the Eastern US, resistance to introducing new tolls can still become significant, as in the cases of the Elizabeth River Tunnels in Virginia and Tappan Zee Bridge Replacement in New York.

In this respect, it is important to keep in mind that all infrastructure projects must ultimately be paid for or funded in one of two ways: (1) government funds raised through taxes; or (2) fees charged to users of the project, such as tolls. Even privately financed PPP projects must be funded by public subsidies, user fees, or a combination. In other words, private financing does not necessarily lead to tolls. In fact, transportation projects utilizing private finance outside the US often do not involve user fees, but rather incur direct payments by the government over time (Garvin, 2009).

Myth 5: PPPs Represent a New and Untested Infrastructure Procurement Policy in the US

Between the late eighteenth century and early twentieth century, Congress shrewdly supported expansion and economic growth using a two-track strategy: spending federal funds to "push" projects considered crucial for developing commerce and trade, and "pulling" projects from the private sector through indirect means such as land grants or franchises awarded to private parties. Such projects are amenable to granting contiguous property rights to their developers or to charging fees from their users.

Governments at all levels throughout the nation used similar approaches to develop infrastructure deemed to be in the public interest. For instance, the first PPP in California can be traced back to 1851 when the Mission Toll Road was opened to the public. At the time, canals and railroads had drained public coffers, forcing the construction of new roads onto the private sector. As a result, private road building enjoyed quite a boom in the far West from 1850 to 1902 (Klein and Yin, 1996). Records indicate that 414 toll roads were incorporated in California during that period (although only 159 are known to have been built) (Klein and Yin, 1996).

The private sector's dominance began to wane when the automobile came on the scene. But when Ronald Reagan became Governor in 1967, he found a large budget deficit and resumed the search for alternative methods of finance. Once again, as public debt rose further in the 1970s, the popularity of PPPs began to increase. They were used for a number of categories of infrastructure including local water, healthcare and prisons. In the 1980s, discussions about PPPs in the state legislature were focused on transportation projects. However, only two PPP projects from this period resulted in construction: (1) the 91 Express Lane (Caltrans, 2009; Garvey, 1999; OCTA, 2011) between Orange and Riverside Counties; and (2) the South Bay Expressway (AASHTO, 2011; FHWA, 2018b) in the San Diego area (Peter, 2011).

During the Schwarzenegger administration (2003–2011) a flurry of activities resulted in the authorization of $20 billion to various transportation projects that contained additional PPP provisions. California had only two significant PPP projects underway at the end of Governor Schwarzenegger's term: (1) the Presidio Parkway (ARUP PB Joint Venture, 2010), a new southern approach to the Golden Gate bridge; and (2) the Long Beach Courthouse. These projects represent two of the latest efforts in California to utilize the PPP model not only in transportation but also in financing essential government buildings.

In sum, the private sector has been a partner in various US infrastructure projects for more than 200 years. The ideology behind allowing the public sector to draw on all potential project delivery systems is based on the conviction that, together, the public and private sectors can provide the best services to meet the growing needs of US infrastructure, with the private sector often tapped for its potential to deliver value and innovation.

Myth 6: PPPs are the Same as Privatizations

The private sector has always been involved in the building and maintenance of infrastructure projects, whether they come in the form of PPPs or traditional public procurement. Likewise, no matter the delivery mechanism, the government always remains closely involved, even underwriting the ongoing delivery of the public service. In PPPs, the assets are not sold to the private sector. The private sector is simply responsible and at risk for service provision. The government still defines what is required to meet the needs of the public in a PPP. Moreover, the government also retains the authority to hold the private sector accountable for meeting these requirements via contract. So, if the private sector fails to deliver, there are a variety of safeguards for the government:

- The contractor is under considerable risk of capital loss should the contract not get off the ground, which offers a very powerful incentive to get the project done on time and on budget.
- The equity investors will only benefit from the project after it is complete and in operation. And the initial investment is sometimes recouped over a long time horizon, which promotes a life cycle approach to project delivery.
- The creditors are more risk-averse than the equity providers. These investors put up most of the money for the projects. The creditors play a huge role in due diligence, ensuring that there are no "bridges to nowhere" being built with their money (because their loans would never be paid back).

Thus, the private sector may play an important role in PPPs, but the public sector still has considerable authority. Moreover, the public ultimately retains ownership of the assets. Notwithstanding the clear evidence dispelling the myth of privatization, one additional element bears further attention. It relates to additional public involvement within the concession arrangement through a minority equity investment.

Consider the case of investment arms of private companies that also have infrastructure operating business units that frequently contract with their parent company's operating business units to provide the engineering, construction, and/or operations and maintenance for PPPs. At commercial close most PPPs have a fixed price, and a date-certain design–build contract that cannot change unless relief events in the commercial agreement or DB agreement occur; typically just *force majeure* events. Hence, the incentive from the equity holders' (or SPV) side is always to drive costs down and reduce delivery time once a deal is struck, not vice versa. Nevertheless, some critics of PPPs have argued that, if corporate entities related to the delivery contractors are the principal or only shareholders in the PPP concession, as was the case in the (England to France) Channel Tunnel, there is the potential for a real – or at least a perceived – conflict of interest to arise in transactions such as change order negotiations related to the provision of the engineering, construction or operations services to the project.

The infrastructure investment units in these companies are typically staffed, operated and evaluated independently of their sister service delivery arms, so the investment arm is in tension with the construction or operations and maintenance arm, and the transactions between them tend to be managed at "arm's length." And it can be argued that the parent company in this case is more committed to the venture than a passive institutional investor would be, since it is holding both an equity and an operational stake in the project and is likely to seek win–win outcomes in negotiations, as opposed to win–lose or self-dealing outcomes.

However, the construction and investment arms of these firms may have common ownership structures, and so there could be real or perceived conflicts of interest in the SPVs. Involving pure financial equity investors such as pension funds, or funds whose goals are strictly to maximize return on equity, helps to manage these conflicts, when combined with SPV corporate articles and bylaws that require recusal of conflicted parties from board decisions, and the appointment of independent directors and probity auditors, as is now often done in Australia (see Chapter 5 in this volume).

In jurisdictions where there is no strong public infrastructure procurement and finance agency with the capacity and expertise to audit PPP projects independently, governmental or public perception of a possible conflict of interest can be a significant concern to state or local agencies. The various levels of government involved can collectively take significant equity stakes in specific PPP projects to mitigate this concern. For example, governments in Canada and Australia have taken stakes of up to 49 percent in some of their most successful PPP projects to date. Taking equity in a PPP project places representatives of the government "at the partners' table" so that they can be engaged in negotiating transactions such as change orders between the equity holders and the construction or operations delivery business units of the equity holders' parent companies.

Having governments take equity stakes in their PPP projects also recognizes the fact that governments always have some residual risk in developing public infrastructure, even when these risks have been contractually allocated to others. The government equity holder gives the PPP projects the perception of being more transparent in evaluating change orders requested by the service providers, or in pricing other transactions between the financing and delivery arms of these enterprises. And, from the private investors' point of view, a local government or a local public pension fund that is a significant stakeholder in a PPP project gives the project some level of "political air cover" against future expropriation of project returns by the local government through forced governmental buyouts, unnecessarily stringent regulation of tolls, or other means. This political air cover can be particularly valuable for PPP projects delivered in countries with a weak rule of law and turbulent politics.

Myth 7: The Private Sector's Profit in PPPs Comes at the Expense of the Public Sector

The idea of a PPP is to harness the private sector in the areas where it can provide additional value for money. In this respect, the objective is to find situations where the private sector can manage to create sufficient profit, while still adding net value for the public sector by aligning interests and allocating risks to the people best able to manage them. This can be done in a variety of ways, such as through accelerated project delivery. Project planners can define risks that are optimally shouldered by the private sector, and those that should remain with the public sector. Any government's interest in PPPs should rest on its ability to find value for money (VfM) from the public investment that does not come at the expense of the public sector.

RECOMMENDATIONS FOR SELECTING AND IMPLEMENTING PPPs

Governments considering the delivery of infrastructure via PPPs should conduct VfM analyses for all proposed PPP projects using consistent, rigorous and transparent processes such as those of Infrastructure Ontario (2012a), the Florida Department of Transportation (FDOT) and the consultants on the Presidio Parkway. Impartial third parties should be retained to assess the most significant risks, and the VfM analysis should be repeated when project scope or other key assumptions underlying the initial VfM analysis change materially.

Very few US state or local governments currently possess their own mature and sophisticated PPP or public infrastructure delivery and finance agencies with the capacity to perform rigorous VfM analyses, and to negotiate PPP concession agreements. Until they can develop this kind of capacity, we recommend that US state and local agencies contemplating PPP projects contract with consultants in project evaluation, engineering due diligence, financial due diligence, PPP contract law, and other areas of expertise needed to develop PPP delivery processes and to negotiate PPP concession agreements that are tough but fair. The transaction advisory units in large global infrastructure engineering, legal and financial services companies can provide many of these services, including conducting rigorous VfM analyses to judge whether a PPP offers the public positive value for money compared to traditional public sector delivery methods.

Government agencies involved in PPP projects should consider taking an equity stake in the concession arrangement when legally, financially and fiscally possible, particularly when there is a concern for a perceived conflict of interest on the part of private parties (due to single organizations or related party organizations in concession agreements). This direct investment into a project gives the public entity access and involvement in the PPP process, and an additional level of oversight to the activities of the concessionaire. Such practices can also help to mitigate residual project risk.

The use of PPP delivery for social infrastructure – schools, hospitals, courthouses, jails, and so on – has been widely and successfully adopted in the United Kingdom, Canada, Australia and other countries, but has been relatively little used in the US to date, aside from its large-scale use to develop military housing (GAO, 2006, 2009) and university residence halls. Public building agencies such as the General Services Administration, which develops and manages federal office buildings, have often leased office space from private developers, similarly to the way that large private firms such as Google or Intel do, but have seldom used PPP delivery approaches to develop new facilities on public land. A few hospitals have been built this way (for example, Seattle Bellevue Children's Hospital). The most visible social infrastructure PPP project recently built in the US is the courthouse in Long Beach, California. There is significant opportunity for other kinds of social infrastructure to be built by PPPs, assuming sufficient scale or complexity to counter the attendant transaction costs, at a time when the US economy could greatly benefit from the large number of resulting construction jobs created, with their high economic multiplier.

The most recent round of California transportation PPPs was initiated by an all-volunteer Public Infrastructure Advisory Commission appointed by the Governor, consisting of a combination of interest group representatives and infrastructure delivery experts, but without any significant funding or staff resources. The one PPP project that was recommended by this commission to date – the Presidio Parkway project described above – achieved financial close in May of 2012. The California Department of Transportation and the local agencies involved in this project were competently advised by a group of consultants with experience on PPP projects in other states and countries. California, along with other states that lack a significant public infrastructure financing capability that are contemplating the use of PPP delivery for civil or social infrastructure, will need to use such consultants to advise them in the near term. In the longer term, they should avail themselves of the expertise, experience, process guidelines and document templates available from mature global public infrastructure delivery and finance management organizations (e.g., Infrastructure Ontario, Partnerships UK and Partnerships BC), and allocate the required resources to begin developing these kinds of analytic and decision-making capabilities for themselves. Interestingly, as of July 7, 2018, Governor Brown, the succeeding California Governor who was elected in 2011, had not yet appointed a chair of the Public Infrastructure Advisory Commission (PIAC), so it was still dormant.[1]

If California would like to develop governmental capacity to harness the many advantages that PPPs can provide its citizens in renovating its existing infrastructure and developing new, sorely needed, world-class infrastructure for the most populous state in the union, the state could begin by augmenting an existing organization such as the California Infrastructure Bank. The California I-Bank already has significant infrastructure project financing and contractual expertise, which could easily be augmented to provide broad-based public infrastructure financing capability by hiring additional staff familiar with PPP processes and methods. The expanded I-Bank should ideally be set up in the executive branch as part of the Governor's office, where it would be relatively isolated from the inherently shorter-term and local political pressures impinging on members of the state legislature. The legislature is the appropriate body to decide what fraction of the state budget should go to infrastructure overall, and through state agencies and commissions such as Caltrans and the California Transportation Commission, to prioritize projects relative to one another for funding. Similarly to Partnerships UK or Infrastructure Ontario (2012b), California's public sector procurement and financing agency can then determine the most appropriate way to deliver the state's projects – via either one of the traditional public sector delivery options, or PPP delivery – and to put in place appropriate procedures for financing and managing these projects through the cognizant state or local agencies for transportation, justice, education, hospitals, and so on.

The environmental review and permitting process should be approached differently for projects that are known PPP candidates. Public agencies should avoid unnecessary prescription, particularly when it is not required to identify environmental impacts, and wherever possible show potential limits of deviation in elevation and alignment in defining the alternatives. Exceptions to this concept would include, for example, cases where it is necessary to define a precise elevation for assessment of noise impacts. If given some flexibility in choosing alignments or designs, the PPP concessionaire can often develop more innovative alternatives. This maximizes the opportunity for technical innovation in subsequent project phases.

PPP concessions should be awarded once most or all significant environmental review processes have been completed. A concessionaire has little or no control over the rate of progress and ultimate outcome of an environmental impact review process, so it should not be expected to bear these risks. The multi-year delays on California SR125 (Outlaw, 2003; SANDAG, 2012), due to the long and drawn-out environmental impact review undertaken after the award of the initial PPP concession, contributed significantly to the subsequent bankruptcy of the concessionaire on that project. As intended in the concession agreement, the bulk of these risks were indeed transferred to the private equity and debt participants in the concessionaire, resulting in its bankruptcy and a significant write-down of the debt. However, this misallocation of risk cast a pall over private investment for future PPP projects in the state for a decade or more.

PPP project concessions should be financially and contractually engineered from the outset to allow and encourage engineering and construction contractors that are PPP sponsors to exit the SPV after construction completion and the project's ramp-up phase. These competitively selected contractors provide their expertise to manage the design and construction risks. Following the completion of construction, they have already profited more or less, based on how skillfully they have managed the engineering and construction risks. It is thus appropriate for them to exit the project equity once revenue operations have been established so that they can free up their capital to deploy their skills and resources for developing new projects. At this point, sovereign wealth funds, pension funds or other institutional investors can replace the delivery partners' equity with longer-term, lower-risk financing, at lower rates of return that better match the institutional investors' intergenerational tenor and more conservative risk–return goals. The sponsoring government agency can, and sometimes does, share contractually in any additional profit that a lower-cost refinancing generates for the equity partners. This optimizes the cost of capital for the project, allowing each party to bring its expertise in managing risks and its financial risk–return goals to bear on the different kinds and levels of risk in the development versus operational phases of public sector projects. And it has the added benefit that it can help the sovereign wealth and pension funds raise the weighted average returns of their investment portfolios closer to their historical target return rates of about 8 percent, far better than the very low returns currently being achieved by most sovereign debt and other traditional pension fund investments.

Even if they plan to exit the project following construction completion, the sponsoring engineers and contractors will still be incentivized to take a life cycle perspective in their design and construction decision-making to maximize the price and expedite the time at which they can exit the project by selling it off to the institutional investors. Aggressive non-compete agreements should be avoided on tolled highways in situations where future demand for the infrastructure facility is likely to far outstrip supply. The SR91 in California engendered significant public resentment when traffic demand on these roads increased rapidly, the commute rush-hour tolls became unaffordable to many lower-income commuters, and the freeways became ever more congested. Governments may have to accept a higher private financing cost in the absence of stringent non-compete agreements, or when they disclose those routes where government improvements are permitted or limited prior to procurement. Otherwise, such projects will not be politically viable as privately operated PPP toll road concessions in the long term. A potential alternative would be to make use of availability payments to fund such projects, as in the I-595 (FDOT, 2009a, 2009b, 2009c) and Presidio Parkway PPP projects (see above), so that they can be operated as freeways instead of toll roads. The governments involved would be far more likely to retain public support for a project if the project were not tolled, even if demand were subsequently to balloon, thus rendering even the new or expanded freeway congested.

NOTE

1. One of the book's editors and co-authors of this chapter served as a Commissioner of this currently moribund California PIAC advisory commission, but resigned after several years of inaction by PIAC, following the election of California Governor Jerry Brown.

2. Stakeholder network dynamics in public–private partnerships

Andrew J. South, Raymond E. Levitt and Geert P.M.R. Dewulf

INTRODUCTION

Public–private partnerships (PPPs) are increasingly utilized for the provisioning of infrastructure assets across the globe. As argued by scholars over the last decade, however, there is still much to understand about the governance of these arrangements and the antecedents to various performance outcomes at different levels (Brinkerhoff and Brinkerhoff, 2011; Hodge and Greve, 2007). This is unsurprising as PPPs generally have long life cycles (often 25–50 years) and there is only a small portion of modern PPPs that have completed such terms. Surprising is the large number of PPPs that continue to be developed, and the number of national and subnational governmental bodies that have or are establishing special PPP units and enabling legal frameworks for PPPs, given a contested spectrum of perceived mixed results and unexpected outcomes (for example, early terminations and renegotiations of previous PPPs) (World Bank, 2014). The continued international interest in PPPs for infrastructure provisioning is in need of a more empirically grounded understanding of PPPs with more attention devoted to developing effective life cycle governance of these arrangements.

The organization and governance of large infrastructure projects are complex in themselves (Flyvbjerg et al., 2005a; Flyvbjerg, 2017), but the organization of an infrastructure PPP adds another level of complexity (Grimsey and Lewis, 2002), as PPPs engage a network of stakeholders from different sectors of society including public, private and civic (De Schepper et al., 2014; El-Gohary et al., 2006; Mitchell et al., 1997). In effect, the project brings together diverse members of a wider organization field including developers, financial interests, architectural firms, engineering companies, state regulators and social movement organizations (Scott, 2014). The "public" domain of public–private partnerships refers to governmental bodies and authorities, and publicly owned companies that typically sponsor the PPP on behalf of the public interest (noting that these organizations may also at times include private sector consultants). The "private" domain refers to private sector organizations involved in proposing on, bidding for and contracting to provide a range of professional services related to the development, finance and operation of the PPP. A third, and less often explicitly addressed, civic sector refers to the general public, including users of the infrastructure (who often pay user fees of some sort), special interest groups and affected municipal governments (Kivleniece and Quelin, 2012; Skocpol and Fiorina, 2004). Stakeholders are organizations and/or collective action groups that interact with each other as a result of the PPP. Stakeholders from the different sectors have different objectives and motivations, different repertoires of action, and often different value systems. Stakeholders also have differing perceptions of the socio-economic value and impact of PPPs, and infrastructure in general. Even physical constraints of the PPP environment are evaluated and mediated by and through stakeholders. Therefore, the issue of which stakeholders, and their interactions, is of interest in this research.

Identifying when each stakeholder is active in a PPP is also important. Infrastructure PPPs are developed and operated over long time periods that can be divided into distinct phases by key milestones with specific activities in each phase. In each phase, different stakeholders are present or absent in varying degrees. The following four phases are differentiated:

- Phase one, identification. This phase stretches from initial ideas and project conception to a published request for proposals (RFP).
- Phase two, procurement. This phase is triggered by the issuance of an RFP by the PPP sponsor, continuing through evaluation of proposals and negotiations, to contract award and financial close.
- Phase three, design/construction. Beginning at financial close, this phase includes design and construction, ending with commissioning of the infrastructure asset.
- Phase four, operate/maintain. This is generally the longest phase, which begins with operational ramp-up and continues through its defined concession term. It may include scheduled upgrades and repairs as well as secondary transactions, where the concession agreement and its operations are sold.

Scholars and practitioners have written about the importance of well-executed "front-end" strategy and planning for the success of large infrastructure projects (Artto et al., 2001; Edkins et al., 2013; Miller and Lessard, 2000). However it is noteworthy that key stakeholders in the latter phases of development, especially the longest and final phase of the PPP (operate/maintain phase), are seldom present in the early identification phase. To the extent that organizational stakeholders from later phases are involved in the early phases, it is generally through the representation of different individuals and at differing levels of management in the stakeholder organization. These stakeholder changes and the PPP stakeholder network changes over time add to the complexity of PPPs. The temporal nature of stakeholder interactions in PPPs is an important component to PPP network behavior and performance, which represents a significant gap in the current literature on PPPs, and therefore a critical component of this research.

A growing body of research illustrates the challenges in cooperation between stakeholders of the public, private and civic sectors over the PPP life cycle (Bryson, 2004; Mahalingam and Levitt, 2007). An important factor in the cooperation problem is the difference in stakeholders' institutional logics. Each type of stakeholder is rooted in a different institutional environment with a unique institutional logic (Saz-Carranza and Longo, 2012; Thornton and Ocasio, 2008). Institutional logics are the belief systems and associated practices of stakeholders (Scott, 2014), observable through their actions and interactions with others. Institutional logics related to formal and informal constraints, related to conceptions noted by North (1991), are identified as: formal institutional logics – those relating to legal and regulative action; and informal institutional logics – those relating to norms and cultures. Thus, in addition to looking at which and when stakeholders are interacting with one another, how they interact (whether formally or informally) is also important. In order to further an understanding of infrastructure PPPs, the purpose of this research was to develop a deeper understanding of stakeholder network changes in an infrastructure PPP as evidenced through stakeholder interactions based on formal and informal institutional logics, across four development phases.

To a surprising extent, PPPs evidence a dynamic stakeholder network as varying participants enter and depart over a PPP's life cycle, including changes in the identity of the network's "anchor-tenant." The concept of anchor-tenant is taken from Padgett and Powell (2012) to describe the primary or dominant stakeholder in the network during each phase. The anchor-tenant shapes the purpose and mode of interaction with the largest number of stakeholders, and influences the interaction between others. A change in the anchor-tenant across phases is the first major dynamic identified. Additionally, in phases where an anchor-tenant and its activities use a formal or informal institutional logic, other stakeholders tend to adopt a similar institutional logic. This leads to changes in the development of formal and informal institutional relationships over the PPP phases. In the identification phase, informal institutional logics and relationships are dominant. In the design/construction and operate/maintain phases, formal institutional logics and relationships are dominant. Additionally, it is evident that the public, private and civic stakeholder groups develop relationships differently. The public and private stakeholder groups rely primarily on formal institutional relations, while civic stakeholders use primarily informal relations. These changes and differences in the dominant institutional logics present in the PPP stakeholder network is the second major dynamic identified.

These findings contribute to an increased understanding of PPPs and suggest ways toward improving PPP governance systems. The results show that infrastructure PPPs change dramatically over their life cycle, suggesting a greater need to consider them as dynamic arrangements. The implication of this finding is that coordination should be organized across phases for effective management of diverse and dynamic stakeholder networks, specifically attempting to involve dominant later-phase stakeholders at the earlier phases. Further, it indicates the need for an overarching governance framework facilitating increased coordination over an infrastructure PPP's life cycle to allow stakeholders from all phases of the PPP to interact with one another while bridging incompatible institutional logics.

LITERATURE

Infrastructure PPP Governance

The interest in infrastructure PPPs is motivated by an urgent need to improve infrastructure around the world, and to find ways to increase the attractiveness of private sector participation in infrastructure development to both governments and private investors. In general the PPP literature has focused on risk in PPPs, the financial structuring of PPP deals, and the collaborative structure of public and private organizations (Grimsey and Lewis, 2002, Grimsey and Lewis, 2005). The primary focus of PPP research in construction and engineering management is governance and management of contractual and relational ties between public, private and civic stakeholders (Tang et al., 2010). It is against this background that PPPs as stakeholder networks, involving public, private and civic stakeholders (Fassin, 2009), are conceptualized. PPPs are unusually challenging to coordinate, due to the presence of multiple stakeholders (Roloff, 2008) and because they go through phases that involve considerable change in the nature of the work to be done, hence changing levels of involvement from stakeholders (Kwak et al., 2009). Because infrastructure PPPs involve such distinct and dynamic stakeholder groups, stakeholder theory is used as a conceptual frame to understand their governance.

Stakeholder Theory and Infrastructure PPPs

Stakeholder theory was developed as a perspective of strategic business management, where a stable organization could evaluate and meet the challenges of its external environment as it "takes into account all of those groups and individuals that can affect, or are affected by, the accomplishment of [the firm's] organizational purpose" (Freeman, 1984). Freeman depicts this external environment as including organizations in the firm's supply chain, government regulators, policy-makers, consumers, media, special interest groups, and so on. This theory was a departure from traditional strategic management theory, in which shareholders or stockholders were regarded as the primary stakeholder of interest to the firm A conventional strategic management perspective considered other stakeholders' interests in a stockholder optimization calculus. Since Freeman's original work, however, the concept of stakeholders has been adopted from the domain of strategic management to areas including business ethics, corporate social responsibility (CSR) and environmental justice (Laplume et al., 2008). These perspectives on stakeholder theory suggest a normative treatment of stakeholders and their "rights" as impacted by a firm's pursuit of its objectives. Given a diversity of stakeholders and their differing focal issues and organizational structures, stakeholder interactions can take many forms. Stakeholder theory is therefore applicable to many contexts, and can be based on different kinds of stakeholder involvement (Wolfe and Putler, 2002).

Most research using stakeholder theory has studied stakeholders within and between firms, and although very few studies have explicitly studied stakeholder involvement in infrastructure PPPs (El-Gohary et al., 2006), the theory has been applied to similar study domains. These include project management (Aaltonen and Kujala, 2010; Newcombe, 2003; Fassin, 2009) and construction management (Kwak et al., 2009). Taken together, these studies provide support for the use of stakeholder theory as applied to infrastructure PPPs. Stakeholder theory is applied here to understand the involvement of public, private and civic sector actor groups in a PPP. Public sector stakeholders of a PPP include the public sponsoring organization, related coordinating authorities, and regulators at various levels. Private sector stakeholders include the private developer organization(s), their consultants, building contractors and suppliers, finance institutions and infrastructure asset operators. Civic sector stakeholders include the user public, non-profit organizations impacted by the PPP, special interest groups and media organizations. These can be conceptualized as a network of different actors, or stakeholder networks. A similarity with other network conceptualizations is that stakeholder networks are often complex networks of interrelated and heterogeneous stakeholders, and PPPs are such complex networks.

The development of an infrastructure PPP involves the management of a network of stakeholders with potentially shifting perceptions and objectives. Developing a cooperative environment with stakeholders would reduce the number of conflicts and minimize opportunistic behavior, therefore avoiding important delays and costs (for example, lawsuits, political fights, social movements). Earlier work in the transaction cost economics literature acknowledges the role of a collaborative environment in the success of contract performance (Freeman and McVea, 2006; Williamson, 1975), yet microeconomists have neglected the importance of individual stakeholders. Other stakeholder research echoes this apparent void, noting that differences between stakeholders in stakeholder networks have been understudied (Wolfe and Putler, 2002). Given that PPPs consist of fundamentally different public, private and civic sector stakeholders, there is strong support for using stakeholder theory to understand stakeholder networks of PPPs.

Infrastructure PPP Stakeholder Networks and Institutional Theory

Institutional theorists analyze social structures, including procedures, rules, schemas and routines that have become established as guiding principles for moderating organizational and social behavior in the face of institutional forces. Institutional theory offers a theoretical foundation in addressing the "processes by which social structures, including both normative and behavioral systems, are established, become stable and undergo changes overtime" (Scott, 2014). Institutional theory posits that institutions and organizations interact in a structuration process leading to shared norms (DiMaggio and Powell, 1983; Meyer and Rowan, 1977; Scott, 2008). This is important in the case of PPPs, as arrangements between public, private and civic stakeholders are predicated on their differing institutional backgrounds, which naturally produces potentially conflicting schemas and situational definitions of and within PPPs (Kivleniece and Quelin, 2012).

The application of institutional theory to infrastructure PPPs is particularly salient because these projects transcend multiple institutional environments. The arrangements of PPPs are often institutionally immature, meaning that many stakeholders may have little or no experience in PPPs and that regulations and norms guiding actions may not be established. Even when stakeholders have PPP experience, the specificity of PPPs suggest that the composition of regulator influences, a diverse stakeholder network and other forces from the broader environmental context are likely to produce a somewhat unique arrangement. Therefore, as stakeholders approach a specific PPP from their differing perspectives and experience (or lack thereof) they will likely rely on their existing institutionalized modes of interaction, regardless of whether it "fits" the situation or is compatible with other stakeholders from other perspectives. Thus, understanding the institutional environment of stakeholders is important to understanding how they act.

Dominant Institutional Logics and Relationships over Infrastructure PPPs Development Phases

Infrastructure PPPs are typically developed over several phases, with varying degrees of stakeholder involvement. This concept is broadly defined, and is used purposely as the field of PPP infrastructure research is still developing. According to an evolutionary realist perspective, theory building starts with broad concepts, and progresses toward more well-defined concepts and relationships between concepts (Azevedo, 1997). The concept of "involvement" is used in other research areas to represent a commitment to influence in some respect, such as in business, corporate social responsibility, social economy (Reed and Reed, 2009), public administration (Vigoda, 2002) or organizational involvement (Zsidisin et al., 2000). In this chapter, the definition of "stakeholder involvement" in a PPP is: the degree to which a stakeholder is central to the PPP. Such a broad definition is motivated by the early stages of PPP research. Figure 2.1 illustrates conceptually how the involvement level of different types of stakeholders might vary between phases, and identifies potential discrete triggering events between phases.

This scheme was developed through a comparative analysis of 18 United States (US) highway PPP cases at various stages of development. The first phase involves the identification of an infrastructure asset for PPP delivery, the second is the procurement of the PPP concession, the third is the design and construction phase (which includes a large portion of the active finance activities), and the final phase is operations and maintenance (which historically has included asset monitoring, performance measures, benchmarking, secondary transactions, and so on).

Figure 2.1 depicts a PPP public sponsor and a private developer involved early in the project, with the sponsor's level of involvement being higher. As the PPP concept progresses through the identification phase, and becomes more probable, both become more involved. At this point civic users may become involved (either by design or spontaneously). As

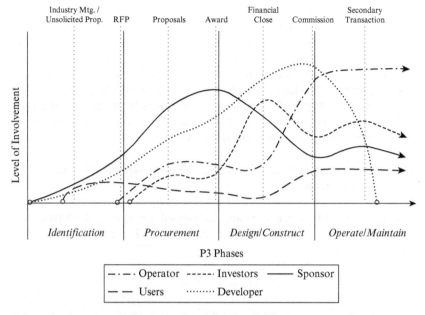

Figure 2.1 Conceptual phases of infrastructure P3 projects, with fluctuating levels of stakeholder involvement

a request for proposals (RFP) is published, private investors and private operators are generally engaged as teams to form and produce proposals. At the time of award, the sponsor is likely to be at its highest level of involvement, and more involved than any other stakeholder. After the PPP concession is awarded, the developer increases its involvement in the PPP during the design and construct phase. Investors are also highly engaged in advance of financial close. The sponsor often begins to reduce its involvement in the project while the operator dramatically increases participation in preparation for the operate and maintain phase. During this last phase, stakeholders' levels of involvement may stabilize. However, as is repeatedly the case in practice, developers of PPPs dramatically decrease their involvement and may seek to exit the arrangement.

The changes in stakeholders' level of involvement over phases are here depicted as gradual, with smooth curves indicating increases and decreases of involvement. However, there may be reason to consider some discrete events, such as the submittal of an RFP, or the signing of an awarded concession agreement, that would produce a steeper increase in stakeholder involvement. Naturally only a few of the key stakeholders in the PPP stakeholder network are identified and depicted in Figure 2.1. The key insight here is that a stakeholder's involvement changes over time in an infrastructure PPP, and thus the composition of the stakeholder network also changes over the phases.

Because multiple stakeholders from differing institutional environments are engaged in the PPP network, stakeholders presumably represent their institutional frame to different degrees. Based on how stakeholder theory and institutional theory relate to infrastructure PPPs, both are relevant and should be combined. Even though stakeholder and institutional theories have not been applied simultaneously to infrastructure PPPs previously, the nature of the phenomenon of phase-based network dynamics can be illuminated by combining these theories. Therefore, stakeholder networks and institutional theory are used as a conceptual framework for analysis in this chapter. Since existing research is not well developed on PPP governance, particularly with respect to stakeholder engagement and management, the framework is used to guide analysis toward theory generation from an in-depth case-based set of observations.

METHOD AND DATA

To empirically understand the involvement of public, private and civic stakeholders throughout the life cycle of the PPP, an exploratory in-depth case study approach is used with the PPP known as California State Route 91 Express Lanes (SR91X). This retrospective case covers more than two decades, from identification of the potential PPP in the early 1990s, to its present-day ongoing operations and maintenance phase.

In case study research the selection of appropriate cases is central to the research design and its effectiveness (Eisenhardt and Graebner, 2007; Flyvbjerg, 2011; Yin, 2013). The SR91X case was selected as it satisfied two important criteria. The primary consideration was selection of a case where the broader environment could encompass a maximal number of potential internal and external forces. This was important as a focus was to search widely for elements that may be found to influence the PPP governance structure. During the time of this case in the 1990s, US public and private sectors were inexperienced with modern PPPs. Particularly in the case of early US PPPs, there was little in the way of a national or state-level "PPP development road map" for public agencies or private developers to follow. Thus, it was important to explore "raw" aspects of PPPs and their emerging fields, with their ensuing unexpected obstacles and unintended consequences. SR91X was the first modern highway infrastructure PPP undertaken in the US since the 1950s.

In order to understand the dynamics of perceptions and reactions as a PPP moves across development phases, it was necessary for a case to have sufficient recordable data in each phase. The US highway transportation sector contains several PPPs that have transitioned into their operations phase. Additionally, due to their high visibility, highway transportation PPPs generally garner widespread publicity, producing a potentially large number of recorded observations accessible through secondary data sources. They are often located in densely populated areas, affect large geographic areas in terms of land disturbed, and assets are normally situated in high-traffic areas where stakeholders are directly and consciously aware of the PPP (particularly during lengthy and disruptive construction timelines). Once operational, high volumes of user-stakeholders interact directly with the PPP, meaning that they actually use (drive on) the asset; as compared to telecom, water and wastewater PPPs where user-stakeholders experience and must pay for a service provided by a PPP asset, but do not interact directly with the asset itself.

The Case

SR91X is a California highway transportation asset including 10 miles of four tolled lanes (two in each direction) along the heavily traveled east–west corridor of State Route 91 between Riverside County and Orange County. The 91 express lanes were constructed in the highway median between the existing non-tolled "general purpose" (or "free") lanes, separated by plastic pylons. The express lanes are tolled using an account-based system of payment, where registered users' vehicles are recorded using automatic photo capture of license plates and/or in-vehicle transponders at no-stop electronic toll gantries. The free-flow aspect of the system allows traffic to maintain highway speeds. A variable congestion-pricing scheme is used for establishing toll rates, and historical travel data is used to determine graduated peak times and rates for lane usage. These published rates are updated on a quarterly basis. The SR91X asset was developed on land controlled by the California Department of Transportation (Caltrans), the state agency responsible for highway, bridge and rail transportation planning, construction and maintenance. Caltrans, the sponsoring agency, entered a franchise agreement (a concession agreement) in 1993 with the California Private Transportation Company (CPTC). CPTC is a special purpose vehicle (SPV), a temporary organization owned by a consortium of corporate owners for the purpose of designing, building, financing, operating and maintaining the asset. The concession agreement contractually allowed CPTC to collect tolls to recover their investment and earn a profit subject to the agreement's terms and conditions.

Case Background

In 1980 State Route 91 had an average of more than 91 000 vehicle trips per day and was becoming one of the busiest stretches of highway in the country. As real estate prices in Riverside County were significantly lower than in neighboring Orange County, and Orange County had thriving employment centers, individuals continued to move east to Riverside County for lower costs of home ownership while maintaining employment in Orange County. The topography of the region illustrates the geographic challenge of building additional capacity anywhere besides the Santa Anna Valley, a single valley connecting these adjacent portions of Orange and Riverside counties. State Route 91 was an effectual "land bridge." As a result, the growing populations in Riverside County and the surrounding Inland Empire increased transportation pressure on the 91. By 1989 traffic on State Route 91 had more than doubled, with an average of more than 188 000 vehicle trips per day.

During the time that State Route 91 was experiencing extreme traffic growth, California continued to face constricted funding sources for transportation and increasing highway construction costs, two factors increasingly present in the 1970s and 1980s. In 1982 California increased the state gasoline tax from $0.07 to $0.09 per gallon. A gasoline tax constituted the primary funding mechanism for state highway construction, but the rate increase failed to match inflation, let alone the growing demands for highway infrastructure. Moreover, in June of 1988 a vote for the Governor's state bond initiative to help close the highway funding gap failed.

In response to the general highway transportation congestion of the greater Los Angeles metro area, the non-profit Reason Foundation published Policy Study No. 111, *Private Tollways: Resolving Gridlock in Southern California* in May of 1988 (Poole, 1988b). Borrowing from European, Asian and Australian examples, the study suggested three innovations that could relieve traffic pressure: congestion pricing, private toll roads, and automatic electronic identification and toll collection. At the time that the bond referendum failed, Robert Poole, Jr, director of the Reason Foundation, wrote an opinion editorial for the *Los Angeles Times* (Poole, 1988a) highlighting findings from the foundation's recent study. After the *LA Times* printed the piece, the Governor's Office of Planning and Research, the new top leadership at Caltrans, and leaders of other government and quasi-governmental organizations began discussing the possibility of private sector participation in the development of public infrastructure. Approximately one year later, California Assembly Bill 680 (AB 680) had passed and was signed into law with immediate effect. Key points of AB 680 stated that (California, 1989):

- California needed an efficient transportation system.
- Public sources of revenue had not kept pace with transportation needs.
- An important alternative was privately funded build–operate–transfer projects (a precursor to modern PPPs) for infrastructure delivery.
- Private entities will have the right to charge tolls to recover investment and operations costs, including a reasonable profit.
- Caltrans should be permitted and encouraged to develop four demonstration projects. SR91X was the first of the four demonstration projects to be completed (one of only two projects that would be completed under this legislation).

Data Collection and Analysis

Primary data was gathered from in-depth and semi-structured interviews of senior-level executives, managers and directors involved at different phases of SR91X. Interview participants were sampled from a cross-section of stakeholders along the project timeline, occupying different positions and roles as employed by various organizations. Access was obtained through chain-sampling of SR91X participants. Interviews began with participants most closely connected to the development and management of SR91X in the early phases of project identification. Interviews focused on critical events, events that materially shaped SR91X and which were the most easily recalled by respondents and verifiable with secondary data sources. In addition to understanding which events were perceived as critical, follow-up questions sought to inform an understanding of why respondents held their perceptions. This was necessary to connect perceptions and meaning to stakeholders' actions following these events. PPPs are comprised of a diverse network of stakeholders, each with differing interests that underpin their identities, objectives and repertoires of action. This approach is consistent with the "new archival" tradition of organization research: employing formal analytic methods; emphasizing organization processes, relations and shared meanings; and an interest in the underlying logics that connect these elements (Ventresca and Mohr, 2005).

Archival collection of more than 120 publicly available media accounts, fact sheets, annual reports, government documents, academic papers, and other similar sources were also collected and coded. These sources, coupled with interview materials, produced a project timeline for SR91X with 110 critical events over a 20-year period. The raw data for this study was this first-order coding and construction of a critical event register from within the project timeline (Figure 2.2 illustrates the general timeline of SR91X).

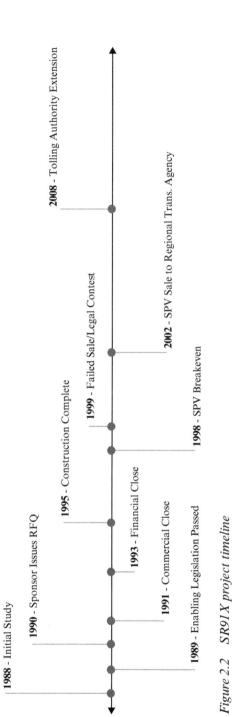

Figure 2.2   SR91X project timeline

Social Network Analysis

The case is analyzed using social network analysis (SNA) (Rowley, 1997). SNA allows the observation of relationships between interacting stakeholders, and theorizing on the importance of those relationships (Knoke and Yang, 2008; Scott, 2000; Wasserman and Faust, 1994). The use of SNA is quite new to stakeholder research.

A second-order coding of the critical event register produced a register of 62 stakeholders and 128 dyadic relationships in four phase-based networks. Each event represented a type of relationship (tie) between stakeholders, and ties were considered present for the PPP phase in which the coded event occurred. These sets of stakeholders and ties were used to construct four network graphs, one for each of the four phases of the PPP development cycle, using open source SNA software (Bastian et al., 2009). The network graphs are displayed in Figures 2.3–2.6.

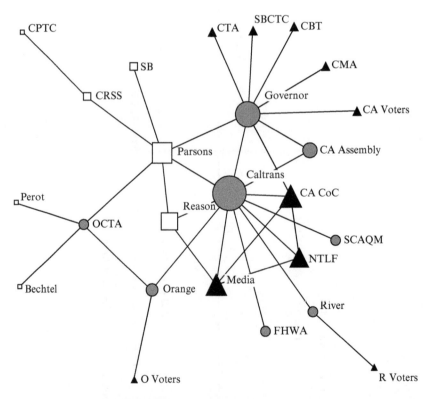

Figure 2.3 Identification phase network

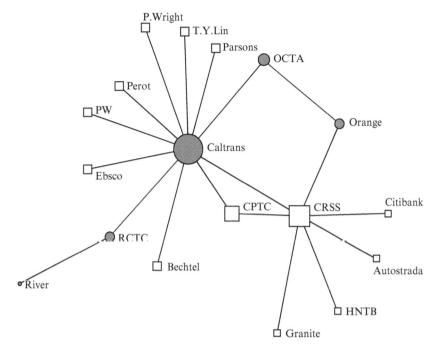

Figure 2.4 Procurement phase network

SNA provides a considerable array of measures and network statistics that represent network properties as a whole. In the present research, we report multiple properties from each of four temporal phase-based stakeholder networks in Table 2.1. "No. Actors" includes the number of actors present in each stakeholder network. "No. Ties" includes the total number of event-derived ties (relationships) in each stakeholder network. "Avg. Degree" represents the average number of ties each actor has in the network. "Network Dia." is the diameter or longest of all shortest paths connecting any two actors (stakeholders) of the network. "Graph Density" is a ratio of the actual number of ties between actors to the total possible number of ties. "Avg. Path Length" is the average number of ties it takes to connect any two actors.

To understand the institutional context influencing these stakeholders, the critical event register was coded again to evaluate whether event-based relationships between each set of connected stakeholders in each phase-based network reflected a formal or informal character. The manner of interaction between stakeholders, coupled with first-hand accounts, provided insights as to the types of relationships between stakeholders

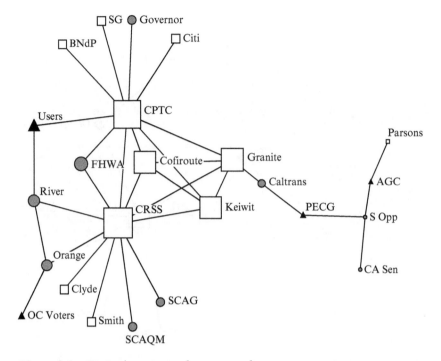

Figure 2.5   Design/construct phase network

based on their individual capital, logics and repertoires of action (Henisz et al., 2012). Formal relationships were primarily contractual or economic transaction-based events. Informal relationships generally represented discourse and other interaction events. These formal and informal sets of relationships were used to derive sub-networks for each of the four PPP development phases. In Table 2.2 we report the same network properties for the formal and informal sub-network of each phase-based stakeholder networks.

SNA also provides for the calculation of individual actor properties within the network. For the purposes of the present research, measures of a stakeholder's centrality in a network are useful for understanding the power and influence of that stakeholder (Jackson, 2008). A specific measure of centrality, eigenvector centrality, calculates the number of connections an actor has, and then factors the relative importance of its neighbors (Bonacich, 1972, 2007). For this research the eigenvector centrality of each actor in the total stakeholder network and each of the two sub-networks for all four phases was calculated.

Stakeholder network dynamics in public–private partnerships 51

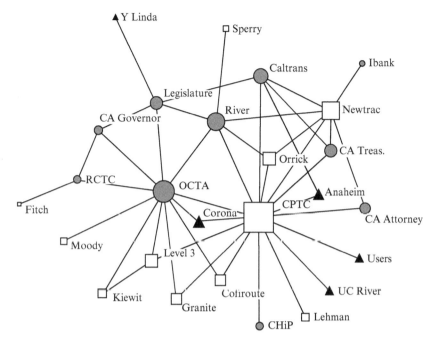

Figure 2.6 Operate/maintain phase network

Table 2.1 Network properties of four phase-based networks

Phase	No. Actors	No. Ties	Avg. Degree	Network Dia.	Density	Avg. Path Length
1 – Identification	25	33	1.32	5	0.110	2.66
2 – Procurement	18	20	1.11	4	0.124	2.29
3 – Design/Construct	24	32	1.33	8	0.116	3.21
4 – Operate/Maintain	26	43	1.65	5	0.132	2.29

RESULTS AND DISCUSSION

Using SNA, 12 networks were constructed. In each of the four phases the total network, the formal sub-network, and the informal sub-networks were mapped. The graphic representations of the total network for each of the four phases are displayed in Figures 2.3–2.6. Each is an undirected network with all relationship weights equal, that is, ties between each dyadic pair of stakeholders were coded as present (represented by a line between

Table 2.2 Network properties of formal and informal sub-networks from each phase

Phase	Network	No. Actors	No. Ties	Avg. Degree	Network Dia.	Density	Avg. Path Length
1 – Identification	Formal	25	12	0.48	4	0.040	2.43
2 – Procurement	Formal	18	10	0.56	3	0.065	1.80
3 – Design/ Construct	Formal	24	22	0.92	4	0.080	2.15
4 – Operate/ Maintain	Formal	26	32	1.23	5	0.098	2.46
1 – Identification	Informal	25	23	0.92	4	0.077	2.43
2 – Procurement	Informal	18	10	0.56	3	0.065	1.96
3 – Design/ Construct	Informal	24	13	0.54	5	0.047	2.06
4 – Operate/ Maintain	Informal	26	9	0.35	5	0.028	2.24

the two) or absent (no line). In each network the individual nodes represent a stakeholder. The size of the node is determined by the stakeholder's eigenvector centrality. Actors were coded by sector and are depicted by the following scheme: public stakeholders = circles; private stakeholders = squares; civic stakeholders = triangles.

Total Network Change Over Phases

In the identification phase of the PPP the dominant position held by Caltrans, the PPPs public sponsor, is readily observable. A number of peripheral stakeholders are engaged, although this graph's density (see Table 2.1) is at its lowest in the PPP life cycle. This is unsurprising as the PPP arrangement is new to the group of stakeholders, and network relationships are still forming. Immediately interesting is network size, the number of stakeholders in the total network. Rather than a gradual build-up of stakeholders over time, the number of stakeholders is quickly established and the total network size remains relatively similar over all phases. This identification phase network of the PPP contains more stakeholders than all but the final phase, while encompassing a relatively short portion of the PPP timeline.

As the PPP progresses to the procurement phase, Caltrans continues in its position as the network's anchor-tenant. Procurement includes requests for proposals, evaluation of proposals, and efforts of the successful private developer to reach financial close. There are a number of private stakeholders (bidders) connected to the public sponsor Caltrans, and then the team of stakeholders connected to CRSS, the winning private developer lead in the PPP deal. It is somewhat surprising that in this phase many of the stakeholders from the first phase (users, interested civic groups, regulators, non-profits, and so on) are no longer active. This phase contains the smallest number of actors in the PPP life cycle. Additionally, the network is somewhat polarized, with only one stakeholder, the purpose-formed special purpose vehicle CPTC, connected directly to both the public and private "sides" of the network.

In the design/construct phase of the PPP there is a change in the anchor-tenant position of the network. The public sponsor quickly loses centrality in the network, and the private developer becomes more central. This also is unsurprising, as the efforts of private stakeholders occupy most of the PPP activities during this phase. However, it is interesting to note that the public sponsors activities are generally channeled through the SPVs design/builder, and not directly to the SPV itself. This observation questions the continuity of the network. In this case the network relationship (termed "partnership" in PPPs) between Caltrans and CPTC is quickly strained and becomes oppositional soon after the design/construct phase. Also interesting in this network is the appearance of the PPP's most vociferous opponent, as the only other stakeholder connected directly to the public sponsor.

The operate/maintain phase exhibits the most connected form of the PPP network, with more ties and the highest density of the four phases. It also represents the highest number of stakeholders engaged in the PPP. At first this is surprising, as the PPP has been in existence for over a decade, and the PPP has been normalized to some degree within the broader environment. However, further examination of this specific case reveals that misaligned objectives between the PPPs purpose and individual stakeholder's objectives and challenges in the fundamental PPP arrangement (stemming from its "liability of newness") have brought into the PPP network a host of new stakeholders. One such misalignment is that of the long-term nature of a PPP, designed to deliver a strong yet capped ROI, and the objectives of key private members of the SPV. The primary SPV members were contractors and developers, who seek to make returns from de-risking construction projects. Once the PPP was operational, and the capital investment costs were captured from the design/construct phase, SPV members were less interested in holding the asset. In this phase, OCTA, a regional transportation authority, becomes the secondary owner of the SPV. Only the asset operator, whose commercial objectives are closely aligned with those of the PPP, remains a stakeholder in the network as original members of the PPP depart from the network.

Perhaps the most interesting membership dynamic within the PPP life cycle is the extent to which stakeholders enter and depart the network. This is readily observable by the dramatic shift in the anchor-tenant position and other highly central stakeholders across the PPP development phases. The phenomenon of dramatic network membership change is also highlighted by the fact that few stakeholders are present in all phases. Only three out of 62 stakeholders, less than 5 percent, are present in all four phases. Those stakeholders present in all phases are: (1) the public sponsor Caltrans; (2) the SPV CPTC; and (3) Riverside County, a local government entity where the physical asset is located. The first two each serve as anchor-tenants at some point in the PPP life cycle. Additionally, 43 of the 62 stakeholders, 69 percent, are present in only one phase of the PPP's development.

Informal and Formal Sub-network Changes Over Phases

The total network can also be divided into sub-networks by each phase and then into the formal and informal networks. The results show that formal networks grow over phases in the number of ties, average degree of centrality and graph density. The results for informal networks show decay over phases in the number of ties, average degree of centrality and graph density. These sub-network graphs are depicted, along with the total network graphs, in Figure 2.7. The network growth and decay patterns are evident in this figure, and illustrate that the formal network goes from being composed of fewer stakeholders that are less interconnected, to a larger number of stakeholders that are more connected. The opposite pattern can be seen for informal networks, going from being more numerous and interconnected to sparse and incomplete. This raised an interesting question for the researchers: why is it that there appears a necessarily dominant mode of interaction? While there were some instances of stakeholders interacting both formally and informally, it was much more usual that stakeholders would interact either in one mode or the other.

Formal and Informal Institutional Relationships in Stakeholder Networks

This work presents new empirical evidence for the extent to which infrastructure PPPs change over phases of the development life cycle. There is evidence of a shift in the type of institutional relationships from predominantly informal to predominantly formal across the four phases. Specifically, in the identification phase, stakeholder networks are composed of primarily informal relationships. However, in the operate/maintain phase the stakeholder network is based on more formal relationships.

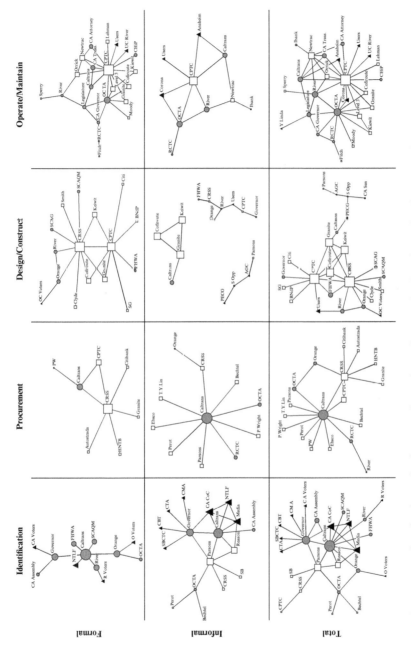

Figure 2.7 Formal and informal sub-networks with total network of each P3 development phase

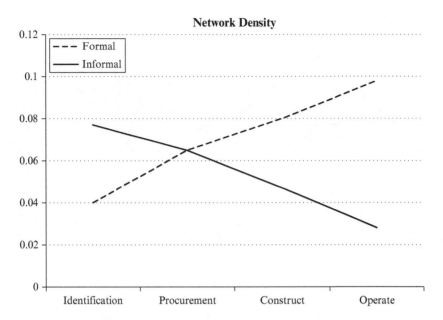

Figure 2.8 Switch in dominant institutional type of relationship in stakeholder networks

The switch in dominant institutional relationships is depicted in Figure 2.8, where it is evident that the dominant institutional relationship type changes as the informal stakeholder sub-network decreases in density and the formal stakeholder sub-network increases.

CONCLUSIONS AND CONSIDERATIONS FOR PPP GOVERNANCE

This research presents an analysis of the changing stakeholder network observed to occur in a highway transportation PPP case. Using various types of data from an in-depth case study, a register of critical events produced a second-order coding of stakeholders and time-based tables of dyadic relationships between stakeholders. Using SNA the relationships between stakeholders were analyzed in order to develop a deeper understanding of stakeholder network change. Through this process it appeared that infrastructure PPPs may be much more dynamic than previously considered. Across four phases of PPP development this dynamism was evident through dramatic changes in the composition of stakeholder networks, and the shifting use of types of institutional logics and resulting relationships. More specifically, it was found that:

1. The stakeholder network is quite fluid, with less than 5 percent of stakeholders remaining engaged throughout the development life cycle, and almost 70 percent participating actively in only one phase.
2. The identity of the stakeholder network's anchor-tenant changes across phases.
3. The dominant institutional logic, and thus types of relationships in the stakeholder networks, also changes, switching from primarily informal to primarily formal across the PPP life cycle.
4. Stakeholder groups (that is, public, private and civic sectors) use institutional logics differently over the PPP life cycle.

Results from a single exploratory case study are necessarily inconclusive, but can produce tentative hypotheses and interesting ideas to be pursued by other investigators. Among these ideas, our research suggests that infrastructure PPP stakeholder networks change significantly over developmental phases, and that such changes present a problem, as any gap in coordination and integration of stakeholders across phases opens the potential for short-sighted opportunistic behavior. Further, as stakeholders' involvement in the PPP life cycle is generally not persistent, issues that do not surface until later in the project are likely borne and "paid for" by those in the later phases. Overly dynamic networks may encourage early-phase actors to push the cost for potential challenges and risks to the later phases. The irony here is that the long-term coupling of stakeholders to asset performance is one of the very reasons why PPPs are championed. This suggests that there is likely to be a need for governance structures that mitigate potential opportunistic behavior and encourage truly long-term participation in the PPP.

As an example of how this might be done, PPPs could be organized so that a private concessionaire will assume overall responsibility for the PPP from procurement and be required to hold it through the operate/maintain phase. Public stakeholders (PPP sponsors) would prioritize infrastructure projects based on political and economic considerations, in the best interest of the civic stakeholders. Given that civic stakeholders primarily interact through informal logics, the public sponsor could include greater informal engagement programs to interact with civic stakeholders. Key private stakeholders who are awarded the PPP concession during procurement could be legally required to take an enduring role in the PPP. This is likely to shift the predominant anchor-tenant role from a developer to a long-term investor (or a developer with a longer financial stake in the asset), whose commercial interests are deemed more closely aligned with those of the PPPs performance. Additionally, the public sponsor could take a more active role in the design–build–finance (DBF) and early operate–maintain (OM) phases for construction coordination and engagement with civic stakeholders (many of whom do not consciously take notice of infrastructure development until it begins to affect their daily routines). Public sponsors typically avoid such roles, but they are often compelled to become involved when challenges arise.

The PPP represents a dramatic shift from the US model of construction company asset developers filling the anchor-tenant position during procurement and DBF phases (taking a few years – a small proportion of the time involved, considering that the project may last 30–50 years), then exiting during the early years of the OM phase, for long-term investors and infrastructure managers to step in. Aspects of this earlier model appeared in the SR91X case when CPTC decided to sell its equity in the project, a development that caused significant turmoil for the sponsor, developer and operator. A departure from the US model would suggest that public authorities may need to support and encourage capacity building and a new institutional frame for long-term investors, and similarly require capacity building within public sponsoring agencies – no small task.

Another idea is suggested by the finding that the stakeholder network's anchor-tenant changes across phases. In the present case, the public sponsor (Caltrans) initially filled the anchor-tenant role in the identification and procurement phases. Later, however, during the design/construct and operate/maintain phases, Caltrans had diminished in terms of centrality and CRSS (initial developer) and CPTC (eventual SPV) become the most central stakeholders in the network, respectively. This change is interesting with respect to the anchor-tenant and its dominant institutional frame. One hypothesis may be that the anchor-tenant sets the dominant frame for the interactions between stakeholders in the network. In SR91X, that anchor-tenant is a public institution, initially. As the network's anchor-tenant shifts, so might the dominant institutional logics and types of relationships. Therefore, the mode of interaction between stakeholders would also likely change. Legitimacy-seeking institutions in the PPP stakeholder network might well be shifting their frames to fit that of the new anchor-tenant, while reconciling their own. Here lies a potential issue. Some stakeholders may not be successful at such reconciliation. For example, civic stakeholders in this case apparently had little or no formal institutional capacity compatible with the anchor-tenant role, and the civic sector diminished their involvement even while the PPP progressed toward operations. Thus, at the height of their observable interaction with the PPP (for example, the user public utilizing the asset, driving on the new highway lanes and paying tolls), their only formal involvement was a transportation/transaction script between the individual users and the PPP operator, which came many years after project conception. Presumably, the public sector stakeholders represent the civic sector stakeholders. Even so, we saw few instances of interaction between the groups, suggesting again that greater engagement with civic sector stakeholders by the public sponsor may be necessary.

3. Toward a unified theory of project governance: economic, sociological and psychological supports for relational contracting*

Witold J. Henisz, Raymond E. Levitt and W. Richard Scott

INTRODUCTION

Extreme governance challenges arise in large, global, cross-sectoral, multi-phased civil infrastructure projects. Over their decades-long lifetimes, such projects evolve through discrete phases: financial and technical feasibility evaluation, conceptual design, detailed design, construction, operations, and renovation and replacement. Each of these phases can be viewed as a discrete transaction, during which key participants and stakeholders rotate into and out of the project. This heterogeneous and shifting mix of counterparties across the project's life cycle creates a heretofore neglected contractual hazard of "displaced agency" – that is, the cumulative costs that can accrue to the participants in a series of interdependent transactions as a result of counterparties' incentives to shift costs or responsibilities to one or more counterparties not represented in the current transaction.

Prior research has argued that relational contracting, while ubiquitous, is most pervasive among multiple, highly interdependent but heterogeneous counterparties (Powell, 1990a) engaging in multiple sequential complex transactions (Argyres and Liebeskind, 1999). As a result, we develop our theoretical arguments drawing upon evidence from a sector dominated by such transactions that is of substantive economic importance: the provision of civil infrastructure projects. Transactions in this industry are characterized by high levels of:

- asset specificity, that is, the magnitude of the difference in value of specialized investments in their use for a given transaction (compared to in their next best use);

- uncertainty and probity, that is, the importance of integrity in process and loyalty to mission and leadership (Williamson, 1999), as public goods that play a catalytic role in the process of development;
- potential for corrupt administration; and
- centrality to a nation's well-being and security.

An important characteristic of civil infrastructure projects is the tightly coupled sequence of interrelated transactions among shifting counterparties with negatively interacting subgoals; that is, one or more subgoals for which a better outcome for one counterparty is worse for the other (Levitt et al., 1999). This raises the relative costs of relying upon neoclassical or trilateral governance as compared to relational contracts. At each stage in the project life cycle, the identity of the counterparties that have these negatively interacting subgoals varies (see Chapter 2 of this volume), but their incentive to pass through or otherwise shift costs to future counterparties or others with a relatively weak voice in the current phase remains constant.

In the very early project shaping phase, planning consultants who seek to ensure follow-on design consulting engagements "conspire" with government officials who seek to take credit for launching ambitious new projects by underestimating total costs and overestimating total benefits consistently (Perkins, 2004). This can saddle future counterparties – particularly future users and/or taxpayers – with enormous liabilities (Flyvbjerg et al., 2003). In the design stage, design consultants and governments can seek to alter the allocation of costs and benefits, often seeking to minimize operating costs that are borne locally at the expense of larger up-front capital costs that are paid for regionally or nationally. Design consultants can also deliberately overdesign projects to avoid even the remote possibility of a failure, for which they could be liable. They seek to ensure their consideration in future work, in part, by avoiding future litigation. This creates higher costs in construction, but is not easily discernible to governments or taxpayers.

An example illustrates this point. The designers of a rapid-transit project specified an 18-inch-thick concrete lining for its tunnel – substantially thicker than needed for structural support – to prevent any water leakage (Levitt et al., 1980). This addressed a specification in the general design requirements created by the local transit authority and its planning consultant that required zero water leakage to eliminate any pumping costs during operations. The hugely increased capital cost would be covered by 90 percent federal funding, whereas the trivial cost of pumping a conventional amount of water leakage with a tunnel designed purely for structural adequacy would have been covered 100 percent from local operating revenues. This kind of "gold plating" of infrastructure introduced during the design phase reduced the engineers' design costs (a more conservative design is generally less costly to develop) and its potential liability, rewarded the operator by reducing its future operating costs, rewarded local politicians by infusing substantial extra federal money into the local economy, but punished taxpayers in other states who subsidized the capital costs of this gold plating.

During the construction stage, low-bid contractors on fixed-price contracts seeking to minimize their cost do battle with the client and engineers over claimed "changes" from the plans or specifications used in bidding. Given the inevitable ambiguities and discrepancies among the multiple sets of necessarily incomplete plans and specifications produced by multiple, fragmented, specialist designers, contrary interpretations that can be claimed to be changes – or rebutted as not being changes – invariably arise after construction begins. Finally, in the operations phase, battle is joined between the market efficiency of certain pricing models versus the equity concerns that shape political and social sustainability, with users and politicians conspiring to shift costs back onto, or revenue from, contractors (Henisz and Zelner, 2005a).

We believe that collective shirking or responsibility-shifting among past, current and future counterparties is a relatively under-analyzed governance challenge, yet one that is critical to performance in a wide array of contexts. The economic, legal, sociological and psychological perspectives on organizations are each increasingly focused on mechanisms that facilitate cooperation among, and reduce the incidence of opportunism by, counterparties or stakeholders in informal agreements that are sustained due to the value of related ongoing or future transactions – that is, relational contracts (Baker et al., 2002; Chan, 2010) – equivalent to the "tit for tat" game theory model of behavior in repeated games (Axelrod and Hamilton, 1981). We build on this prior work by integrating these perspectives to examine the governance of relational contracts in the face of the hazards of displaced agency.

We set out the beginnings of a framework based on institutional theory (Scott, 2008) that integrates a range of mechanisms to enhance the efficacy of relational contracts, drawing on:

- regulative institutional supports (for example, laws, regulations, contracts and their enforcement through mediation, arbitration or litigation, and the shadow of the future);
- normative institutional supports (for example, socially shared expectations of appropriate behavior, and social exchange processes); and

- cognitive institutional supports (for example, creating shared identities, scripts or conceptual frameworks to bridge differences in values or interests).

Finally, we present a set of propositions that begins to develop a contingent, integrated project governance framework based on transaction, counterparty, relationship, field and country-level project characteristics that can guide future research on engineering project organizations to better predict, and ultimately manage, the incidence and efficacy of different regulative, normative and cognitive supports for relational contracting.

THEORETICAL POINTS OF DEPARTURE

We begin with a brief overview of key points of departure from the literatures of economics, law, sociology and psychology.

Transaction Cost Economics (TCE) and Game Theory

Economic and legal perspectives on governance focus on financial incentives and formal legal structures that can impose sanctions to enforce financial contracts, and to constrain and motivate the behavior of counterparties. Economic approaches initially had the strongest purchase in the analysis of atomistic markets or bilateral contracts but, integrated with their legal counterparts, have been usefully extended to examine contractual versus hierarchical governance (Williamson, 1979). The focus within law and economics on incentives and sanctions generates insights into the codifiable elements of contractual governance and their "legal/regulative" institutional supports (Scott, 2008) as well as the delineation of court-sanctioned zones for managerial discretion. This focus highlights the substantive differences between the functioning of markets and hierarchies, particularly where market-based contracts involving significant uncertainties are necessarily incomplete.

Research on relational contracting incorporates the role of reputational capital in repeated games. Under certain assumptions regarding the reaction of principals and agents to reneging or shirking – for example, triggering "tit-for-tat" responses (Axelrod and Hamilton, 1981), punishment strategies or community enforcement – reputational capital can cast further light on important distinctions in the functioning of different governance mechanisms. Despite the growing interest in relational contracting within organizational economics, the scope of strategic behavior for a contractor who wishes to minimize the hazard of "displaced agency" remains limited in such frameworks to the *ex ante* design of governance mechanisms that provide financial incentives or other sanctions to enhance efficiency. We demonstrate that such efforts to craft unified, trilateral or network governance mechanisms are frequently insufficient to mitigate this hazard. We assert that, while important and widely adopted, these legal and economic governance mechanisms are only a subset of the mechanisms that can be employed to generate cooperation among and limit the hazard of opportunistic behavior by counterparties, particularly those that are distant to the immediate transaction within a multi-party, multi-phase network of interdependent transactions.

Sociological and Psychological Points of Departure

In contrast to their economic and legal counterparts, sociological and psychological perspectives on governance focus on underlying patterns of human behavior that financial incentives and legal sanction can enhance or moderate, but can never fully subsume. These approaches have enjoyed the strongest purchase in micro-level studies of employment relations, teams, workplace interactions and influence campaigns. Their focus on behaviors that can shape individual perceptions, shared beliefs, affect and group dynamics generates insights into the informal and behavioral elements of governance and the normative and cognitive bases for their enforcement.

Across a wide array of contexts, compliance with or the successful invocation of psychological perceptions, collective norms or senses of identity has been shown to alter individual behavior (Gächter and Fehr, 1999; Nee and Ingram, 2001; Ring and Van de Ven, 1994). While the existence of financial incentives and legal sanction is acknowledged, and the potential for positive or negative feedback between such regulative institutional supports and these normative and cognitive counterparts is occasionally studied, this literature does not focus on the best means to enhance cooperation among and minimize opportunism by counterparties with the explicit aim of improving transactions' financial performance. A large body of literature does, however, link these constructs to individual and group-level satisfaction, innovation, learning and other potentially performance-related outcomes. Such individual and group-level outcomes reduce the collective shirking which is at the core of "displaced agency" and are, therefore, core elements of relational governance.

We link these disciplinary perspectives by drawing on the insights on institutional theory (see Greenwood et al., 2008; Scott, 2014). Specifically, we draw on Scott's assertion that human behavior in societies is regularized and made predictable by three kinds of "institutional pillars":

1. Regulative institutions – laws, regulations, contracts and their enforcement through price-based incentives, mediation, arbitration or litigation. Regulative institutions are enforced coercively via sanctions imposed by governmental or private organizations using their police power or formal authority when they are violated.
2. Normative institutions – for example, socially shared expectations of appropriate behavior, and social exchange processes. Individuals who violate normative institutions are punished by their fellow group members through social sanctions such as ridicule, isolation or ostracism.
3. Cultural-cognitive institutions – shared identities, beliefs and conceptual frameworks to bridge differences in values or interests. Persons who behave in ways that conflict significantly with their own cognitive-cultural institutions punish themselves by experiencing acute "cognitive dissonance."

These three kinds of institutions are carried and propagated in different ways – see Scott (2008) for a fuller discussion – but they all serve to enforce behavior that is "appropriate," as judged by the state or formal organization, relevant social groups and the individual, thereby making our collective social world more predictable and manageable most of the time.

Both the legal-economic bases of TCE and the sociological and psychological behavioral insights about relational contracting are fragmented and limiting for addressing the governance challenges we have described. We believe that Scott's "three institutional pillars" framework provides a powerful way to unify the heretofore disparate and fragmented insights from TCE, sociology and psychology into a more unified theory that can allow us to better understand and manage relational project governance.

Based on a five-year ethnography of alliance partnering in Australia, Clegg et al. (2011) claim that normative and cognitive governance mechanisms, assiduously applied, can almost completely replace regulative governance mechanisms. We make the weaker claim that regulative, normative and cognitive mechanisms, contingently applied and carefully aligned, can serve as complements rather than substitutes for one another in an overall governance framework.

REGULATIVE, NORMATIVE AND COGNITIVE GOVERNANCE MECHANISMS

Each transaction in the multi-phase life cycle of a large, long-lived infrastructure project is potentially a one-off transaction and, therefore, too infrequent to justify large fixed governance costs independently. It is nevertheless a tightly coupled element in a sequence of related transactions linking multiple heterogeneous and shifting counterparties over a lengthy time interval, ranging from several years to multiple decades (see Chapter 2 in this volume). Within this complex system, there exist one or more residual claimants (for example, end users, taxpayers, lead designers, lead construction contractors and facility operators) who stand to gain financially if cooperation is enhanced and/or opportunistic behavior reduced in a manner that improves the efficiency of the system. Sizeable potential gains from improvements in the efficacy of relational contracting in this multi-trillion-dollar sector can accrue to citizens who ultimately pay for and use these public goods, and shareholders of the corporations that increasingly finance and deliver them.

In the rest of this section, we elaborate the application of each of Scott's (2008) three institutional pillars to infrastructure projects separately. In the subsequent section, we attempt to integrate them in a manner that gives rise to concrete propositions regarding the relative incidence and efficacy of these governance supports for relational contracting holding constant the contractual hazards; that is, high asset specificity, uncertainty and probity with low frequency and high displaced agency. Specifically, we draw attention to: (1) the structure of the relationships among counterparties to those interdependent transactions; (2) a comparison of the short-term or one-off benefits of opportunistic breach to a given counterparty versus gains to trade that can accrue to the network of counterparties absent any opportunistic breach; and (3) the existence of complementary institutional supports.

Regulative Governance Mechanisms

Building on work by Williamson (1985, 1975, 1996), one branch of the construction management literature has followed the logic of TCE in arguing that managers in the position of residual claimant should pursue a cost minimizing alignment between the governance of an individual transaction and that transaction's contractual hazards (e.g., Eccles, 1981; Gunnarson and Levitt, 1982). TCE asserts that where these hazards are high, opportunistic behavior can be mitigated in unified governance structures where all of the life cycle project costs and benefits of a project are born by a single entity; that is, the local government agency or private entity that will plan, finance, design, build, operate and maintain the facility over an extended period. Alternatively, coordination can be enhanced and opportunistic behavior mitigated through carefully specified contractual incentives with appeal to neoclassical contracting (that is, trilateral governance) or through sharing ownership among stakeholders (that is, network governance supported by ownership) or relying upon the shadow of the future (that is, network governance supported by reputational capital).

Unified Governance

As compared to traditional TCE logic, the level of contractual externalities between counterparties in one phase (for example, planning) and another (for example, construction or operation) is so great as to require extensions to the governance mechanisms typically deployed for intertemporal, bilateral or even multilateral contracts. *In extremis*, these frameworks suggest that a reliance on unified governance over the project life cycle can address these concerns; traditionally through self-performance of all project phases by governments, or through long-term public–private partnership infrastructure contracts with private concessionaires for life cycle delivery of infrastructure to citizens as a 25–99-year service.

We can examine various levels of unified governance over the life cycle of infrastructure projects. As a first step, a design–build construction contractor unifies detailed design and construction services and tenders a proposal to the client to maximize the value that can be delivered for a given budget. The client then picks the design–build tender that offers its organization the greatest perceived value for its intended purpose. In addition, design–build contracting allows construction to begin before design is complete, with the potential to save considerable time over a more conventional, sequential design–bid–build approach.

However, only relatively sophisticated construction buyers can specify their requirements well enough at the conceptual design stage to pick a design–build or "engineer, procure and construct" (EPC) contractor that will optimally satisfy its needs and wants for the project. As a result, this approach tends to be used by sophisticated buyers of relatively well-specified facilities such as industrial plants, warehouses, standard office buildings, highway segments or bridges. For other buyers, the subsequent buyer's remorse at what they have bought, or the *ex post* renegotiation costs incurred with the design–build construction contractor, can outweigh the savings in time and the increases in value from alleviating the agency problem between the design and construction actors, if acting independently.

The design–build approach can be further unified both upstream and downstream so that the same entity plans, finances, designs, builds, owns and operates the facility. However, even this extensive internalization of the delivery process can generate a situation of displaced agency in which the ultimate costs of the project are passed on to third parties – end users – who will ultimately pay higher taxes or user fees such as highway tolls to fund the delivery of the infrastructure service, but who are unable to assess accurately the risks that they are bearing, or have no choice but to accept them. While such forward shifting of costs may serve strategic purposes, especially for political actors with time horizons no longer than the next election cycle, contractors, investors and bondholders need to understand these long-term risks and incorporate them within their financial models.

Few if any public or private organizations are capable or willing to internalize the full set of transactions involved in infrastructure service provision. Such integration does occur, often through the creation of a specialized project company – termed a special purpose vehicle or SPV – that is jointly governed by a consortium of private companies and regulated as a long-term, service concession for provision of a public good by the public sector. This delivery approach is typically referred to as a public–private partnership (PPP). In a PPP transaction, end users and the governments that represent them are at a bargaining power disadvantage to obtain redress for opportunistic behavior during the design and construction phases of the project, given the difficulty of replacing the incumbent financiers and contractors. In what has been called the "obsolescing bargain" (Vernon, 1980; Vernon and Vernon, 1977), power shifts to the host government once the project has been completed. The completed asset, being large, costly and immovable, is highly location-specific; and tolls or other user fees paid to the concessionaire are typically set by the host government and can be arbitrarily reduced in the name of economic or political expediency. Thus, some form of multi-party governance that relies upon neoclassical or relational contracting seems inevitable.

Moreover, a conflict-of-interest problem arises when contractors that will design, build and operate the project are also part of the consortium that sponsors the project's equity. They then have two ways to make profit: payment for their design–construction or operation services; and income from their share of the investment returns for the life cycle delivery of the infrastructure service.

The Channel Tunnel project, in which all of the initial equity in the Transmanche Link concessionaire was held by five British and five French contractors, provided a clear instance of this kind of conflict of interest. Transmanche Link (TML), the consortium of five British and five French contractors that built the tunnel, initially provided the majority equity stake in the project. The construction contract for the tunnel was written up during this period and it allocated almost all of the construction risk to shareholders, while the contractors participated in decisions and renegotiated their payments for construction services based on redesign, differing site conditions and other contingencies that led total project costs to increase from the original 1987 estimate of £4.7 billion to more than £11 billion. At the time, the construction companies had an incentive to estimate construction costs optimistically to promote investment in the project. The initial public offering in 1987 raised an additional £770 million, providing the vast majority of the equity for the project company, now called Eurotunnel, and diluting the shares held by the construction companies to 7 percent. Subsequently, as the magnitude of cost overruns and overoptimistic estimates of the travel demand for the tunnel became clear, TML eventually agreed to bear a share of cost overruns; but the effect on Eurotunnel's investors and bondholders was far more dramatic, including several major financial restructurings, the suspension of interest payments from 1995 through 1997, and an eventual write-off of half of the £6 billion debt.

Trilateral Governance Structures

One means to mitigate opportunism in such transactions is through the use of external commitment or bonding mechanisms such as an appeal to arbitration, or other kinds of alternative dispute resolution of contractual disputes, or through commitments to complete the project from financial guarantors such as surety bonding companies. In theory, the reliance on independent and impartial third-party rulings could mitigate the risk of complex and always incomplete contingent contracts, particularly in the aftermath of unexpected shocks or contingencies that render rigid adherence to the terms of the contract excessively costly to one counterparty or another. However, one or both parties may face incentives to tilt the playing field in their favor by directly or indirectly stimulating political intervention into the dispute resolution process. The aim of such influence tactics is typically to avoid the uncertainty of the dispute resolution process and to use political or regulatory intervention to secure a more favorable and potentially expeditious outcome. Whether in disputes regarding toll road construction in the United States (Sullivan, 1998), independent power projects in South East Asia (Henisz and Zelner, 2005a; Wells and Ahmed, 2007; Woodhouse, 2006) or oil pipelines in Central Africa (Pegg, 2009), investors placing undue reliance on such contractual remedies to restrain such *ex post* political intervention have frequently met with bitter disappointment.

Network Governance Supported by Shared Ownership

The cost of writing general contracts and pursuing third-party intervention of disputes about their interpretation can be prohibitive for infrequent and highly idiosyncratic transactions (Williamson, 1979), particularly those embedded in relationships involving multiple shifting counterparties sequenced over multiple phases. In these cases, creating a significant, long-term economic stake for the most influential counterparties – the "selectorate" (Mesquita et al., 1999) – can align their interests. This should increase long-term political support for sustaining fair levels of reimbursement to private firms that develop the infrastructure, and thereby prevent opportunistic behavior against private infrastructure sponsors by future governments. Examples of such co-option include local hiring quotas, contract volume set-asides to local business entities and the like to compensate and co-opt locals, who could otherwise be vociferous opponents if they felt that they would be inconvenienced by construction or penalized by costs of operation of the facility. Such "economically inefficient" policies can shift the political calculus around a project, thereby creating a more enduring governance solution than pure economic principles might allow (Williamson, 1999).

Local pension fund investments and local set-asides similarly align many citizens' interests with those of the infrastructure project sponsors. Clark (2000) and Vives (1999) set early frameworks, suggesting that infrastructure projects had the potential to enhance risk-adjusted returns while matching pension fund obligations for long-term payouts. Clark (2000) also showed that infrastructure investments have had a negative correlation with other asset classes that are commonly held in pension fund portfolios, and thus could provide the added benefit of diversification. Australian pension funds have financed much of that country's infrastructure investment over the past decade; Chilean and Argentinean pension funds have held small infrastructure investments since the 1990s through infrastructure funds and securitizations.

Network Governance Supported by Reputational Capital

Even in the absence of an ownership stake, counterparties may perceive an economic benefit to cooperation and a cost to opportunism, particularly if their interactions are repeated and specific assets are at stake (Bercovitz et al., 2006). Assuming that counterparties are willing to punish opportunistic behavior by avoiding subsequent transactions with counterparties observed to be opportunistic, numerous formal economic interests (MacLeod, 2007; Weigelt and Camerer, 1988) can generate benefits to amassing reputational capital (that is, the demonstration of cooperative or non-opportunistic behavior). Such models have long been used to model the incidence and utility of warranties, bonus pay, community enforcement and the investment in reputation (MacLeod, 2007).

Baker et al. (2002) examine the variable impact of reputation on the actions of individual counterparties under different regulative governance mechanisms (for example, within one organization, in a bilateral employment relationship, within an alliance or joint venture) highlighting how the choice of (a sequence of) regulative governance mechanism(s) can be influenced by the relative importance to performance of one or the other counterparty engaging in opportunistic or non-cooperative behavior (over a given time period). In a study of infrastructure project administration, Chan (2010) found that the reputational concerns of a concessionaire, based on having two or more simultaneous ongoing or planned future projects at risk in a region, led concessionaires to renegotiate relationally rather than pursue litigation when faced with government requests to renegotiate infrastructure delivery agreements.

The Limits of Regulative Mechanisms

The economic and legal literature has expanded the scope of inquiry substantially, but it still perceives the strategic choice variable under the control of the residual claimant seeking to mitigate "displaced agency" as the *ex ante* choice of a regulatively (that is, legally and contractually) supported governance mechanism. This choice is influenced by characteristics of the transaction (that is, contractual hazards) and/or the relative importance of non-cooperative or opportunistic behavior by counterparties. While this choice variable is clearly one that is considered carefully within civil infrastructure projects, an equally and potentially even more important set of governance choices for the residual claimant revolve around ongoing efforts to increase the incidence of cooperation and reduce the incidence of *ex post* opportunism over the life of the relationship (Ring and Van de Ven, 1994). These efforts occur within a given governance structure and its regulative supports. They emphasize and seek to manipulate normative and cognitive supports for relational contracting. Such an extension is particularly important as the chain of counterparties expands in scope and the ability to contract with or even directly identify the full range of relevant counterparties becomes increasingly difficult.

Normative and Cognitive Governance Mechanisms

Another branch of the project organization and management literature has developed what it refers to as a partnership model for project development. Instead of emphasizing financial and legal incentives that alter the pay-offs to cooperation versus opportunistic defection, they emphasize tapping into and/or manipulating pre-existing social structures and psychological processes so as to alter behavior within an existing governance structure.

Social Exchange in Pre-existing Communities

The power of shared identity and interpersonal ties to alter behavior is well established in the sociological and psychological foundations of management (Ring and Van de Ven, 1994; Turner, 1987) as well as marketing (Heide and Wathne, 2006; Jap and Anderson, 2007; Jap and Ganesan, 2000; Wathne and Heide, 2000). Shared backgrounds, worldviews and prior interactions shift the pattern of behavior in negotiations or renegotiations toward collaboration (Gächter and Fehr, 1999; Hoffman et al., 1998; Nee and Ingram, 2001). This can be particularly important for transactions characterized by high contractual hazards where the ability to codify all relevant contingencies is prohibitively expensive, if not infeasible. This view diverges from the previously discussed economic literature on reputational capital. The normative and cognitive perspective on relational contracting asserts that increases in cooperation and reductions in opportunistic behavior can occur due to the threat of non-pecuniary social sanction, even in the absence of a contractual obligation that could be enforced or a rational economic calculation based on the shadow of the future. Furthermore, the strength of this sanction and resulting counterparty behavior can be altered by featuring counterparties that are elements of a potentially sanctioning group more prominently, or by emphasizing or otherwise increasing the salience of participants' group membership and identity.

Counterparties who perceive that they have shared identity as members of a social group may eschew opportunistic behavior because they perceive the costs of defection in terms of ostracism from the peer group, or loss of reputation among, or other social sanctions by, actors within that peer group, to outweigh the benefits (North, 1990). Prominent examples of the use of such mechanisms include the Maghrebi traders (Greif et al., 1994) and numerous other ethnic trading networks (Landa, 1995) including the Jewish diamond merchants in New York (Richman, 2005), as well as stewards of common pool resources (Ostrom, 1990, 2005).

In the context of infrastructure delivery, company efforts to overcome the problem of the "last mile" of pipe or wire in water, telephone and electricity distribution frequently rely upon a sense of shared identity in a group within which failure to cooperate may result in social sanction. In each of the three cases we describe below, the provision of information, monitoring and enforcement by an identifiable peer and community member is designed to trigger reciprocal cooperation in the form of payment, overcoming the limitations of purely financial or legal incentives on relatively poor customers who often feel entitled to the supply of these basic public services.

In Argentina, more than 850000 households belong to water co-operatives and, according to Hwang (2008), the degree of community participation is positively associated with cross-sectional variation in their financial and operational performance. She argues that at least three complementary causal mechanisms are at play. First, users are generally more willing to pay fees to a local organization in which they have a stake than to a large multinational corporation with other priorities. Second, the social ties add "governance value" in the opposite direction, too. Consumers can rely on social ties between themselves and the co-operative's managers – who are generally also community members – to get low pressure, a leaky pipe or other service problems attended to in a timely manner by the co-operative's staff. Finally, Hwang (2008) suggested that the co-operatives promote interaction between members and help to form additional social capital within the community, which reinforces the importance of social sanctions.

In the Philippines a subcontractor of Manila Water relies on local monitoring via Aquadors (that is, individuals who reside within a neighborhood and sell water to clients through connections from their own line, receiving 20 percent of sales as their salary). The Aquadors also take responsibility for reading meters to clients and billing them daily. As of June 2008, the subcontractor supplied water to more than 125000 people. In addition to alternative providers, Manila Water has made direct efforts to engage local community members. The company also maintains a "Walk the Line Policy," which requires all company employees to walk from house to house and meet customers, creating a personal link between the user and service provider.

A similar mechanism was used in the Republic of Georgia by electricity distributors. Relying upon cultural norms that sharply differentiate between theft from a neighbor and theft from the government or business, distributors both save money by installing fewer meters and lower their enforcement costs by relying on self-policing, while still increasing payment rates (Gorst, 2006). The success of this program stands in stark contrast to the failures of the same managerial team when working for United States (US) investor AES, which incurred more than a $200 million loss in its investment in electricity distributor Telasi, partly due to its reliance on the economic incentives and legal enforcement enabled by individual metering (Henisz and Zelner, 2005b).

The Power of Procedural Justice

Managers seeking to tap into such social sanctions to support relational governance among stakeholders to an infrastructure project can either rely upon norms of social exchange (Gouldner, 1960) among members of existing social structures (Jones et al., 1997) as described above or, in the absence of such pre-existing social structures, can demonstrate that, despite their outsider status, they follow norms of distributive justice (Blau, 1964; Homans, 1958) or procedural justice (Lind and Tyler, 1988; Thibaut and Walker, 1975) in the hope that the observation of such legitimate behavior engenders reciprocal cooperation. The former strategy relies on collective norms within existing social structures, whereas the latter constructs new social structures by invoking existing social norms of procedural justice.

While the leveraging of social sanctions within pre-existing networks of social ties can enhance cooperation among members of such a network, reliance upon an existing network may be infeasible in many circumstances where the scope of relevant stakeholders exceeds the scope of pre-existing social networks. In these instances, a growing body of psychological research (Tooby et al., 2006) argues that managers can still craft a sense of community by following decision-making processes that are perceived as fair or legitimate (Camerer and Fehr, 2006; Charness and Rabin, 2002; Fehr and Simon, 2000), thereby eliciting cooperation and reducing the likelihood of opportunism among counterparties – even those who are not linked via a network of pre-existing social ties to (employees of) the provider.

Theories of procedural justice (Lind and Tyler, 1988; Thibaut and Walker, 1975) emphasize that opportunistic behavior can be constrained, even in the absence of perceived reciprocity (Gouldner, 1960) or distributive justice (Blau, 1964; Homans, 1958), through shared information on the activities, contributions and rewards of other actors in the network; perceptions that concerns about the pattern of activity, contribution and rewards can be voiced, heard and responded to; and perceptions that the behavior of actors toward their peers is fair and consistent. Together this sharing of information, right to an effective voice and perceptions of fairness in the application of decision rules constitute a procedurally just process to which stakeholders may respond cooperatively even where outcomes deviate from their individual self-interest (Dal Bó et al., 2008). For related applications see Kim and Mauborgne (1993a, 1991, 1996, 1995, 1993b, 1998, 2002) in multinational management; Husted and Folger (2004) in transaction cost economics; Artz and Brush (2000) in buyer–supplier relations or alliances; Korsgaard et al. (1995) on teams; Arnstein (1969) and Choguill (1996) in community development; Jap (2001) in marketing; and Krick et al. (2006) in corporate social responsibility.

Partnering

These insights about shared identity and procedural justice have a long history of application to the management of counterparty relationships in the context of large-scale project management in the form of the "project partnership" model as well as participatory models of stakeholder engagement (Krick et al., 2006). Weston and Gibson (1993) cite core elements of partnering as "trust, shared vision and long-term commitments" that encourage "contracting parties to change their adversarial relationships to a more cooperative, team-based approach" by forming a "team mentality for the benefit of the project." Freedom of speech, openness and innovation are harnessed to craft win–win incentives collectively that maximize opportunity in the face of shared risks (Crowley and Karim, 1995). Harback et al. (1994) draw the analogy to a shift from the design of the best prenuptial agreement to a focus on the win–win goals and give-and-take behaviors needed for a successful marriage. Participatory models of stakeholder engagement likewise emphasize transparency and voice as means to foster shared purpose and identity, overcoming suspicion and distrust.

Quantitative empirical analysis supports the hypotheses that successful partnerships experience lower cost escalation, fewer change orders and greater participant satisfaction (Gransberg et al., 1999; Sarkar et al., 1998). Qualitative studies of a Hong Kong railway extension (Bayliss et al., 2004), as well as comparative case studies undertaken by the governments of Hong Kong (Chan et al., 2004) and the United Kingdom (Latham, 1994), provide richer supporting evidence in support of this argument, as do case studies of Terminal 5 at Heathrow Airport in London (Gil, 2009), Sutter Health's process of hospital construction (Fischer et al., 2017), the Taralga wind farm in New South Wales, Australia (Gross, 2007), the Ohio River Bridges Project (Bailey et al., 2007), the Capital Beltway extension (Groat, 2004, 2006) and Chevron's onshore liquid natural gas processing facility in Angola (Angola LNG, 2006).

While there is no single agreed-upon formula for the construction of a successful partnership, key elements suggested by the literature include repeated multi-stakeholder workshops that result in a "partnership agreement" early in the project life, and frequent follow-up on its implementation (Larson, 1997; Weston and Gibson, 1993), well-articulated objectives (Crane et al., 1999; Weston and Gibson, 1993), the a priori design of a dispute resolution or problem escalation process (Larson, 1997; Weston and Gibson, 1993), buy-in from participants including top management (Larson, 1997; Weston and Gibson, 1993), and an emphasis on holistic multi-level multi-stakeholder results-oriented problem-solving as opposed to an individualistic or hierarchical task-oriented approach (Barlow, 2000). The collective definition of the goal, and a plan for achieving it that includes supporting incentives and other reinforcements at each stage of this process, is central to success (Crane et al., 1997; Wilson et al., 1995). Frank up-front discussion of what constitutes "fair dealing" helps to create norms that guide future behavior (Larson, 1997; Ring and Van de Ven, 1992). More recently, scholars have emphasized the use of sophisticated shared simulations and visualizations to allow group visualization and joint evaluation of project outcomes for different scenarios (Shrage, 2000), and networked communications among project team members (Cheng et al., 2001) to facilitate interparty negotiations and foster shared identity.

Cognitive Frames

In some cases, managers can neither tap into pre-existing social structures nor demonstrate adherence to pre-existing social norms due to the unwillingness or inability of external stakeholders to engage directly with the focal organization. In these instances, managers may still strategically generate psychological contracts (Rousseau, 1995) or draw upon "social skills" (Fligstein, 1997), communication or influence campaigns to alter preferences of counterparties indirectly. Managers may enhance coordination and reduce the incidence of opportunistic behavior by counterparties by crafting the perception that counterparties' individual or organizational identity is linked to that of the manager's organization – for example, the project company set up as a special purpose vehicle for privatized infrastructure delivery projects – despite the lack of a formal social or contractual connection.

Managers with strong social skills possess this "ability to induce cooperation among others. Skilled social actors empathetically relate to the situations of other people and, in so doing, are able to provide those people with reasons to cooperate" (Fligstein, 2001, 112). Despite a lack of formal organizational linkage and a targeting of individuals, these strategies, by taking advantage of individuals' inherent desire for factional or group membership, construct a sense of connection that is sufficiently strong to mirror the patterns of behavior observed of group members outlined above.

In contrast to collective norms which grow less efficient as the scope of counterparties expands, social skills that create a link between a desired behavior and an individual's sense of identity are more readily scalable (Scott and Lane, 2000). They frame inspiring shared high-level goals and "stories that help induce cooperation from people in their group that appeal to their identity and interests, while at the same time using those same stories to frame actions against various opponents" (Fligstein, 2001, 113). Frames enable individuals to "locate, perceive, identify and label" (Goffman, 1974, 21) events and occurrences even if the targeted counterparty has limited or no direct exposure. Most importantly, they create a link between an individual's sense of self and a course of action amenable to the designer of the frame.

Similar insights relating constructs of identity to the governance of large multinational organizations have previously been applied by scholars seeking to craft a knowledge-based view of firm organization as a contrast to a transaction cost logic. While we disagree with the underlying premise of the strong form of that literature's critique of transaction cost theory's focus on opportunism (Conner and Prahalad, 1996; Ghoshal and Moran, 1996; Kogut and Zander, 1992, 1996), we do agree that the underlying mechanism of shared identity formation can enhance coordination and reduce the incidence of and impact of opportunistic behavior, whether within the boundary of a firm or outside of it (Dyer and Chu, 2000, 2003; Helper et al., 2000; Lubatkin et al., 2007).

In response to these framing efforts, counterparties to a transaction or set of transactions may alter their behavior because they perceive actions or goals of the network to be legitimate due to the congruence of these actions or goals with their own individual or organizational interests or beliefs (Suchman, 1995, 574) or to the best possible behavior given the tension posed by their multiple identities (Davis, 2007). Such intrinsic motivation may be cued through the use of unified imagery (for example, logos, terminology, color schemes or other branding campaigns), stories (Polletta, 1998), rituals (Taylor and Whittier, 1992) or symbolic actions (for example, associations with charities or causes) (Ansell, 1998; Elsbach, 1994). Counterparties may also be prominently featured in the imagery and actions so as to co-opt their individual or organizational identity (Elsbach and Glynn, 1996). Frequent and substantive interaction between counterparties reinforces this sense of shared identity (Dutton et al., 1994). As in the case of collective norms, a growing body of economic and psychological research highlights the importance of the words, frames or belief systems invoked to support or critique an otherwise identical argument (Levin et al., 2002; Levin et al., 1998; Tversky and Kahneman, 1981a, 1981b).

Employees may prefer to work for a company they perceive to be socially responsible, accept lower wages or benefits, or exert greater effort (Besley and Ghatak, 2005; Bhattacharya et al., 2008; Brekke and Nyborg, 2008; Collier and Esteban, 2007; Greening and Turban, 2000; Kim et al., 2010; Preston, 1989; Turban and Greening, 1997). Suppliers of other factors of production could make similar choices influencing the cost of capital or production (Bruyn, 1991; Mackey et al., 2007; Porter and Kramer, 2006; Sparkes and Cowton, 2004; Waddock, 2000).

In studying the motivation of electrical workers on two large coal-fired power plants in the south-western United States, Borcherding (1972) interviewed two workers doing essentially identical tasks in the power plant's control room. The worker on the first project reported that he was "terminating cables for one of the steam safety systems"; the worker on the second project reported that he was "lighting up the Southwestern United States!" The fact that the project manager on the second project had framed the project in an exciting way clearly paid off in multiple dimensions. The second project had smoother labor relations, higher productivity, lower absenteeism and less delay.

Similar framing battles occur in the public policy-making process. Advocates of a policy or position typically frame an event or occurrence as unjust, offer a solution (that is, their preferred policy or position) to that injustice and mobilize external stakeholders for action (Benford and Snow, 2000). They construct frames via discourses that interpret a series of events based on the presentation and/or obfuscation of a subset of those events; strategies that seek to draw in new supporters by bridging frames, amplifying values or beliefs of potential supporters, extending frames to new issues or, if needed, transforming the content of the frame itself; and engaging in collective struggles between competing frames (Benford and Snow, 2000).

At each stage of this process, two prominent tactics are the strategic dissemination of information and the undertaking of actions (for example, the provision of costly goods or services potentially followed by the publicization of these acts) designed to alter preferences about the focal organization, a policy of importance to that organization or another stakeholder or set of stakeholders. Given the heavy resource demands of such a campaign, successful diffusion is facilitated where a frame can either directly tap into individuals' sense of self (Gamson, 1992; Snow and McAdam, 2000) or indirectly do so by connecting with political (McAdam et al., 1996) and cultural (Tarrow, 1992) opportunity structures (for example, a pre-existing conflict or debate closely linked to members' identities and over which members are willing to expend resources).

TOWARD AN INTEGRATED THEORY OF PROJECT GOVERNANCE

We have established the existence of regulative, normative and cognitive supports for relational contracting in civil infrastructure projects (that is, documenting that project sponsors in the position of residual claimant expend effort to craft the correct financial incentives and punishments *ex ante* as well as to tap into and manipulate peer group sanctions and individual psychological incentives *ex post*). We now seek to outline a means to integrate the economic, legal, sociological and psychological perspectives on governance in a manner that gives rise to testable propositions for subsequent empirical research.

Our conception of "relational contracting" extends beyond microeconomic notions of repeated contracting – in which the "shadow of the future" mitigates opportunism – to include a variety of sociological, social psychological and cognitive psychological mechanisms that buttress contracts and their enforcement by legal means or extralegal third-party arbitrators. The propositions below, with their supporting arguments, provide some initial theoretical points of departure to propose that normative and cognitive supports for relational contracting will be needed and found more frequently as a function of selected project and counterparty attributes. Additional research is needed to identify where specific normative or cognitive supports add the most value, and should therefore be used.

First, we draw upon the inability of the economic and legal perspectives to solve the contracting problems in multi-counterparty, multi-phased, long-lived transactions such as civil infrastructure concessions to highlight additional baseline transactional features that enhance the likelihood and importance of relational contracting for these extremely challenging governance regimes. Second, we draw upon the nature of the collective norms and cognitive frames invoked by the sociological and psychological perspectives to highlight baseline counterparty relationship features that have the same effect. Finally, we combine these diverse theoretical perspectives to offer predictions on the relative incidence of *ex ante* regulative governance mechanisms versus *ex post* normative and cognitive governance processes in support of relational contracts.

Prior research has highlighted the importance of temporal linkages across repeated contracts between identical counterparties (Argyres and Liebeskind, 1999), and in related contracts between different counterparties (Granovetter, 1985; Jones et al., 1997; Powell, 1990b; Chan, 2010), as well as the importance of the "gains from trade" and the "gains to shirking or opportunistic behavior" (Baker et al., 2002) to the ability to sustain relational contracting based upon the shadow of the future. We join these three elements together to highlight the particular contractual hazard of displaced agency (that is, the costs that accrue to a series of interdependent transactions as a result of counterparties' incentives to pass through or shift costs or responsibilities to a counterparty not fully represented in the current phase of the transaction) to the long-term detriment of the current residual claimant.

Proposition 1: As displaced agency costs rise, the need for relational contracting increases.

Holding constant the level of displaced agency, a number of country-level and network-level characteristics alter the relative costs or competencies of relational contracting. The degree of variation in the composition of teams from project to project – termed the "relational instability of the project network" by Taylor and Levitt (2007) – tends to be much higher in countries with liberal market economies such as the United Kingdom (UK) and US, compared to countries with coordinated market economies such as France, Finland, Sweden and Japan (Hall and Soskice, 2001) in which multiple counterparties tend to work together more frequently on successive projects. This exacerbates the tendency for opportunistic behavior by a given party and renders governance of the transaction more challenging in liberal market economies.

Proposition 2: The incidence of relational contracting in the presence of displaced agency will be higher in coordinated market economies than in liberal market economies.

Transaction-level asset specificity gives rise to contractual hazards that may require investment in formal governance mechanisms to overcome and achieve gains from trade. In contrast, mutual dependence upon a relationship – whether due to characteristics that are transactional, counterparty-level (for example, a lack of knowledge of alternative counterparties), or country-level (for example, formal regulatory restrictions on altering the identity of the counterparty) – may generate a self-regulating sanctioning mechanism via the shadow of the future that allows transactions to continue even in the absence of investments in formal regulative governance mechanisms. Counterparty dependence upon within-group resources as compared to potential external substitutes will reduce the cost of relying upon social sanctions, further advantaging relational contracts. At the extreme, where each counterparty is entirely dependent upon and only interacts with a small number of other counterparties within the network of coupled sequential transactions on this or a broader set of projects, the potential cost to them of failing to cooperate or behaving opportunistically is much larger than when counterparties are more anonymous (that is, numerous and atomistic) and, as a result, are indifferent between contracting within the network or outside of it.

Proposition 3: The incidence of relational contracting in the presence of displaced agency increases with the mutual economic dependence among counterparties.

Mutual economic dependence provides a strong economic rationale for continued cooperation. However, as highlighted above, a similar outcome can be engendered through appeals to collective norms or cognitive frames particularly in the presence of shared backgrounds, world-views and prior interactions. In place of, or in complement to, the economic shadow of the future, the presence of a common identity or dense network of relationships creates a "social shadow of the future" as well as the potential for immediate social or cognitive sanctions for opportunistic behavior.

Proposition 4: *The incidence of relational contracting in the presence of displaced agency increases in the presence of shared backgrounds, world-views and prior interactions among counterparties.*

Having established that these baseline country-level and network-level factors alter the relative costs and competences of relational contracting, we next consider how variation in the structure of economic pay-offs or social relations could impact the effectiveness of normative and cognitive supports for relational contracting, compared to their regulative counterparts. One obvious potential change, particularly in the rapidly globalizing realm of civil infrastructure, is the extension of an existing network into a new geographic or political market and/or so as to incorporate new suppliers with heterogeneous past experiences and relevant beliefs. Expanding the project team to include unfamiliar new participants creates exposure to new counterparties for whom both mutual economic dependence and shared backgrounds, world-views and prior interactions are relatively lower than for pre-existing counterparts (Johnson et al., 2002; McMillan and Woodruff, 1999a, 1999b; Orr, 2005).

Proposition 5: *The expansion of the scope of tightly coupled sequenced transactions to include new counterparties (for example, new end consumers, a new geographic market, new intermediate suppliers or new political authorities) is positively associated with the incidence of normative and cognitive supports for relational contracts.*

Where co-location is prolonged and contact frequent, the slow incremental process of identity shaping through social construction, messaging and strategic communications has a greater likelihood of altering behavior and of justifying the substantial costs in terms of time and resources involved. By contrast, more diffuse or ephemeral ongoing transaction networks make the justification of such expenses more uncertain.

Proposition 6: The duration and intensity of counterparty interactions is positively associated with the incidence and efficacy of normative and cognitive supports for relational contracts.

Our final two propositions highlight interdependencies between the efficacy of regulative and normative or cultural supports. First, while investments in the latter mechanisms develop a sense of shared identity that can enhance the likelihood of cooperation, that tendency toward cooperation by some counterparties could be thought to increase the benefit of opportunistic defection by others who seek to capture or divert rents that the cooperative counterparty has left exposed. We believe that the prevalence of normative and cognitive supports for relational contracts in civil infrastructure despite this risk – particularly in the pre-operation phase – can be traced to the limited potential benefits to any one counterparty from shirking, as compared to the system-wide benefits to cooperation, of which a significant portion in any phase of the project accrues to a single residual claimant (for example, lead designer, construction contractor or operator). That is, the pay-off matrix for the counterparties resembles a "stag hunt" (that is, coordination) game rather than a "prisoner's dilemma." By contrast, where substantial asymmetries exist – particularly insofar as any individual counterparties face relatively large benefits from non-cooperation or opportunism as compared to cooperation – the efficacy of collective norms or cognitive processes will be substantially reduced. Below some level, the need to construct contractual safeguards or legal limitations on counterparty discretion dictate a shift to stronger regulative supports in either unified hierarchical or fragmented market governance structures.

Proposition 7: The ratio of the gains from trade to the residual claimant within the tightly coupled sequenced transactions to the gains from non-cooperation or opportunistic behavior is positively associated with the incidence and efficacy of normative and cognitive supports for relational contracts.

Finally, drawing on the frameworks of Ring and Van de Ven (1994) and Husted and Folger (2004), we note the mutually reinforcing nature of regulative, normative and cognitive institutional supports for relational contracting. Contracts on complex, long-lived projects are necessarily incomplete and involve high levels of uncertainty regarding the magnitude and distribution of potential future pay-offs achievable through cooperation. Success in achieving those potential pay-offs will be a function of ongoing assessments of the negotiations, commitments and executions based on efficiency and equity grounds. Where counterparties have shared backgrounds, world-views and prior interactions, and subsequently interact more intensively over a longer period of time, the resulting normative and cognitive institutional supports for relational contracting reinforce the efficacy of the regulative institutional supports such as formal contracting or rational cooperation in response to the economic shadow of the future. Similarly, the presence of formal contractual commitments and a clear economic pay-off from reciprocal cooperation reinforce the sense of shared identity. This argument is consistent with a growing body of recent literature highlighting the complementarity of formal and informal governance mechanisms (Gulati and Nickerson, 2008; Mayer and Argyres, 2004; Poppo and Zenger, 2002; Zaheer and Venkatraman, 1995).

Proposition 8: *Normative and cognitive institutional supports for relational contracting are complementary to their regulative counterparts.*

CONCLUSION

The *ex post* governance of relational contracts can be supported by regulative normative and/or cultural-cognitive institutions (Scott, 2008). Regulative institutional supports legally or economically sanction individuals who violate contracts or exceed an allowed range of managerial discretion. Normative institutional supports socially sanction individuals who violate values, beliefs and scripts for appropriate behavior in various social settings that are deemed to be appropriate by a collective body. Cultural-cognitive institutional supports sanction individuals psychically (that is, through cognitive dissonance) when their actions violate internalized frames or schemas for naming, categorizing and understanding tangible and intangible concepts in the world; or a set of values, beliefs and scripts (Schank and Abelson, 1977) that define and guide appropriate behavior in different settings from the perspective of various groups (for example, church, company, agency or family) to which an individual considers that they belong.

We used a heretofore neglected source of contractual hazards – displaced agency – to examine the relative efficacy of these institutional supports for relational contracting in infrastructure contracts, especially for long-lived, public–private partnership, infrastructure service concessions. While we have developed this analysis in the context of the provision of civil infrastructure services, we believe the arguments to be quite general. We believe that the problem of a residual claimant eliciting cooperation among counterparties linked through a series of sequenced and highly interdependent transactions, and whose pay-off structure mirrors that of a coordination game rather than a prisoner's dilemma, is ubiquitous in many project-based settings. We have referenced numerous detailed examples from the development of infrastructure projects as well as highlighted related literature on teams, buyer–supplier contracts, alliances, diversified multinational corporations, corporate social responsibility and community development.

We do not dismiss the central importance of contractual mechanism design and partner selection in market and trilateral governance structures, administrative fiat in unified governance structures, the alignment of economic interest in bilateral and network governance structures, and the value of strategic choice about how to govern an individual transaction. We seek to highlight, however, that purely regulative institutional supports for relational contracting may, under certain conditions, usefully be complemented *ex post* by systematically developing collective norms and a cultural-cognitive sense of shared identity.

Integrated project delivery (IPD) – the approach used to develop Terminal 5 at Heathrow (Gil, 2009) and the Sutter Hill Camino Hospital in California (Khanzode et al., 2008; Fischer et al., 2017) – embraces all three kinds of institutions to implement and buttress effective relational contracting:

1. Regulative: the economic interests of all key contractors are aligned by using reimbursable cost contracts for design and construction with a shared incentive pool to be divided among the contractors according to a predetermined formula, based on overall project outcomes rather than each contractor's individual outputs. To create a social shadow of the future, the team are promised that they will be kept together and hired for multiple projects subject to satisfactory performance on each project.
2. Normative: key design and construction professionals from all involved firms are collocated in a "big room" workspace, creating a further sense of shared identity, social exchange and shared destiny. They use a shared three-dimensional (3-D) computer-aided design (CAD) building information model to integrate each team member's design information into a unified virtual design and construction model, and are thus collectively accountable for its accuracy and completeness.
3. Cognitive: a great deal of effort is spent by the client and its project management team on shaping shared identity early in the project through numerous goal alignment sessions during the conceptual design phase.

However, these normative and cognitive institutional supports come at a cost. The allocation of ownership or rights of employment locally may reduce competition, thereby raising the costs of capital; or lead to suboptimal innovation, particularly in capital-intensive or uncertain technologies. Leveraging of pre-existing social ties for monitoring and enforcement opens the door to abuse, including nepotism, insular networks and outright corruption. "Fair processes" for decision-making are lengthier and tend to require more frequent iteration and revision of initial plans. Influence strategies require careful assessment of the identity and preferences of key stakeholders and the ties that connect them, as well as analysis of the best means to influence the collective policy outcome or preference and, finally, the execution of such a strategy. Furthermore, successful framers share many characteristics with propagandists and con artists. Where the price premium for market governance is not too high or the capacity and political legitimacy for unified internal governance exists, relational contracting will often be at a cost disadvantage. In contrast, where contractual hazards are high, invoking all of these costly mechanisms to buttress the effectiveness of relational contracting can be an important complement to neoclassical contracting or unified governance, particularly in the face of displaced agency costs, among mutually economically dependent counterparties with shared backgrounds, world-views and prior interactions, and where the scope for individual gain from opportunistic behavior is limited as compared to the potential collective gains from cooperation.

Empirical research to explore these propositions could begin with the construction of a representative sample of large infrastructure projects including data on the identity of key contractors and subcontractors as well as the size, scope and timeline of the project. This data could be further supplemented with press coverage of these projects from which information on project schedules and delays, stakeholder identity, and opinions on the project and frames invoked by these stakeholders could be coded. A survey could then be sent to each of the contractors to identify the magnitude of traditional contractual hazards (that is, asset specificity, frequency, uncertainty and probity), displaced agency costs, the nature of the pay-off structure, their degree of economic dependence on the counterparties to this project, as well as decision-making processes that adhere to norms of procedural justice or project partnership. Though such a data collection effort would be time-consuming it would generate enormous insight into the strategic decision to supplement the regulative supports for relational contracting with their normative and cognitive counterparts. Comparative cases including multiple projects led by the same lead contractor that appear substantively different in terms of their governance would provide additional insight to the nascent case studies currently examining these topics (Caldwell et al., 2009; Zheng et al., 2008). Parallel empirical efforts in other domains where relational contracting dominates, such as biotechnology alliances, open source software and global supply chains, would be needed to address questions of generalizability convincingly.

An interdisciplinary governance framework, particularly if supported by empirical analysis, offers the possibility of connecting strains of literature that share a common objective – that is, enhancing cooperation and reducing opportunistic behavior so as to improve organizational performance – but have operated in relative isolation due to the disparate and heterogeneous theoretical bases for the regulative, normative and cognitive supports for relational contracting. Whereas a large body of scholarship has already highlighted the understudied nature of alternative institutional supports for contracting (Bradach and Eccles, 1989; McEvily et al., 2003; Ouchi, 1980), we need further theoretical and empirical work examining precisely when, where and why regulative, normative and cognitive supports of relational contracting can effectively mitigate contractual hazards. By integrating these perspectives in our analysis of the contractual hazard of displaced agency, we have highlighted not only their complementarity, which is well understood in the literature (Bercovitz et al., 2006; Poppo and Zenger, 2002; Ring and Van de Ven, 1994, 1992), but also certain boundary conditions within which individual supports are more or less effective.

We hope that scholars and practitioners in a broad range of fields and contexts, who share an interest in the mechanisms by which a set of actors who share a common high-level goal such as delivering a new infrastructure asset, but who also encounter difficulties in coordinating their behavior because of potentially misaligned specific local interests and time frames, can structure their interactions to improve performance, and will build upon the insights here to construct an interdisciplinary theory of the economic, legal, organizational, sociological and psychological elements of governance and subject it to empirical analysis.

NOTE

* Adapted from: Henisz, W.J., Levitt, R.E., and Scott, W.R. (2012). Toward a unified theory of project governance: economic, sociological and psychological supports for relational contracting. *Engineering Project Organization Journal*, 2(1/2), 37–55, with permission from the Engineering Project Organizations Society.

4. Stakeholders, issues and the shaping of large engineering projects*
Wen Feng, Donald R. Lessard, Bruce G. Cameron and Edward F. Crawley

INTRODUCTION: STAKEHOLDERS, ISSUES AND THE SHAPING OF LEPs

Large engineering projects (LEPs) are significantly shaped by the multi-type and networked relationships between LEPs and their stakeholders in both market and non-market environments. As explained in Chapter 2 of this volume, public–private partnership (PPP) projects are large, complex engineering projects that involve long-term relationships between a dynamic group of powerful stakeholders from the public, private and civic sectors across their life cycles, and so are especially challenging to manage. This chapter advances a multidisciplinary network approach, namely the stakeholder value network (SVN), as a lens to examine, understand, model and manage stakeholder relationships in LEPs such as PPP infrastructure projects. The SVN approach brings together knowledge from three domains: engineering systems, organizational sociology and strategic management. Specifically, the focus of this chapter is on exploring the underlying connections between stakeholders and issues; extending the methodological framework of the "stakeholder-based SVN" to the "issue-based SVN"; as well as discussing the strategic implications of the issue-based SVN and demonstrating the benefits of the integration of stakeholders and issues.

Since the twentieth century, LEPs, sometimes also called "superprojects" (Levitt, 1984), "megaprojects" (Flyvbjerg et al., 2003) or "macro-projects" (Bolonkin and Cathcart, 2009; Merrow, 2011), have become a remarkable phenomenon emerging from the interactions between human society and the natural environment, such as telephone networks, electric grids, national highways, oil fields, space stations, and so on. These LEPs are made possible by technological advancement, especially after individual "inventions begin to be connected" (de Weck et al., 2011, 3) into large and complex systems. The main contents of LEPs can be categorized in the following way (Lessard and Miller, 2013): "LEPs are games of ambition in which sponsors aim to build solutions to unmet needs. LEPs may involve the development of major engineering breakthroughs, pushing the engineering envelope of production systems through major capital investments, and/or developing new institutional constructs that allow diverse project actors and stakeholders to collaborate."

Meanwhile, the impacts of LEPs are far-reaching from multiple perspectives. On the one hand, LEPs not only substantially improve the quality of human life, but are also strongly connected to the productivity and competitiveness of a country (Hirschman, 1957) and "constitute one of the most important business sectors in the world" (Miller and Lessard, 2000, 1). On the other hand, LEPs also bring potential externalities (overuse of natural resources, environmental pollution, and so on) as well as unintended consequences (traffic congestion, power outrages, and so on), and further, because of their scale and complexity, LEPs are challenging to shape and execute, and often go terribly wrong, with serious implications for their sponsors, other stakeholders and society at large. In particular, for the shaping of LEPs, Lessard and Miller (2013) point out:

> the "fuzzy" front-end of opportunity or the shaping of LEPs, where the project concept, the projects sponsors and core team, and the engagement of various stakeholders co-evolve through the concerted efforts of a small number of players interacting with many emergent factors, [is a crucial but often-overlooked aspect of LEPs.] . . . LEPs are not simply selected. Instead, they are shaped over multiple episodes through strategic moves with risk resolution in mind. In "one off" multi-party projects, these early stages include not only developing the project concept, but also the project coalition itself . . . [In addition,] [f]ront-end shaping is most important for LEPs that are pioneering in either the technical or institutional domain, or both. Many LEPs are pioneering in that they require significant departures from business as usual.

A critical element of the shaping of LEPs is associated with the multi-type and networked relationships between the LEPs and their various stakeholders, in both market and non-market environments. In this chapter we advance a multidisciplinary network approach, namely SVN (Cameron, 2007; Cameron et al., 2008; Cameron et al., 2011b; Feng, 2013; Fu et al., 2011; Hein et al., 2017; Sutherland, 2009), as a lens to examine, understand, model and manage these stakeholder relationships in LEPs. It brings together knowledge from three domains: engineering systems, organizational sociology and strategic management.

First, engineering systems: LEPs are typical "engineering systems," that is, systems "characterized by a high degree of technical complexity, social intricacy, and elaborate processes, aimed at fulfilling important functions in society" (de Weck et al., 2011, 31). The tools and models for managing the structural complexity of engineering systems – more specifically, the dependency structure matrix (DSM, a.k.a. design structure matrix) (Eppinger and Browning, 2012; Feng et al., 2012a) and the utility model of network exchanges (Cameron et al., 2011a) – make it possible for us to analyze the interorganizational relationships between the LEPs and their stakeholders quantitatively.

Second, organizational sociology: in the eyes of sociologists (Stinchcombe, 1965), interorganizational relationships provide the microfoundations for broader social structures, which in turn shape the organizational actors and their activities, and also determine the power, conflict, authority, identity and other interesting phenomena on the macro level. Specifically, we apply social exchange theory (SET) (Malinowski, 1920; Lévi-Strauss, 1949/1969; Homans, 1958; Emerson, 1976) to unify both social and economic relationships into a common framework for analysis, and then to link these relationships to macro-level phenomena, especially the power of stakeholders.

Third, strategic management: in order to better understand the power of stakeholders, the importance of strategic issues simply cannot be ignored; not only because of the underlying connections between stakeholders and issues from the perspective of network analysis, but also because of the inseparability of these two concepts in the context of strategic management, as recently proposed by management scholars (Frooman, 2010; Lucea, 2007; Mahon et al., 2004; Roloff, 2008). Following these proposals, the main focus of our chapter is to develop the "issue-based SVN" as a practical means to integrate the strength of stakeholder theory (Freeman, 1984; Freeman et al., 2010) and strategic issue management (Ansoff, 1980; Chase, 1982, 1984) for the shaping of LEPs. Based on this development, we will also compare and contrast the issue-based SVN with the more traditional "stakeholder-based SVN" to demonstrate the benefits of this integration.

The remainder of our chapter is organized as follows. First, we build up the theoretical foundations along with three key assumptions for the SVN approach as background. Second, we discuss the connections between stakeholders and issues, develop the concept of the issue-based SVN from the stakeholder-based SVN, and generate three propositions about the strategic implications of the new concept. Third, we briefly demonstrate the kinds of insights one can get from a rigorous multi-relational network analysis of the issue-based SVN. We conclude with a discussion of the merits of our approach and a few promising directions for future research.

THE SVN APPROACH AND ITS THEORETICAL FOUNDATIONS

We first define five important concepts and introduce three ways of mapping stakeholder relationships. After that, we briefly lay out the theoretical foundations and key assumptions for the SVN approach.

Concepts and Definitions

- SVN: a multi-relational network consisting of a focal organization (that is, LEPs in the context of this chapter), the focal organization's stakeholders, and the tangible and intangible value exchanges between the focal organization and its stakeholders, as well as between the stakeholders themselves (Feng, 2013).
- Value exchange: the processes during which the specific needs of stakeholders (including the focal organization) are satisfied at a desirable cost (Crawley, 2009).
- Value flow: derived from the specific needs of each stakeholder, a value flow is the output of one stakeholder, and at the same time, the input of another.
- Value path: a string of value flows connecting a group of stakeholders.
- Value cycle: the value path beginning from and ending with the same stakeholder (for example, the focal organization).

Mapping Stakeholder Relationships

There are three canonical ways to map the relationships between stakeholders: the "hub-and-spoke" model, the "stakeholder-based SVN" model, and the "issue-based SVN" model. As Feng et al. (2012b) have demonstrated, the hub-and-spoke model, which only includes direct relationships between the focal organization and its stakeholders, is typically incomplete as it allows important stakeholder relationships and balances to be ignored; and the "stakeholder-based SVN" model is superior to the hub-and-spoke model by capturing the impacts of both direct and indirect stakeholder relationships. Compared to the stakeholder-based SVN model, the issue-based SVN model also includes both direct and indirect relationships between stakeholders, but only those relevant to a specific "issue." Since the issue-based SVN is a subset of the stakeholder-based SVN, it involves a smaller number of stakeholders and relationships and hence reduces the modeling complexity.

The first step in creating either of these network models is to map the stakeholder relationships, and no prior theory is needed to do so. However, in order to make sense of the more complicated relationship maps in anything but the most trivial of cases, it is necessary to analyze the networks quantitatively, which requires a new theory.

Theoretical Development of the SVN

Based on the above discussion, multiple types of relationships are the key to analyzing the strategic implications of the SVN systematically. In the social sciences, social and economic relationships are two basic and distinct types of interactions between individuals or organizations. Although they are different in many ways and are often studied separately by sociologists and economists, two ambitious efforts have been made in recent years to unify both social and economic relationships into a common framework for analysis. One is the new economic sociology (NES), which begins with social relationships and uses the concept of "social embeddedness" to study various economic phenomena (see the work of Harrison C. White, Mark S. Granovetter, Ronald S. Burt, Paul J. DiMaggio and Joel M. Podolny, among others). The other is social exchange theory (SET), which begins with economic relationships and uses models analogous to economic exchange, but based on the exchange of favors and reciprocal obligations between individuals, to study various social situations (see the work of George C. Homans, Peter M. Blau, Richard M. Emerson, Karen S. Cook and Peter P. Ekeh, among others). These two efforts can be viewed as dual theories, echoing the distinction of "structure versus process" by Van de Ven (1976), or "structural versus relational" by Granovetter (1992), or "structuralist versus connectionist" by Borgatti and Foster (2003), for the relationships between either individuals or organizations.

Following the NES approach, Rowley (1997), Mahon et al. (2004) and Lucea (2007) propose the application of social network analysis (SNA) for stakeholder research. SNA views stakeholder relationships as empty social ties without content, and studies the impacts of network structures on stakeholders' behavior. The strength of this approach lies in providing a way to measure the structural properties of the whole network (network density, and so on) and the structural position of individual stakeholders (degree, closeness and betweenness-centralities, and so on), with a rigorous basis in graph theory. The weakness of this approach lies in the separation of the different types of relationships: only a single type of relationship (for example, economic or social) is put into one network and all these structural measurements are defined for this single-relational network.

In order to overcome this weakness of SNA, we develop a new network approach following SET – the SVN analysis – which views multiple types of stakeholder relationships as value exchanges and studies the strategic implications of the exchanged value flowing through the whole stakeholder network. Under the SET framework, social relationships involve the exchange of socially valued favors and obligations, and so can be viewed as an extension of economic relationships (Coleman, 1990; Emerson, 1976; Homans, 1961). Thus, "concepts and principles borrowed from microeconomics" (Cook, 2000, 687) can be applied to conduct "the economic analysis of noneconomic social situations" (Emerson, 1976, 336).

Specifically, we apply the classic concept of "utility" in economics to create a mathematical model for the purpose of comparing the relative importance of value flows in the SVN: each value flow, no matter what type it is, is assigned a numeric score according to the satisfaction level perceived by the stakeholder who receives the benefits from that value flow. These value flow scores are comparable and actually reflect the degrees of desire for stakeholders to be involved in the relevant direct value exchanges. Further, these scores, or the importance levels of value flows, provide a basis to rank the relative importance of value paths and value cycles, which are then taken as the basic units to measure the aggregate impacts of both direct and indirect stakeholder relationships for the focal organization. Based on the SET, we posit that all the stakeholder relationships are formed by the use of subjective utility analysis (rational choice theory) and the comparison of alternatives (behaviorist psychology).

From the above discussion, value flow and value path are obviously two essential concepts in the SVN analysis, and it would be helpful to link these concepts with similar ones in SET. In SET, a pair of value flows between two stakeholders represents a "restricted exchange" (Lévi-Strauss, 1949/1969), which is defined as a two-party reciprocal relationship that may be shown as AδB. A closed value path, or a value path beginning from and ending with the same stakeholder, actually represents a "generalized exchange" (Bearman, 1997; Ekeh, 1974; Lévi-Strauss, 1963; Malinowski, 1920; Sahlins, 1965), which is defined as the univocal reciprocal relationships among at least three parties in the exchange situation that may be shown as AδBδCδA.

Key Assumptions for SVN

Having reviewed the relevant literature, we formulate three key assumptions, which have a solid foundation in SET, for the SVN analysis:

- Relationship types: social exchanges are the extension of economic exchanges (Coleman, 1990; Emerson, 1976; Homans, 1961), and thus monetary and non-monetary relationships between stakeholders can

be analyzed in a common framework, with the use of subjective utility judgments as well as comparison of alternatives.
- Exchange patterns: multilateral and indirect value exchanges exist widely in the strategic behavior of modern organizations (Levine and Shah, 2003; Olson, 1965; Westphal and Zajac, 1997), and thus the value cycles for the focal organization can be taken as the basis to understand the impacts of indirect relationships between stakeholders.
- Strategic implications: stakeholder power is the outcome of both exchange relations and network positions (Blau, 1994; Emerson, 1972b; Molm, 1990) and thus, network statistics can be constructed from the sample space of value cycles to measure the power of stakeholders, as well as other metrics of interest.

ISSUE-BASED SVN AND THREE PROPOSITIONS

In this section, we first examine the underlying connections between stakeholders and issues from the perspective of network analysis, and also review several recent proposals from management scholars for integrating stakeholders and issues. Next, we discuss the motivations for us to integrate issues into the above SVN approach. Finally, we generate three propositions about the strategic implications of issue-based SVN.

Connections between Stakeholders and Issues

Based on their deep appreciation for network analysis in the social sciences during the past century, Laumann et al. (1983) point out that "nodal attributes," "relations" and "participation in specified events or activities" are three foci to define the boundary of a network. We further infer that "actors," "relations" and "events" are three types of basic units in network analysis. It is straightforward to understand the inclusion of "actors" and "relations" because we can easily find the corresponding concepts in graph theory (vertices/nodes and edges/links, respectively), in the social sciences (individuals/organizations and individual/organizational relations, respectively), as well as in our SVN approach more specifically (stakeholders and stakeholder relationships, respectively). However, it is not that intuitive to identify a concept similar to the "events" in the SVN approach. After an intensive investigation of relevant literature, we argue that the concept of "issues" is the most appropriate way to match the concept of "events."

In the field of strategic management, "issues" are a mature and important concept, which often means "events, trends, or developments that could have a negative impact on the organization's ability to reach its objectives if left unattended" (Mahon et al., 2004, 171) or, more accurately, "focal and concrete events such as a project, a product, or a firm policy that generate gaps between the expectations of a number of stakeholders and the firm's behavior" (Lucea, 2007, 26). Thus, "stakeholders" and "issues" are essentially connected in the way that both of them provide the foci for the definition of the network's boundary as well as the subsequent network analysis.

Others who have sought to integrate issues with stakeholders via a network approach include the following:

- Mahon et al. (2004) employ SNA to make "a number of theoretically grounded conjectures about the delicate relationships between stakeholder behavior and issue evolution" (Mahon et al., 2004, 170).
- Lucea (2007) develops the concept of "global issue space" as an integrative framework that "helps make sense of the multiple relations established between a focal firm and its stakeholders across issues and geographies" (Lucea, 2007, 16).
- Roloff (2008) identifies two types of stakeholder management in companies' practice – "organization-focused" and "issue-focused" – and then demonstrates that "issue-focused stakeholder management dominates in multi-stakeholder networks" (Roloff, 2008, 233).
- Frooman (2010) introduces the idea of an "issue network" and argues that "members of an issue network can be identified as those with grievances, resources, or opportunities" (Frooman, 2010, 161), by drawing on concepts from the fields of social movements (sociology) and interest groups (political science).

We observe that the above proposals are still in the early stages of modeling the ties between stakeholders and issues; most of them only focus on justifying the need of integration, developing theoretical hypotheses and/or building descriptive models. More importantly, except for the proposal from Lucea (2007), none of the other three provide an analytical and instrumental framework, nor do they address the importance of a multi-relational approach.

Integration of Issues and SVN

After understanding the strong connections between stakeholders and issues, now we propose to integrate "issues" into the SVN approach (that is, stakeholder-based SVN). The motivations of our proposal are mainly threefold:

- Stakeholder relationships and issue evolution are intricately intertwined with one another: on the one hand, stakeholders may be involved in multiple issues (Mahon et al., 2004); on the other hand, the interaction of multiple issues may be shaped by the awareness and influence of stakeholders (Bigelow et al., 1991, 1993). Bigelow et al. (1993) summarize: "Stakeholders are only mobilized around issues, and issues only emerge when stakeholders advocate them."

- Each method has its own strength and weakness: as discussed before, the stakeholder-based SVN model provides better descriptive accuracy than the hub-and-spoke model through the inclusion of indirect stakeholder relationships. However, without the consideration of "issues" it is difficult to see through the causal mechanisms behind the balance of stakeholder relationships and to use such an understanding to formulate meaningful strategies.
- Last but not least, a focus on "issues" provides a practical principle to restructure large SVN networks in order to reduce modeling complexity, as the stakeholders and relationships included in the issue-based SVN model are generally fewer than all the stakeholders and relationships included in the stakeholder-based SVN model.

Three Propositions for Issue-Based SVN

We are now ready to generate testable propositions on the strategic implications of the integration between stakeholders and issues. Specifically, we are interested in ranking the importance of different issues as well as understanding the inherent connections between stakeholder power and their relationship balance.

In order to rank the importance of different issues, we need to compare the characteristics of each issue-based SVN; that is, the subset of the SVN model obtained by excluding the stakeholders and relationships irrelevant to that specific issue. Drawing on a common principle of network analysis in the social sciences, "network density" – the proportion of the maximum number of possible edges that are actually present in a network – is arguably the most common measurement for the characteristics of a whole network (Wasserman and Faust, 1994, 101). We use the relative density of each issue-based SVN to rank the importance of each related issue. Specifically, if an issue-based SVN has a higher density than others, we interpret that it is more important than other issues because: (1) a higher density indicates a higher concentration of critical relationships from the perspective of the recipient stakeholders; (2) a higher density indicates more efficient communications between stakeholders (Rowley, 1997, 897); and (3) a higher density indicates a larger likelihood for stakeholders to establish shared behavioral expectations (Oliver, 1991, 171). Thus, we derive the following proposition:

Proposition 1: The importance of a specific issue increases with the network density of the SVN based on that issue.

Second, in order to understand the power of stakeholders in the issue-based SVN, we resort to SET – the theoretical foundation of our SVN approach. Recall the third key assumption stated before: stakeholder power is the outcome of both exchange relations and network positions. More specifically, here we apply power-dependency theory (Emerson, 1962, 1964, 1972a, 1972b) to link the relative power between two stakeholders to the balance of their value exchange relationships. In Emerson's theory, the power of actor "a" to actor "b" in an exchange network equals the dependency of actor "b" on actor "a", or simply written as $P_{ab} = D_{ba}$. Further, as he points out, dependency is a function of both the value of that source and its availability from alternative sources. This dependency can be measured by aggregating the exchange relationships between two stakeholders in the issue-based SVN. A more detailed explanation can be found in Feng (2013). Thus, we derive the following proposition:

Proposition 2: For a specific issue, the power of Stakeholder A over Stakeholder B increases with the dependency of Stakeholder B on Stakeholder A in value exchange relationships around that issue.

Last but not least, based on our relevant work (Feng et al., 2012b; Feng, 2013), we must recognize the importance of indirect relationships in measuring the stakeholder balance and thus in predicting the relative power between two stakeholders. As stated in the second key assumption for the SVN approach: multilateral and indirect value exchanges exist widely in the strategic behavior of modern organizations, and thus the value cycles for the focal organization can be taken as the basis to understand the impacts of indirect relationships between stakeholders. We thus extend Emerson's notion that relative power is based on relative levels of dependency in exchange relationships, to include indirect as well as direct relationships. We postulate that this is also true for the issue-based SVN:

Proposition 3: For a specific issue, the stakeholder dependency based on both direct and indirect relationships is more accurate than the stakeholder dependency based only on direct relationships to describe the relative power between those two stakeholders.

INSIGHTS FROM ISSUE-BASED SVN

In our original paper (Feng et al., 2013b), we conduct a detailed SVN analysis for a retrospective case study of a large real-world engineering project, Project Phoenix, first on a stakeholder basis and then on an issue basis. At the end of this case study, we perform three tasks: (1) validating the strength of the SVN approach in general; (2) testing three propositions generated previously regarding to the strategic implications of issue-based SVN; and (3) demonstrating the benefits of integrating stakeholders and issues.

Specifically, in Project Phoenix, there are four different issues (that is, local economic stimulus, general economic performance, local environmental protection, and national strategy supply security) emerging from 74 relationships (that is, value flows) between 14 stakeholders (including the focal organization itself). Further, we successfully demonstrate: (1) either the stakeholder-based SVN model or the issue-based SVN model would have overcome the blind spots in the "Managers' Mental Model," based only on data that would have been available to them; (2) the issue-based SVN model arrives at the same conclusions as the stakeholder-based SVN model, with a much simpler analysis; (3) the issue-based SVN model has the greatest normative power since it identifies those stakeholders that place large values (positive and negative) on particular issues and can thus link them internally, as well as those stakeholders that are "closest" to each other to effect this "issue trade"; and (4) under the above circumstance, generalized exchanges, which include more than two parties in value exchange, can help to shed light on formulating "indirect" strategies to negotiate with stakeholders with positive balance and those with negative balance simultaneously.

In this chapter, we choose not to repeat the detailed analysis for the stakeholder-based SVN and issue-based SVN of Project Phoenix, but only showcase two critical insights that one can get from a rigorous multi-relational network analysis of the issue-based SVN: one is the importance of different issues (see Figure 4.1) ranked by the network density of each issue-based SVN, and the other is the power balance (see Figure 4.2) characterized by the net transaction value between a focal organization (Project Phoenix – PP) and one of its stakeholders (Local Public, LOP). To help readers have a vivid impression of the issue-based SVN, we also provide the stakeholder map for the issue of "local economic stimulus" in Project Phoenix (see Figure 4.3).

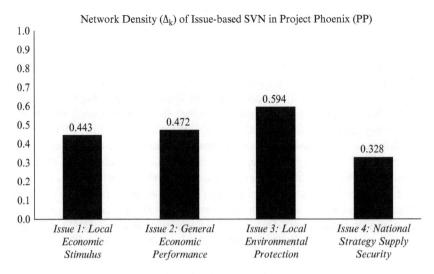

Figure 4.1   Importance of four different issues in Project Phoenix

CONCLUSIONS AND FUTURE WORK

Motivated by the underlying connections and potential synergies between stakeholders and issues in the shaping of LEPs, we first extended the concept of the "stakeholder-based SVN" to the "issue-based SVN" and then generated three propositions regarding the strategic implications of the issue-based SVN. Through a retrospective case study of a large real-world engineering project, which is detailed in Feng et al. (2013b), the benefits of the integration of stakeholders and issues were clearly demonstrated:

- Reduced complexity: the issue-based SVN is generally a subset of the stakeholder-based SVN, and can thus reduce the dimensionality of network models.
- Simpler analysis: the issue-based SVN is able to overcome the blind spots of the "Managers' Mental Model," but with a much simpler analysis than the stakeholder-based SVN.
- Normative power: the issue-based SVN helps project managers to see through the causal mechanism behind the relationship balance. Specifically, issue-based SVN identifies those stakeholders that place large values (positive and negative) on particular issues and thus can link them internally, as well as those stakeholders that are "closest" to each other to effect one or more "issue trades."

Stakeholders, issues and the shaping of large engineering projects 99

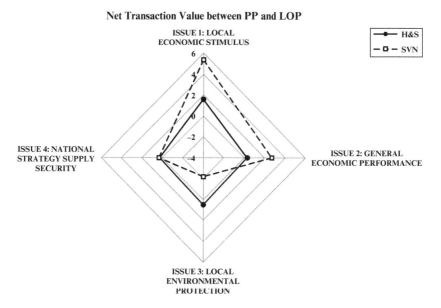

Note: "H&S" is the "Hub-and-Spoke" model; SVN is the Stakeholder Value Network. The solid line shows the power balance between PP and LOP if only the direct H&S relationships are included. Based on the comparison between the dashed SVN line and solid H&S line: (1) The power balance from the SVN model was closer to the empirical facts in this case study; (2) In the meantime, the power balance from the SVN model reveals more possibilities for PP and LOP to make an "issue trade", since their relative power with respect to the four issues is more imbalanced across different issues.

Figure 4.2 Power balance between Project Phoenix (PP) and Local Public (LOP) across four issues

At the same time, we would like to point out the following limitations of the SVN approach:

- Normative justification. The SVN approach is mainly developed with the goals of descriptive accuracy and instrumental strength, and thus lacks a consideration of normative justification. It is in the spirit of Freeman's strategic and egocentric view of stakeholder management. The issue-based SVN can thus be a valuable tool for proponents of PPP projects or other large engineering projects who seek to identify powerful opposing stakeholders early in the conceptual design stage, when it is still relatively easy to make changes in the project's scope and design, and to identify issues that can be used to make trade-offs with the opponents that will allow the

100   *Public–private partnerships for infrastructure development*

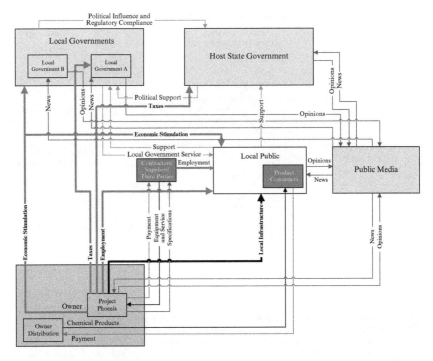

Figure 4.3   Stakeholder map for the issue of "local economic stimulus" in Project Phoenix

project to proceed without unduly compromising its attractiveness to the sponsors.
● Meso-level networks. The SVN approach often deals with the inter-organizational networks on the meso level of human society, and the linkage between the SVN and other networks at the individual, micro or macro levels has not been fully understood. Again, this makes the technique attractive to PPP projects whose stakeholders can be meaningfully dealt with at the organizational level.
● Static characteristics. The SVN approach is static and more like a "snapshot" for the value exchanges among stakeholders at a specific temporal stage, and thus is unable to illustrate the longitudinal evolutions of the network. This is not necessarily a concern when applying this method to PPP projects because, as pointed out in Chapter 2 of this volume, the composition of the stakeholder network and the centrality of different stakeholders in PPP projects changes dramatically across project phases, so trade-offs across project phases may not be as relevant.

- Homogeneous utility. The SVN approach utilizes multi-attribute utility theory (MAUT) as a powerful tool to quantify the value flows based on the subjective utilities of the recipient stakeholders; but for simplification, the same utility function is used for all stakeholders, and additionally, the utility function has not been calibrated with experimental data.
- Egocentric distortion. Value cycles, the representation of generalized exchanges, are the basic units to measure the impacts of indirect stakeholder relationships in the SVN model (both stakeholder-based and issue-based), but the sample space of important network statistics is centered on the focal organization and thus omits those cycles bypassing the focal organization, which may cause distortions of the network structure from a descriptive perspective, as well as of the resulting stakeholder strategies from an instrumental perspective.
- Strategy implementation. Last but not least, the SVN approach does not provide practical guidelines to effectively implement the derived strategies for stakeholder engagement (for example, how to avoid the social dilemmas of moral hazard and free-riding), and these guidelines are much desired in the real world. We have made some progress toward addressing this limitation: in Feng et al. (2013a), we discuss the application of "structural" and/or "exchange" strategies for the focal organization to engage its stakeholders and reposition itself in the SVN. Further articulating these limitations will actually help with the appropriate usage of the SVN approach, and also the identification of the directions for future development and improvement.

Although the above is by no means a complete list, one should not be intimidated by these limitations. As wisely commented by Box and Draper (1987, 424), "Essentially, all models are wrong, but some are useful"; and, "Remember that all models are wrong; the practical question is how wrong do they have to be to not be useful" (Box and Draper, 1987, 74).

NOTE

* Adapted from: Feng, W., Lessard, D.R., Cameron, B.G., and Crawley, E.F. (2013b). Stakeholders, issues, and the shaping of large engineering projects. Engineering Project Organizations Conference, Devil's Thumb Ranch, Colorado, July 9–11, by permission of the Engineering Project Management Society.

PART II

Governance mechanisms in PPP planning, delivery, contracting and management

Private delivery of infrastructure services through public–private partnership (PPP) concessions reprises approaches that were used in colonial times in the United States (US), and as early as the twelfth century in Europe (for example, for the Old Stone Bridge over the Danube River in Regensburg, Germany that was financed by urban salt traders and repaid its investment through bridge tolls). However, during the last century, most Organisation for Economic Co-operation and Development (OECD) countries had their government agencies finance and procure infrastructure assets and operate them using the agencies' staff. The full-blown design–build–finance–operate–maintain (DBFOM) concession approach for delivery of infrastructure as a service by private concessionaires has been reinstituted during the last few decades as part of a movement toward outsourcing government functions that legislators in some countries felt could be more effectively and efficiently provided by private concessionaires.

Some of the most mature PPP jurisdictions are the United Kingdom, Canada and some of its provinces, and Australia and some of its states. Based on earlier problems with the governance approaches that they started with, these mature PPP jurisdictions have evolved governance practices that address previous shortcomings and can thus be a source of tried and tested governance approaches for countries and regions such as the United States that are now beginning to adopt this project delivery approach for some of their civil and social infrastructure.

In Chapter 5, Raymond E. Levitt and Kent Eriksson describe findings from a set of interviews with a broad set of participants in the governance of PPPs drawn from government agencies, equity investors, lenders, industrial partners and regulators in three eastern states of Australia (Victoria,

Queensland and New South Wales). The interviews adopted a broad focus on governance practices, starting with the way in which legislatures allocate funds to infrastructure and prioritize infrastructure projects, through PPP concession procurement approaches, to the internal governance of the equity and debt partners in infrastructure concessions and their construction and operations delivery partners. The mature governance practices now being used in Australia provide models for countries, regions and municipalities newly engaging in PPPs to evaluate and consider adopting or adapting, in order to accelerate the maturity and effectiveness of their own PPP governance regimes.

Chapter 3 in Part I laid out how PPP concession contracts between government agencies and their PPP concessionaires must allocate a variety of high-stakes risks among their participants over decades-long periods. Governments, economies, technologies and even regional demographics can change significantly enough over this extended period that the necessarily "incomplete" PPP concession contracts will never fully address the resolution of all possible contingencies. Thus, the administration of PPP contracts can benefit from various relational mechanisms to buttress their administration when unexpected contingencies arise, as they almost always do. The equity and debt investors in PPP concessions, and their engineering, construction and operations contractors are acutely aware of the nature and magnitude of these risks, and typically incur large legal expenses to try and understand how the key risks have been allocated contractually at all levels and how the ambiguities that will inevitably arise in such long-term contracts will be administered. The relational mechanisms described in Chapter 3 can support the administration of a long-term PPP concession contract, but the contract itself will ultimately be the basis for resolving claims, arbitration and litigation whenever the stakes are high enough and the claims cannot be adjudicated and resolved relationally to the satisfaction of all counterparties.

In Chapter 6, Duc A. Nguyen and Michael J. Garvin present the results of a study that explored how a sample of existing US highway PPP contracts have managed the allocation of 15 risk sharing methods between the client agency and its concessionaire in two different and complementary ways: *ex ante* specification versus *ex post* resolution. The goal of the chapter is to uncover the categories of risk for which each approach works best. A more detailed discussion of alternative mechanisms for allocating what is perhaps the most difficult risk to assess and allocate – uncertainty in the ultimate user demand and willingness to pay for the use of a PPP infrastructure service – is discussed in greater detail in Part III, Chapter 8.

5. Mitigating PPP governance challenges: lessons from eastern Australia*

Raymond E. Levitt and Kent Eriksson

INTRODUCTION

A great deal has been written about the pros and cons of delivering civil and social infrastructure services via public–private partnership (PPP) concessions (Tang et al., 2010), but much less about the governance challenges arising from potential conflicts of interest between the various public and private parties within different phases of PPP infrastructure projects over their 25-year or longer life cycles. The early phases of PPPs involve planning and selecting which infrastructure elements to develop, a very different phase from the infrastructure design and construction phase which, in turn, is very different from the operations and maintenance phase. In PPP infrastructure service delivery, the public and private sectors both need to be governed for coordinated and aligned work over these very different life cycle phases. The governance challenge is that the goals and practices of public and private sectors differ significantly; at the same time the set of participants changes across the life cycle phases (South et al., 2015; and Chapter 2 in this volume).

PPPs combine private and public actors in society, so it is natural to look to research that takes the public sector perspective on PPPs, and combine that with research that takes the private sector perspective. The public sector perspective has been adopted by researchers in public policy fields such as political economics, public economics and political administration. This research focuses on how government legislators and executive agencies prioritize projects, and organize the regulatory framework and agencies for infrastructure service delivery (Boardman and Vining, 2012; Vigoda, 2002). Private sector perspective PPP research has been carried out by researchers in management, finance and engineering. This research focuses on productive organization of work and contracts and relationships between actors (Cruz and Marques, 2013; Kwak et al., 2009). The public perspective research is thus more concerned with public governance and utility, whereas the private perspective focuses more on efficient production for creation of profit.

Governance of infrastructure PPPs lies at the intersection of public policy, management, finance and engineering, yet there is currently very little cross-disciplinary research on PPP governance. We therefore look to current practice to develop a research agenda for PPP infrastructure services. This chapter summarizes insights about PPP governance challenges and lessons learned from more than two decades of experience with alternative approaches for addressing a variety of governance challenges confronting economically, environmentally and socially sustainable investment and delivery of infrastructure in three eastern Australia states (Victoria, New South Wales and Queensland). We choose to study Australia because it is one of the most experienced countries with respect to governance of PPP infrastructure service delivery (Johnston, 2010; Matos-Castaño et al., 2014; Osei-Kyei and Chan, 2015). We discuss and draw insights about the following five areas of governance:

1. Prioritization of federal and state funds to address the wish-list of infrastructure needs and desires of all regional and sectoral claimants for new or enhanced infrastructure services.
2. Deciding whether a prioritized project should be delivered via a PPP concession or as a traditional government-financed and operated project.
3. The procurement process to short-list and select concession companies, termed special purpose vehicles (SPVs), to deliver PPP projects.
4. Internal decisions of the SPV board and its key executives over the life cycle of the concession.
5. Contracts between the SPV and its construction and operations contractors.

These empirical observations of current practice suggest that public utility, institutions and coordination issues are of importance for PPP infrastructure service, and lead us to form a governance model for infrastructure service delivery.

PRIOR RESEARCH ON PUBLIC–PRIVATE PARTNERSHIPS

The history of public and private collaboration to develop and deliver infrastructure can be traced back in history to the Stone Bridge of

Regensburg developed by its salt merchants in mediaeval times, but the formalized arrangement known as a public–private partnership is a much more recent phenomenon. Research on public–private partnerships has adopted the perspective of the public in political economy, public economics and public administration (Boardman and Vining, 2012; Hodge and Greve, 2007; Iossa and Martimort, 2015; Vigoda, 2002). Of these, the first two focus on the economics of public–private partnerships, whereas public administration focuses on public sector management and governance of PPPs (Vigoda, 2002).

In the economics literature, theories on rational expectations have motivated research on PPPs. Public utility is governed by public agency (Pongsiri, 2002), contracts that safeguard against opportunistic behavior (Iossa and Martimort, 2015; Ho and Tsui, 2009) and/or by self-organized sharing of "common pool" resources (Ostrom, 1990). Infrastructure service has thus been studied from the perspective of public utility, and governance has been studied through contracts, self-organization and agency. PPP research in the fields of finance, management and engineering has generally adopted the perspective of the private sector (Kivleniece and Quelin, 2012; Tang et al., 2010). This body of research focuses on the efficiency of hierarchies versus markets, and which of these is most suitable for production of infrastructure services (Rufín and Rivera-Santos, 2010; Gunnarson and Levitt, 1982). The research uses theories about markets, relationships and contracts (Kwak et al., 2009), and theories on work organization (Liu et al., 2015).

Infrastructure is primarily studied and conceptualized as an asset in PPP research (Tang et al., 2010). Although not explicitly studied, infrastructure service can be conceptualized as social interaction and exchange among the participants in infrastructure delivery (Levitt et al., 2010), and governance is implemented through organization of work for design, construction, planning and maintaining the infrastructure.

Comparing public and private perspectives on PPP research, it is clear that research on the public side revolves around how the system surrounding the infrastructure service leads to distribution of public utility, whereas the private perspective takes the delivery approach as a given, and focuses on how to deliver the service as efficiently as possible. Put simply, the public perspective research studies how to govern the selection of projects to pursue and delivery approaches for delivering them; whereas the private perspective research studies how to optimize the delivery of the infrastructure service, given a project and delivery approach chosen by the government. However, little or no research is available on how this should be done in practice. Considering the public side in particular, the public government and agencies weigh public utility and cost in a number of ways, such as health, economic benefits and socio-economic progress, as they prioritize which infrastructure projects to build or enhance (Afonso et al., 2005).

Public choice models are important because political environments that limit the feasibility for policy change are associated with less infrastructure investment (Henisz, 2002). As societal progress brings changes in citizens' socio-economy, health and urban life, there is a need for a corresponding evolution in models of public utility that can guide public government in the prioritization of public funds to address the wish-list of infrastructure needs and desires of all regional and sectoral claimants for new or enhanced infrastructure services (Rauch, 1995). Commonly, infrastructure investments are based on engineering assessment of public needs, political outcomes, socio-economic effects, and urban and environmental sustainability (Gramlich, 1994; Koppenjan and Enserink, 2009). However, infrastructure development and maintenance is expensive, and governments find it increasingly difficult to fund infrastructure. The search for alternative public governance models has resulted in models involving private capital, and the United Kingdom (UK), France, Canada and Australia have led the field.

Politically elected government usually decides whether a prioritized project should be delivered via a PPP concession or as a traditional, government-financed and operated project. Increasingly, private capital – especially institutional capital – wishes to invest in infrastructure, and there is a resulting growth in PPP infrastructure. In case the private sector is involved, the government has to decide at what phase of infrastructure service delivery they should be involved, and how the private sector participation should be governed (Koppenjan and Enserink, 2009). Examples range from projects in which the private sector is involved only in construction, or only in operation and maintenance, to those in which the private sector takes care of financing, development, design, construction, operation and maintenance.

The UK and Australia, early adopters of PPP governance models, have continuously evolved their PPP governance models, as they have learned from both successful and less successful experiences. Their models represent current best practice and are designed to govern in a way that balances the short-term profit orientation of the private sector with public service, ownership, risks and finance (Johnston, 2010). Tendering for a PPP infrastructure project is very costly: several million dollars for each bidder on a large project. So, it is especially important to design the procurement process so that a small number of concession companies are short-listed and selected to tender.

Studies that have reviewed success factors of PPP infrastructure project procurement generally point to the importance of a well-defined business proposition for the private sector, strong public sector governance, transparent communication between public and private sector, and elaborate risk management (Liu et al., 2016; Osei-Kyei and Chan, 2015; Ismail, 2013; Zhang, 2005; Aziz, 2007). Common practice is that the private sector companies form a special purpose vehicle: a private, limited liability corporate entity, owned and financed by private companies, that will provide public infrastructure service according to performance specifications provided by the cognizant government agency. In many cases, enabling legislation is enacted for each SPV individually, meaning that politically elected officials decide on the legislation, and that government agencies implement the legislation by supervision of, and cooperation with, the concessionaire (Kwak et al., 2009). The organization, structure and management of the SPV contains the conflict between the short-term profit orientation of private actors, and the high-quality, low-cost, long-term infrastructure service provision that the public sector wants.

Traditionally, infrastructure development is divided into different phases, each involving partially different sets of public and private stakeholders (South et al., 2015). The organization of the SPV should reflect the long-term orientation inherent in public infrastructure service delivery. This is currently problematic, as design and construction phases traditionally involve actors that are more transaction-oriented and are, therefore, near-term-focused; whereas operations and maintenance is a more long-term phase. There is a surprising dearth of research that covers infrastructure PPP change across life cycle phases, but research on PPP infrastructure risks (Grimsey and Lewis, 2002; Bing et al., 2005) and stakeholder management (El-Gohary et al., 2006) provides some insights into overall project governance. Extending the SPV organization, structure and management requires organizational arrangements that achieve a balance between the interests and operational style of short and long-term-oriented phases and stakeholders.

Finally, formulation of contracts between the SPV and its construction and operations contractors need to be considered for how they allocate risks and responsibilities within the SPV, and for how relationships with the government should be conducted. Within the SPV, contracts need to reflect the long-term responsibility of the SPV board, and its relationships to private participants in the project. The contracts within the SPV are between private companies, so there is both considerable past practice, and an established legal framework in common-law countries such as the United States (US) and Australia to utilize in contract making. Contracts between the government and the SPV are different, because they are between a private and a public actor, and the legal institutions in that area are still emerging (Hart, 2003). For instance, many PPP infrastructure developments have required enabling legislation specifically designed for that PPP. Because PPP infrastructures are complex and extend over long periods of time, involving many actors, the SPV will always face an incomplete contract situation, where outcomes are uncertain and therefore cannot all be specified beforehand (Hart, 2003). The government authorities that oversee the infrastructure may issue additional requirements if environmental specifications are not met.

For infrastructure PPPs, the contracts must specify procedures for the interaction between government and private actors in case of contract dispute. As described in Chapter 3 of this volume, success in the administration of one-off, long-term, high-uncertainty transactions requires more than traditional legal contracts alone; the contracts must be buttressed by relational mechanisms between the public and private parties to the project (Williamson, 1979; Henisz et al., 2012). As we go on to report the findings of a study of best practices in PPP infrastructure, namely that of Australia, we will consider how governments in three of Australia's eastern states – Victoria, Queensland and New South Wales – have handled governance across the life cycle phases of infrastructure PPPs.

RESEARCH METHODOLOGY AND APPROACH

The insights presented in this chapter are derived from a set of semi-structured interviews that the first author conducted with more than 20 senior executives drawn from key participants in PPP investment and delivery – governmental PPP bodies and infrastructure agencies, pension funds and aggregators of pension funds, infrastructure developers, investment banks, investment arms of construction firms, lawyers and bankers – over a two-week period during December 2015 in three Australian states: Victoria, New South Wales and Queensland. To encourage free-flowing, candid discussion, interviews were not recorded. Extensive notes were taken, coded, redacted and analyzed. The insights about ways to mitigate the significant governance challenges of PPP delivery that have evolved from this shared experience over more than two decades can provide high-level guidance to federal and state agencies in countries such as the US that have had far less experience delivering infrastructure services via PPP concessions, and can serve to generate a set of focused research questions for academics to explore in greater depth.

KEY FINDINGS FROM THE INTERVIEWS

The sample of respondents in these interviews was relatively small: about 20 interviews of 1–2 hours each in the three eastern states of Australia. Nevertheless, when they had been coded and analyzed, some clear and consistent findings about the history and evolution of present PPP governance models in Australia emerged from the set of interviews. These insights are summarized in this section.

Prioritization of National Infrastructure Needs

Australia's national Parliament has created an infrastructure agency to help it develop a prioritized list of national infrastructure needs. The agency is called Infrastructure Australia, and it has a mandate to prioritize and advance nationally significant infrastructure, and to advise government at national and state levels. Like similar agencies created in the UK and elsewhere, a group such as this provides some influence over which regional or sectoral projects will receive national funding, but it is challenging to insulate this kind of professional bureaucracy from high-level political pressures when the party in power in the government changes, or when new projects that were not previously prioritized are proposed by state, municipal or regional governments, or presented as unsolicited proposals by private infrastructure concessionaires.

State-Level Governance Issues

Three Australian state governments – Victoria, Queensland and New South Wales – have established independent statutory bodies to prioritize statewide infrastructure needs. Infrastructure Australia and federal legislators will still make the final calls on funding projects at the state level, but cannot easily ignore the state priorities to favor regional or other special interests. To the extent that these agencies publish and widely disseminate their prioritized lists of statewide projects, it becomes increasingly difficult for the legislature to completely ignore their rationally prioritized projects and to justify to the public investing in a lower-priority project, or one that had not previously been considered.

Sponsors of unsolicited, "market-driven" PPP proposals must justify sole-source negotiation between the government and the SPV, rather than an open call for proposals, based on their "uniqueness." These proposals have only occasionally been accepted; and virtually all of the handful that have been accepted thus far involve expansion of the scope of existing assets. The perceived extreme difficulty of managing the interface between the entrenched concessionaire and a new concessionaire whose construction or operations might interfere with the existing concessionaire's operations has been the only justification for claiming "uniqueness" that appears to have been accepted thus far as a basis for such sole-source unsolicited proposals. This basis for justifying "uniqueness" clearly runs the risk of increasing the concentration of ownership of infrastructure concessions in a given sector by expanding the number and scope of facilities already being operated by existing PPP concessionaires. For example, in the Australian roads concession sector, Transurban is already a dominant player in Australia, and has had expansions of its existing concessions approved.

The expansion of the scope of an existing asset has typically been proposed as being "free to the public"; that is, without the need for up-front government funding or additional availability payments. The proposals that have been accepted to date typically request a lengthened concession period for the underlying asset and, in some cases, increases in tolls; for example, sharply increased tolls for heavy vehicles, which disproportionately damage roads. So the unsolicited infrastructure proposals typically claim that there is no cost to the state or federal government for the unsolicited proposal. However, from a public benefits point of view, this claim is misleading. Taxes or user fees, or a combination of these two sources, must ultimately pay for all infrastructure services. So, even if no new, tax-supported government funds are being sought for the unsolicited proposal, the new project will ultimately require incremental taxpayer and/or user funding – via the additional availability payments to be made over the lengthened concession terms and/or the longer toll collection period and higher tolls – in addition to the public's payments of taxes and user fees for all other existing and new projects. Thus, we argue that the new infrastructure advisory agencies at federal and state levels should still rank any unsolicited proposals against the existing list of prioritized projects to determine whether and when they will be developed, even if they do not seek near-term additional government funding for their development and delivery.

Choosing PPP versus Traditional (Design–Bid–Build or Design–Build) Delivery Approaches

During the late nineteenth and twentieth centuries, most developed countries adopted a strategy of public finance, public and/or private design, private construction and public operation of infrastructure. Starting late in the twentieth century, the UK and several Commonwealth countries – notably Canada and Australia – began using an alternative infrastructure delivery model in which the government selected projects to be delivered and then contracted for the financing, design, construction, operation and maintenance with private concessionaires. This public–private partnership model spread to Latin America, Eastern Europe and other parts of the world, promoted by the multilateral development banks.

The United States was very late in adopting this approach, although infrastructure such as roads, bridges and ferries had often been provided under concessions during colonial times. The federal, state and local tax exemption for interest payments associated with public financing of infrastructure has undoubtedly tilted the choice in favor of public financing of infrastructure in the US until very recently, when full or partial tax exemption has also been extended to private developers of public infrastructure. In choosing between PPP and traditional delivery of prioritized infrastructure assets, most countries that allow PPP delivery use some version of a "value for money" (VfM) analysis, in which the total costs for public versus private financing, operation and maintenance of an infrastructure asset over its life cycle are compared. In this comparison, public financing bears lower interest rates than private financing in most developed countries that have sound credit ratings, even without the tax exemption described above for the US. So the PPP alternative must demonstrate enough savings through greater efficiency and quality of design, construction and maintenance, as well as in the expected value of the construction cost overrun and demand shortfall risks that the private party would assume under a given PPP concession regime to compensate for the lower cost of public financing, in order for it to be selected.

This VfM process has been quite controversial at times. It is very difficult to capture the full cost of public financing and supervision of design and construction; and public maintenance is seldom provided at the same level of quality as is required in PPP agreements. Moreover, determining the expected value of risk transfer for construction cost overruns and user demand shortfalls requires considerable judgment. These judgments can be – and have frequently been – challenged by advocates of one or the other delivery approach. In spite of this, mature jurisdictions such as the UK, Ontario in Canada and the three Australian states listed above have developed standardized VfM procedures that employ impartial experts to make these judgments based on historical data wherever available, and running Monte Carlo simulations on the set of probabilistic variables to determine the expected value of the interacting risks being transferred. The standardization and professionalization of VfM analyses have contributed to their broader acceptance over time. The Australian government and Infrastructure Australia develop national standards for VfM, and VfM has emerged as a relatively standard process for selecting the delivery approach when comparing PPP delivery to traditional delivery of infrastructure assets.

PPP projects have historically often been viewed as off-balance-sheet financing, especially when they were 100 percent funded by user fees. Because of this, they were excluded from budgetary planning by governments and from credit evaluations by credit rating bureaus. However, a PPP with fixed, periodic availability payments – increasingly used for surface transportation projects – is essentially equivalent to a bond from a budgetary perspective, since it commits future funding resources from the government to this project over multiple decades. An emerging approach for a government jurisdiction to evaluate infrastructure project delivery alternatives in a more comprehensive way, therefore, considers the impact of the life cycle fiscal commitments associated with PPP versus traditional delivery of an infrastructure project on that government's long-term future "budget resilience." This approach has been called "value for funding" (VfF) (Kim and Ryan, 2015b).

VfF stochastically embeds the future financial commitments incurred by using a conventional design bid build or design build delivery approach compared to a PPP delivery approach for a given procurement, in the context of all of the government's other projected fixed and uncertain revenues and expenses over the PPP concession's term or the project's planned lifespan. This embedded and integrated analysis compared to a stand-alone analysis of the financial implications of alternative delivery approaches for the project allows the governmental entity to determine the impact of these two approaches on the "budget resiliency" of the jurisdiction that will deliver the project, and thereby to determine whether either or neither delivery approach is the preferred choice. Ongoing research by Stanford's Global Projects Center is developing methods and tools for conducting VfF analysis of infrastructure project delivery.

Governance Issues between the Government Agency and the SPV

Government infrastructure agencies in all three states covered by this study stated that they were not concerned about internal SPV governance issues and so did not typically review SPV shareholder agreements. They believed that their concession contracts with the SPVs, which had fixed availability payments and penalties for violations of operational performance requirements, placed these governance risks squarely on the SPV's owners and lenders, and thus insulated the government and public from harm due to any conflicts of interest internal to the SPV. The Australian government provides detailed contract templates that can be used by states (https://infrastructure.gov.au/infrastructure/ngpd/index.aspx). There are templates for traditional contracting, alliance contracting and public–private partnerships. The contract templates specify cost, governance, performance, value for money, and many other factors for each development phase of the project. These documents show that the Australian institutions for infrastructure development are mature and well developed. There is one exception, however.

Some of the earliest Australian PPP concession SPVs were to be funded purely from patronage tolls and were sponsored by investment banks acting as developers. The investment banks garnered significant management fees for packaging the projects and winning the bids – often based primarily on using more optimistic demand forecasts than other bidders – and then listed and sold their equity via an initial public offering (IPO), either immediately or shortly after financial close. Some of these listed shares lost much or all of their value when the demand forecasts in the SPV proposals turned out to have been highly optimistic and the SPVs went into bankruptcy. Partly as a result of this experience, Australian government agencies now typically exert some control over the identity and ownership structure of their counterparty to the SPV agreement across the project life cycle, although not over its internal governance. Australian SPV concession agreements now typically contain a number of constraints on any "change of control" of the SPV, or even on significant changes to its capital structure at different project phases, to avoid equity participants selling out their stakes to public shareholders or unknown others too soon in the concession term without the agency's knowledge or consent. Violation of these concession terms would constitute a serious breach of contract by the SPV, and no interviewees reported the occurrence of any such breaches.

Clearly, the longer investors are required to hold their equity in the infrastructure asset, the more closely their goals become aligned with the government's goals for long-term, low-cost, high-quality delivery of infrastructure services to its citizens, and hence the fewer real or implied conflicts of interest are likely to arise. From this point of view, pension funds, pension aggregators, sovereign wealth funds and others are the ideal majority investors in infrastructure concessions, provided that they can access the necessary design, construction and operations expertise to bid competitively and realistically and to manage these infrastructure services well over their life cycle.

The PPP investment arms of design–construction contractors typically have heavily overlapping ownership with the contractors; often 100 percent common ownership (Bing et al., 2005). They should not generally be majority equity partners in PPP infrastructure assets. They are not long-term asset holders, typically seeking to exit after construction has been completed. Moreover, equity participation in the PPP concession can generate conflicts of interest between construction profits and infrastructure returns that pose risks to other purely financial equity investors, lenders and the public. The Channel Tunnel project, in which five British and five French contractors owned all of the initial equity in the Eurotunnel concessionaire and were also the builders of the project, showed how serious these conflicts can be, especially when a project is not yet fully designed at the beginning of the concession term (Henisz et al., 2012).

One approach that has been proposed to address this conflict, while still bringing the requisite expertise into the concession, is to create well-aligned investment platforms for investing in multiple infrastructure concessions comprised of engineers, contractors, operators and long-term, institutional investors such as pension funds, in which the long-term investors would hold large or even majority stakes in the concessions. When design–construct contractors or infrastructure operators (collectively termed "industrial investors") hold large enough minority equity stakes to give them SPV board representation in SPVs in which there are also pure "financial" equity investors such as pension aggregators (for example, Queensland Investment Corporation in Australia), or infrastructure development funds that are not majority-owned by industrial partners, shareholder agreements generally require the designers', constructors' and/or operations contractors' nominated directors to recuse themselves from voting on board resolutions involving construction cost or time extensions, operating issues or similar SPV board of directors matters in which they are interested parties. Some financial investors go further and assert that directors nominated by design–construct or operations partners or their firms' investment arms should be excused from the meeting and should not even participate in board-level discussions on matters in which their holding company's construction or operations arm is an interested party.

Executives from the infrastructure finance arms of some construction firms argue that their firms are truly independent business entities; that they are personally, organizationally and individually independent of their parent company's construction arms; and they are incentivized based on their investment arm's long-range financial returns, not on the profits of their sister companies' construction arm. In addition, some of them state that they have developed a history of holding infrastructure investments far into the operating concession phase, so that their goals are very well aligned with the goals of the financial investors. These firms have sometimes been able to establish sufficient trust with the purely financial investors to get these conflict-of-interest recusal clauses for industrial directors in the SPV shareholder agreements waived when their parent firm's engineering, construction or operations subsidiary holds the design, construction and/or operations contract for the SPV.

Australia has very strong fiduciary requirements in its corporation laws that require corporate directors to act strictly in the interests of the companies on whose boards they serve; in this case the SPV's board rather than the SPV directors' previous or current employers' boards. In addition, all three states surveyed engage "probity auditors" across the phases of tendering, SPV selection, financial and commercial close, design–construction and operations to assure good governance of the SPV companies. Nevertheless, when delivery partners or their investment arms hold enough SPV equity to gain one or more seats on the SPV board, a virtually unanimous opinion among all of the executives interviewed in this study is that appointing an experienced independent board chairperson with no employment or financial ties to either the financial or the industrial partner companies in the SPV has proven to be extremely valuable in tapping the delivery partners' deep construction or operations expertise for the benefit of the SPV, while providing strong governance to address real conflicts of interest when they arise, and keeping contentious board-level discussions on track. Several experienced Australian senior executives now make a career out of serving as independent board members, independent board chairs and senior executives in concession SPVs.

The state of New South Wales (NSW) in Australia has added another innovation in the public–private partnership governance of its overall portfolio of infrastructure assets: "asset recycling." In NSW's asset recycling program model, an independent government infrastructure agency (InNSW) prioritizes needed infrastructure assets in the state, contracts for the design and construction of each prioritized infrastructure asset, finances its development and tolls the asset. When and if the asset becomes operational and has achieved a commercially viable ramp-up in demand and revenue, the state sells a long-term lease on the asset to a private entity – typically a professional infrastructure operator, a pension fund or a fund of pension funds – to operate and maintain the asset and collect the tolls or other user fees to repay its investment in the lease. The proceeds from the concession sale are placed into a dedicated state infrastructure asset recycling fund (RestartNSW) and can only be used by RestartNSW to develop future infrastructure assets.

The asset recycling mechanism relies on a new vision of the role of government as an efficient, effective and risk-taking investor in infrastructure. Using a dedicated and ring-fenced fund to ensure that the proceeds of the lease of existing assets be used solely to fund new infrastructure – and not to use these funds to pay off other government obligations such as underfunded pensions, as some other jurisdictions worldwide have done – increases public support for the asset recycling program and public willingness to accept the resulting toll payments. So it can be a way for governments to increase funding sources for new infrastructure development. However, it requires that the government is able to structure a competitive bid process to drive up the lease sale price; prioritize new projects effectively and secure funding for their operation and maintenance; and finally, that the agency can effectively acquire the skills and knowledge to take on construction risk and potentially also user demand risk. (See Chapter 12 in this volume for additional detail about this asset recycling program.)

Governance Issues Related to the SPV Design and Construction Agreement

In their PPP concession agreements with the government, the PPP SPVs typically agree to very strict limits on making any claims for additional payments from the government for construction cost or time overruns. The concession agreements typically even disallow claims for extra time or cost due to differing site conditions, or significantly worse than average weather, with exceptions only for a limited and very specific set of *force majeure* situations such as storms or floods larger than the 100-year return period. These concession agreement terms are then passed down to the SPV's design, construction and operations contractors, to prevent construction or operations claims from impairing the SPV's equity, potentially triggering debt defaults or renegotiations due to violations of loan covenants. In fact, part of the due diligence process by lenders involves a "gap analysis" of any differences in contract terms at the two levels – government to concession, and concession to contractor – that could impair the SPV's equity. Tough, firm, fixed-price contracts that set very tight conditions between the SPV and the designer-constructor for making construction claims also simplifies or eliminates many potentially conflictual governance issues within SPVs owned by both industrial and financial equity investors.

Institutional Investors' Internal Governance Issues

US and Canadian pension funds have historically not been direct investors in new, greenfield infrastructure projects; with a small number of notable exceptions such as the Ontario Teachers' Pension Fund and the Dallas Firemen's Fund. Traditionally pensions have required extensive internal committee review and approval of significant financial commitments in, or changes to, their investments. The same has been true for some of the pension aggregators, with internal committees that can create delays for urgent decisions that need to be made by the SPV boards. This has made them unattractive partners to infrastructure developers and builders who are able to delegate more decision-making authority to their SPV directors and managers.

But this mismatch in authority in the SPV–pension fund investor relationship is beginning to change. Increasingly, Australian aggregators of pension funds wanting to invest in greenfield infrastructure assets have been acquiring and/or developing significant internal capacity and/or relationships with external advisors that allow them to invest directly in the equity of greenfield infrastructure assets. The most experienced pension aggregators have changed their internal governance accordingly to allow them to appoint board representatives in the SPVs who are authorized to make substantial financial commitments and decisions without prior approval from their own or the participating pensions' investment review committees or boards. This makes them more attractive SPV partners in greenfield infrastructure projects for the traditionally more experienced and empowered representatives of industrial equity investors and professional infrastructure fund equity investors in PPP SPVs.

SUMMARY OF THE AUSTRALIAN MODEL FOR PPP INFRASTRUCTURE SERVICE DELIVERY

The description of practices and models used for PPP infrastructure service delivery in Australia shows that private and public actors there have developed working practices and models for infrastructure service delivery that address many of the key governance challenges. The Australian experience shows the benefits of having professional national and state-level infrastructure units that are independent of the legislatures to prioritize national infrastructure needs. The model for national needs prioritization is mature. Parliament has created an agency that provides analysis of national infrastructure needs, and advises government at all levels on its prioritization. Government ultimately decides which infrastructure assets to develop, guided by these priorities, and uses rigorous value-for-money analyses to select the delivery approach used to finance and develop the selected infrastructure assets.

In the Australian case, coordination over the different life cycle phases of an infrastructure asset is also increasingly being governed by stipulating that the SPV concession must be owned and governed by its initial investors for an extended time period, including design, construction, and a ramp-up period of several years of operation and maintenance. The division of responsibilities between private actors and the public is governed by an elaborate and precise performance contract that stipulates the responsibilities of the private actors in operation and maintenance of the asset. Thereby, the government can use contract enforcement to achieve the desired infrastructure service for the public. The governance of SPV boards and companies is overseen by licensed probity auditors, and SPV boards often have independent board chairs.

The Australian case shows that the relationship between private investors and private infrastructure service providers can be made clear and can be governed so that long-term stewardship of the asset is promoted. The mature set of governance arrangements that they have evolved significantly mitigates the problems of changes in the active participants and their conflicting sets of interests across life cycle phases, since the long-term operating responsibility for the concession increasingly bridges over and mitigates the broken agency and resulting incentive incompatibility of a conventional publicly financed, design–bid–build process across the successive phases of the provisioning and use of infrastructure services (Henisz et al., 2012), as discussed in Chapter 3.

CONCLUSIONS

The Australian PPP experience over almost three decades now points to a future model for infrastructure service delivery. In such a model, the government selects infrastructure projects, guided by a non-partisan, expert infrastructure prioritization panel. For the prioritized infrastructure assets determined by the panel and approved by the legislature, the government then either:

1. Finances and develops an asset itself and sells the up-and-running "brownfield" asset to an operator, with the proceeds placed into an infrastructure asset recycling fund, as described above; or
2. Issues a concession to a private concessionaire for the delivery of infrastructure service for an extended period with the private entity responsible for financing, designing, constructing, operating, and maintaining the infrastructure service.

The government supervises each infrastructure asset's service performance levels at arm's length to safeguard public interest. The government also provides a relatively standardized national set of institutional frameworks, with contracts and authorities necessary for the institutional governance of the relationship between private and public actors, guided by the public's long-term interest in high-quality, effective and cost-efficient infrastructure services.

NOTE

* This chapter has been adapted from Raymond E. Levitt and Kent Eriksson (2016). Proceedings of the 2016 Engineering Project Organization Conference, Cle Elum, Washington, USA, June 28–30, 2016, by permission of the Engineering Project Organization Society.

6. Contractual risk sharing mechanisms in US highway PPP projects

Duc A. Nguyen and Michael J. Garvin

INTRODUCTION

Infrastructure public–private partnerships (PPPs) are an outgrowth of the contemporary movement in government to alter the public service delivery paradigm. Risks and contracts are central to these arrangements. In fact, the PPP paradigm is founded, rather significantly, on the concept of risk allocation through contracts. The transfer of risk, through the contractual framework, is often the basis for the decision to deliver public services by a PPP arrangement and movement of assets off the public sector balance sheet. Contracts serve as the vehicle for tangibly distributing benefits and risks in PPPs, typically for the better part of 30 years or more. Ideally, the contractual framework is structured to balance the interests of the public and private sectors to promote reasonable outcomes for both parties. Yet, uncertainty with time and the limitations of contracts challenge the efficacy of PPP arrangements since unpredictable, incalculable events are inevitable.

Within this context, researchers have examined contract-related issues in PPPs. One theme of investigation has focused on risk identification and allocation (Akintoye et al., 1998; Bing et al., 2005; Chou and Pramudawardhani, 2015; Chung et al., 2010); this work has pinpointed perspectives of various risks and which risks are retained by the public sector, transferred to the private sector or shared. Another theme has more specifically explored contract design through the lens of contract economics. Specifically, incomplete contract theorists recognize the limitations of contracts in complex, long-term transactions such as PPPs, so they contend that *ex post* opportunistic hazards are best handled through counterparty renegotiation, or through empowering concessionaires with ownership and decision rights (Crocker and Masten, 1991; Hart, 1995; Hart and Moore, 1988; Chung and Hensher, 2016). Hence, PPP contractual designs must address two related issues: (1) alignment of principal–agent interests through information revelation versus agent empowerment; and (2) *ex ante* versus *ex post* treatment of contingent circumstances. Researchers have addressed the first issue. Hart (2003) explored the boundaries between public service provision by either a public or a private organization; he compared a bundled approach using a single contract with a private party for facility construction and service provision with a "conventional" approach using separate contracts with private parties for facility construction and service provision. Among Hart's conclusions was that bundling promoted advantageous investments overall as long as service requirements were adequately specified. In other words, a properly incentivized agent will act in the interests of the principal. With respect to *ex ante* versus *ex post* treatment of contingent situations, very little research has explored this issue to date.

Building from a companion investigation that determined how risks were allocated and provisioned in 21 highway PPP project contracts in the United States (US) (Nguyen et al., 2018), this chapter investigates contracting practice to determine how PPP contractual frameworks are structured. Fifteen risk sharing mechanisms were uncovered, and these are further examined to gauge the propensity to specify *ex ante* treatments versus *ex post* resolution, which also provides an indication of the timing of transaction costs. This examination is based on the premise that uncertainty drives risk sharing overall, and its severity pushes contracting parties toward reduced *ex ante* specification. Consequently, this work takes a step toward determining whether PPP risk sharing mechanisms rely on *ex post* solutions, which would indicate that such mechanisms are intentionally left incomplete.

BACKGROUND

Transaction Cost Economics

The firm, contracts and transaction cost economics (TCE) are three closely connected concepts in the field of economics. Coase (1937) posited that one of the reasons for a firm to exist is that there are costs of using the price mechanism (the entrepreneur will choose to produce a good/service or to acquire that good/service from somewhere else, depending on which method has the lower price). The costs include: costs for discovering the relevant prices, costs of negotiating contracts, and costs for concluding a contract. These costs are reduced, though not eliminated, if there is a firm. Coase coined the term "transaction costs" (but did not define the term) and started the foundation of transaction cost theory. One noticeable characteristic of transaction costs is that the bigger a firm becomes, the more its internal marginal costs for organizing transactions will grow. At a point where its internal transaction costs are equal to the costs of conducting the transactions in the open market, it is no longer efficient for the firm to get bigger. An analogy to PPPs is that when the government cannot bear large transaction costs if it develops projects itself, it seeks more outside services from the private sector.

After decades, Coase's idea of TCE still had no root academically (Coase, 1937). This changed when Williamson (1979) treated transaction costs systematically to deal with problems arising from firm and contract; the ideology of transaction cost economics adopts a contractual approach to the study of economic organization. Williamson (1996) defined transaction costs as: "the ex-ante costs of drafting, negotiating, and safeguarding an agreement and, more especially, the ex post costs of maladaptation and adjustment that arise when contract execution is misaligned as a result of gaps, errors, omissions, and unanticipated disturbances; the costs of running the economic system." This definition not only described components of transaction costs but also delineated their causes. In determining dimensions of TCEs, Williamson (1996) characterized three factors: (1) the frequency of transactions; (2) the degree and type of uncertainty of transactions; and (3) the asset specificity of transactions. The last factor assesses the degree to which "the transaction [is not] transferable without sacrificing productive value" and was rated by Williamson as most important among the three factors.

Williamson paid particular attention to bounded rationality and opportunism – behavioral assumptions – when considering the cost of a transaction, because "they serve to delimit the study of contract to the feasible subset" (Williamson, 1996). Speaking of behavioral assumptions, Williamson wrote:

> Transaction cost economics pairs the assumption of bounded rationality with a self-interest-seeking assumption that makes allowance for guile. Specifically, economic agents are permitted to disclose information in a selective and distorted manner. Calculated efforts to mislead, disguise, obfuscate, and confuse are thus admitted. This self-interest-seeking attribute is variously described as opportunism, moral hazard, and agency. (Williamson, 1996)

In the context of PPPs, Ho et al. (2015) categorized three types of opportunism that increase project transaction costs: (1) principal–principal problem: where the controlling principal exploits passive stakeholders; (2) firm hold-up problem: renegotiation induced by the concessionaire; and (3) government-led hold-up problem: when the bargain balance shifts to the government and it induces renegotiations (for example, to decrease tolls or raise taxes). These opportunism problems in PPPs are unique compared with those in other types of contract governance.

Incomplete Contracts

In a perfect world, contracts would not need to be modified or updated since everything would be anticipated and planned for in advance, or there would be no cost for engagement of a third party (for example, a court) to resolve problems. In reality, however, transaction costs are pervasive and substantial, so long-term contracts are always incomplete (Hart, 1988). Hart defined an incomplete contract briefly as one that "contains gaps or missing provisions." For an incomplete contract, events will occur that make it desirable for the parties to depart from what was specified in the contract: they may want to revise the contract; they may disagree about the meaning of the contract; and lastly, disputes may occur so parties will need to bring in a third party to determine a solution (Hart, 1988).

These high costs are caused by: unforeseen contingencies (describable and indescribable), cost of writing contracts, cost of enforcing contracts and cost of renegotiation (Anderlini and Felli, 1999; Maskin, 2002; Tirole, 1999). Ayres and Gertner (1989) also listed asymmetric information distributed between parties as an additional factor influencing transaction costs. Given that transaction costs are undeniable, and reasonable contractual parties cannot design a contract that precisely predicts all contingencies in the future, some mechanisms have been investigated to make contracts "less" incomplete.

First, Hart (among others) focused on the notion of property rights theory (Grossman and Hart, 1986; Hart, 2009, 1988). The idea of property rights theory, simply put, is that for events that happen in an incomplete part of a contract, the party which has the residual right on the asset (of the transaction) reserves the decision right. Second, parties can rely on norms to cover the incomplete part of the contract (Anderlini and Felli, 1999; Ayres and Gertner, 1989; Maskin, 2002). Norms have two forms: default rules and immutable rules. Default rules govern unless the parties contract around them, while immutable rules always govern even if the parties attempt to contract around them (Ayres and Gertner, 1989). The advantage of using norms is that it requires minimal costs to write and implement contracts (Anderlini and Felli, 1999). Third, parties may rely on renegotiation as the mechanism for revising the terms of trade as they each receive information about benefits and costs over time (Hart and Moore, 1988). Renegotiation has been the most common approach to deal with incompleteness of long-term contracts (Roberts, 2015). Finally, Crocker and Masten (1991) and Crocker and Reynolds (1993,

145) suggested that contracting parties may elect to leave a contract intentionally incomplete since they "face a trade-off between the costs of drafting a more complete document and the losses associated with incomplete agreements." Essentially, their work indicated that the level of incompleteness in practice was a function of the magnitude of these respective costs. Transaction attributes such as technological uncertainty or remote contract performance periods increased *ex ante* drafting costs, so less exhaustive frameworks were preferable.

In PPPs, researchers have examined contractual design and incompleteness issues, such as Athias and Saussier (2007) who described three contract strategies: one termed a "flexible contract" where the parties plan to renegotiate once uncertainty unfolds; one termed a "rigid contract with renegotiations" where the parties cannot commit not to renegotiate, but attempt to prevent renegotiation; and one termed a "rigid contract" where the parties commit not to renegotiate. Their work indicated that contractual designs that balance flexible and rigid features will minimize transaction costs. Yet, the vast majority of this literature is theoretical and normative, focusing on what contracting parties ought to do.

A much smaller body of literature has examined how PPP parties contract in practice and whether their actions align with or depart from prevailing theory. For instance, Chung and Hensher (2015) reviewed several contractual risk management mechanisms in a case study of the M4 highway PPP in Australia. The contractual areas included changes by government, handback, sovereign risk and technological risk, as well as some incentive schemes associated with these areas. The authors traced contract enforcement throughout this project's concession period, and connected successes and challenges of the contract management process with how the mechanisms were designed. A strength of their work was that it followed the contract enforcement process from concession start to finish, to assess risk mechanism effectiveness. However, the research investigated only a few areas in a single case study, so this limits generalization of the research observations. Clearly, an opportunity to more comprehensively explore how PPP contractual frameworks are structured exists to determine the nexus of theory and practice.

METHODOLOGY

Overview

A companion investigation determined how risks were allocated and provisioned in 21 highway PPP project contracts in the US (Nguyen et

Table 6.1 PPP highway projects investigated

Project	Jurisdiction	Commercial close	Value ($ mil)
Chicago Skyway	Chicago	2004	$1800
Indiana Toll Road	IN	2006	$4600
Colorado (CO) Northwest (NW) Parkway	CO	2007	$600
I-495 Capital Beltway Express	VA	2007	$2068
SH 130: Segments 5 and 6	TX	2007	$1380
I-595 Express Lanes	FL	2009	$1760
Port of Miami Tunnel	FL	2009	$651
North Tarrant Express (1 and 2A) (NTE 1–2A)	TX	2009	$2000
I-635 LBJ Managed Lanes	TX	2009	$2600
PR-22 and PR-5	PR	2011	$1136
Elizabeth River Tunnels	VA	2011	$2100
Presidio Parkway (Phase II)	CA	2011	$362
I-95 Express Lanes	VA	2011	$922.6
East End Crossing	IN	2012	$763
North Tarrant Express (3A and 3B) (NTE 3A–3B)	TX	2013	$1350
US 36 Managed Lanes – Phase 2	CO	2013	$175
I-4 Ultimate Improvements	FL	2014	$2323
I-77 High Occupancy Toll (HOT)	NC	2014	$655
Rapid Bridge Replacement Program	PA	2015	$1119
Southern Ohio Veterans Memorial Highway	OH	2015	$819
SH 288 Toll Lanes	TX	2016	$425

al., 2018). This research investigated contracting practice to determine how PPP contractual frameworks are structured. Numerous risk sharing approaches were uncovered in the 21 projects investigated (see Table 6.1) ranging from deductible to negotiation and event mechanisms; hence, 15 risk sharing structures were further examined to: (1) determine the nature and frequency of usage; and (2) gauge the propensity to specify *ex ante* treatments versus *ex post* resolution, which also provides an indication of the timing of transaction costs. This examination is based on the premise that uncertainty drives risk sharing overall, and its severity pushes contracting parties toward reduced *ex ante* specification. Consequently, do PPP risk sharing mechanisms rely on *ex post* solutions, suggesting that such mechanisms are intentionally left incomplete?

Contract Analysis Approach

The presence, frequency and content of the 15 risk sharing provisions in the 21 contracts were analyzed based on selected rules of coding to determine the characteristics and features of the risk sharing provisions (Krippendorff, 2013; Weber, 1990). A classification scheme was adopted to categorize the sharing provisions, and the level of specification provided an indication of *ex ante* drafting effort.

The level of completeness of each mechanism reflects the effort required of the contractual parties to implement the mechanism when its corresponding risk occurs. Such efforts correlate to the level of specification of the mechanism. A more specific mechanism, one with high specification, requires more *ex ante* effort – hence *ex ante* transaction costs – and vice versa. Therefore, the specification level of a mechanism indicates its completeness. A qualitative assessment of risk sharing contractual provisions was conducted to determine whether it had a high, medium or low level of specification. The specification level was surmised based on two characteristics of a provision: its procedures and its definitiveness. Most provisions establish procedures for treatment of a contractual situation or event; however, a provision may not be definitive in its treatment. In other words, the provision is inconclusive regarding its treatment. A definitive provision has established *ex ante* how a risk or contractual event will be handled; whereas a provision that is procedural has established how the contracting parties will interact regarding the risk or event, but it is not conclusive: its resolution will occur *ex post*.

Each risk sharing mechanism was classified into three groups of specification: high, medium and low. The high group includes mechanisms related to a risk where procedures are described and treatment of the risk is definitive. The low group includes mechanisms where procedures are described, but treatment of the risk is inconclusive or left open. The medium group has procedures described, and treatment of the risk is partially definitive.

FINDINGS

Risk Sharing Mechanisms and Usage

As previously explained, 15 unique sharing mechanisms were identified in the contracts analyzed. Table 6.2 presents these sharing mechanisms in the order of their frequency of usage; in total, 552 instances of these mechanisms were identified in the contracts. For some risks, only single mechanisms were used. For example, "network" risk in project IH-635 was

Table 6.2 Risk sharing mechanisms identified

Mechanism	Description	Risks addressed most often
Relief event (128/552 – used 128 times out of 552 times a sharing mechanism was identified)	Events with negative impacts on a project (e.g., losses in time, money) but cannot be avoided or reduced by reasonable efforts of the private party. The private party is excused from contract non-conforming penalties. It can then be compensated with extended time (most times) or some other forms, including monetary compensation. In some cases, events only qualify for relief if the consequences exceed insurance coverage. In case of relief events with financial compensation, a "relief events allowance account" often exists which is deposited by the public party. This account is prioritized to pay for extra work and delay costs. In case of extension of time, the private party will file a document explaining the delays caused by a relief event; if the public party agrees, it will extend the term of the project (construction phase or operation phase). If disputes occur, parties will follow dispute resolution procedures as designed in the contract.	Socio-political opposition, change in law, risks that can cause delay and loss in construction (e.g., rights of way, site geology, archaeology and fossils), risks that are caused by the public sector (e.g., permits, changes by the public authority, network, latent defects of existing assets), and risks caused by natural disasters.
Compensation event (69/552)	Events that are not caused by the concessionaire and that have negative impacts on the concessionaire, and are in special situations where the government must financially compensate the concessionaire. Situations that most likely lead to compensation include faults by local, state or federal governments and changes made by governments.	Risks that are caused by the public sector (e.g., some qualifying changes in law, delay caused by the government, changes by the government, revenue payment, network, latent defects of existing assets, termination for convenience).
Delay event (54/552)	Delay events usually apply to the same events as relief events and are treated similarly. Delay events and relief events were mutually exclusive in the project contracts analyzed.	Used for the same risks as relief events.

External reference (43/552)	Risks whose impacts are calculated based on some external factors at the time those risks occur, or at other times as agreed by parties. An example is that of the Consumer Price Index (CPI) – an external factor – which is considered to calculate impact by inflation. Another example is "fair market value" of the project which is used as a base value for parties to negotiate when a project is terminated early.	Inflation, interest rates before financial close, special purpose vehicle (SPV) default, termination by the government.
Force majeure event (41/552)	Events that have unpredictable causes in both time and consequences but occur from outside of the project system. Causes may be civic or natural. Consequences vary from delays and losses in revenues, to catastrophic damage to project assets. *Force majeure* events are usually insured through obligations. However, some causes have high policy premiums and some are even uninsurable. Contracts require the private party to buy minimum insurance plans, which may include plans to protect the projects from natural disasters such as storms and earthquakes. Uninsurable *force majeure* risks may include disasters caused by humans such as wars and terrorism. Once the risks happen and the consequences are too great for the insurance plans to cover, the contracts usually treat these events as relief or delay events and negotiations likely follow.	Socio-political opposition, terrorism, natural disasters such as earthquakes or named storms, floods.
Further interpretation (38/552)	Some risks need to be broken down for the parties to determine appropriate mechanisms. For example, when a latent defect is detected, parties must investigate the cause and when it might have occurred before deciding how the loss will be treated. Another example is environmental risks: parties must know that the risk is or is not pre-existing.	Used mostly with change in law and environmental risks, since the cause of these risks determines subsequent actions of parties. For instance, not all changes in law become subject to compensation: only a few, including discriminatory changes in law that affect a small group of the private sector, will qualify.

129

Table 6.2 (continued)

Mechanism	Description	Risks addressed most often
Negotiation (36/552)	Using this mechanism, the parties state that they will negotiate based on outcomes of the risks. This does not necessarily lead to an amendment of the contract. This mechanism is distinguished from renegotiation, where the result is an amendment of the contract.	Used mostly with SPV default and termination by the government.
Extension (24/552)	In some relief and delay events when the contract explicitly states that the term of the contract will be extended so that the losses of the concessionaire will be recovered.	Used with permits, site geology, socio-political opposition risks.
Deductible (23/552)	Specified amount of loss must be borne by a party before applying other sharing mechanisms.	*Force majeure*, changes by the government, environmental risks (pre-existing), existing latent defects, right of way and easement risks.
Proration (21/552)	Parties share the losses (or gains) on a pro rata basis.	Changes by the government, right of way and easement, and interest rates before financial close.
Extra work costs and delay costs (21/552)	The costs that surpass estimated costs due to causes related to public party or relevant governments or nature of the project, and are provisioned or agreed by parties to apply compensation mechanisms.	*Force majeure*, changes by the government, environmental risks (pre-existing).
Insurance (21/552)	The mechanisms that the two parties use to transfer part of the risks to a third party; the risks are usually large in consequence and have high uncertainty. The private party is (most of the time) obligated to buy insurance plans. Particular plans with minimum deductibles are required for particular assets in both construction and operation phases. If the insurance requirements are not met due to high premiums or lack of market supply (uninsurable) then further tasks	*Force majeure*.

	(e.g., consulting insurance experts) will be undertaken by parties to prepare for the risks. Projects in different areas have different requirements on insurance. For example, projects close to oceans have higher insurance requirements on storms; some projects have higher insurance requirements on earthquakes. Residual losses after insurance coverage will then be treated by other sharing mechanisms as agreed in the contracts.	
Cost adjustment (18/552)	Provisions in the contracts usually depend on estimated costs of work (e.g., in the base case model). When actual costs change significantly (determined by parties' agreement), costs that are the basis of other calculations are adjusted correspondingly.	Inflation, payment for services in availability payment (AP) projects.
Relief event for the government (12/552)	Similar description as relief event for the concessionaire, but in this case the government is the party which has extended time (e.g., for making payments) and is exempt from non-conforming penalties	Payment for services in AP projects, existing latent defects.
Maximum reimbursement (3/552)	A compensation or sharing mechanism is conducted until some agreed values are reached.	Used rarely with some risks such as network, payment for services.

Table 6.3   Tandem use of risk sharing mechanisms

	(1)	(2)	(3)	(4)	(5)	(6)	(7)	(8)	(9)	(10)	(11)	(12)	(13)	(14)	(15)
(1) Relief event		33	0	1	25	27	3	15	13	12	13	14	0	0	0
(2) Compensation event	33		14	0	4	23	3	0	1	3	2	4	0	0	1
(3) Delay event	0	14		0	14	7	0	7	1	1	7	2	0	0	0
(4) External reference	1	0	0		0	0	32	0	0	0	0	0	7	0	0
(5) *Force majeure* event	25	4	14	0		0	0	5	6	3	21	3	0	0	0
(6) Require further interpretation	27	23	7	0	0		0	0	2	3	0	3	0	0	0
(7) Negotiation	3	3	0	32	0	0		1	0	0	0	0	0	0	0
(8) Extension	15	0	7	0	5	0	1		0	1	0	0	0	0	0
(9) Deductible	13	1	1	0	6	2	0	0		8	0	0	0	1	0
(10) Prorated	12	3	1	0	3	3	0	1	8		1	0	0	0	0
(11) Insurance	13	2	7	0	21	0	0	0	0	1		3	0	0	0
(12) Extra work costs & delay costs	14	4	2	0	3	3	0	0	0	0	3		0	1	0
(13) Cost adjustment	0	0	0	7	0	0	0	0	0	0	0	0		3	0
(14) Relief event for the government	0	0	0	0	0	0	0	1	0	0	1	3			0
(15) Maximum reimbursement	0	1	0	0	0	0	0	0	0	0	0	0	0		

treated by a compensation event. However, for most risks, multiple mechanisms were used together. For example, in provisions related to "change in law" risk in IH-635, compensation event, relief event and negotiation were used in tandem for this risk.

As explained, mechanisms were often used in tandem, and Table 6.3 depicts how often a mechanism was used with another mechanism. For instance, row 5 shows that there were 25 cases where the *force majeure* event risk sharing mechanism and the relief event mechanism were applied to risks at the same time; however, there were only four cases where the *force majeure* mechanism and the compensation event mechanism were applied to risks in tandem.

Ex Ante Treatment vs. *Ex Post* Resolution

The classification of each risk sharing mechanism follows.

High specification
Highly specific mechanisms include deductible, insurance and maximum reimbursement provisions. In a deductible provision, the deductible amount – which requires *ex ante* effort – and the party which first bears it are set and are definitive. Therefore, once the risk happens, the parties will not likely need to spend too much effort to determine each party's required tasks or loss. For instance, the Elizabeth River Tunnels contract utilized a deductible to handle latent defects as provisioned in Section 8.11:

> (A) the Concessionaire will be solely responsible for the Net Cost Impact for performing Excess Rehabilitation Work up to $5 million in the aggregate ("Excess Rehabilitation Work Deductible"); and (B) the Department will be solely responsible for the Net Cost Impact for performing Excess Rehabilitation Work in excess of the Excess Rehabilitation Work Deductible but less than or equal to $20 million.

This provision is indicative of the deductible schemes found in the contracts analyzed, and it is conclusive regarding who bears the cost of excess rehabilitation work.

An insurance provision in a contract often stipulates the assets, the deductible amount and the maximum coverage that the private developer must purchase. Government must expend effort (or rely on standard provisions or consultant advice) to stipulate insurance requirements, because each project is located in a different area and has its own characteristics that affect its vulnerability to different kinds of threats (for example, natural disasters). The following provision from Colorado Northwest Parkway dictates the government's requirements:

> The Concessionaire shall obtain All Risk Property Insurance at full replacement cost, covering all loss, damage or destruction to the Parkway, including improvements and betterments; provided, however, that the limits of such coverage may be based on a probable maximum loss analysis, subject to the Authority's Approval of such probable maximum loss analysis by an independent third party that is reasonably acceptable to the Authority, which Approval shall be provided prior to Closing. (Section 13.1)

In these requirements, the private party must also obtain approval from the government before it purchases the insurance plan; the provision is procedural, but it is definitive since coverage amount and scope are set. The *ex post* contractual effort of the parties to seek compensation of insured assets, on the other hand, only requires that the insured follow the policy requirements, with the government expending little to no effort.

Low specification

Mechanisms with low levels of *ex ante* specification include the event mechanisms and negotiation. Event mechanisms (that is, relief, delay, compensation, *force majeure* events) require limited *ex ante* efforts but potentially large *ex post* efforts by the parties. The *ex ante* effort is likely low since the uncertainty associated with the risk is high, so the parties cannot specify all the necessary parameters during contract formation. For situations categorized as event mechanisms, parties will base their decisions on how the risks actually occur.

The Portsmouth Bypass contract, Section 15, stipulated a representative procedure for relief, which is summarized as follows. The concessionaire must: complete a "time impact analysis," prove that the event affected the project's critical path, prove that the event could not be avoided by reasonable efforts, and provide evidence of the causes of the event. The government then reviews the information and decides whether and how to grant relief. If the concessionaire agrees with the government's decision, then the decision is followed; if the concessionaire disagrees with the government, then the provision indicates:

> If the Parties cannot agree on the extent of any delay incurred or relief from Developer's obligations under this Agreement, or the Department disagrees that a Relief Event has occurred (or as to its consequences), or that Developer is entitled to relief under this Article 15, the Parties shall resolve the matter in accordance with the Dispute Resolution Procedures. (Portsmouth Bypass, Section 15.3)

The relief provision has a number of stipulations, but these are procedural rather than categorical; hence, the parties will expend considerable effort *ex post* to remedy the situation.

Negotiation is another process associated with high *ex post* transaction costs in the literature. By choosing negotiation, parties again structure a provision, such as this provision from I-595:

> If and only if FDOT, in its sole discretion, is interested in the proposed Business Opportunity, FDOT and Concessionaire shall thereafter negotiate cooperatively and in good faith to formulate a structure, terms and conditions and written agreement(s) for such Business Opportunity and its use and development. (Project I-595, Section 21.2)

Here, the parties will expend effort *ex post* and are more exposed to other types of uncertainty: uncertainty associated with human behaviors and opportunism. This is why "good faith" – a general but susceptible commitment – is usually stated in negotiation provisions.

Medium specification
The remaining mechanisms – proration, external reference, further interpretation, cost adjustment, extra work costs and delay costs, and extension – fall into the medium category, since these mechanisms require both *ex ante* and *ex post* effort, but less than that of the other two groups. Compared to the highly specific mechanisms, more effort is necessary if risks are realized. A representative proration provision follows: "The Parties shall negotiate in good faith to determine the Refinancing Gain. FDOT will receive a payment equal to 50% of any of Refinancing Gains received in connection with any Refinancing other than an Exempt Refinancing" (Project I-4, Section 16.4.3). In this provision, parties must define the ratio (50 percent) beforehand, that is, the definitive portion; as well as expend additional effort to determine the refinancing gain once refinancing occurs, that is, the procedural portion, which will add some *ex post* transaction costs to the process. Another example provision, employing the further interpretation mechanism, also illustrates the timing of transaction costs:

> Discovery of (i) subsurface or latent physical conditions at the actual boring holes identified in the geotechnical reports included in the Reference Information Documents that differ materially from the subsurface conditions indicated in such geotechnical reports at such boring holes, excluding any such conditions known to Developer prior to the Proposal Due Date, or (ii) physical conditions within the Project Right of Way of an unusual nature, differing materially from those ordinarily encountered in the area and generally recognized as inherent in the type of work provided for in the Agreement, excluding any such conditions known to Developer prior to the Proposal Due Date or that would become known to Developer by undertaking reasonable investigation prior to the Proposal Due Date. (Project IH-635, Exhibit 1, page 53)

This means that the loss due to actual site geology conditions will be compensated by the government if they "differ materially" from known conditions; similarly, it is procedural and somewhat definitive since baselines for judgments of material difference are prescribed: the Reference Information Documents and those ordinarily encountered. Though this interpretation seems simpler than negotiation, agreement on whether conditions "differ materially" may or may not be easy for the parties.

Summary of results
The three groups of mechanisms can be depicted schematically by degree of completeness and timing of transaction costs (Figure 6.1), where

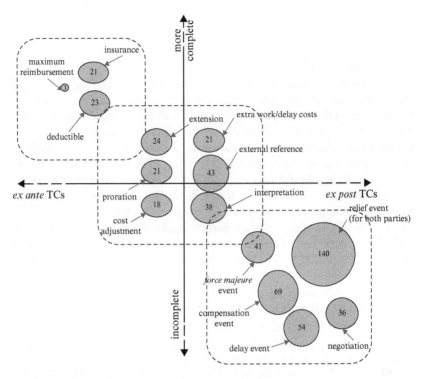

Figure 6.1   Classification of risk sharing mechanisms

provisions in the high group are in the upper left quadrant, the medium group are at the intersection of the two axes, and the low group is in the lower right quadrant. Each provision is sized according to its frequency of use in the contracts analyzed.

Each mechanism is positioned within the group for illustrative convenience; this does not indicate its location along the two continua. Some differences in the level of specification between mechanisms in the various contracts would shift a mechanism's location along each continuum, but it would still remain within its quadrant.

DISCUSSION AND IMPLICATIONS

The findings related to the structure of risk sharing mechanisms suggest that when this strategy is employed it tends to rely on event mechanisms more often than not; these are less complete than other mechanisms such as deductible schemes or insurance. Figure 6.2 depicts the frequency of

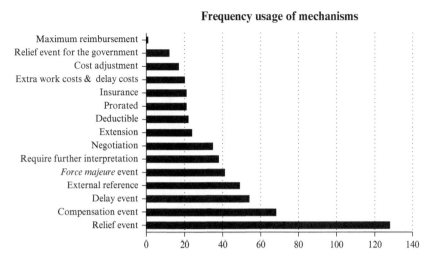

Figure 6.2 Frequency of risk sharing mechanisms

the mechanisms used in the analyzed contracts; the prevalence of the event mechanisms is clear. These were categorized into the low group with respect to *ex ante* specification. While procedurally complex, they are not definitive. This suggests that contract designers do leave contracts incomplete, as suggested in the literature (Crocker and Reynolds, 1993; Iossa and Martimort, 2012; Rausser and Stevens, 2009). The presence of mechanisms ranging from more complete to less complete is also aligned with recommendations by Athias and Saussier (2007) to balance rigid (non-negotiable) with flexible (negotiable) contractual structures.

However, the strength of these findings is limited by the qualitative assessment approach employed to evaluate the mechanisms as well as the tendency of contract designers to use these mechanisms in tandem; in other words, a less complete mechanism such as a relief event can be used in conjunction with a more complete mechanism such as a deductible. This combination would shift this specific treatment in the quadrant space presented previously toward the middle, that is, completeness and both *ex ante* and *ex post* transaction costs; the research did not assess these combinations due to the number of permutations found in the contracts.

Yet, the design of these contracts has incorporated implicit flexibility. The implicit flexibility is found in the event mechanisms that provide a framework for addressing uncertainty as it resolves. These mechanisms are imperfect since they depend on *ex post* negotiation, so they are subject to opportunistic behavior and information asymmetry. Relational mechanisms, however, may mitigate such behavior. Indeed, governance that unifies contractual and relational theories and practices and that embraces the alignment of stakeholder interests will likely produce better outcomes for PPP projects and society. Future research could track the performance of the risk sharing mechanisms as the US highway PPPs evolve throughout project life cycles, hence providing empirical assessment of these mechanisms' efficiency. Moreover, the findings point toward the need to explore behavioral theories and practices further to understand how stakeholders perceive and interact during PPPs.

CONCLUSIONS

As long-term contracts, PPPs potentially face many issues such as contract incompleteness, high transaction costs and incentive problems. Yet, these procurements are also challenged by the overarching emphasis on preserving the public interest in infrastructure procurement and service provision. Building off a companion investigation that identified risks and risk allocation in 21 US highway PPP projects, this chapter examined how highway PPP contracts are structured to determine what choices governments make with respect to contract formation and enforcement, by examining whether risk sharing mechanisms employed were structured to specify *ex ante* treatments or to rely on *ex post* resolutions in such mechanisms.

Fifteen risk sharing mechanisms were identified in a companion investigation and ranged from deductible to negotiation and event mechanisms. Based on the content of the contractual provisions, each mechanism was qualitatively assessed and categorized by its level of completeness and timing of transaction costs; mechanisms such as relief events were classified as incomplete with *ex post* transaction costs, while mechanisms such as deductible and insurance were classified as more complete with *ex ante* transaction costs. The frequency of risk sharing mechanism use was also determined. Event mechanisms were the prevailing method by far for risk sharing in the contracts analyzed (55 percent of risk sharing strategies employed an event mechanism). The prevalence of these mechanisms suggests that the parties do leave risk sharing provisions incomplete; however, the strength of this finding is limited by the assessment approach adopted as well as the risk sharing mechanisms' permutations; the latter means that mechanisms were often used in tandem, which complicates the assessment process, but it does indicate the relative complexity of the risk sharing schemes adopted.

Results show that contract practices in US highway PPPs are aligned with contract theories. As one of the first investigations to examine how contracts are structured and what contract formation and enforcement choices PPP practitioners make, this research can serve as the basis for future research, including: (1) complementary research in different international markets and market sectors; and (2) tracking the performance of the contract mechanisms as the US highway PPPs evolve throughout project life cycles, hence providing empirical assessment of the contract mechanisms' efficiency.

ACKNOWLEDGMENTS

The authors gratefully acknowledge the support for this research provided by the US National Science Foundation Grant #1334292. All conclusions and opinions expressed are those of the authors and not of the US National Science Foundation.

PART III

Leveraging institutional capital and governmental fiscal support for PPPs to enable the "golden handshake"

In nearly all public–private partnerships (PPPs), the engaged private entity establishes a special purpose company exclusively for its intended functions – that is, asset development and service provision – and a number of private entities provide funds or services to the company. Further, the special purpose company arranges the financing package that includes a combination of equity and debt. Indeed, the introduction of private capital into infrastructure development, expansion and modernization is one of the hallmarks of PPPs.

Part III of our book examines two topics of increasing interest among policy-makers and practitioners interested in PPP investment and finance: the role of institutional investors in the PPP marketplace, and the fiscal support that governments might provide to enhance PPP viability.

In Chapter 7, Ashby H.B. Monk and Rajiv Sharma delve into the widely held belief that institutional investors such as pension and sovereign wealth funds are ideally suited to invest in infrastructure assets, thanks to their relatively stable and inflation-adjusted cash flows. Yet, the flow of such funds into infrastructure investments has generally fallen short of expectations.

To explore why this is the case, they describe institutional investor characteristics, and examine how they typically access infrastructure. Their findings show that while a variety of financial products are offered, unlisted equity investments into PPP projects or privatized assets are most common. Moreover, such investments in PPP special purpose companies can occur indirectly through an infrastructure fund, or directly in such companies. In the former case, investment consultants play a significant role in aligning institutional investors with infrastructure funds. In the latter case, the institutional investors have in-house resources to facilitate and manage the investment.

Subsequently, Monk and Sharma look at governance issues of pension fund infrastructure PPP investors to conclude that larger funds seemingly have clearly defined policies related to infrastructure investments and sufficient inhouse expertise whereas smaller funds rely heavily on financial intermediaries whose substantial management and "carry" fees guarantee lower returns to the funds, and which may result in principal–agent issues for the funds that rely on intermediaries. They conclude by describing three recommendations for improving equity PPP investor governance: re-intermediation, collaboration and in-sourcing.

In Chapter 8, Ting Liu and Michael J. Garvin examine forms of fiscal support to mitigate revenue risk that are increasingly offered by governments to improve the viability of PPP arrangements. Such fiscal support is typically direct or indirect in nature. Direct support includes up-front cash subsidies, availability payments (APs) and shadow tolls, while indirect support includes governmental guarantees, tax breaks and subordinated governmental loans. These mechanisms all reduce the revenue risk transferred to PPP special purpose companies, since some portion or all of the revenue risk is retained by a government. However, such fiscal support can have unexpected consequences if governments do not adequately consider or properly structure such mechanisms.

While existing work has considered various aspects of these fiscal support arrangements, a comprehensive framework to guide governments when selecting among alternative ways to provide such fiscal support remains underdeveloped. Consequently, Liu and Garvin introduce a framework that evaluates a fiscal support mechanism against two criteria: (1) how much it increases a PPP project's leverage; and (2) how much financial exposure it creates for the government agency. Borrowing capacity is quantified for the first criterion while budget at risk is quantified for the second. Accordingly, these two criteria can be used to assess alternative fiscal support mechanisms to identify a dominant mechanism and to consider trade-offs among mechanisms. Liu and Garvin conclude by illustrating and discussing the framework using a hypothetical example.

7. The role of institutional investors in financing PPP infrastructure
Ashby H.B. Monk and Rajiv Sharma

INTRODUCTION

It is widely held that large institutional investors with long-term liabilities and a low risk appetite, such as pension funds and sovereign wealth funds, are ideally suited to invest in infrastructure assets. However, despite the theoretically ideal match between a large source of capital and a large infrastructure asset, the uptake among institutional investors has been slow. This chapter seeks to shed light on the role that institutional investors can play in infrastructure development and in particular the market for public–private partnerships (PPPs). We do this by illustrating in detail the unique characteristics of these investment organizations and the methods through which they have traditionally accessed infrastructure PPPs.

Over the last three decades, the processes of privatization, liberalization and globalization have enabled institutional investors to invest in infrastructure assets around the world. These investors are attracted by infrastructure's investment characteristics, such as low competition, predictable and stable cash flows, and inflation protection. Despite these favorable characteristics, a number of barriers still prevent the steady flow of capital into the space. To be fair, the lack of investor interest is also the result of some bad investor experiences during the early stages of development in the market. The inherent complexity and heterogeneity of infrastructure assets, and a lack of clarity around the true risks associated with these types of investments (for example, political, reputational, environmental and governance), led to some less than satisfactory outcomes. Further uncertainty also arises from the financing mechanisms used by financial intermediaries to facilitate access to these assets, as well as the funding and regulatory frameworks enforced by government institutions.

The confusion and uncertainty surrounding these factors has meant that institutional investor capital has not been channeled into infrastructure assets as freely as one would expect or hope. Furthermore, the adoption of PPPs and the privatization of infrastructure assets have varied significantly, with the United States lagging Western Europe, Australia, Canada and other parts of the world. In this chapter, we examine some of the key characteristics of institutional investors, specifically as these pertain to their infrastructure investments. We also highlight the political forces that have enabled infrastructure assets to come to market, as well as the economic trends that have led to the growth in institutional investor capital. We then look in detail at the governance of pension funds, the largest investors in infrastructure assets, to understand why and how they are deploying capital into the assets. The deeper analysis of investor characteristics provides insights into why the capital flows have been stymied, which allows us to then offer suggestions for improvements to the process.

PRIVATE INVESTMENT IN INFRASTRUCTURE

Private provision of infrastructure is not new, as railways, bridges and canals were often built, owned and operated privately during the nineteenth century. This early era of private infrastructure provision was motivated by entrepreneurialism and the growth of market ideals, a core tenet of classical liberal economists of the time. The virtues of "free-market," "laissez-faire" economics and the idea of an individual's rational pursuit of wealth were preached by pioneering liberals Adam Smith and David Ricardo (O'Neill, 2009; Harvey, 2005). Through their theories of *Homo economicus* and comparative advantage of free trade,[1] it was claimed that economic and political matters could be separated and that economic activities operated best without government interference (Heilbroner, 1983). Built upon the classical liberal ideal of the self-regulating market, and based on the writings of economists Friedrich Hayek and Milton Friedman, the belief has been that government interference to compensate market failures would create more problems than solutions (O'Neill, 2009).

However, in the post-Great Depression and World War era of the twentieth century, the Keynesian model of policy based upon universal access to publicly controlled infrastructure seemed to dominate the provision of infrastructure networks (O'Neill, 2009). Leading economist John Maynard Keynes proposed that the role of government was much more than a "passive overseer," as assumed by classical liberals. Regarded as a controlled form of capitalism, Keynesianism advocated large government spending to create new jobs and increase consumer spending (Peter, 1989). The political implementation of Keynesian theory in many industrial countries led to a period following the Second World War of high economic growth rates, high wages and low inflation. However, as a result of the oil shocks in the 1970s and subsequent effects of stagflation (a situation of simultaneously rising unemployment and inflation rates) and falling corporate profits, a novel way forward was sought to revive the doctrine of liberalism under new conditions of globalization.

Neoliberalism was thus subscribed to as a common set of ideological and political principles dedicated to the worldwide spread of an economic model that emphasized free markets and free trade (Harvey, 2005). Neoliberalization over the last three decades has transformed the role of government from the domineering Keynesian model back to a facilitator of the market, acting as an arbitrator and enforcer of the rules of the new game (Clark, 2000; Harvey, 2003; Peck and Tickell, 2002). The accompanying public policy agenda has consisted of deregulating the economy, liberalizing trade and industry, and privatizing state-owned enterprises. It has been this simultaneous movement of globalization and neoliberalization that has led to the splintering of urban infrastructure networks and placed the ownership and financing responsibilities for some of these assets into the hands of global private financial institutions.

Economic theorists have recently argued that in cases of market failure, the allocation of responsibilities to the private or public sector will depend on whichever sector will add the greatest value to the community, based on the principle of comparative advantage (Officer, 2008). Using the idea of property rights, governments are likely to have a comparative advantage when it is difficult to establish a clear property right to the activity, whereas the private sector may be more effective and efficient in producing or delivering the good or service when a clear property right can be established (Officer, 2008). Through the neoliberalization process and engagement of private actors, the property rights of urban infrastructures have been more clearly defined by governments using the tools of PPPs, privatization and regulation.

The investment vehicles that make up the global institutional infrastructure market are made possible by governments that have adopted privatization or public–private partnership policies. The adoption of private involvement for infrastructure investment and management has varied significantly by geography. Within Organisation for Economic Co-operation and Development (OECD) countries, the United States of America (USA) has lagged other jurisdictions considerably such as the United Kingdom (UK), Western Europe, Australia and Canada. Privatization differs from PPP arrangements in that the government transfers complete ownership of the asset to private players. In this case, the private investor takes on all of the risk of the investment (O'Neill, 2009; Macquarie, 2009). Privatization can involve individual asset sales, sales of interests in state-owned companies, and outright sales of companies via initial public offerings (IPOs) or auctions. There is also a growing secondary infrastructure market enabling private institutions to acquire assets from other private players. PPPs, on the other hand, are long-term leasing contracts that stipulate specific services to be rendered, such as construction, maintenance and operations.

While the decision to privatize or delegate urban infrastructures is often split along the lines of political parties, many city, state and national governments, independent of political affiliation, are now considering alternative sources of financing out of a pure fiscal necessity. In the wake of the global financial crisis and other austerity measures, the infrastructure investment challenge today is different to that faced by governments following previous economic downturns: never in history have so many nations around the world had such a high level of debt on their national balance sheets. As Clark (2000) posits: "if the urban fabric of the Anglo-American countries is to be sustained and enhanced, pension funds are the obvious and only likely source of new investment over the coming years of the 21st century."

THE RISE OF PENSIONS AND THEIR SUITABILITY FOR INFRASTRUCTURE INVESTMENTS

The Great Depression of the 1930s and the Second World War can be seen as having a significant impact on both the development of the welfare state and the influence of pension funds in the Anglo-American world. While it is evident that local government authorities created a number of small pension funds in the nineteenth century, it was not until after the Great Depression that widespread development of pension funds occurred (Clark, 2000). The Depression swept away the life savings of many, and created a feeling of insecurity that shook the very foundations that economies had been built upon. The spread of pension plans can thus be attributed, at least in part, to a shift in the social and political atmosphere that has prevailed since the 1930s: from then on, people were acutely aware of the need to provide for old-age economic security. As financial positions strengthened and the ability to influence worker conditions improved, retirement services became a priority in both the public sector and private companies.

Since the end of the Second World War and through the turn of the last century, pension benefits have become an integral component of employees' wages. And in order to secure these pensions, governments and companies funded these liabilities. As such, there has been a net flow of assets into pension funds of immense proportions, due in large part to the baby boom generation entering peak earning years and the requirement of private plans to be fully funded. As a result, the pension fund industry has become the single largest source of savings in the global economy, with both the funds themselves and their market representatives (second-order intermediaries) today playing a core role in capital markets. In the Anglo-American countries of the UK, USA, Canada, Australia and New Zealand, employer-sponsored pension plans have proliferated and coverage of the private workforce has greatly expanded.

Funded plans generally take one of two forms: defined contribution or defined benefit. Defined contribution (DC) plans do not promise a final benefit or retirement value. Instead, they rely on the flow of contributions and the accumulated performance of individuals' investments to generate a personal retirement annuity for the plan beneficiary. DC plans are therefore particularly sensitive to individuals' investment decisions and often vulnerable to the short-term performance of investments (Clark and Evans, 1998). In contrast, defined benefit (DB) plans require an employer to commit to a formula for determining retiree annuities. Consideration is thus given to the expected inflow of contributions and the expected outflow of benefits, matching them through the use of investments that seek to maximize returns consistent with the time profile of expected benefits that will have to be paid out.

The key distinguishing characteristic between DC and DB plans is that the DC framework focuses on the value of the assets currently endowing a retirement account, whereas the DB plan focuses on the future flow of benefits that the individual will receive upon retirement (Bodie et al., 1988). In a final average pay DB plan, retirement benefits are implicitly indexed to inflation, at least during the employee's active years with the firm. Greater benefits accrue toward the end of the employee's working life, or are "backloaded." If inflation increases significantly over the course of a worker's life, the backloading effect is more pronounced. In contrast, backloading or frontloading in DC plans is independent of inflation, as employers can achieve any backloading pattern by simply choosing an appropriate pattern of contribution rates over the course of the employee's career (Bodie et al., 1988). An investment in the infrastructure asset class with a long-term horizon and inflation-linked, volatility-protected cash flows thus provides an attractive proposition for DB plan administrators looking to match liabilities. In a DC plan, a DC participant values an infrastructure investment in a similar way to a DB sponsor but without the pressing need for matching liabilities. A concern for DC plan providers is the illiquidity of infrastructure assets. DC plan providers prefer to make more liquid investments to be able to trade out of their assets quickly and reduce the risk of losses. For these reasons, DB plan providers have invested more in infrastructure assets than DC plan managers.

DB pension fund investment strategies have traditionally followed convention by allocating funds to a mixture of equity products, fixed-income products and property investments (Muralidhar, 2001). While the investment opportunities associated with infrastructure assets have been extremely varied in nature, there seems to be a growing acceptance amongst the investment community of what the key characteristics should be for the asset class to be an attractive proposition for pension funds. Firstly, the extended life of infrastructure facilities and long-term nature of the concession rights for associated investments make them a suitable match for the long-term liabilities of a pension fund. The accompanying cash flows of infrastructure investments are usually stable and predictable due to the usually monopolistic characteristics of the assets, with high barriers to market entry and inelastic demand for use of the assets. Infrastructure investment cash flows such as user tolls, airline charges or rail tickets are often inflation-linked, providing pension funds with protection against volatility and inflation. Pension funds may also use infrastructure as a diversification strategy, as returns tend to have low correlations with returns on other asset classes (Beeferman, 2008; Macquarie, 2009; Probitas Partners, 2010). After pension funds, a variety of other long-term investors might find infrastructure a suitable asset class. For example, sovereign wealth funds (SWFs) have invested in infrastructure assets globally. These funds are usually created in resource-rich geographies, where the proceeds from commodity sales are used by the government to diversify their economy. Other SWFs have been created from budget surpluses in order to help governments to provide budget relief in the future. The various types of sovereign funds – which include stabilization funds, savings funds, reserve investment funds, development funds and pension reserve funds – have different objectives, which will influence the way they invest and what they invest into. The total assets under management of SWFs around the world has increased to US$8.4 trillion (Kalb, 2015).

HOW INSTITUTIONAL INVESTORS ACCESS INFRASTRUCTURE

As is the case for other asset classes, there are a number of different vehicles on offer for pension and sovereign investment in infrastructure. Both debt and equity vehicles have been used by investors to access core economic infrastructure. The infrastructure asset class is heterogeneous and not all investments satisfy the same risk–return qualities. The vehicle selected for investment will therefore depend both on the nature of the asset and on how the investor has defined and allocated infrastructure in their portfolios. The various investment vehicles for infrastructure are summarized in Figure 7.1.

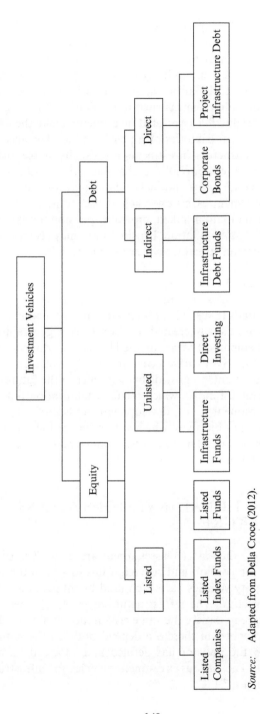

Source: Adapted from Della Croce (2012).

Figure 7.1 Infrastructure investment vehicles

There are a large number of financial products available to invest in infrastructure, and a large amount of variability within each of the infrastructure products on offer (that is, no two airports or roads are exactly the same). As the market continues to grow and information about the asset class becomes more readily available, the existing vehicles will become refined and new offerings will emerge. This section provides a snapshot of where the market has been and what trends might arise in the future for institutional infrastructure investment. Market analysis suggests that unlisted equity investment has been the most popular vehicle for institutional investors to access core economic infrastructure to date (Probitas Partners, 2010). This is highlighted in Figure 7.2's graph depicting the results of a survey of 75 institutional investors, conducted by data provider Preqin. The survey conducted by Preqin consisted mainly of pension funds and sovereign wealth funds but also included insurance companies, banks and other smaller institutional investors. Project financing in the survey referred to investments made into debt for infrastructure projects. The graph shows that all unlisted vehicles – unlisted funds, direct investments, co-investments – are the most common for institutional investors. Co-investments are a form of direct investing where institutional investors partner up with other investors to invest together in an asset. Unlisted equity refers to equity investment in a company that is not listed on a stock

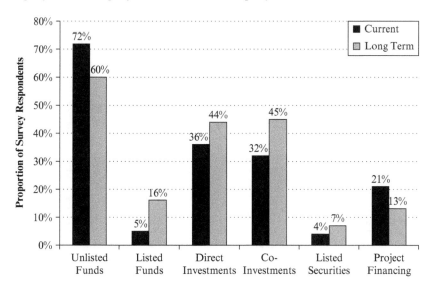

Source: Preqin (2010).

Figure 7.2 Preferred infrastructure investment vehicle

exchange. The value of the company is not therefore directly affected by general stock market sentiment.

Despite the wide variety of financial products on offer, unlisted equity investments into PPP projects or privatized assets predominate for institutional investors. Because of the heterogeneity of infrastructure assets and underlying information asymmetries, long-term relations between institutions and individuals are often central to the infrastructure investment process, with reliance on financial intermediaries. Whether an investor invests directly in the asset class or utilizes financial intermediaries will depend in large part on the size and internal resource capability of the investor. The governance and internal resources of a pension fund will determine the extent of reliance on investment consultants or fund managers. The relational form of infrastructure investing can take one of two main structural forms, indirect or direct, with variations illustrated in Figure 7.3.

The indirect investment method involves the pension fund investor deploying its capital as a "Limited Partner" in an infrastructure fund, passing on all responsibility to the fund manager for the investment. Investment consultants have played an increasingly important role in the indirect relational infrastructure investment process, providing advice to small and medium-sized pension funds for investing in infrastructure. The

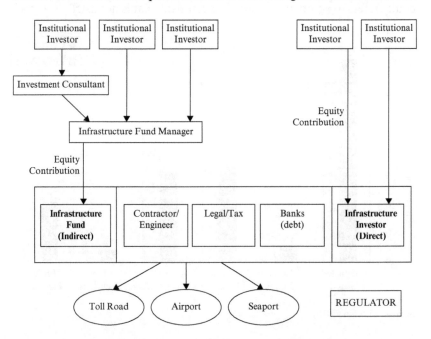

Figure 7.3   Methods of institutional infrastructure investment

investment consultant usually initiates the process by advising the investor of the benefits of an allocation to infrastructure. Once the investor has agreed to invest in infrastructure, the consultant then provides advice on suitable managers through which to invest. The selected manager's role in the process is to source appropriate assets to invest in on behalf of institutional investors.

As shown in Figure 7.3, the second, direct method refers to a pension fund investor foregoing the consultant and the manager by investing directly in infrastructure assets. This means that these investors have the in-house resources to be able to source assets, finance the investments, and manage or maintain them.

Direct investments can be made alongside co-investment partners in a consortium consisting of other pension fund investors and infrastructure fund managers. The equity arrangement in a consortium of direct investors varies from asset to asset. In a co-investment arrangement, it is usually the fund manager or largest pension fund investor in the consortium that leads the transaction. We discuss the co-investment method of investing in more detail below.

The very large pension funds capable of directly investing in infrastructure will have a separate division of the fund's investment team solely focused on infrastructure investments. Medium-sized to large funds may have one member of the investment committee dedicated to infrastructure with the responsibility of overseeing due diligence on fund managers and making recommendations to the wider committee. It is likely that this person would not be entirely focused on infrastructure and would have other asset classes to look after as well. The smallest funds would most likely have no dedicated infrastructure asset analysts, and based on a collective trustee or investment committee decision employ the advice of an investment consultant for an allocation to the infrastructure asset class.

The attachment of early infrastructure funds to the investment banking industry has resulted in numerous conflicts of interest. The fees charged by managers have sometimes been excessively high, resembling private equity fees, despite private equity returns being higher. This has typically involved a base management fee of 1–2 percent and performance fees of 10–20 percent, with an 8–12 percent hurdle rate (Inderst, 2009). Investors have also been concerned over the short time horizon of fund managers, with most funds offering closed-end models around ten years. Investors, on the other hand, are attracted to the asset class for the long duration of investments which can be held for up to 30 to 50 years. While some fund managers have aligned their fund conditions more closely to investor interests, the issue of excessive fees is still widely perceived as a barrier to investment.

DATA ON THE INFRASTRUCTURE PPP EQUITY INVESTOR UNIVERSE

This section provides greater detail on the infrastructure investor universe to understand how investors access infrastructure PPP projects. The data for this section was obtained through a detailed document and database review of industry-based publications, case study interviews on seven different pension funds of varying size and characteristics, as well as surveying the pension fund clients of three of the largest global investment consultants by size of assets under advisement. This was part of a research project conducted by one of the authors between 2010 and 2012.

Analysis of Pension Funds in the Market and Vehicles Utilized for Infrastructure Investing

A document and database review was conducted in order to examine the types of equity investors in the global infrastructure market and the types of investment vehicles employed by investors looking to invest in this field. A summary of the various industry-based publications is provided here.

Probitas Partners, an investment management and advisory firm, published the Infrastructure Market Review and Institutional Investor Survey 2010 which included an online survey of 160 senior investment executives from pension funds, "fund of funds" managers, family offices, endowments and foundations, conducted during the second half of September 2009. Of the respondents that were active investors in infrastructure (the largest percentage of which were pension funds), 52.6 percent invested through closed-end infrastructure funds, compared with 15.7 percent investing via direct investments. Fourteen percent of infrastructure investors made co-investments, while 8 percent in each case invested through publicly traded infrastructure vehicles and funds of funds (Probitas Partners, 2010).

In the Preqin database of unlisted infrastructure funds, pension schemes accounted for the largest share of infrastructure investment, at 44 percent (Preqin, 2009). The same database shows that 10 percent of infrastructure investors have assets under management of less than $1 billion, 36 percent have assets under management between $1 billion and $10 billion, and 32 percent of investors have assets under management between $11 billion and $50 billion. Less than a quarter of investors have assets of more than $50 billion (Preqin, 2009).

The Global Alternatives Survey conducted by financial services company Towers Watson and the *Financial Times* newspaper records that more than 60 percent of assets under management in the world's top 50 infrastructure funds at the end of 2009 were managed on behalf of pension funds; that is, $108.6 billion out of the total $179 billion of assets in infrastructure funds. This represented the highest proportion of pension funds for the five alternative asset classes (infrastructure, real estate, private equity, hedge funds and commodities) covered by the survey. The survey also shows that the largest manager of pension fund assets across all asset classes was the infrastructure fund manager Macquarie Group, which manages $52 billion of assets on behalf of pensions. There is a high concentration of assets under the top five infrastructure managers: Macquarie Group, Brookfield Asset Management, Alinda Capital Partners LLC, Industry Funds Management and Goldman Sachs account for 80 percent of all infrastructure assets under management (Towers Watson, 2009).

Infrastructure Investor 30, collated by PEI media, is a ranking of firms which have formed the greatest amount of direct infrastructure investment capital over a five-year period starting January 1, 2005. The list includes fund managers, pension funds and infrastructure developers, based on the amount of capital they have invested directly in infrastructure. Out of the top 30 firms, headed by Macquarie Group, only eight are pension funds, with the majority (19 out of 30) being investment fund managers (PEI Media, 2010). Table 7.1 summarizes the findings of these industry-based publications.

Two key findings can be deduced from the analysis of industry-based publications. Firstly, it is clear that pension funds are the largest investors in the global infrastructure investing market. Secondly, the predominant structural form of investing in infrastructure is through the fund management route, as the majority of pension funds in the

Table 7.1 Summary of infrastructure investor universe statistics

Name	Year	Organization type	Study type	Results
Probitas Partners	2010	Investment Management/ advisory	Pension fund survey of method of infrastructure investment	52.6% fund manager 15.7% direct 14% co-investment
Preqin	2009	Data provider	Types of investors in infrastructure funds	44% pension funds (largest)
Towers Watson	2009	Investment consultant	Types of investors in infrastructure funds	>60% pension funds
PEI	2010	Media/data provider	Top 30 direct infrastructure investment capital providers	19 fund managers 8 direct pension fund investors

market do not have sufficient resources and in-house capability to make investments directly.

The Governance Challenges of Pension Fund Infrastructure PPP Investors

A survey was conducted on the pension fund clients of three investment consultants with combined assets under advisement of US$7 trillion (as at January 2011), in order to understand the characteristics of pension funds that utilize investment consultants for infrastructure investing. From the survey, it was found that the average proportion of total clients that invest in infrastructure was 4.5 percent. The average allocation of each client to infrastructure was 5.1 percent. Eighty-two percent of the funds surveyed were from pure DB schemes and 95 percent of funds invested in unlisted infrastructure vehicles.

Figure 7.4 shows the distribution of pension fund clients that invest in infrastructure by size of assets under management. It can be seen that the majority of clients (89 percent) had fund sizes ranging between £0 and £5 billion, with few funds greater than £5 billion.

From the client survey undertaken and interviews conducted, the institutional equity investor universe can be segmented by the method of infrastructure investing employed. Firstly, the "small to medium" size range of funds that utilize investment consultants for investing would typically have assets under management between £0 and £5 billion. This could be put alongside a "medium to large" fund size range of £5 billion to £15 billion, and a "large" category consisting of pension funds with size greater than £15 billion. The majority of "medium to large" and

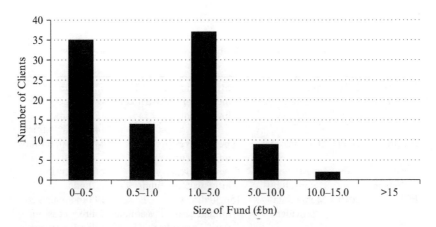

Figure 7.4   Distribution of pension fund clients by size

"large" pension funds would have sufficient in-house capability that they would not require the services of an investment consultant to invest in infrastructure assets.

The size ranges of the three pension fund categories identified are not intended to be strict categories. Instead the three categories provide a useful gauge by which to classify funds in the investor universe, and thus determine the likely method of infrastructure investing utilized. The sample of pension funds used is not representative of the entire infrastructure investor universe and therefore the categorization method does not cover all possibilities of classifying funds. The three categories, however, help to conceptualize the responses of pension funds used in this case study and provide a framework to further understand the decision-making process of pension funds when investing into infrastructure. The size ranges are based on figures for assets under management for funds surveyed as at September 2010.

The governance characteristics of the funds in each of the three different categories based on the interviews and survey are detailed below. In order to analyze the governance characteristics of the different categories of funds, the "best-practice" governance framework outlined in Clark and Urwin (2008a) was utilized, specifically looking at the "people," "process" and "organizational coherence" of these organizations.

As outlined in Clark and Urwin (2008a), "organizational coherence" refers to the pension fund's organizational strategy and mission, including the consideration of clarity and focus of investment objectives. The "people" aspect refers to the skills and expertise of those involved in investment decision-making, including trustees, investment and general purpose committee members as well as external consultants. Finally, the "process" of best-practice governance refers to how investment decision-making is organized and implemented.

How Small to Medium Funds Access PPP Infrastructure Investments

The funds interviewed at the lower end of this size category started their operations very much as "amateur-like" organizations where the board of trustees and investment committee were made up of industry personnel without any real financial expertise. Such funds then progressed toward more "professional" institutions as the importance of retirement planning and a fiduciary responsibility became apparent for its members. This has meant recruiting people within the fund's industry who also have a certain degree of experience dealing with investment issues. More frequent meetings are held and an investment committee and general purpose committee have been set up where they did not previously exist.

With such humble beginnings, these small funds had to employ the services of external consultants from the start for actuarial services, and subsequently for investment consulting advice. The general sentiment amongst board members has been to keep the same advisors through the development of the funds and for advice on investing in new areas such as infrastructure. The reliance on external advisors is so great that trustees find it hard to voice their own opinions. As one trustee member stated, "Members feel uncomfortable making investment decisions for the fund without consultant advice." In this way, investment consultants have been instrumental in introducing small funds to the infrastructure asset class and have acted as thought leaders for smaller funds to access infrastructure investments. The main reason that consultants have advised clients to invest in infrastructure has been for diversification and in order to match the long-term liabilities of the funds.

A number of small funds had initially thought of gaining access to the infrastructure asset class through publicly listed infrastructure and utilities companies; however, the advice of consultants has been not to make infrastructure investments by themselves, and to use the unlisted fund market instead. Once the investment consultants have narrowed down the range of fund managers according to the most suitable products for their client, each manager will go through a "beauty parade" process before the investment committee and board make their final selection. The final selection of fund manager can be made quite arbitrarily. The final decision could be made due to an affinity with a particular asset in the portfolio of a certain fund manager, as infrastructure assets tend to strike a loyal, sentimental chord with the general public. A well-regarded name and reputation is also an important criterion in selecting a fund manager.

Most of the funds in the small to medium category had a structure provided by statute with responsibilities of the board and various subcommittees defined so that actions are carried out for the benefit of plan members. These funds, however, lacked a clear investment objective or mission statement apart from recognizing the need to match the long-term liabilities of the fund through their investments. A key distinguishing factor of the organizational coherence of the small funds was the limited ability to provide an appropriate resources budget for the investment functions of the fund.

The "people" governance aspect could also be seen as a factor contributing to the indirect procedure of infrastructure investing being preferred by small to medium funds. The smaller funds were restricted by their requirement to appoint board members and committee members from within their organization. The level of financial expertise and the skill set available to fill these positions were thus limited. Board members and investment committee members took up their positions on a part-time basis, further restricting their ability to carry out their role as effectively as might be possible. Little or no compensation was given to the board and committee members of most of the small to medium funds for their role in making decisions on infrastructure investment.

Perhaps the most significant effect on institutional performance is leadership at the board level, and particularly by the chairperson. In the small to medium fund environment, where expertise is often lacking amongst committee members, the importance of showing strong leadership and being accountable for making tough decisions was made apparent during the interviews. It was perceived by one fund that the external advisors "hunt in packs," influencing the perceptions of committee members, and so it is very hard to go against their advice. It was recalled by one chairman that he did not agree with the advice of a consultant on a particular decision. A lack of expertise amongst the committee members forced them into the mindset that they must take the advice of the consultant, leaving the chairman helpless in his position to voice his concerns. It is very easy for a chairman of a small to medium fund to be forced into the mentality that it is safer to take the advice of consultants, especially in the current pensions crisis climate.

The infrastructure investment "process" of small to medium funds, as outlined above, is mainly initiated by the investment consultant. The decision to invest and the selection of a fund manager can be quite arbitrary, particularly in the case of a new type of financial product such as infrastructure. Such a selection process by external managers falls short of the best-practice investment process which calls for "selection by rigorous application of fit for purpose criteria as well as a clearly defined mandate, aligned to specific goals" (Clark and Urwin, 2008a). The arbitrary nature of the investment process for small to medium funds in many ways reflects the lack of a clear mission statement and ability to attract relevant expertise or skilled personnel. The final decision-making responsibility of investment issues falls to the board members, who may be contacted informally in order to quickly approve a decision reached by the investment committee. Thus arrangements can be made to ensure that investment decisions are not restricted by prearranged quarterly or less frequent meeting times.

How Medium to Large Funds Access PPP Infrastructure Investments

In between the small to medium and the large direct investor funds are a group of mid-size funds. These medium–large funds are large enough in size that they have the institutional resources to make investment decisions without the need of investment consultants; however, they do not have the in-house resources to make direct investments in infrastructure assets. These funds usually have one or two people looking after the infrastructure mandate (although infrastructure will not be their sole focus) and who will carry out the due diligence and selection process of fund managers. The size of these funds enables them to attract interest from fund managers themselves, which facilitates their own process of sourcing appropriate vehicles to invest through. Quite often, fund managers will approach medium to large pension funds to provide information on their product and service offerings. Once a fund manager has been selected, which usually requires general investment committee and board approval, the fund divests all responsibility for investing its capital to the fund manager.

The medium to large funds are of a size large enough to have special significance for a provincial or even national community, and a mission statement and investment objective is usually clearly defined. It was perceived from the interviews that the obligation to these funds' members was very important to the investment executives, and the underlying mission of the fund was engrained in the investment operations of the institution.

The investment management team of the medium to large funds could be seen to exhibit a similar skill set to the managers of large funds, although the investment manager in the medium to large funds generally had a much more varied role, primarily due to there being only one person, with responsibilities involving researching the industry, carrying out due diligence on managers, as well as cross-checking the investment analysis carried out by the selected managers. The leadership function in the medium to large funds is slightly different to that of the small funds in that greater expertise can be called upon around the board table when making decisions. The medium to large funds are not as reliant on external consultancy advice, reducing the principal–agent problem when deciding how to invest in infrastructure. The due diligence process and selection of fund managers is more thorough than that employed by small to medium funds. Quite often a request for information (RFI) process is carried out by the funds to identify potential managers. This is followed by a request for proposal (RFP) to narrow down the selection to around four or five candidates, who are subjected to an elaborate survey consisting of more than 100 questions around the investment philosophies, strategies and business practice of the manager. The process is concluded by an on-site visit to the fund manager before the final selection is made with board approval.

Such a process is in line with best-practice measures for funds that recognize their restricted resource capability and have effectively utilized external agents to emphasize diversity and limit risk. Medium to large funds, while not being able to lead direct investments on their own, have started to join consortiums in the co-investment or club models as minor partners.

How Large Funds Access PPP Infrastructure Investments

At the far end of the spectrum lie the large pension funds which have developed specialist management companies or dedicated teams for different investment asset classes including infrastructure. These pension funds have the in-house resources and capability to source deals, carry out due diligence on investments, provide finance and manage the assets they invest in. In contrast to the smaller funds, strong leadership was required not only to start investing in a new sector such as infrastructure, but also to start up a new management division within the fund to focus solely on infrastructure assets (Clark and Urwin, 2008b). In these funds, global teams of up to 40 have been set up to manage the infrastructure mandate of the fund, commanding a portfolio allocation of up to 20 percent of the total assets under management. All aspects of the investment process are controlled within the fund, although external contractors may be used prior to making investments in order to gain construction, legal or tax and accounting advice. The expertise and level of resources contained within these institutions are comparable to those of the fund managers that smaller pension funds invest through. Board members of these large funds are chosen by the parent company or in some cases the finance ministry via a rigorous selection process designed so that only those with specialist expertise in investment, business and finance are appointed. In certain circumstances, it was observed that large direct investors would sometimes utilize the services of a fund manager or investment consultant when working on a specific investment where the external advisor could bring specific expertise to the investment analysis process.

While inheriting a structure provided by statute, the large funds often have a clear mission statement with specifically defined goals for their infrastructure investments. This was made apparent in the interviews and is usually explicitly stated on the company's website. Risk analysis forms a crucial part of the investment analysis process for direct investments in infrastructure. The infrastructure investment team is not able to make commitments over a certain size without board approval. With sufficiently experienced personnel on the board, a cross-check of the risks and other issues pertaining to infrastructure investments is obtained before a final commitment is made. Because a significant amount of analysis is done in-house by the large funds, a greater amount of information must be digested in the investment analysis process. This means that the decision-making process may take longer, especially before gaining the final board approval. In summary, however, the substantial size of the large funds in the infrastructure market has enabled them to sufficiently resource each element in the investment process and governance chain with an appropriate time and resources budget. As can be seen from the market analysis above, such resource capability is restricted to only a few pension fund investors in the market.

We believe that it is imperative for institutional investors to define the aim, strategy and resourcing requirements before pursuing the direct investing route. In terms of the "people" aspect for the governance of direct infrastructure investors, the skill set required for infrastructure investment is different to what an institutional investor may be used to. An understanding that infrastructure investments are transaction-oriented as opposed to market-oriented is essential (requiring origination, structuring, execution and risk analysis skills), and that such investments are long term and place an emphasis on asset management (overseeing management and improving efficiency). It was also noted that remuneration must be able to attract appropriately skilled people from competing employers (Clark et al., 2011).

The "process" for direct investing requires risk control functions to work within tight time frames, with relevant committee members having the experience to appraise analyst reports and asset allocation investment targets while also being able to facilitate the in-house team's long-term performance (Clark et al., 2011). The large funds are often the leading members of a co-investing or club/partnership consortia.

Summary

The segmentation of the investor universe for infrastructure equity into the three categories described provides an understanding of how institutional capital is channeled into infrastructure assets in very different ways even among the same types of funds. The larger funds appear to have a clearly defined policy on the allocation of funds to infrastructure and will be looking to invest in core economic assets that suit the profile that they have defined for the asset class. Their investment decisions are based on sufficient in-house expertise and investment knowledge amongst the board of trustees. The smaller funds are hugely reliant on the advice of financial intermediaries, not only for asset allocation but also for the choice of infrastructure fund manager. Both pieces of advice will affect the vehicle and type of asset invested in. As mentioned, such a reliance on external service providers can lead to principal–agency issues and a misalignment of interest between client and service provider. We look at how these issues can be addressed in the next section.

IMPROVING EQUITY PPP INVESTOR GOVERNANCE: RE-INTERMEDIATION, COLLABORATION AND INSOURCING

The analysis carried out above highlights how the infrastructure investor market is segmented and, as a result, how investors actually invest in infrastructure projects. It is clear that there are a large number of investors that rely heavily on financial intermediaries. This poses some principal–agent problems. This issue is similar to that faced in the construction industry, termed "broken agency," where conflicts may arise between the short-term contractors that bear short-term risk, and the managers who bear the long-term risk and rewards of the project (Sheffer and Levitt, 2010). In the infrastructure investment process, investors may approach infrastructure with a long-term horizon in mind, but may use intermediaries that have a much shorter-term focus. This is usually because asset managers in the unlisted fund model are constrained by a time horizon (usually ten years) and therefore are looking to make investments with the idea of selling them off soon after. The holding period of investments in this fund model is usually 4–5 years, which is much shorter than the time period that investors have been expecting from the asset class. Asset managers will charge both a management fee and a performance fee for investing investors' money on their behalf. The combination of shorter time horizon and high costs has forced investors to consider alternatives.[2]

In an ideal world, investors would consider bringing the investment management function for infrastructure in-house, where internal employees would be responsible for the origination, analysis, due diligence, execution and management of their infrastructure investments. There is significant data that shows that the costs of internally managing an infrastructure program are a lot lower than hiring external managers to invest in infrastructure assets (Andonov, 2013; Metrick and Yasuda, 2010; Fang et al., 2015). As highlighted earlier, to move from indirect to direct investing in infrastructure is a significant undertaking and very difficult to achieve for many smaller investors (Clark and Monk, 2013; Clark et al., 2011). As institutional investor assets under management increase, however, moving to a direct model will need to become a serious consideration. This has been observed in Australia, where compulsory superannuation has meant that superannuation funds have ballooned in size. As a result, the cost economics of continually using asset managers has driven these funds to consider the direct model of investing.

So, what solutions are there for those funds that are unable to insource for infrastructure investing? We draw upon economic sociology and contract theory to offer some suggestions for how institutional investors can achieve more alignment. Drawing upon social network theory, we believe that investors need to develop their social capital. Social capital is defined as the external relationships of an individual or an organization. Most investors recognize the importance of their financial and human capital, but underappreciate the value of their social capital. In many ways, we believe that it is the network of an asset manager that provides the most value to the investment management process. A string network enables better deal sourcing and business performance through assisting portfolio companies. This has been evident in other asset classes such as venture capital (Sahlman, 1990; Hochberg et al., 2007). We believe that investors that also invest time and resources into building their own network will go a significant way toward improving their organizational capability and finding opportunities. Investing in social capital can be achieved even by the small to medium fund category of investors by simply attending roundtables and conferences specifically set up to help facilitate long-term investing, and by taking a conscious, deliberate and structured approach toward managing the relationships of the organization with other peer investors, and useful individuals and organizations alike. Investment opportunities and organizational enhancements can be sourced through many different means and by many different interactions. The idea is to build an ecosystem around an organization which helps to facilitate the decision-making process in order to achieve its long-term investment objectives. Investors right across the spectrum should be able to cooperate, collaborate and ultimately co-invest with trusted peers and partners in a more aligned way than the traditional indirect fund model for infrastructure investment.[3]

While a number of asset managers have abused their position of power in their relationship with investors, there are also managers that have been able to add significant value to their investors, albeit while taking significant fees. As mentioned, a large number of investors will be unable to "dis-intermediate" with their asset managers, and so we call for investors to "re-intermediate" with their managers. Re-intermediation is a call for more alignment in the relationship between asset owners and asset managers. At the core of re-intermediation is the need for a more "relational" approach to the contract between asset owner and asset manager, as opposed to the "classical" form of contract that seems to have prevailed in the traditional model. Just as relational contracting has been called upon in Chapter 3 of this volume as a way to gain more alignment between various contractors in a PPP, we believe that relational contracting norms should be applied by investors in their relationships with asset managers. In the decades leading up to the financial crisis of 2008–2009, the relationship between investors and asset managers seemed to move away from client and service, to investors just simply funding the business of managers. In many cases the limited partner–general partner (LP–GP) contract between investors and their managers could be more associated with classical contracting norms such as short-term, discrete transactions, where the identities of parties are irrelevant, and the terms and limits are carefully outlined with limited flexibility. We argue that the investor–manager relationship should be more akin to relational contracting norms such as long-term, repeated exchanges based on trust, reciprocity, cooperation and mutual dependency, and where the personal involvement of parties is important. We acknowledge that adopting a "relational" approach to investor–manager contracts might not be feasible, given the time constraints required and the potentially large number of manager relationships that an investor might have. There are also challenges for smaller investors who may be writing smaller checks and therefore would receive a service that is commensurate with the amount that they are investing. At the very least, however, smaller investors should be demanding complete transparency on the fees and incentives of the infrastructure funds that they are investing into. They should also be fully aware of the underlying risks of the investment that they are invested into, as well as how the fund structuring may distort and even add further risks to their investments.

In terms of fund characteristics, relational infrastructure contracts would be more suited to open-ended funds or funds of length greater than 15 years, as this would be more appropriately matched to the long-term liabilities of institutional investors and more suited to developing the type of partnership required. There is now greater appreciation of the diversity of risk–return profiles of infrastructure assets, and this should be reflected in the fees charged to investors. It is understandable that a fund investing in greenfield assets in the emerging markets carrying greater risk will charge a higher fee compared to a fund investing into brownfield assets in developed countries. Management fees should just cover the cost of running the fund on a day-to-day basis, as opposed to providing a source of profit for the manager. Given the large size of funds, a level of 2 percent management fee, common for private equity funds, is considered too high, particularly for brownfield, core economic infrastructure assets in OECD countries (Towers Watson, 2009), and that figure should be closer to around 0.5 percent. A key consideration here is whether the total fee and portfolio construction costs for an investor are greater than the illiquidity and risk premium of investing in these assets.

Re-intermediation and collaboration are key tenets of the research we have conducted for addressing the infrastructure investor governance problem. We have conceptualized the collaborative model of investing, which essentially alludes to the new vehicles being set up by institutional investors to access assets such as infrastructure alongside more aligned

Figure 7.5 Collaborative model infrastructure investment vehicles

partners. The vehicles associated with the collaborative model include joint ventures between investors (usually larger in size) and development, construction companies or other investors. Co-investment platforms are where investors pool their capital together, in an open-ended, longer-term fund structure, independent of an asset manager. In a co-investment platform, one large investor would usually take the lead, or a new team would be set up to manage the investments. Smaller investors have the opportunity to join such an initiative, which should be more aligned than a traditional unlisted infrastructure fund. Platform companies or seeding managers is the third type of vehicle that defines the collaborative model for infrastructure investing. Platform companies are usually created by large investors to seed a specific team or group of individuals who have an excellent track record in a specific area or opportunity of interest to the investor. The idea behind a platform company is that the investor is able to set the terms of the vehicle in a more aligned fashion, while the seeded team does not have to worry about raising further capital to make investments. These new collaborative model vehicles are summarized in Figure 7.5.

Many investors have started to see the benefits of the collaborative model, and the number of these types of vehicles being formed has increased since the financial crisis. The vehicles have been set up with the intention to get as close to the underlying infrastructure assets as possible. They represent the newest trends for pooling the (predominantly equity) capital together to invest into the long-term concession projects being offered by governments. A lot of these vehicles will be investing in the PPP opportunities that have been looked at in this book, through an alternative procurement process with a preferred bidder being awarded the contract. We have also started to see a number of governments which have recognized the value of true long-term investors such as local pension funds and have decided to partner with these investors directly. We detail some of these initiatives in the next section.

EXAMPLES OF THE "GOLDEN HANDSHAKE"

The "golden handshake," in our world, is represented by matching PPP projects with long-term investors such as pension funds and sovereign funds. A certain number of governments have recognized the importance of partnering with true long-term investors in this way and have thus come up with initiatives to help facilitate the flow of long-term institutional capital into their infrastructure projects.

The first example we would like to highlight that represents possibly a truer form of the golden handshake is the Quebec provincial government and CDPQ Infrastructure partnership in Canada. In this case, the provincial government, which had been under pressure as the second most indebted Canadian province with a large infrastructure investment gap, announced that it would hand over the planning, financing and management of new infrastructure projects to the province's major pension fund, Caisse de Depot et Placement du Quebec (CDPQ). The arrangement can be seen as a more integrated design–build–finance–operate–maintain (DBFOM) PPP model. After the government has identified its infrastructure investment needs, through the agreement, the pension fund has the discretion to select the projects that will help generate a commercial return for its clients and help propose solutions to the government. Various rounds of dialogue between CDPQ and the government will then proceed, after which the government will either accept or reject the proposal. CDPQ will assume full responsibility for all aspects and stages of the project, including planning, financing, execution and operations. The projects that are selected will be removed from the government's balance sheet, providing some budgetary relief.[4]

Such an arrangement allows the government to form a relationship with a trusted long-term partner to help solve its infrastructure investment needs. A key component is that the projects selected by CDPQ have to be able to generate revenues. By investing in the projects and overseeing their operation, execution, financing and planning, the citizens of Quebec not only benefit from improved infrastructure, but they also benefit from the proceeds of the investment helping to secure their retirement through the pension fund. It must be noted that CDPQ is a large, experienced direct investor in infrastructure with significant capability to carry out the function of investing and managing assets. This program was designed to help fund greenfield projects, which historically have been too risky for pension funds to invest in. CDPQ will supplement its in-house expertise by working with well-aligned and complementary partners who will help to undertake the stages of construction, logistics and operations. By being involved at the earliest stage of project origination, CDPQ Infrastructure will be able to carry out substantially deeper research and due diligence, and mold the design of the project to ensure mutually beneficial outcomes.

The first project, a new integrated light rail network linking downtown Montreal with the airport, is under way for the new partnership. The project will have construction costs of approximately $6.04 billion, and requires government investment to complement CDPQ's investment. The project is expected to add more than $3.7 billion to Quebec's gross domestic product over four years and to enable $5 billion in private real estate developments along the route.

The second example to highlight here is that of the Queensland (Australia) government's sale of its motorway network to the local defined benefit pension fund manager Queensland Investment Corporation (QIC).[5] In 2011, the Queensland government transferred Queensland Motorways (QML), a 70 km road network consisting of two major tolled motorways, to QIC under a long-term concession which valued the asset at AU$3.088 billion. There were a number of factors that contributed to the sale. Firstly, it must be recognized that the Queensland government had professionalized its services in developing alternative procurement programs for infrastructure assets, and the local defined benefit pension fund had also professionalized its services to be able to conduct direct infrastructure investments. In the lead-up to the sale, system upgrades and the global recession had necessitated increased tolls for users, but in 2010 the entity still reported aggregate deficiencies of equity of more than AU$500 million from its major shareholder, the state government. The Queensland government's finances were also deteriorating, with the state's credit rating being downgraded in 2009 and the state budget forecasting a deficit of AU$1.9 billion. QML was identified as an asset to sell or lease in order to address the government's budget shortfalls.

At the same time, the state actuary was completing its three-year review of the state's defined benefit pension and found that the fund's liabilities exceeded its assets by more than AU$1.4 billion. As a result, and after weighing up the relative disadvantages and advantages of putting QML through a standard competitive tender process, the Queensland government began an exclusive negotiation with QIC on the transfer of a concession agreement for QML. A key rationale behind the transfer was that value would ultimately be captured by the retirees of Queensland. The shared liabilities between QIC and the government reduced the concerns over the valuation of the asset for the public. The valuation and due diligence process also benefited from QIC's experience of evaluating infrastructure investments globally and in Queensland itself. Following consultations with external advisors and independent valuations being commissioned, both entities agreed on a market value of AU$3.088 billion.

Following the sale transfer, QIC was able to make significant operational and efficiency improvements to the network, including adding new assets to the system by acquiring a failed tolled motorway and two other Brisbane city council-owned roads. In late 2013, the board of QIC was presented with a unique challenge in that the QML asset had grown sufficiently in size and value that it was over-represented in the pension fund's portfolio of assets. The concentration of QML in QIC's portfolio was so great that the fund was forced to assess the divestment of all or part of QML. It was decided that the entire QML asset would be divested (in order to maximize the value of a sale), at a time when competition for operating brownfield infrastructure assets was extremely high. QIC sold QML to a consortium consisting of a local pension, Middle Eastern sovereign fund and local road operator for AU$7.057 billion, realizing a profit of AU$3.8 billion for the pension fund over a four-year period. The sale was made between a pension fund and a consortium that also consisted of long-term investors. In normal circumstances, QIC would have held on to QML, being a long-term investor; however, the high level of locational concentration risk resulting from the significant incremental value created for this toll road network led to the sale, a decision that was in the best interest of the beneficiaries of the pension fund.

Both of the cases above provide examples of how the golden handshake between governments looking for long-term capital for their infrastructure projects, and long-term investors such as pension funds and sovereign funds, can come to fruition. What is crucially required is a government that has the ability to procure assets for alternative financing and pension funds or sovereign funds with the expertise to execute infrastructure investments and asset management appropriately. There are challenges with the model, including the conflict of interest of each entity in satisfying each of its beneficiaries appropriately; that is, pension funds should only be investing in assets that maximize commercial return in order to carry out their fiduciary obligation. Certain projects of the government, however, may not be the best commercially viable projects available. What is evident here, though, is the desire for governments to partner up with true long-term investors, whose long time horizons point to a closer alignment with the public interest.

CONCLUSIONS AND FINAL THOUGHTS

It is clear that filling the global infrastructure investment gap will require private capital catalyzed through government facilitation efforts. It is also clear that large, long-term institutional investors such as pension funds and sovereign wealth funds will be called upon to improve their capabilities and provide a large amount of that private capital. Understanding the governance and decision-making process of institutional investors is thus crucially important to help unlock this capital into the PPP projects and facilitate what has termed the "golden handshake." In many ways this chapter illustrates how the golden handshake can be executed in the most efficient way: that is, long-term institutional capital being matched directly to the long-term concession projects. We also illustrate, however, why the ideal golden handshake may not be able to be replicated in abundance around the world because of structural and institutional constraints at the investor and governmental level.

Our research agenda is tasked with understanding innovative strategies that can work within these constraints. Our overarching objective is to understand how more long-term institutional investor capital can flow more efficiently into long-term projects that desperately need it. We believe that re-intermediation is a way forward for investors to find more alignment with their asset managers. Our research would indicate that re-intermediation is occurring, with a number of investors consolidating the number of managers they use to invest in assets such as infrastructure, preferring fewer, deeper relationships. Similarly, the number of collaborative investment vehicles being formed in the last decade has increased immensely to more than 100, with many investors opting for this approach as their default for infrastructure.

The QIC and CDPQ examples have shown that governments are starting to recognize the importance of partnering with true long-term investors when going through a PPP or privatization process. The examples also emphasize the importance for investors to build their social capital so that they can not only build their organizational capacity, but also know about these opportunities as they arise. Further work is being carried out to continually monitor the institutional investor trends and also to further understand how these investors can make the most of their competitive advantages of scale of capital and time horizon when allocating their capital. Further work is also being conducted to understand how governments, particularly in the United States, can build the institutional capacity to be able to procure the assets in an effective way and identify the right long-term investment partners to help address their infrastructure investment needs.

NOTES

1. *Homo economicus* is the view that people are isolated individuals whose actions reflect mostly their material self-interests. Ricardo's theory argued that free trade would lead

to a win–win situation for trading partners because it would enable countries which had a comparative advantage to specialize in the production of those commodities. See Heilbroner (1983) for more discussion.
2. For more information on the limited partner–general partner (LP–GP) fund model, please see Monk et al. (2017).
3. For more information on the application of social network theory collaboration strategies for infrastructure investing, please see Monk et al. (2017).
4. For further information on the CDPQ–Quebec example, please see World Economic Forum (2016).
5. The case study on QIC and QML can be found at Bennon et al. (2017b).

8. Framework to assess fiscal support mechanisms for mitigating revenue risk in transportation public–private partnerships

Ting Liu and Michael J. Garvin

INTRODUCTION

Governments worldwide have increasingly used public–private partnerships (PPPs) to deliver infrastructure as an alternative to conventional approaches; in these arrangements, the private sector assumes responsibility for a project's life cycle activities and costs as well as the associated risks that are contractually transferred. Although PPP project selection has traditionally focused on project candidates whose anticipated revenue streams (for example, tolls) are sufficient to cover all capital and operating expenses, PPP delivery can still be viable for projects that are not financially self-sustaining. In such cases, governments must provide additional support to enable these projects to reach financial close. This assistance can take a wide range of forms, collectively termed fiscal support mechanisms.

In the United States (US), the significance of such mechanisms has risen since the global financial crisis and recent bankruptcies of several PPP toll concessions: South Bay Expressway in California, Indiana Toll Road in Indiana, and SH 130 Segments 5 and 6 in Texas. Traffic levels lower than forecasts were a driving factor in each project's financial troubles (Dezember and Glazer, 2013; Samuel, 2010; Mallett, 2014; Reinhardt, 2017b). Since toll revenue is used to pay debt service and equity dividends, concession contracts are susceptible to changes in demand (Charoenpornpattana et al., 2002). Demand will depend on a toll road's condition and management as well as the accessibility of alternative non-tolled routes; further, the global financial crisis illustrated that toll road demand is far more sensitive to macroeconomic conditions than previously thought (Bain, 2009). Additional research has also illustrated that demand forecasts are frequently wrong, erring on the side of being too high

(Flyvbjerg et al., 2005b). A PPP bankruptcy that results from revenue risk indicates that a public agency successfully transferred this risk to the private sector, so taxpayers were insulated from this burden. Outcomes such as this in the US, however, can impact the market and future procurements. Consequently, PPP highway procurements have transitioned toward other approaches where governments assume revenue risk by providing fiscal support (Cruz and Marques, 2012; Parker, 2011).

Governmental fiscal support is typically direct or indirect in nature: direct mechanisms provide funds to the project without contingencies or expectation of repayment; whereas indirect mechanisms are just the opposite. Direct support includes up-front cash subsidies, availability payments (APs) and shadow tolls; while indirect support includes governmental guarantees, tax breaks and subordinated governmental loans. These mechanisms decrease the revenue risk transferred, since a government retains some or all of it. However, if governments do not adequately consider or structure fiscal support, then unexpected consequences may occur. For example, the Mexican government employed guarantees in its toll road program and incurred significant unanticipated costs following the 1994 Mexican economic crisis, when actual revenues turned out well short of forecasts (Brandão and Saraiva, 2008; Ruster, 1997). Some studies have also identified that inadequately designed guarantees or support mechanisms typically result in disproportionate guarantees and *ex post* renegotiations (Cruz and Marques, 2012; Xu et al., 2014). Hence, the choice of fiscal support mechanisms in PPPs is significant, but existing research focused on this decision is limited.

Accordingly, this chapter presents a framework to assist governments in their assessment of alternative fiscal support mechanisms in a PPP project where they assume a portion or all of a project's revenue risk. Such a framework can improve governmental funding and budgeting decisions related to revenue risk. In particular, the framework evaluates and compares APs, flexible-term contracts and minimum revenue guarantees (MRGs) for toll-funded highway PPPs. The chapter first further discusses governmental support mechanisms and relevant literature. Subsequently, the framework is introduced and illustrated with a conceptual example. Finally, conclusions are drawn.

GOVERNMENTAL SUPPORT MECHANISMS

Overview

Public sector agencies are often faced with demand for infrastructure that does not cover its own costs, or the acceptance of user fees is challenged by socio-political dynamics. In such cases, a project may be deemed worthwhile from a socio-economic perspective but is not financially self-sufficient. Such projects can still be delivered as PPPs if made suitably attractive to the private sector through various mechanisms.

Typical mechanisms found in the literature and in practice include: (1) change in policy or law; (2) technical assistance; (3) monetary support; (4) financing support; (5) guarantees; and (6) usage/service fees (Gonzalez et al., 2015). The first two are forms of general support. A government may opt to modify a policy or law to strengthen the confidence of the private sector regarding its commitment to a project or to enhance its feasibility. Similarly, a government can assist and fund technical studies necessary to assess or implement a project. The remaining mechanisms are fiscal support. A government can provide monetary support in the form of capital contributions or in-kind grants of land. It may also offer governmental loans or credit enhancements that improve financing options. Guarantees typically backstop revenue shortfalls or other types of risks; while usage/service fees are payments by the government directly tied to project asset usage (shadow tolling) or service (availability payments).

Clearly, these mechanisms are illustrative, and other mechanisms exist. Regardless, a government has an array of available options to consider. The choice will likely hinge on the economic and socio-political feasibility of a particular alternative (Garvin and Gonzalez, 2013).

Fiscal Support Mechanisms that Address Revenue Risk

In a toll-funded, "patronage" PPP highway project, the revenue risk is typically transferred to the private concessionaire. Often, tolling is governed by schedules and conditions to minimize excessive pricing, so traffic volume determines overall project revenue. In cases where a government decides to retain the revenue risk or share it with the private sector, three plausible mechanisms include:

- Availability payments (AP). A government makes periodic performance-based and inflation-linked payments to a concessionaire (Sharma and Cui, 2012), and it retains all revenue risk and sets toll rates. Concessionaires are insulated from revenue risk, and they have little incentive to increase a project's traffic through their development and management practices.
- Flexible-term contract. An agreement where the duration of a concession is not fixed, but it ends once a target cumulative revenue is reached, least present value of revenue (LPVR), developed by Engel et al. (2001). Chile has employed this mechanism frequently (Vassallo

and Soliño, 2006), but its use elsewhere has been relatively limited (Cruz and Marques, 2012). It creates uncertainty for a project's financing since the concession period is unknown (Cruz and Marques, 2012; Nombela and de Rus, 2004). An adaptation suggested by Vassallo (2004) minimizes this issue since a government will pay any remaining LPVR once the maximum concession term is reached.
- Minimum revenue guarantee (MRG). Public agencies provide funds to concessionaires when revenue falls below an agreed threshold. MRGs have been implemented in Chile, Columbia, Peru and South Korea (Carpintero et al., 2015; Vassallo, 2006). A form of MRG, which is described subsequently, is also found in a recent PPP project in the US (Nguyen et al., 2018). MRGs are occasionally paired with excess revenue sharing (ERS) mechanisms where governments cover revenue shortfalls but share in revenue windfalls.

Trends in the US indicate an increasing use of such mechanisms. Table 8.1 depicts characteristics of highway PPPs delivered as design–build–finance–operate–maintain (DBFOM) arrangements from 1993 to 2017. Since 1990, 24 such projects have reached financial close: 14 (58 percent) have used the revenue risk payment structure, 5 (21 percent) have used the availability payment plus toll structure, and 5 (21 percent) have used the pure availability payment structure. The distinction between the availability payment plus toll and the availability payment structures is that the public agency levies and collects tolls in the former, whereas in the latter no toll is implemented. As illustrated, the revenue risk structure was predominant in the early years. However, from 2009 to present it is clear that the types of structures used are more balanced. Some public agencies have elected to keep control of toll rates to achieve affordability or traffic throughput objectives, while others have chosen to eliminate known challenges associated with tolls altogether (Garvin, 2015). In addition, the I-77 HOT (High Occupancy Toll) Lanes project in North Carolina included a revenue guarantee to share revenue risk through a contractual arrangement called the developer ratio adjustment mechanism (DRAM). The DRAM provisioned that, in a given year during the DRAM period from substantial completion until final maturity of the US Transportation Infrastructure Finance and Innovation Act (TIFIA) loan, if the next year's projected annual TIFIA total debt service coverage ratio (TIFIA DSCR) is below 1.0, then the project company is entitled to request that NCDOT make payments sufficient to cover the expected debt service shortfall (DRAM payment). The DRAM payments are, however, subject to restrictions: (1) in any year, the DRAM payment cannot exceed $12 million; and (2) during the DRAM period, the aggregate payments cannot exceed $75 million.

Table 8.1 Contemporary highway PPPs (DBFOM arrangements)

Project	State	Payment structure	Contract length	Financial close	Contract value ($100K)
Dulles Greenway	VA	Revenue risk	43	1993	350
SR 91 Express	CA	Revenue risk	50	1993	135
SR 125 (South Bay Expressway)	CA	Revenue risk	35	2003	658
I-495 Capital Beltway Express	VA	Revenue risk	80	2008	2068
SH 130: 5&6	TX	Revenue risk	50	2008	1328
I-595 Express Lanes	FL	Availability + toll	35	2009	1834
Port of Miami Tunnel	FL	Availability	30	2009	1073
North Tarrant Express (1&2)	TX	Revenue risk	52	2009	2047
I-635 Managed Lanes	TX	Revenue risk	52	2010	2615
Elizabeth River Tunnels	VA	Revenue risk	58	2012	2089
Presidio Parkway (Phase II)	CA	Availability	30	2012	365
I-95 Express Lanes	VA	Revenue risk	73	2012	923
East End Crossing	IN	Availability + toll	35	2013	981
North Tarrant Express (3A&B)	TX	Revenue risk	52	2013	1328
Goethals Bridge Replacement	N/A*	Availability + toll	40	2013	1436
U.S. 36 Managed Lanes Phase 2	CO	Revenue risk	50	2014	113
I-4 Ultimate Improvements	FL	Availability + toll	40	2014	2323
I-69 Phase 5	IN	Availability	35	2014	325
Rapid Bridge Replacement	PA	Availability	28	2015	899
I-77 HOT Lanes	NC	Revenue risk	50	2015	655
Portsmouth Bypass	OH	Availability	39	2015	429
SH 288 Toll Lanes	TX	Revenue risk	52	2016	819
I-66 Express	VA	Revenue risk	50	2017	3685
Central 70	CO	Availability + Toll	30	2017	1170
				Total	$29 648

Note: * Procured by the Port Authority of New York/New Jersey.

Relevant Literature

Mechanisms to mitigate revenue risk in PPPs

Given the significance of revenue risk in PPPs, scholars have examined mechanisms to mitigate or manage revenue risk from a variety of perspectives. One avenue has focused on theoretical studies of decision-making of various parties. Engel et al. (1997) and Nombela and de Rus (2001, 2004) developed models and explored the implications of flexible-term contracts; whereas Feng et al. (2015) created models to assess the impact of MRGs on toll pricing as well as road quality and capacity.

Another extensive line of research has examined government support using real options. Numerous authors have studied MRGs. Huang and Chou (2006) and Cheah and Liu (2006) modeled MRGs as real options and assessed their value. Chiara et al. (2007) structured MRGs as simple multiple-exercise real option models. Brandão and Saraiva (2008) valued minimum traffic guarantees and established a cap on cumulative government expenditures; similar work was done by Jun (2010), Ashuri et al. (2011) and Iyer and Sagheer (2011). Others have quantified a government's fiscal liability from MRGs using various metrics (Ashuri et al., 2011; Almassi et al., 2012; Wibowo et al., 2012); whereas Wibowo and Kochendoerfer (2010) created a methodology to quantify the contingent liability associated with MRGs. These studies generally found that MRGs and other mechanisms should add value in PPPs.

Some empirical work has also examined fiscal support mechanisms. Vassallo (2006) interviewed practitioners and experts in Chile to determine that flexible-term arrangements using the LPVR mechanism encountered strong opposition from concessionaires initially, but the mechanism did reduce anticipated renegotiations. Carpintero et al. (2015) analyzed PPP toll road project data in Latin America from 1990 to 2010 to conclude that flexible-term contracts, MRGs and APs did not reduce renegotiation rates.

Finally, a host of work has focused on augmenting particular mechanisms. Nombela and de Rus (2004) introduced the least present value of net revenue (LPVNR), where operations and maintenance costs are deducted from revenue, to improve flexible-term arrangements. Vassallo (2006) proposed modifying flexible-term contracts by fixing the concession duration and requiring governments to pay the LPVR balance, to attract more private participants. Shan et al. (2010) created a "collar" structure by combining a put (MRG) and a call (ERS) option; whereas Ashuri et al. (2011), Rocha Armada et al. (2012), Sun and Zhang (2014), Carbonara et al. (2014) and Wang and Liu (2015) focused on optimal MRG and ERS threshold structures. Engel et al. (2013) adjusted a flexible-term arrangement by pairing a revenue cap with a minimum income guarantee for projects with modest demand. Lastly, Sharma and Cui (2012) investigated optimizing concession duration and annual payments in AP projects.

Comparing fiscal support mechanisms
Certainly, the previous section highlights the attention given to fiscal support mechanisms that address revenue risk in PPPs. However, only

a handful of studies have suggested methods to assess alternative fiscal support mechanisms, such as Irwin (2003), who developed a qualitative framework to help governments analyze which fiscal support mechanisms to employ in PPPs. Wibowo (2004) used a real option approach to contrast fiscal support alternatives using expectations of a government's contingent liabilities and a concessionaire's negative net present values (NPVs); results demonstrated that minimum revenue/traffic guarantees are potentially better than comparable direct subsidies. Interestingly, the findings of Brandão et al. (2012) were similar.

FRAMEWORK TO ASSESS FISCAL SUPPORT MECHANISMS[1]

Existing research has undoubtedly explored fiscal support mechanisms that mitigate revenue risk in PPPs. A comprehensive framework, however, to guide governments when selecting such fiscal support mechanisms remains undeveloped. Further, such a framework should consider the perspectives of a PPP's chief stakeholders: the government, concessionaires and lenders. Lenders' concerns are particularly important since their decision-making necessarily influences a project's capital structure, which impacts rates of return and the need for public fiscal support. In light of the trends observed in the US (and elsewhere), the need for such a framework is quite timely. Subsequent sections describe the framework's conception and illustrate it with a hypothetical example.

Conception

The work of Fisher and Babbar (1996) provides a solid foundation for building a framework. Their conceptual framework considered alternative fiscal support mechanisms against two criteria: (1) impact on ability to raise financing; and (2) government financial exposure. From their perspective, a mechanism such as an MRG would have a moderate impact on ability to marshal financing, while creating relatively low financial exposure for a government; whereas a debt guarantee would have a high impact on financing capacity, while generating moderate financial exposure for a government. Hence, governments face a trade-off between these criteria when considering alternative mechanisms, so metrics approximating their criteria are needed; these are subsequently developed, and a trade-off, comparative framework is described.

Ability to raise financing

Governments offer financial support to projects with revenue risk to make them bankable and to reduce their weighted average cost of capital (WACC). A project's WACC is determined by the costs and weights of both equity and debt: WACC = $w_e * C_e + w_d * C_d$, and the value of each variable depends on a project's risks. For instance, alternative fiscal support mechanisms can each decrease a project's financing cost primarily by increasing a project's leverage. These are key notions of the proposed framework: increased borrowing capacity (BC) is a proxy for reducing a project's financing costs, and the characteristics of a fiscal support mechanism will impact BC.

In practice, lenders calculate a project's BC based on annual cash flows available for debt service (CFADS) over the loan life subject to coverage ratios such as debt service coverage ratio (DSCR) and loan life coverage ratio (LLCR). CFADS is the amount of cash available to service debt after payment of all essential operating expenses (equation 8.1, below, where O&M = operations and maintenance). DSCR is annual CFADS divided by the annual debt service. LLCR is equal to the present value of CFADS over the loan life, $PV(CFADS)$, divided by the outstanding debt. Since annual debt service and DSCR can be adjusted through structuring debt repayment schedules, our framework uses LLCR instead to determine the project's BC at financial close (equation 8.2, below). Lenders and underwriters generally use a very conservative forecast of demand to determine CFADS. LLCRs also vary widely based on whether the project is exposed to revenue risk. The required LLCR for CFADS with safe revenue is generally between 1.2 and 1.3, while the market LLCR for CFADS with revenue risk is generally between 1.5 and 1.9 (Khan and Parra, 2003).

$$CFADS = Forecasted\ Gross\ Revenue - O\&M\ Cost \quad (8.1)$$

$$BC = \frac{PV(CFADS)}{LLCR} \quad (8.2)$$

Government financial risk exposure

Fiscal support linked to project revenue risk may create contingent liabilities and claims for the government, which increases the challenge of public budgeting. In order to better meet overall fiscal constraints, a stochastic analysis is needed not only of the expected value, but also of the volatility of the government's financial exposure (Kim and Ryan, 2015a). The concept of value at risk (VaR) was first introduced to improve risk management in finance and insurance (Embrechts et al., 2013). It takes volatility into account and indicates a threshold loss value given a probability level (say P5, P10). The VaR of a government's budget – budget at risk (BaR) – provides a better view of government liabilities, and a more informed decision is possible, especially if a project's traffic forecast is optimistic. Therefore, BaR ($VaR[PV(CF_g)]$) is adopted as the primary indicator of government financial exposure, while expected value ($E[PV(CF_g)]$) is a secondary indicator. $PV(CF_g)$ is the present value of a government's cash flow, where a positive value denotes net cash inflow and a negative value indicates cash outflow:

$$\text{Government financial exposure} = \{VaR[PV(CF_g)], E[PV(CF_g)]\} \quad (8.3)$$

These two indicators can be calculated through stochastic modeling and Monte Carlo simulation.

BaR–BC comparative framework

To facilitate comparison, the indicators are combined in a two-dimensional coordinate space (see Figure 8.1). The BC is on the y-axis, illustrating the leverage or marginal benefit of government fiscal support. The BaR is on the x-axis, illustrating the maximum potential cost of fiscal support given a certain probability level, for example, 5 percent.

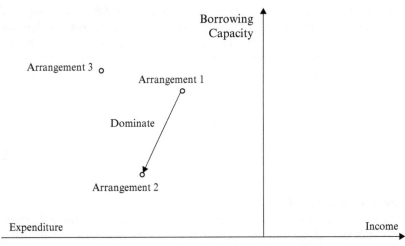

Source: Liu et al. (2017).

Figure 8.1 Fiscal support assessment framework – BaR versus BC

To illustrate the framework's comparative approach, three fiscal support mechanisms, Arrangements 1–3, are depicted in Figure 8.1. A point on the top right dominates a point on the bottom left; consequently, Arrangement 1 dominates Arrangement 2. However, a point on the top left and a point on the bottom right cannot be directly compared. For example, Arrangement 3 has a lower cost of financing than Arrangement 1, but government BaR is higher. In this case, other factors such as government's budget flexibility for this project and maximum debt to equity ratio required by lenders or applicable regulations are needed to narrow the range of feasible options. If Arrangement 3's BC exceeds the maximum debt ratio desired by the procuring agency, or the government BaR is higher than desired, then Arrangement 3 should be rejected since it offers more fiscal support than is necessary or affordable. However, if Arrangement 3 does not violate these other considerations, then further analysis between Arrangement 1 and 3 is needed. Non-financial issues such as transparency, accuracy of incentive mechanisms, regulatory difficulties, government's preferences, and so on, should be taken into consideration.

In practice, each fiscal support mechanism can have various structures. For example, MRGs can take annual minimum revenue thresholds of 70 percent, 80 percent, and so on, of forecasted revenue. The BC and government BaR with each support structure can be determined and plotted in this coordinate system. Figure 8.2 depicts a schematic of the range of outcomes for certain fiscal support mechanisms. On the y-axis, a base case depicts borrowing capacity when revenue risk is completely transferred to

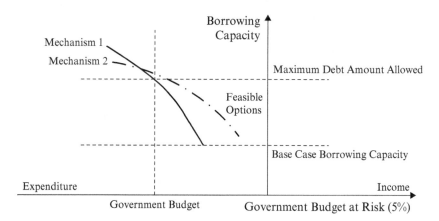

Source: Liu et al. (2017).

Figure 8.2 Illustrative comparison of fiscal support mechanisms

a concessionaire; a maximum acceptable leverage ratio constraint is also shown. On the x-axis, a range reflects a public agency's budget flexibility for given confidence interval. Combined, these create a two-dimensional space for feasible fiscal support option frontiers. A fiscal support mechanism frontier on the upper right will dominate a feasible frontier on the lower left. As illustrated in Figure 8.2, fiscal support Mechanism 2 is a better choice than Mechanism 1, given the conditions and constraints.

Illustration

The framework is further illustrated using a notional example. Presume that a public agency is considering three fiscal support mechanisms to mitigate a project's revenue risk in a toll-funded highway PPP: (1) an AP structure; (2) a flexible-term contract with a maximum duration plus possible government payback; and (3) an MRG combined with ERS. The public agency conducts or commissions the studies necessary to estimate the project's capital and operating parameters such as capital expense, LLCR, annual average daily traffic (AADT), traffic volatility, O&M expense, and so on. Further, it develops a stochastic model to forecast the project's revenue and formulates estimates of BC and BaR following the methodology of Liu et al. (2017) for a base case scenario where no fiscal support is offered and for each of the three fiscal support mechanism scenarios.

Sufficient simulations of the project's revenue are run, and probability distributions of $PV(CF_g)$ for each scenario are generated. Subsequently, BC and BaR (5 percent quantile of $VaR[PV(CF_g)]$) are calculated, and decision-makers identify an acceptable level of government exposure; these are plotted in the proposed framework's BaR–BC coordinate space in Figure 8.3, where BC is represented as the percentage of debt to capital.

For the presumed parameters, the public agency can evaluate the results of each scenario. First, the base case scenario does not expose the government monetarily, but its BC is quite low; the project is unlikely to attract private interest without some form of support. For instance, the agency could consider an up-front subsidy or credit enhancement if the other scenarios prove undesirable. Second, the flexible-term contract with a maximum duration scenario plus government payback is within the acceptable government exposure level, but it too has a low BC and as modeled this cannot be increased; similarly, this mechanism is not likely to draw lender or equity investor interest. Third, the MRG and ERS frontier depicted indicates that it has thresholds within the acceptable exposure level; lower guarantee (such as 65 percent of expected revenue)

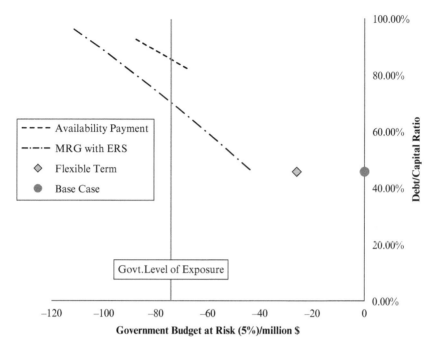

Figure 8.3 Hypothetical comparison of base case and alternative fiscal support scenarios

and higher revenue sharing (such as 135 percent of expected revenue) thresholds are in the lower right, while the opposite is in the upper left. Hence, the agency could opt for modest MRG and ERS levels and remain within its acceptable exposure range while possibly attracting private interest; in this circumstance, the relatively high BC and the possibility of capturing all of the net revenue up to the ERS threshold could entice private investors. Fourth, the AP frontier has the highest BC overall, and up to a point it outperforms any MRG with ERS structure; consequently, if the government can sustain appropriations of the necessary budgetary resources, then this is most likely the preferred mechanism under this set of project conditions.

Of course, the public agency will want to conduct sensitivity analysis of key parameters such as capital expense and revenue volatility to further evaluate the results; such tests will shift the outcomes associated with each mechanism. For instance, higher traffic volatility (and consequently revenue volatility) will shift the location of the frontiers for the MRG and ERS and AP scenarios, likely bringing them closer to one another.

Hence, if higher traffic volatility is plausible, then MRG and ERS may prove preferable to AP. Additionally, the formulation described in Liu et al. (2017) includes a coefficient parameter β ($0 \leq \beta \leq 1$) for the AP structure; this coefficient determines how much project toll revenue that the government commits toward funding the project versus directing it elsewhere: a value of 1 means complete commitment to the project, while a value of 0 means full diversion. Hence, an agency can assess the results based on how it plans to use the project tolls that it collects.

CONCLUSION

The proposed framework can help government agencies to evaluate the efficacy of alternative fiscal support mechanisms that mitigate revenue risk in PPP projects. Given the shifts under way in the US market and elsewhere, such decisions are increasingly important as governments conduct project planning and feasibility studies. The framework itself, and the formulation in Liu et al. (2017), relies on data that a PPP project's key stakeholders would have at hand during preliminary planning, so it is quite practical. Moreover, this is precisely when public agencies should consider what type of fiscal support, if any, to offer.

The "borrowing capacity" indicator assesses the marginal benefit of mitigating revenue risk for a fiscal support mechanism while the "government budget at risk" indicator estimates the cost of such fiscal support. Together, the indicators provide public agencies the ability to identify a potentially dominant support strategy as well as trade-offs between alternative strategies, while also taking into account the interests of PPP investors and debt providers. Certainly, additional refinements to the framework are possible, but it provides a basis for making better decisions about alternative fiscal support mechanisms for PPPs.

ACKNOWLEDGMENTS

The authors gratefully acknowledge the support for this research provided by the National Science Foundation Grant #1334292, the Stanford Global Projects Center, and the National Natural Science Foundation of China #71572089. All conclusions and opinions expressed are those of the authors and not of the National Science Foundation or the Global Projects Center.

NOTE

1. In the "Framework to Assess Fiscal Support Mechanisms" section, the subsections "Ability to raise financing," "Government financial risk exposure" and "BaR–BC comparative framework" are reused from Liu et al. (2017) with permission from the American Society of Civil Engineers (ASCE).

PART IV

The evolution of mature PPP institutional fields

As described in previous chapters, public–private partnerships (PPPs) pose difficult – even "wicked" – governance challenges. Among these, one of the most basic is the problems that are posed for managers attempting to craft a governance structure capable of combining the strengths (and weaknesses) of two differing forms of organizing: public and private. In Chapter 9, Casady, Eriksson, Levitt and Scott first spell out the quite fundamental differences represented by these two arrangements: the public systems privilege procedural rationality as they pursue controversial and often vague goals, while the private gives priority to achieving a quite specific set of outcomes and is rewarded for doing so efficiently. These represent vastly differing governing logics. This chapter also: (1) reminds us that contemporary public systems have begun to incorporate into their own structures elements from private systems; and (2) observes the wide variety of ways in which these two forms are being brought together in various combinations.

However, as currently constituted, PPPs create partnerships that attempt to respect the different roles played by public and private forms by incorporating components of each into a temporary project organization and company, termed a special purpose vehicle (SPV), that is charged with financing, designing, constructing, operating and maintaining a specific facility. As detailed in earlier chapters, each of the two types of partners brings both strengths and weaknesses to the project. The public side typically lacks technical expertise and is likely to be weak on contract negotiation and oversight skills. The private side lacks experience in dealing with multiple, legitimate stakeholders, including public representatives and private non-profit interest groups, and is likely to be unfamiliar with the volatility of public systems.

Other important types of challenges confronting PPPs described in earlier chapters include:

- the relatively long duration of projects – often extending up to 50 years from project conception to operational obsolescence;
- the dynamic nature of stakeholder involvement and relative influence as various types of staheholder participants come and go, their participation and power changing over the course of the project;
- the difficulties that project organizational forms generally confront in capturing and carrying forward lessons learned from one project to another.

To elaborate on this last challenge, it has often been observed that project organizations, including PPPs, suffer from being "one-off" organizations: structures constructed in order to plan, construct and operate a single facility or facility component. Combinations of participants, often from multiple companies, agencies and countries, are assembled by developers to design, produce and operate a specific chunk of infrastructure. Often these participants have no previous experience with one another and no expectation of continuing to work together beyond the span of a specific project. They may share no common history and often do not anticipate a shared future. For this reason, they have been described as being "learning disabled": unable to benefit from the experience of past shared interactions and unable to make full use of the lessons learned through their collaborative experience.

Ingredients for a solution to many of these types of problems besetting PPP project organizations have been developing gradually over the past three decades. Beginning in the 1990s in the United Kingdom (UK), steps were taken to address the lack of capacity within the public sector to plan and oversee public infrastructure projects with the creation of Private Finance Panels at the national level to identify and encourage the development of PPP projects (Allen, 2001). The structure was later replaced by Partnerships UK, a structure including both private and public officers, to facilitate the coordination of prospective and ongoing PPP projects (Farrugia et al., 2008). These ideas and organizing models were gradually diffused to other countries – primarily, former British colonies – and applied at both regional and national levels. Countries such as Australia, Canada and South Africa have spawned a variety of planning, coordinating and support systems to enable the sustained development of PPP programs. One of the factors facilitating success has been that these units shifted their attention from individual projects to programs: collections of projects which were evaluated and selected for their suitability, and reviewed and ranked for their feasibility and priority. Once launched, these coordinating agencies would offer project managers various types of technical, political and financial support. The chapters in Part IV provide an overview of some of these types of supporting structures.

As suggested by Casady and co-authors in Chapter 9, we can put these developments into a wider theoretical context. Organization theorists have long proposed the value of adopting an "organizational field" perspective, in which it is recognized that every type of organization operates in a broader framework consisting of other organizations – both similar and different. The field has been usefully defined as referring to other organizations similar to the focal organization, which it competes with and learns from, as well as to other different types of organizations which provide essential inputs or markets or exercise various support and oversight activities (see DiMaggio and Powell, 1983; Scott, 2014, Ch. 8). Fields are composed of organizations linked together in fateful relations and shared common meanings. While some kinds of fields remain somewhat fragmented and contested, others become more "structurated" over time, as relations become thicker and more important and as consensus increases regarding who does what and why. A "mature" field is one in which these patterns of relations, activities and meanings are settled: the nature of the common enterprise and the division of labor among participants is accepted as natural. Within some regions, as described in Chapter 9, a collection of organizations supporting PPPs have begun to develop into a mature field.

Jooste and Scott (2011) provide a more specific framing for these structures, depicting them as an "enabling field": a network of public and private organizations that, in combination, provide support and oversight of infrastructure projects within a given jurisdiction. These networks vary over time and across regions in their specific components and structural features, but provide a variety of services to projects. These include:

- undertaking research and disseminating PPP information and best practices;
- setting policy and proposing legislation on PPPs;
- proactively identifying projects and guiding their development;
- offering a variety of consulting services;
- funding PPP studies or project development;
- assisting in monitoring PPP contracts;
- capturing and retaining examples of best practice (Jooste and Scott, 2011, 381).

In this manner, these organizational systems help to overcome some of the governance challenges commonly confronting isolated project organizations.

In Chapter 10, Garvin assesses the institutional maturity of the United States (US) PPP infrastructure field in 2018, and suggests ways in which it could be further matured. Among his recommendations is the creation of a national enabling unit to prioritize and advance infrastructure development that would be comparable to Infrastructure Australia. In Chapter 11, Casady and Geddes propose the adoption and adaptation of a federal-regional framework of PPP-enabling organizations, similar to the federal and provincial or state infrastructure prioritization and "packaging" agencies that exist in Canada and Australia, that could facilitate and support the rational prioritization, selection, financing and delivery of both conventionally procured and PPP infrastructure projects in the US. Consequently, both of these chapters describe means for enhanced coordination, implementation and oversight of PPPs in the US.

9. (Re)assessing public–private partnership governance challenges: an institutional maturity perspective

Carter B. Casady, Kent Eriksson,
Raymond E. Levitt and W. Richard Scott

INTRODUCTION

Engineering project organization (EPO) is a specific field where "engineering, social science, business and public policy are integrated as foundational pillars within the context of infrastructure development" and used to meet multiple stakeholder objectives (Chinowsky, 2011, 3). Within this interdisciplinary research domain, "there remains a bias towards project-based research over broader issues within the [EPO] community" (Sakhrani et al., 2017, 17). One critical area of inquiry that remains understudied in the EPO field is the role of institutional maturity in infrastructure project governance. Institutional maturity represents well-developed norms, rules and cultural-cognitive beliefs involved in socio-economic development. Governance challenges which plague infrastructure development tend to stem from weak and conflicting institutional and organizational goals, norms and expectations (Scott et al., 2011). By their nature, infrastructure projects are burdened by economic and political uncertainty, distributional issues and prolonged environmental impacts.

The distinct project life cycle stages, diverse stakeholder networks (Hodge et al., 2010), high degrees of "broken agency" (Henisz et al., 2012), and unique, transaction-specific characteristics (Vining et al., 2005; Williamson, 1981, 1985) associated with infrastructure projects make them costly, complex, politically contentious and inherently challenging to execute (Boardman and Vining, 2012). From planning, design and construction through operations and maintenance, the changing composition and interaction of multiple stakeholders, skills and professions within infrastructure projects gives rise to complex organizational, political and social governance issues (Scott et al., 2011). When administered poorly, these projects are ripe for corruption and opportunism, both of which persistently threaten the governance, efficacy and transparency of infrastructure contracting (Spiller, 2011; Obermann, 2007). As a result, many researchers have shown in traditionally procured infrastructure projects that:

- infrastructure planners systematically overstate project benefits and underestimate costs (Flyvbjerg et al., 2002);
- engineers indemnify themselves against potential liability risks by producing overly conservative designs (Levitt et al., 1980);
- contractors both exploit design ambiguities to obtain contractual change orders that increase their remuneration and avoid additional investments that could improve project life cycle costs by building cheaply to meet minimum design specifications (Henisz et al., 2012); and
- governments favor building new infrastructure assets over maintenance investments, thereby increasing future repair and replacement costs (Bennon et al., 2017a).

In light of these governance challenges, collaborative institutional arrangements between the public and private sector known as public–private partnerships (PPPs) have emerged as an alternative project delivery mechanism to procure infrastructure assets. Public–private partnerships generally refer to long-term contracts between governments and private partners which "[bundle] together basic project-delivery functions, including facility design, construction, operation, maintenance, and financing, along with the transfer of significant infrastructure delivery-related risks to private partners" (Casady and Geddes, 2016, 1).

Around the world, PPPs have been widely touted for their ability to overcome some of the shortcomings of traditional infrastructure procurement and deliver benefits such as on-time and within-budget delivery, access to new forms of capital, novel financing solutions, design innovation, optimized risk sharing, and life cycle costing. However, these collaborative arrangements hold their own unique governance challenges. While previous research efforts in EPO have examined PPP governance issues in some detail (see, e.g., Mahalingam, 2010; Garvin, 2010), the role of institutions in the successful planning, execution and enforcement of PPPs remains largely understudied.

To address this knowledge gap, this chapter attempts to "broaden the [EPO] research agenda [and] break out of the confines of . . . more traditional engineering project topics" by tracking the evolution of institutional drivers affecting PPP governance (Sakhrani et al., 2017, 17). To do this, we first outline the institutional and organizational challenges involved in collaborative governance arrangements between the public and private sector. Then, we use this extant theory to define PPPs as a unique form of collaborative governance for infrastructure project delivery. Next, we employ an interdisciplinary, institutions-based analysis to examine the institutional maturity of the US PPP market. Finally, this chapter concludes by summarizing our theoretical contribution and offering a few normative recommendations for institutional reform of PPP governance in the United States.

INSTITUTIONAL AND ORGANIZATIONAL CHALLENGES IN COLLABORATIVE GOVERNANCE

While public and private governance systems are both inherently political systems defined by control and the use of power (Hult and Walcott, 1990), these systems are governed by distinct and conflicting institutions and organizations. In the starkest terms, private organizations engage in profit-making serving private interests, while public agencies serve the public interest providing common goods. Private firms are fundamentally guided by the market and search for business that generates a return on investment. The norms and rules of this system are governed and enforced by shareholders, corporate managers and board representatives through business relationships, contracts and fiduciary obligations, all in the name of commercial gain (Daily et al., 2003). Conversely, public sector entities strive to maximize public utility and preserve the public interest through legislation, regulation and adjudication (Bingham et al., 2005). Within the government bureaucracy, governance is overseen by elected officials and policy-makers and administered by program managers who must balance competing economic, environmental and social objectives.

Taken together, these differences between the public and private sector are further complicated by two additional factors. First, public organizations are generally expected to provide oversight over private organizations through corrective measures and incentives. Second, government agency goals and objectives tend to be more numerous, vague and conflicting than those found in private systems. Policy-makers and program managers working in public sector institutions define and scope problems, assess strategic options, analyze policy implications, and make decisions in the absence of certainty (Bell, 1985; Chamberlin and Jackson, 1987). This uncertainty and controversy causes the public sector institutions to focus on "the processes by which goals are established, challenged, and reestablished" rather than actual government outcomes (Hult and Walcott, 1990, 62). Some of the primary process values exhibited by public organizations include:

- Structured rationality: processes that incorporate relevant expertise and information into agency decision-making.
- Accountability: procedures that hold governing officials responsible for their actions.
- Representativeness: processes which enable affected stakeholders to participate in the shaping of policies.
- Legitimacy: public sentiment that assumes a given policy decision has been formulated in acceptable ways, through justifiable procedures (Hult and Walcott, 1990, 63–67).

In applying these processes, public agencies place great emphasis on the structure of rule-like frameworks and the development of "patterned ways in which to discover and articulate goals, select among means, and cope with uncertainty and controversy" (Hult and Walcott, 1990, 36). Through these processes and patterns of decision-making, agency formation and framework development provide structure for the surrounding institutional environment. However, this also explains why government agencies, unlike private companies, appear to be governed by constraints. Their priorities favor established rules, processes, norms and objectives more than performance outcomes and accomplishments. As a consequence, most public agencies operate "inefficiently." Many lack profit-maximizing incentives which promote efficient resource allocation and institutional goal alignment (Wilson, 1989).

Under pressure to become more efficient, public agencies are increasingly scrutinizing and revising their administrative objectives and decision-making processes. This process has been variously described as governments reinventing, downsizing, privatizing, devolving, decentralizing, deregulating or delayering. They are increasingly subjected to performance tests and are contracting out more of their traditional public sector responsibilities to private non-governmental actors (Salamon and Elliott, 2002, 1). Through broader engagement of private actors in public service provision, public sector organizations are seeking to promote higher levels of accountability and improve the range and depth of policy options considered in serving the public interest (Mashaw, 1985). This greater reliance on the expertise and organizational proficiency of private firms to execute certain public services is forcing public sector institutions to explore collaborative governance models such as public–private partnerships (Andrews and Entwistle, 2010). PPPs are inherently difficult to craft and execute because of extant differences in the goals, norms and beliefs of the public and private sectors (Bryson et al., 2006). Successful collaboration within these collaborative governance agreements thus requires reconciliation of their conflicting institutional and organization constructs. This is especially true in infrastructure project delivery, where the public and private sectors are not exclusive spheres of action but rather co-dependent domains, working together to successfully provide public services and solve complicated public problems (Salamon and Elliott, 2002). In the following section, we elaborate on this blending of public and private domains by discussing the collaborative governance challenges of infrastructure PPPs. We also touch upon factors which promote the institutional maturation of PPP-enabling environments.

INFRASTRUCTURE PUBLIC–PRIVATE PARTNERSHIPS: A UNIQUE COLLABORATIVE GOVERNANCE FORM

Public and private collaborative endeavors are not new (Wettenhall, 2003, 2005; Bovaird, 2004; Hodge and Greve, 2007). In fact, according to Kettl (1993, 4), "Every major policy initiative launched by the [United States] federal government since World War II – including Medicare and Medicaid, environmental cleanup and restoration, antipoverty programs and job training, interstate highways and sewage treatment plants and even security in post-conflict zones – has been managed through public–private partnerships." However, PPPs only emerged as a popular mechanism for governments to engage private firms in infrastructure project delivery after the United Kingdom's (UK) private finance initiative (PFI) during the early 1990s. Since then, governments around the world have been increasingly incorporating private sector expertise, resources and risk management proficiency into infrastructure project delivery through the use of public–private partnerships (PPPs). PPPs generally bundle various infrastructure project phases – including facility design, construction, financing, operations and maintenance – into long-term contracts with private consortiums. These contractual arrangements typically involve a significant transfer of risks from the public sector project sponsor to private, third-party actors and link remuneration to performance of the contracted service (Casady and Geddes, 2016, reprinted this volume, Chapter 11). Together, these two unique features of PPPs – bundling phases and taxpayer/private partner risk sharing – allow governments to holistically address multiple stages of the project life cycle without developing the technical, financial and physical resources needed to deliver and maintain these projects themselves. Depending on how public agencies construct these innovative procurement agreements, PPPs can take on a wide range of structures (see Figure 9.1).

Across the PPP spectrum, from design–build (DB) contracts to design–build–finance–operate–maintain (DBFOM) agreements and long-term

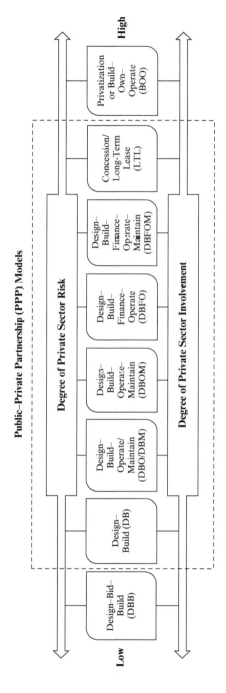

Figure 9.1 Spectrum of PPP model types

leases and concessions, governments must balance trade-offs between contractual incentives, project flexibility and institutional dynamism (Bennett and Iossa, 2006; Martimort and Pouyet, 2008; Iossa and Martimort, 2015). When properly executed, PPPs can deliver significant social value through life cycle costing, asset maintenance, and allocation of complex, infrastructure delivery-related risks to parties best positioned to manage those risks (Hodge et al., 2010; Engel et al., 2014). Some potential benefits of PPPs include design innovation, enhanced technological implementation, access to new pools of private capital, and better on-time and within-budget delivery (Hodge and Greve, 2007; Raisbeck et al., 2010; Lammam et al., 2013; Casady and Geddes, 2016).

Despite these documented benefits, PPPs can also create issues for public agencies. For example, a long-standing concern with PPPs continues to be the loss of flexibility associated with long-term contracts (Ross and Yan, 2015). As a procurement model, infrastructure PPPs characteristically exhibit high transaction costs and long tendering periods (KPMG, 2010; Reeves et al., 2017). Moreover, PPPs may not always provide the public sector and taxpayers with adequate value for money (VfM) (HM Treasury, 2012; Burger and Hawkesworth, 2011). In some cases, PPPs can even create budgetary problems for governments (Hellowell and Vecchi, 2015). Finally, PPPs, by their nature, force governments to engage private institutions in complex, co-dependent relationships, networks and exchanges over the provision and maintenance of public infrastructure assets (Grimsey and Lewis, 2007; Yescombe, 2011). Throughout these interactions, public sector entities must activate, orchestrate and maintain relevant stakeholder networks across the project life cycle while modulating contractual incentives to elicit publicly desired outcomes (South et al., 2015). PPPs thus "require, rather, aggressive management by a strong, competent government" (Kettl, 2011, 6). If governments lack the capacity to engage private firms in these complex, networked environments, successful planning, execution and stewardship of PPP contracts becomes especially challenging (Geddes and Reeves, 2017).

Therefore, PPP arrangements require strong political commitment and well-designed governance mechanisms that promote the public interest (Buxbaum and Ortiz, 2007). While successful stewardship of PPPs can be attributed to a variety of different factors (see, e.g., Grimsey and Lewis, 2007; Hodge and Greve, 2005; Yescombe, 2011; Levitt and Eriksson, 2016), effective PPP governance generally includes:

1. sophisticated, long-term, relational contracts to manage dynamic, multi-stage networks of diverse stakeholders such as designers, contractors, financiers and operators (see, e.g., Wettenhall, 2003);

2. standardized procurement laws and commercial transactions which maximize competitive tendering and minimize transaction costs (KPMG, 2010); and
3. a strong institutional environment supported by international best practices (Opara et al., 2017; Martin et al., 2013).

These factors, taken together, help broadly define a government's ability to develop a trustworthy network, regularly measure PPP performance, and successfully align public and private interests. However, this criterion is by no means exhaustive. Successful collaboration between public and private actors in PPP projects also depends heavily on accountability. Accountability is important because surrounding networks of actors and institutions ultimately condition collaboration between the public and private sectors (Bingham and O'Leary, 2014). These interactions shape the institutional environment surrounding PPP arrangements and may adversely influence the government's oversight capacity to promote fairness, transparency and contractual compliance (Kee et al., 2007). To avoid instances of corruption and regulatory capture, governments can track mutual influence, participation rights and transparency within PPPs along six dimensions: risk; costs and benefits; political and social impacts; expertise; collaboration; and performance measurement (Forrer et al., 2010). Using this framework, governments may be able to form an overarching alignment of public and private interests (Brinkerhoff, 2002; Brinkerhoff and Brinkerhoff, 2011).

Overall, public–private partnerships have grown in popularity around the world as an alternative infrastructure procurement model. While many governments globally have turned to PPPs in order to break the government monopoly on infrastructure development; inject competition and flexibility into infrastructure contracting; enhance the public sector's technical, financial and physical capacity to deliver projects; and improve infrastructure service quality, traditional infrastructure procurement methods still offer governments, in most projects, the ability to "[internalize] transactions, [minimize] legalisms involved in complex contractual negotiations with external actors, and [provide] a more stable framework for bargaining" (Salamon and Elliott, 2002, 31). PPPs should therefore not be regarded as a panacea for the shortcomings of traditional infrastructure provision. Governments should rather assess "the net gains to the public offered by [PPPs]" compared to governments' more traditional project delivery methods (Forrer et al., 2010, 482). In total, PPPs offer governments a unique alternative form of governance for infrastructure project delivery (Brinkerhoff, 2007; Greve and Hodge, 2010; Skelcher, 2010), one that requires proper safeguards and a mature institutional setting to ensure "public services are not compromised for the sake of private profits" (Forrer et al., 2010, 477).

GOVERNANCE CHALLENGES IN THE UNITED STATES: AN INSTITUTIONAL MATURITY ASSESSMENT

In markets where PPPs are successful, strong institutional platforms help to shape and deliver policy, prepare and procure projects, and manage and regulate project agreements (Farquharson et al., 2011). These institutional settings generally mature over time through the ongoing structuration of organizational fields (Scott and Meyer, 1994), and typically involve broad facilitating factors of PPP development such as "market potential, institutional guarantees, government credibility, financial accessibility, government capacity, consolidated management, and corruption control" (Yang et al., 2013, 301). Regulative and normative interactions, characterized by legislating, agency development and legal precedents, enhance the structural organization of PPP-enabling institutions by clarifying responsibilities, interfaces, procedures and processes both within and between market actors and the public sector. In leading PPP jurisdictions, such as Australia, Canada and the United Kingdom, as well as other countries across Europe, Asia and Latin America, this long-term structuration process across decades of projects has yielded significant cross-national differences in the institutional frameworks governing PPPs. Despite global trends toward procedural standardization, contract specification and elaboration of procurement details, many countries around the world still employ a wide variety of different PPP approaches and most lack national PPP models (Hodge, 2013; Siemiatycki, 2013). This diversity in the ongoing growth of PPP legislation and agency work across institutional settings has created distinct PPP-enabling fields within an elaborately networked and regulated market environment (Jooste and Scott, 2012).

While many leading PPP jurisdictions around the world have been successful in navigating the institutional dynamics of PPP project governance and established "mature systems of government regulation, as well as [normalized] market rules" (for example, Canada, Australia), weak institutions and scarce institutional capacity in other nations have made governance of the PPP process especially challenging (Wang et al., 2018, 296). In the United States (US) in particular, "[p]ublic procurement authorities often fail to appreciate the significant differences between PPPs and traditional forms of procurement and the implication of these differences for the level of resources, the unique skills, the output-based nature of the contracts, and the new processes and institutions required" (Farquharson et al., 2011, 23) Consequentially, the US lags far behind many leading PPP jurisdictions in the development of sufficient PPP project governance mechanisms at the federal, state and municipal levels.

This relatively slow adoption of the PPP procurement model in the United States is institutionally rooted (Geddes, 2011; Bennon et al., 2017a). Federal, state and local consensus on a clear PPP policy rationale, supported by robust legal, regulatory and investment frameworks, is inherently challenging because the distribution of powers and responsibilities of infrastructure provision in the US is significantly fragmented across different levels of government (Albalate et al., 2015). For example, historical bifurcation of infrastructure investment priorities between federal, state and municipal governments has created an unbalanced funding model which disincentivizes enhanced private investment in US infrastructure via PPPs. Election cycles accentuate the misalignment in federal, state and local investment priorities by creating political incentives that favor new infrastructure projects over adequate maintenance for existing infrastructure assets. This, coupled with the tax exemption for public bonds, has significantly tilted the playing field in favor of government financing, operations and maintenance of US infrastructure projects (Bennon et al., 2017a).

As a result, PPPs in the US have been executed on a relatively ad hoc basis. Wide variation in PPP governance exists across state lines, within specific infrastructure sectors, and amongst cities as well as some metropolitan transit agencies. The absence of cohesive project prioritization guidelines, uniform procurement procedures, standardized contracts and robust project pipelines has created an unstable policy environment devoid of the technical capacity, regulator autonomy, decision-making predictability and process transparency found in more mature PPP markets. Consequentially, the US has experienced limited adoption of the PPP model and a relatively uneven distribution of PPP procurements, concentrated predominantly in more populated states where larger markets exist for potential users or customers (Albalate et al., 2015). For instance, large states such as California, Virginia, Florida and Texas have each delivered upwards of ten PPP projects, while many others have yet to complete a single procurement (Istrate and Puentes, 2011; Geddes and Reeves, 2017). Moreover, some states trying to deliver experience and build confidence in their PPP procurement capacity have only been able to procure a handful of "pathfinder" projects (Bennon et al., 2017a). In total, the US's unique institutional setting, characterized by divergent national and regional priorities and dissimilar infrastructure processes, has hindered the widespread adoption of PPPs as an alternative means of infrastructure procurement.

Despite these institutional barriers, the use of PPP projects in the United States is continuing to grow. Between 1985 and 2016, roughly 498 PPP projects, with a value of $116.5 billion, were closed in the United States (PWF, 2017b; Geddes and Reeves, 2017). This total includes design–build (DB) projects which are not traditionally regarded as PPPs. Of this total, $48 billion has been invested in 36 DBFOM and long-term lease projects since 1993 (PWF, 2017c). This increased PPP activity is largely driven by ongoing economic, political and social consequences of the US's enormous infrastructure deficit. For instance, local jurisdiction debt-stress and tax burdens are forcing governments toward enhanced private involvement in infrastructure contracting (Albalate et al., 2015; Boyer and Scheller, 2017; Bel and Fageda, 2009). Moreover, increasing healthcare and pension obligations, declining discretionary budgets and growing public opposition to tax increases are exacerbating declines in federal, state and local funding for infrastructure investment (Cawley, 2013; DeCorla-Souza et al., 2013; Engel et al., 2014). Taken together, these challenging conditions have made the adoption of PPPs "a pragmatic rather than a political decision" (Albalate et al., 2017, 41).

To accommodate this growing pragmatism, PPP-enabling legal, regulatory and investment frameworks are emerging across the United States. At the federal level, legislative measures and supporting federal institutions have become increasing favorable toward PPP procurement (see Iseki et al., 2009 for a detailed assessment of PPP-enabling federal legislation). Within the US Department of Transportation, entire offices are now dedicated to promoting PPPs as an alternative infrastructure delivery mechanism. For example, the Federal Highway Administration's (FHWA) Office of Innovative Program Delivery (OIPD) offers technical guidance and public sector capacity support for innovative financing and project management arrangements such as public–private partnerships. Likewise, the passage of the Fixing America's Surface Transportation (FAST) Act in 2015 led to the creation of the Build America Bureau, an entity designed to serve as "the single point of contact and coordination for states, municipalities and project sponsors looking to utilize federal transportation expertise, apply for federal transportation credit programs and explore ways to access private capital in public private partnerships" (Build America Bureau, 2017). Operating under the Office of the Undersecretary for Transportation Policy, this nascent bureau replaced the Build America Transportation Investment Center (BATIC) and assumed responsibility for streamlining access to credit and grant opportunities as well as encouraging the adoption of best practices in project development, delivery, financing and management. Some of the Bureau's core responsibilities include:

1. centralized project coordination, project-level technical assistance and alternative project delivery assessment;
2. federal credit enhancement via the Transportation Infrastructure Finance and Innovation Act (TIFIA) and Railroad Rehabilitation and Improvement Financing (RRIF) direct loans, loan guarantees and standby lines of credit;
3. management of the tax-exempt Private Activity Bonds (PABs) program for prospective PPP concessionaires; and
4. administration of Infrastructure For Rebuilding America (INFRA) grants for projects that address critical issues on US highways and bridges (Build America Bureau, 2017).

Together, federal institutions such as the Bureau and OIPD work to encourage PPP use by addressing the aforementioned institutional barriers favoring traditional project delivery. While their role is paramount in the formation of a mature institutional setting for US PPPs, their influence should not be overstated. Because infrastructure provision happens primarily at the state and local levels, "developments at the federal level are often limited in scope and effect and typically provide only general guidelines for PPP implementation" (Geddes and Reeves, 2017, 159).

Naturally, laws and agency formation at the state and local levels have a more direct effect on the US's institutional capacity to engage in PPPs. This is evidenced by the ongoing proliferation of general administrative law, sector regulations and specifically stipulated PPP contract provisions across the United States (Queiroz and Lopez Martinez, 2013). In 2017, 35 states, the District of Columbia and one US territory had enacted PPP statutes (see Figure 9.2).

While the adoption and favorability of PPP-enabling laws has typically followed local demand-side, supply-side, and political and institutional drivers such as state debt and urban travel demand (Geddes and Wagner, 2013; Albalate et al., 2017; Boyer and Scheller, 2017), rather than traditional public finance considerations such as federal highway aid (Geddes and Wagner, 2013), the implementation of these statutes has not been consistent. Widespread variation currently exists between state-level PPP-enabling environments. Depending on how the institutional framework surrounding PPP procurement is structured, these statutes can either provide a supportive environment for PPP procurement or undermine PPP activity. Overall, difficulties associated with balancing contractual flexibility and public-interest protections have created large disparities in PPP favorability between states (Geddes and Reeves, 2017; Iseki et al., 2009). Despite these challenges, a growing body of procurement law and jurisprudence across the US is slowly laying the legal and regulatory foundation for a successful US PPP market.

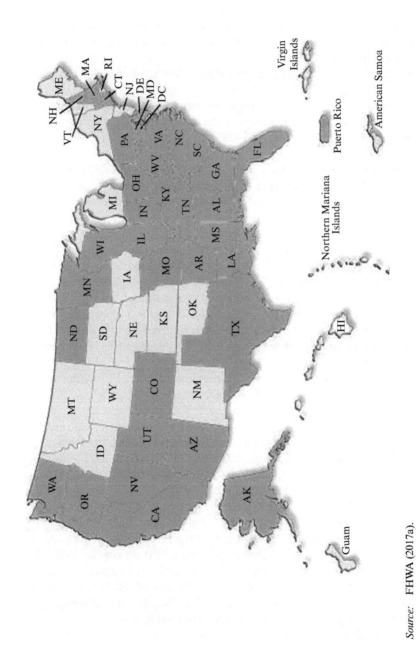

Source: FHWA (2017a).

Figure 9.2   PPP-enabling legislation across the United States

To complement these ongoing legal and regulatory developments, PPP-enabling organizations are also beginning to develop at the state and municipal level. For example, a handful of states and some municipalities (including Virginia, California, Washington, Michigan, Oregon, Colorado, Georgia and Washington, DC) have established PPP units to promote procurement accountability, standardization and transparency. Typically found in leading PPP jurisdictions, these units are designed to provide stewardship through the PPP procurement process by assisting governments with project scoping, performance specification, business case development, identification and allocation of risks, market sounding, bid evaluation and selection, and contract monitoring, among other project delivery tasks (Istrate and Puentes, 2011). When appropriately structured, PPP units enable governments to navigate the complexities of PPP proceedings with greater consistency, transparency and legitimacy. Since the development of PPP units across states, territories and municipalities is still in its infancy, the US should consider establishing PPP units on a regional and national level to capture some economies of scale and avoid duplicating institutional capacity across states and localities (Casady and Geddes, 2016).

In summary, the US PPP market continues to face significant institutional challenges. The slow development and maturation of PPP-enabling institutions, governance frameworks and public organizational structures has created an all-too-common impediment hindering the widespread adoption of PPPs as an alternative procurement model (Bennon et al., 2017a). While progress is being made in some areas at the federal, state and local levels, many private firms and public agencies still do not believe current US institutions (for example, laws, rules, social norms and policy) offer enough incentives, transparency and accountability for the US to successfully deliver a coordinated PPP program (Geddes and Reeves, 2017). The prevalence of inconsistent PPP procurement procedures, dissimilar legal and regulatory environments across state lines, and minimal use of PPP-enabling organizations such as PPP units, are just some of the many ongoing institutional challenges affecting PPP project development and governance in the US PPP market. In order for the US to improve its PPP governance capacity and mature into the world's largest PPP market, more US public agencies at the federal, state and municipal levels will need to address existing knowledge gaps, share and adopt international best practices, and "reform institutions or build new organizations to assess and manage new models for infrastructure procurement and assets management" (Bennon et al., 2017a, 24; Boyer, 2016).

CONCLUSIONS

The field of engineering project organization has traditionally confined itself to more conventional, project-based engineering topics (Sakhrani et al., 2017). In doing so, this interdisciplinary domain has neglected broader issues affecting infrastructure project governance. One area in particular that has garnered relatively little attention is the role of institutional maturity in successful governance of public–private partnerships. Our research addresses this gap in the EPO literature in the following ways. First, we document the differing institutional and organization constructs in the public and private sector which make collaborative governance agreements between them challenging to execute. Next, we draw upon this extant theory to define PPPs as a unique form of collaborative governance for infrastructure project delivery. More specifically, we articulate how public agencies pursuing PPP contracts must navigate diverse organizational forms, competing stakeholder interests, and complex regulative, normative and cultural-cognitive domains, all while upholding the public interest. Finally, this chapter highlights the critical role that institutional maturity plays in the successful planning, execution and enforcement of PPP contracts. By applying this interdisciplinary theoretical perspective to the US PPP market, our research efforts offer a broad institutional assessment of the public sector's capacity to effectively steward PPP projects. Moreover, this assessment highlights various institutional deficiencies across the United States that require further development and reform.

Overall, PPP projects, in the US and around the world, present governments with a unique governance task. Public sector institutions facing vague, competing and dynamic policy objectives are increasingly using PPPs to overcome shortcomings in traditional project delivery and to enhance their technical, financial and physical resource capacity to execute large, complex infrastructure projects. While PPPs offer some attractive potential benefits for governments such as on-time and within-budget delivery, life cycle asset maintenance, design innovation and enhanced access to private capital, these alternative procurement mechanisms also contain embedded challenges across many stages of the project life cycle, from planning, design and construction through to financing, operations and maintenance. High transaction costs, long procurement timelines, budgetary problems and lost government flexibility are just some of the issues that can arise from PPP contracting. These problems ultimately stem from a lack of maturity in the underlying institutional environment. Evaluating the institutional maturity of diverse PPP markets thus serves as a powerful tool for isolating PPP governance shortcomings and identifying areas for institutional reform.

NORMATIVE RECOMMENDATIONS FOR INSTITUTIONAL REFORM IN THE US PPP MARKET

Successful PPP governance requires an enabling institutional setting that promotes efficient and equitable delivery of infrastructure assets while safeguarding the public interest. Leading PPP jurisdictions such as Canada, Australia and the UK have undergone extensive institutional maturation processes to promote robust environments for successful PPP governance. In all of these jurisdictions, elaborate legal structures, economic policies and social norms have emerged to help balance the inherently conflicting interests of public and private actors. These mature settings typically have:

1. clear policy rationales for PPPs;
2. streamlined PPP legislation;
3. transparent approval processes;
4. robust project pipelines;
5. consistent frameworks for project selection, preparation and procurement;
6. standardized commercial contracts;
7. clear dispute resolution procedures; and
8. multiple PPP units managing the preparation, solicitation and evaluation of PPP bids (Farquharson et al., 2011).

In contrast, US institutional capacity for PPPs remains in its infancy. The absence of an enabling institutional environment for PPPs in the United States is largely driven by the public sector's lack of political will, project preparation capacity, and trust in the private sector to properly design and structure PPP projects. The US can improve its institutional capacity for PPPs by "establish[ing] clear, predictable and legitimate institutional framework[s] supported by competent and well-resourced authorities" (OECD, 2012, 8; see also World Bank and DFID, 2009). For a more detailed review of PPP governance mechanisms, see World Bank and DFID (2009) as well as OECD (2012).

Institutional reforms that could immediately improve PPP governance in the United States might include, but not be limited to:

1. enhanced political commitment to PPPs as an alternative delivery mechanism;
2. overarching policy guidance and sector-specific models "that may respond, in a logical, consistent, and consultative way, to inevitable changes in policy and the market" (Farquharson et al., 2011, 19);

3. consistent PPP legislation and procurement procedures at the federal, state and local levels;
4. transparent infrastructure project prioritization using non-partisan, expert panels; and
5. adoption and utilization of PPP advisory units at the regional and national level.

These recommendations are representative of more mature PPP markets, and the "US can capitalize on the tested experience of its international counterparts" to implement them (Garvin, 2010, 402). However, careful consideration must also be given to the transferability of PPP international best practices (Acerete et al., 2015). This is especially true at the state and local levels, where more research is needed on the localized development of PPP-enabling institutions (Boardman et al., 2015; see also Van den Hurk et al., 2016). Additionally, if PPPs are going to be successful in the United States, further work is required on comprehensive performance metrics for public–private partnerships (Boardman et al., 2005). Overall, successful PPP governance in the United States requires public agencies to close the knowledge gap, adopt international best practices, and establish credible processes supported by an enabling institutional environment. While PPPs should not be expected to solve all of America's infrastructure needs, these alternative procurement mechanisms have a specific role to play in delivering needed infrastructure across the United States.

10. Transportation public–private partnership market in the United States: moving beyond its current state

Michael J. Garvin

INTRODUCTION

At the outset of the twenty-first century, the public–private partnership (PPP) market in the United States (US) seemed on the cusp of growth. Factors such as infrastructure systems in need of modernization and expansion, government agencies searching for new sources of capital, capable domestic and international private enterprises ready to do business, and private sources of equity and debt attracted by attributes of infrastructure investments were converging to heighten optimism about the US market. The economic recession of 2008–2009, however, altered the infrastructure discourse. "Shovel-ready" projects became more important than prospective PPPs. The crisis slowed or stopped financial markets. To stimulate a recovery, the American Recovery and Reinvestment Act of 2009 allocated monies across multiple economic sectors, with $48 billion available for transportation infrastructure and $27 billion committed to highways (Recovery, 2009). States were required to obligate 50 percent of allocated highway funds by 120 days (USDOT, 2009); all 50 states met this aggressive deadline (Lew and Porcari, 2017). In addition, the Transportation Investment Generating Economic Recovery (TIGER) Discretionary Grants program made $1.5 billion available for high-impact transportation projects, while up to $200 million was allocated to the Transportation Infrastructure Finance and Innovation Act (TIFIA) credit program. The TIGER program was sustained annually through 2017, and it was typically oversubscribed (Lew and Porcari, 2017). In 2018, TIGER was replaced by the Better Utilizing Investments to Leverage Development (BUILD) Transportation Discretionary Grants program; BUILD grants were essentially the same as those of its predecessor, and applications for

FY18 funding were due in July 2018. Plus, the continuing significance of the TIFIA program for transportation infrastructure projects is well known.

Other federal initiatives were started as the nation endured the recession. For instance, the Federal Highway Administration created the Office of Innovative Program Delivery, which continues to provide resources to the transportation community to enhance delivery strategies; now, one of its four centers is the Center for Innovative Finance Support – which works with the US Department of Transportation's Build America Bureau – where special emphasis is given to PPPs. Further, market activity aided by federal support did continue. For example, Florida's I-595 Express project was financed by $781 million in bank loans, a $681 million TIFIA loan and $208 million in equity; an indicator that the capital markets would support strong projects (Halai, 2009). Subsequently, nine additional US highway PPP projects reached financial close from late 2009 through 2013, with private equity investment and TIFIA loans totaling over $2.4 billion and $3.8 billion, respectively (PWF, 2017a).

Yet, more recent transaction flow in the US highway PPP market has remained modest at best. In 2014 and 2015, three projects reached financial close each year, only one closed in 2016 and only two closed in 2017. Certainly, the recession made public officials and investors more cautious, and possibly the mixed track record of PPPs tempered activity. Further, some public and private institutions and organizations do not see major issues with the US infrastructure delivery and financing system; rather, it just needs its funding stream multiplied. Seemingly, such interests were bolstered during the 2016 election campaign when then candidate Trump proposed to invest $1 trillion in improving America's infrastructure if elected. When the Trump administration presented its FY 2018 budget, however, only $200 billion in direct federal infrastructure funding over the next ten years was included (ARTBA, 2017; Reinhardt, 2017a). In fact, the administration's goal is to leverage federal funds to incentivize non-federal investments that will total $1 trillion through its Infrastructure Initiative (White House, 2017). Two of the Infrastructure Initiative's four principles are to give state and local governments incentives to generate their own resources and to leverage private funds through PPPs. So, the Trump infrastructure plan places local autonomy and PPPs at the forefront, though key details are still not settled (Davis and Kelly, 2017; Reinhardt, 2017a).

Thus, the US has traveled a rather unique path over roughly the last two decades to wind up again at a point where PPPs perhaps are poised to emerge as one cornerstone of infrastructure development. A key question is whether state and local agencies are prepared to implement such arrangements. In the transportation sector, 35 states, the District of

Columbia and Puerto Rico currently have enabling legislation allowing some form of PPPs, but only a handful are active and fewer are experienced. Inexperienced public agencies are certainly at a disadvantage compared to seasoned consultants or private infrastructure developers. Hence, a broader and deeper understanding of PPP arrangements for infrastructure remains essential if public agencies expect to engage the private sector productively in infrastructure provision. Accordingly, this chapter revisits an appraisal of the US transportation market in 2009, which drew on the author's experience with PPP cases and participation in a scanning tour of international PPP programs in 2008. The chapter proceeds as follows. First, following some brief background information, it presents a refined framework to differentiate project delivery and PPP models from one another to further enhance understanding of these arrangements. Second, it reconsiders international PPP policies and practices in place in 2008 to assess their relevance to the current state of practice in the US; importantly, the US market has made strides in the last decade, but international experience remains quite salient to the path forward. Finally, recommendations for action in the US are renewed to reflect lessons learned from international experience as well as recent market developments.

BACKGROUND

PPP literature has increased as adoption of this approach to infrastructure development has grown, and publications may be found in archival, institutional and popular sources (e.g., Hodge and Greve, 2007; Kwak et al., 2009; Wang, 2015; World Bank, 2014; OECD, 2012; Thornton, 2007; Fitzgerald, 2015). Archival topics have ranged from general characteristics of PPPs to quantitative methods for mitigating revenue risk. Institutional sources have generally focused on policy and implementation guidelines. Finally, popular literature includes periodicals that focus on project or public finance. For instance, a popular business magazine ran a story about the long-term leases of the Chicago Skyway and the Indiana Toll Road, speculating about the potential value of such arrangements for infrastructure assets (Thornton, 2007). More recently, such leases have been rebranded as "asset recycling," and they are again in the debate as a means to fund needed infrastructure investments (Poole, 2017).

Given the literature available, what is the merit of this chapter? First, it has an American perspective that is based on the author's knowledge of cases of contemporary PPP-type arrangements shown in Table 10.1 as well as America's infrastructure history (Garvin, 2007a). Further, the information about PPPs collected during the international scan of Australia,

Table 10.1 Case histories in the US and Canada

First generation cases	Second generation cases
AB 680 Projects (CA)	407 ETR: Solicitation 2 (Canada)
Santa Ana Viaduct Express	Chicago Skyway Lease (Chicago, IL)
SR 91 Express Lanes	Eagle P3 (Denver, CO)
SR 125	East End Crossing (IN)
Mid-State Tollway	Elizabeth River Tunnels (VA)
Confederation Bridge (Canada)	Hudson-Bergen Light Rail System (NJ)
Cedar River Water Treatment Plant (Seattle)	I-4 Ultimate Improvements (FL)
	I-495 Capital Beltway Express (VA)
Dulles Greenway (VA)	I-595 Express Lanes (FL)
407 ETR: Solicitation 1 (Canada)	I-77 HOT Lanes (NC)
Pocahontas Parkway: Development (VA)	I-81 Improvements (VA)
	Indiana Toll Road Lease (IN)
Tolt River Water Treatment Plant (Seattle)	JFK AirTrain (New York City)
	Lake Pleasant Water Treatment Plant (Phoenix)
	North Tarrant Express (TX)
	Pocahontas Parkway: Lease (VA)
	SH-130: Segments 5 and 6 (TX)
	South Bay Expressway (CA)

Source: Adapted from Garvin (2010).

Portugal, Spain and the United Kingdom provides recent perspectives of more than 50 active public and private sector market participants. Finally, the original account is reassessed for its relevance to present-day circumstances in the US. Hence, the chapter provides a pragmatic account of the current state of US practice relative to international experience.

DEFINING PUBLIC–PRIVATE PARTNERSHIPS

Despite an increasing transition into the mainstream, PPPs are still loosely defined and often mischaracterized. Currently, the Federal Highway Administration (FHWA) (2017b) defines PPPs as: "contractual agreements between a public agency and a private entity that allow for greater private participation in the delivery of transportation projects. Typically, this participation involves the private sector taking on additional project risks, such as design, construction, finance, long-term operation, and traffic revenue." Vives (2008) considers PPPs as any arrangement for service between the public and private sectors, whereas Savas (2000) qualified PPPs as arrangements between governments and private entities where traditional public services are performed by the private sector; his perspective is comparable to the FHWA's present definition. While narrower than the characterization by Vives, both are quite broad.

Many definitions characterize PPPs as long-term, contractual arrangements between the public and private sectors. The attention here on a definition of PPPs is motivated by the continued need to create a shared understanding of what they are, based on positive analysis of PPP policies, practices and projects. A slight modification to prior definitions proposed by the author (Garvin, 2007b; Garvin and Bosso, 2008) is suggested: "an infrastructure public–private partnership is a long-term contract between the public and private sectors where mutual benefits are sought and where the private sector at least provides operations and maintenance services and puts private [equity] at risk." The definition is based on perspectives gained during the scanning tour as well as recent literature on the topic. For instance, public and private officials in the countries visited during the scanning tour described programs and projects that aligned with this definition. Further, Yescombe (2011), among others, characterizes PPPs as long-term contracts where asset development and service provision are combined, and a special purpose company arranges the financing that typically is a mix of equity from the company's sponsors and debt provided by bonds or commercial loans. Notably, the definition excludes design–build, design–build–finance and the sale of infrastructure assets to the private sector. While presenting some unique challenges, design–build is a derivative of design–bid–build, while design–build–finance only adds the provision of short-term financing to a private entity's scope of services. An asset sale is "privatization," which is an important distinction. PPPs are governed by contracts and contract law, whereas privatized infrastructure is owned by regulated enterprises where public commissions have significant governing authority.

At the project level, PPPs could easily be considered as project or service delivery systems; a shift that might prove beneficial. Figure 10.1 then would aid in distinguishing between delivery systems. Adapted from Miller's (1995) quadrant system, the vertical axis considers the payment mechanism for project services, ranging from owner payment to user fees, and the horizontal axis reflects life cycle activities from segregated to integrated. Greater integration increases the risk borne by service providers, since a single entity responsible for all life cycle activities takes substantially more risk than independent providers of each life cycle activity. Further, shading is used to delineate who is responsible for arranging a project's financing. While a project's payment mechanism and life cycle activities

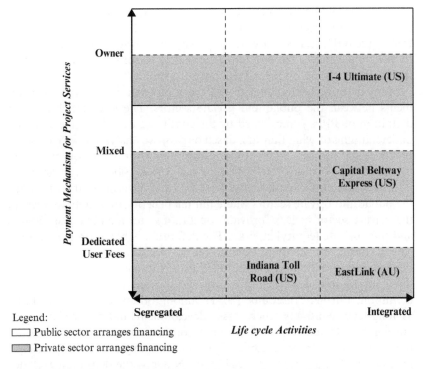

Figure 10.1 Framework to distinguish project/service delivery systems

will fall along a continuum, an 18-cell matrix is illustrated to simplify plotting any delivery approach based on where project payments for the project originate, how integrated life cycle activities are, and which sector is responsible for arranging the financing.

Several projects are plotted to illustrate the framework. The I-4 Ultimate project in Florida is a design–build–finance–operate–maintain (DBFOM) arrangement with direct payments from the government based primarily on service availability, that is, availability payments (APs). It plots in the shaded portion of the upper right cell of the framework. The Capital Beltway Express in Virginia is also a DBFOM arrangement where the concessionaire arranged the financing and is collecting user fees as payment for its services; however, it also received a significant public capital contribution (more than $400 million) to fund the project, so it plots in the shaded portion of the middle right. The EastLink project in Australia is another DBFOM delivery where the concessionaire arranged the financing, but it is relying solely on tolls as payment for services situating it in the shaded lower right. The Indiana Toll Road plots in the shaded portion of the bottom middle cell since the concessionaire is leasing an existing toll road from the public authority; it arranged the financing, payments are solely from existing tolls and life cycle activities are somewhat integrated because the leasing consortium must operate and maintain the roadway while implementing periodic rehabilitation and targeted capital improvements. The PPP label is likely here to stay, but Figure 10.1 is still useful to differentiate PPPs by their project delivery characteristics.

INTERNATIONAL PRACTICE AND US STATE OF PRACTICE

Policies and practices in place in Australia, Portugal, Spain and the United Kingdom (UK) in 2008–2009 were documented during the scanning tour; for brevity, these nations are henceforth referred to collectively as "the nations visited." Several practices in place in 2008–2009 are characterized; subsequently, the current state of practice in the US is considered to gauge where America stands comparatively roughly a decade hence.

International Practice[1]

Project identification
A common attribute among the nations visited was the importance of long-term transportation and highway plans in their capital programming process. PPP candidate projects were typically identified from requirements in each country's overall master plan. Another common perspective was that projects with reasonable to significant scale and complexity were viewed as PPP candidates. For instance, in the United Kingdom a Private Finance Initiative (PFI) strategy was considered first for any major highway scheme (or plan) exceeding £7.5 million. However, schemes valued at less than £100 million were likely to offer better value if delivered conventionally. While scale can offset the substantial transaction costs involved in these projects, both attributes are likely to introduce meaningful risks throughout a project's life cycle. Long-term risk assumption by the private partner was seen as a driver of innovative project concepts and solutions.

Project analysis and selection
The United Kingdom and Australia employed similar methods for analyzing and selecting projects for PPP delivery. Each developed quantitative estimates for a conventional approach, called a Public Sector Comparator (PSC), and for a PPP approach. Subsequently, a value-for-money (VfM) analysis was conducted to determine whether VfM was generated,

contrasting the PPP strategy against the PSC; if so, a PPP strategy was followed. This philosophy is succinctly explained by Froud (2003) in that value for money can only be achieved in a PPP if private sector expertise, innovation, competitive efficiency and risk transfer can overcome the increased transaction, contracting and negotiation costs – not to mention the additional need for economic profit. VfM/PSC analysis methods are somewhat controversial. Comments from UK elected officials are illustrative of concerns about such methods:

> To justify the PFI option, departments have relied too heavily on public sector comparators. These have often been used incorrectly as a pass or fail test; have been given a spurious precision which is not justified by the uncertainties involved in their calculation; or have been manipulated to get the desired result. (Committee of Public Accounts, 2003)

Despite such criticism, the methodology does promote use of a systematic and auditable process, as opposed to an expedient or politically motivated one, for making a project delivery decision.

Neither Portugal nor Spain followed VfM methods. Each country conducted a feasibility analysis during project planning to determine whether most of a project's market risks were transferable to the private sector. If so, then a project was likely to move forward as a PPP. Additional assessments were done of the expected rate of return. If the expected rate was too high or too low, then the government would modify the project by either increasing a project's scope to lower the rate or including subsidies or other types of financial support to increase the rate.

Procurement regulations

Portugal, Spain and the UK operated under the standards and procedures for public procurement of the EU. Generally, the basic principles are comparable to those of the United States that encourage fair competition and selection of the most economically advantageous offer. Procurements may be open, restricted, negotiated, or a competitive dialogue. In an open procurement, bids from interested parties are received after a public notice, whereas in a restricted procurement bids are submitted by invited parties. Use of negotiated and competitive dialogue procurements is by exception. A negotiated procedure is allowed when the nature of the work and its risks precludes effective pricing at the time of submission of bids. Hence, a binding proposal is made after the parties have negotiated a project's scope and conditions; the proposal is then evaluated according to stated criteria. A competitive dialogue is permissible when a public agency cannot adequately scope a project itself due to its complexity. Chosen participants dialogue about the project's scope until a preferred participant is selected.

In Australia, each state had jurisdiction over its procurement process subject to national policies and regulations.

Procurement processes
The principal difference in procurement processes between the nations visited was the extent of negotiation, where Spain employed the least and the UK the most. Spain used an "open competition" model devoid of negotiations. The government typically issued a call for tenders, and interested parties submitted binding and compliant proposals. Respondents could offer up to three alternatives to their base proposal. No discussion between the government and proposers occurred beyond standard requests for clarification or information. An award was based on the most economically advantageous tender.

Alternatively, the UK typically employed a negotiated procedure, although its PFI policy also permitted restricted and competitive dialogue. The mix of in-house staff and consulting advisors involved depended on project complexity and scale. Primary stages of the process were: pre qualification, tender and contract award. The tender stage typically involved: (1) issuing of tender documents, including a model contract, an "illustrative design" to demonstrate a feasible design solution, and draft contract schedules; (2) disseminating tender circulars and responses to queries; (3) submission and assessment of tenders; and (4) identification of the provisional preferred bidder (PPB) and subsequently the preferred bidder. Negotiations between the public sector and tenderers occurred over contract provisions and technical requirements. Once negotiations concluded, tenderers submitted proposals in accordance with the revised contract.

Demand risk
Demand or market risk is often problematic in PPP arrangements since forecasting traffic volumes *ex ante* is complicated by multiple factors. The philosophies observed in Spain and Australia offered an interesting contrast to its treatment. Spanish law allowed the government to establish a threshold for a specific demand-risk variable and bidders to propose upper and lower boundaries; additionally, a limit for the lower boundary was usually set to ensure that bidders assumed meaningful demand risk. If actual conditions turn out different from the expected conditions, the contract could be rebalanced by adjusting pre-established parameters such as the toll rate. For instance, an arrangement could select gross revenue for the threshold and the toll rate and the contract's duration as parameters for adjustment. Further, 80 percent of the annual gross revenue forecast could be established for the lower boundary. If the winning bidder proposed

upper and lower boundaries of 130 percent and 70 percent, then as long as actual annual gross revenue falls within this range no changes would be made. However, if actual gross revenue falls below 70 percent, then a rebalancing occurs. An option may be to raise the maximum toll rate until gross revenue increases back into the established boundaries. Similarly, if actual gross revenue exceeds the upper boundary, then a rebalancing action is triggered. Vassallo and Gallego (2005) provide more detailed discussion of this demand-risk handling approach.

In Australia, the philosophy regarding demand risk was quite different. All highway PPPs through 2009 in New South Wales, Victoria and Queensland were pure tolled projects. All were structured so that private investors, both equity and debt-holders, would take the downside market risks. In other words, if revenues or rates of return do not turn out as anticipated, then private investors bear the consequences. Investors and lenders generally accepted these conditions and had confidence that the market could remedy financial hardships through restructuring financing arrangements. More recent contracts, however, included sharing provisions between the government and the concessionaire should the upside exceed predefined thresholds. This precludes "windfall" gains by the concessionaire.

An issue related to the demand risk is competing or parallel facilities. In the nations visited, protections afforded the private sector for competing facilities were modest but disclosed. In some instances, an alternative free route was required if the PPP highway facility was tolled as a matter of policy. Usually, governments had the right to proceed with any highway network expansion or enhancement identified in its long-range transportation plan. However, the trend was toward defining within the contract what rights the government had in the vicinity of a highway facility. For instance, a contract would identify particular corridors or roads that the government was free to expand or improve. This practice delineated what flexibility the government had and established conditions that private concessionaires could take into account when developing their proposals.

Performance measures

Unquestionably, performance measures or key performance indicators (KPIs) were central to the most recent PPP projects in the nations visited. Each country utilized KPIs to generate the outcomes that it desired for its PPP projects, and they were the basis for incentives and penalties – primarily during the operations phase of a project. For instance, Spain used KPIs to manage safety, heavy vehicles, congestion, winter weather conditions and toll collection times, as well as other elements. In a particular contract, the concessionaire was required to sustain adequate driving conditions during winter weather; if road closures were mandated or tire chains were required, then fines of €1800/hour or €600/hour would be levied. In Victoria, Australia's EastLink PPP, the government's KPI regime focused on customer service, road maintenance, landscape and environment, and tolling accuracy. If performance thresholds were not met, the concessionaire was at risk financially up to $17 million annually. The concessionaire was required to distribute any abatement amounts to EastLink's customer account holders in the form of toll credits, rather than paying them back to the government. Although ConnectEast – the concession company formed to develop, finance and manage Eastlink – was sold to new owners in 2011, these conditions remain in place until the contract expires in 2043.

US State of Practice

Project identification and analysis

Today, a number of public agencies in the US use qualitative screening guidelines to identify candidate PPP projects; common criteria are whether a candidate addresses priorities in state, regional or local transportation plans and has sufficient complexity (VDOT, 2017). Moreover, the Center for Innovative Finance Support in the Office of Innovative Program Delivery of the US Federal Highway Administration (FHWA) has developed the P3-SCREEN tool to aid public agencies in assessing whether a project is plausible for delivery as a PPP; one of its key assessments is consistency of a project with an agency's long-range transportation plans (FHWA, 2018a).

Similarly, the impetus in the US is toward increased utilization of VfM-based techniques. Over the past few years, FHWA has created the P3-VALUE analytical tool to introduce practitioners to VfM analyses (FHWA, 2018a). In addition, states that are active in the market, such as Indiana and Virginia, describe quantitative assessment procedures for PPPs in their implementation guidelines, including the use of VfM-like methods (INDOT, 2013; VDOT, 2017). Several high-profile PPPs have also published VfM studies such as the I-595 Improvements project in Florida and the Presidio Parkway-Phase II project in California. Hence, the US has moved toward adoption of techniques like those used in Australia and the UK. These, however, warrant caution: the techniques are somewhat complicated and subject to manipulation.

Regulatory frameworks

Currently, the US lacks anything comparable to the overarching regulatory framework found in the EU. In 2017, 35 US States, the District of Columbia and Puerto Rico had legislation in place enabling PPPs in the

Table 10.2 Key elements of US transportation PPP-enabling legislation

Item	Jurisdictions
Allows conversion of existing roads to toll roads	15 (40.5%)
Limits duration of PPP agreement	18 (48.6%)
Prohibits non-compete provisions or requires alternative routes	11 (29.7%)
Requires state legislative approval, review or other involvement	28 (75.7%)
Requires approval, review or other involvement by other entities	27 (73.0%)
Establishes a public PPP advisory body	12 (32.4%)
Allows solicited and unsolicited proposals	22 (59.5%)
Requires request for competing proposals or other process for unsolicited proposals	19 (51.3%)
Specifies evaluation criteria for PPP proposals	17 (45.9%)
Allows for multiple types of procurement	19 (51.4%)

Source: Adapted from Pula (2016).

transportation sector (alternatively, 15 US states had no legislation). The enabling statutes vary quite a bit from jurisdiction to jurisdiction. Using the classification scheme of Pula (2016), 27 jurisdictions have broad legislation whereas ten have limited or project-specific legislation. Table 10.2 summarizes some key aspects of existing legislation.

As shown, current legislation addresses many issues such as conversion of existing roads to toll roads, limitations on contract durations and provisions, regulatory approvals and reviews, and types of procurement. For instance, 28 jurisdictions (roughly 75 percent) mandate some form of involvement of state legislatures in PPPs; for instance, Kentucky requires that any PPP project valued at over $25 million be approved by the state legislature, whereas California requires legislative review of projects but not approval. Similarly, 27 jurisdictions require some form of involvement by other entities; New Hampshire, the most recent state to enact legislation in June 2016, established a seven-member PPP Infrastructure Oversight Commission to comment on, approve or deny all requests for proposals. While providing public entities this sort of authority can enhance PPP oversight, it creates variability among the states and considerable political risk: projects can incur significant costs to both the public and private sectors as they progress through planning and procurement processes, but remain at risk if necessary approvals or reviews are still pending.

Nearly two-thirds (22 or 59.5 percent) of the Acts allow both solicited and unsolicited proposals; yet, only three do not require a call for competing proposals or another process if an unsolicited proposal is received. Unsolicited proposals have some advantages, since a private entity is very likely to propose projects with a strong business case; however, such proposals may conflict with public sector priorities and cause unanticipated transaction costs. Roughly half (19 or 51.4 percent) allow multiple forms of procurement for PPPs, which essentially gives the executive entity in charge of procurement (most likely a unit within a state Department of Transportation) flexibility with regard to this process; while this has its advantages, it essentially allows the executive entity to decide how to procure private sector PPP services.

Procurement processes
In many respects, the variances in the enabling legislation in the US are manifested in the procurement approaches adopted from jurisdiction to jurisdiction. Table 10.3 depicts characteristics of highway PPP projects that reached financial close in the US from 1993 to 2017. Over time, the PPP models used and the procurement approaches have fluctuated. The earliest projects were primarily demand (or revenue) risk arrangements procured using both competitive and non-competitive processes. More recent projects have varied more in the models used, but procurements have trended toward competitive procedures. Generally, competitive procurements have followed a multi-phase process where qualifications of respondents are assessed in the initial phase, and short-listed respondents participate in subsequent phases where some form of best-value techniques are used to select the preferred proposer. A fair number of PPPs implemented in the US, however, are the consequence of unsolicited proposals that are permitted in more than half of the jurisdictions allowing PPPs, such as the Capital Beltway Express in Virginia, or pre-development agreements (PDAs), such as SH 130 Segments 5 and 6 in Texas. On receipt of an unsolicited proposal, most public agencies must solicit competing proposals, as was the case in the nations visited; though, often, additional proposals are not received. PDAs, however, are fairly unique to the US. In most instances, a public agency engages a private partner to assist in analyzing and scoping an identified transportation need (or set of needs), and the private partner typically has "first rights" to or the opportunity to pursue the project (or projects) resulting from the PDA. The basic rationale for using a PDA stems from the more market-driven approach by the private partner to identify and scope viable PPP projects: theoretically the private partner has a considerable commercial imperative to select projects that will prove to be economically viable. This logic has not necessarily worked as intended; for example, the concession company formed to develop, finance and manage SH 130 Segments 5 and 6 declared bankruptcy in August 2016 and was reorganized under new ownership in June 2017.

Table 10.3 Highway PPP characteristics 1993–2017

Project	Jurisdiction	Close	Model	Procurement approach*
Dulles Greenway	VA	1993	DBFOM: Demand	NC: Unsolicited proposal
SR 91 Express	CA	1993	DBFOM: Demand	C: Scoring of unique proposals
SR 125 (South Bay Expressway)	CA	2003	DBFOM: Demand	C: Scoring of unique proposals
Chicago Skyway	Chicago	2004	Asset lease: Demand	C: Highest qualified bid
Indiana Toll Road	IN	2006	Asset lease: Demand	C: Highest qualified bid
Pocahontas Parkway II	VA	2006	Asset lease: Demand	NC: Sole source negotiation
I-495 Capital Beltway Express	VA	2008	DBFOM: Demand	NC: Unsolicited proposal
SH 130: 5 and 6	TX	2008	DBFOM: Demand	NC: Pre-development agreement
I-595 Express Lanes	FL	2009	DBFOM: AP	C: Multi-phase best value
Port of Miami Tunnel	FL	2009	DBFOM: AP	C: Multi-phase best value
North Tarrant Express (1 and 2)	TX	2009	DBFOM: Demand	C: Multi-phase best value
I-635 Managed Lanes	TX	2010	DBFOM: Demand	C: Multi-phase best value
PR-22/PR-5	PR	2011	Asset lease: Demand	C: Multi-phase best value
Elizabeth River Tunnels	VA	2012	DBFOM: Demand	NC: Pre-development agreement
Presidio Parkway (Phase II)	CA	2012	DBFOM: AP	C: Multi-phase best value
I-95 Express Lanes	VA	2012	DBFOM: Demand	NC: Unsolicited proposal followed by competing proposal
East End Crossing	IN	2013	DBFOM: AP	C: Multi-phase best value
North Tarrant Express (3A and B)	TX	2013	DBFOM: Demand	NC: Pre-development agreement
Goethals Bridge Replacement	NY/NJ PA	2013	DBFM: AP	C: Multi-phase best value
U.S. 36 Managed Lanes Phase 2	CO	2014	DBFOM: Demand	C: Multi-phase best value

Table 10.3 (continued)

Project	Jurisdiction	Close	Model	Procurement approach*
I-4 Ultimate Improvements	FL	2014	DBFOM: AP	C: Multi-phase best value
I-69 Phase 5	IN	2014	DBFOM: AP	C: Multi-phase best value
Rapid Bridge Replacement	PA	2015	DBFOM: AP	C: Multi-phase best value
I-77 HOT Lanes	NC	2015	DBFOM: Demand	C: Multi-phase best value
Portsmouth Bypass	OH	2015	DBFOM: AP	C: Multi-phase best value
SH 288 Toll Lanes	TX	2016	DBFOM: Demand	C: Multi-phase best value
I-66 Express	VA	2017	DBFOM: Demand	C: Multi-phase best value
Central 70	CO	2017	DBFOM: AP	C: Multi-phase best value

Notes: * Delineates the general process used. C = competitive; NC = non-competitive.

Demand risk

By and large, treatment of demand risk in the US has followed the Australian model, where private entities in such arrangements have fully borne this risk. A recent exception is the I-77 HOT Lanes project in North Carolina where demand risk was shared. This project included a provision called a developer ratio adjustment mechanism (DRAM), where the public agency agreed to financially support the private developer if revenues fall short during the payback period of the project's federal TIFIA loan (Nguyen et al., 2018). Further, some agencies are considering threshold arrangements like those used in Spain as a means to manage demand risk between public and private agencies. Most recent PPP arrangements in the US also include revenue-sharing provisions if actual revenues exceed a predefined threshold, and they follow similar protocols for competing facilities: governments hold the rights to make improvements in their transportation networks except in specific corridors or routes identified in the contractual agreement (Nguyen et al., 2018). In a number of jurisdictions, however, enabling legislation precludes the inclusion of any protection against competing facilities for the private sector.

Performance measures

Extensive KPI regimes are typical in US PPP contracts, particularly more recent ones. For instance, the Elizabeth River Tunnels project in Virginia utilized a "noncompliance points system" to identify concessionaire acts, omissions, breaches or failures to perform its obligations under the project's contract; such occurrences result in the assessment of points that can trigger remedies set forth in the agreement (Nguyen et al., 2018). Analogous systems are common in other US highway PPP arrangements.

RENEWED RECOMMENDATIONS FOR THE US PPP MARKET

Whether the Trump administration's Infrastructure Initiative triggers more PPP projects or not, their effective use in the US requires shifts in the national environment. While the state of practice in the US has advanced since the time of the scanning tour, the experience of the international community remains relevant for improving PPPs.

Normalization

In a number of European countries, PPP programs are driven primarily by the national government. Plus, European Union regulations create shared standards across national boundaries. This generates market consistency and stability across these nations. The situation is different in Australia; it, like the US, operates under a federalist system where states have significant autonomy, particularly in matters of infrastructure and procurement. This is not inappropriate since the context of projects in general and PPPs specifically will influence matters ranging from stakeholder engagement to risk allocation (Dewulf et al., 2016; Nguyen et al., 2018). However, 50-plus unique markets for PPPs in the US will discourage private participation and increase transaction costs. Hence, some amount of standardization is essential. The FHWA, primarily through its Office of Innovative Program Delivery, has produced materials to enhance consistency across the US market, such as its model contract provisions and guidance documents for public agencies covering topics such as PPP best practices and performance-based specifications. Other national initiatives include the Build America Transportation Investment Center Institute (BATIC), which is geared toward promoting public sector capacity building in the use of project finance techniques.

In the case of Australia, its states in many respects incrementally standardized their practices. New South Wales was the first to implement PPPs and Victoria followed. They learned from each other as their programs evolved. Queensland came next, using the experience of its sister states to its advantage. To some extent, the US is already following this model. Early movers such as Florida, Indiana, Texas and Virginia have shared knowledge with more recent entrants such as Colorado, North Carolina and Pennsylvania. However, Infrastructure Australia has emerged as a national independent body to prioritize and progress nationally significant infrastructure. While its mandate is broader, it has played an important role in PPPs. It helped to establish the National PPP Policy and Guidelines that apply to all Australian, state and territory government agencies (Infrastructure Australia, 2008). It also coordinates the National PPP Working Group that has representatives from all levels of government. At the very least, Infrastructure Australia coordinates activities across the PPP space. The US should seriously consider following suit, since initiatives across America remain fragmented. Notwithstanding the efforts of the FHWA, individual states and professional organizations – such as the American Association for State Highway and Transportation Officials (AASHTO), the PPP Division of the American Road and Transportation Builders Association (ARTBA) and the Association for the Improvement of American Infrastructure (AIAI) – an independent, empowered and resourced "Infrastructure America" body could harmonize PPPs in the US. Moreover, Michigan recently took comparable action at the state level with the formation of the Michigan Infrastructure Council and the Water Infrastructure Council; these councils will track state assets and develop investment strategies (Lamb, 2018).

Training

The nations visited emphasized the importance of institutional capacity for PPP program effectiveness. PPPs present a variety of challenging tasks throughout a project's life cycle for public sector officials. Over time, the nations visited have relied less heavily on external consultants as their PPP staff competencies improved. Deliberate actions such as establishment of best-practices groups supported capacity development. Just as the need for complementary expertise from legal and financial consultants will not go away, neither will the need for institutional capacity to advance.

Currently, America does not lack PPP educational programs or resources. Again, the FHWA offers training such as PPP webinars and has promulgated public agency decision support systems such as its P3-SCREEN and P3-VALUE analytical tools. Others – such as AASHTO, BATIC and ARTBA – provide additional training and support. Yet, the fragmentation problem persists. Where should a state or a municipality initiating or considering PPPs turn? A unit such as "Infrastructure America" could be the answer. Its coordination of PPP resources and training is consistent with the role it would play as a normalizing agent just discussed.

CONCLUSION

While the future direction of the current administration's Infrastructure Initiative is unclear, the US will likely continue its gradual shift toward increased provision of infrastructure services by the private sector. The international community understands that their highway PPP programs must both preserve the public's interest and attract private participation, which are somewhat conflicting objectives. To balance the two, the state and its citizens must receive marginal value at a reasonable price, while private participants need reasonable risk–reward profiles and transaction costs.

Various practices used by the nations visited have enabled such outcomes. Project analysis methods identify life cycle value drivers and suitable risk allocation strategies. Public decision-makers focus on project outcomes, so that they can determine customer needs and create KPIs to satisfy them. While procurement processes vary, they share an emphasis on competition, transparency and accountability as well as minimizing transaction costs.

Clearly, the US has matured as federal, state and local experience with PPPs has increased over the last decade. Yet, its PPP market is still evolving. Moreover, efforts to advance it need better coordination and suffer from a plurality of interests rather than solidarity. Perhaps the question is not whether a body like "Infrastructure America" should exist, but rather, could it? The answer lies in whether national PPP leaders can marshal the conviction and the perseverance necessary to build "Infrastructure America" with the right balance of power for effective PPP policies and practices in the US federalist system.

ACKNOWLEDGMENTS

The scanning tour described in this chapter was sponsored by FHWA/ AASHTO; the opinions, findings and recommendations presented are the author's alone and do not necessarily represent the views of the FHWA or AASHTO.

NOTE

1. In the "International Practice" subsection, the sub-subsections "Project identification," "Project analysis and selection," "Procurement processes," "Demand risk" and "Performance measures" are reused from Garvin (2010) with permission from the American Society of Civil Engineers (ASCE).

11. Private participation in US infrastructure: the role of regional PPP units[1]

Carter B. Casady and R. Richard Geddes

INTRODUCTION

Public–private partnerships (PPPs) are used globally to incorporate private sector skills, resources and risk management expertise into various aspects of infrastructure project delivery. "Public–private partnership" has become an expansive term to describe bundling together basic project delivery functions, including facility design, construction, operation, maintenance and financing, along with the transfer of significant infrastructure delivery-related risks to private partners. When properly designed, executed and enforced, PPPs can create social value through on-time and on-cost delivery, synergies between various bundled project components, innovation in project design, incorporation of global expertise, access to new sources of capital, increased technological adoption, and reliance on life cycle costing and life cycle asset maintenance, among other important benefits (Reinhardt, 2011; US Department of Treasury, 2015). Conversely, poorly negotiated and executed PPPs can generate substantial social costs. They are frequently renegotiated (Guasch, 2004) and may be undertaken for political expedience rather than net social benefit (Engel et al., 2014). Therefore, ensuring careful end-to-end management of the PPP process is crucial.

Globally, PPPs have emerged as the main contractual vehicle to facilitate private participation in infrastructure. The United States (US) lags behind other developed countries that have successfully used them for decades. This includes neighboring North American countries. For example, Canada has attracted about six times the amount of private investment in infrastructure in recent decades via PPPs, per dollar of gross domestic product, relative to the United States.

PPPs are an important tool for addressing numerous endemic US infrastructure problems. Although the United States has benefited from well-designed and well-developed infrastructure systems across sectors for decades, many facilities now suffer from years of deferred maintenance. Some systems, including many roads, local streets, bridges, tunnels, airports, and water and wastewater systems, require major renovation and fresh investment. In addition to simply restoring those facilities to a state of good repair, reconstruction today would benefit from an array of innovative technologies, new materials and new designs not available at original construction.

There is widespread agreement that PPPs can add value, and policies have been adopted at both the state and federal levels to encourage their use. Thirty-four US states have adopted PPP-enabling laws designed to create the stable legal and institutional framework necessary to attract the long-term, irreversible investment required to deliver many infrastructure services (Geddes and Wagner, 2013). Moreover, financial instruments, such as private activity bonds (PABs) and Transportation Infrastructure Financing and Innovation Act (TIFIA) loans, were created to encourage private investment in infrastructure. In January 2015, the Obama administration expanded the PAB concept to urge the creation of Qualified Public Infrastructure Bonds (QPIBs). It emphasized those instruments' value in promoting PPPs, stating that "QPIBs will extend the benefits of municipal bonds to public private partnerships, like partnerships that involve long-term leasing and management contracts, lowering the cost of borrowing and attracting new capital" (Chappatta, 2015). Additionally, in July 2016, Transportation Secretary Anthony Foxx announced the creation of the Build America Bureau (Build America Bureau, 2017) within the US Department of Transportation (USDOT). The new bureau will combine several major PPP-related programs, including TIFIA, the Railroad Rehabilitation and Improvement Financing (RRIF), the PAB program, the Build America Transportation Investment Center, and the new $800 million FASTLANE grant program under one large umbrella (US Department of Transportation, 2016).

Many countries worldwide have also turned to PPP units to facilitate private participation in infrastructure (Kim, 2015). Although their precise structure varies, PPP units are typically independent governmental or quasi-governmental entities. They usually provide pre-project screening, prioritization, education, support and expert advice to public sector project sponsors wishing to use PPPs. In addition to providing education and training to public officials, these units universally strive to ensure that PPP contracts promote the public interest. Dedicated, specialized PPP units are a policy tool that remains relatively understudied and underused in the United States, however.

PPP units have been used globally to facilitate PPPs and successfully attract risk capital into infrastructure investment. Countries with established units include Australia, Canada, China, Ghana, India, Indonesia, Israel, Japan, Kenya, Malawi, New Zealand, the Philippines, Singapore and the United Kingdom, among many others. More recently, Albania, Egypt, Mozambique, Nigeria, Tanzania and Turkey have created such units.

To our knowledge, we are the first to explore regional PPP units as a tool to facilitate greater private participation in infrastructure delivery in the United States. Each of our proposed regional PPP units includes several economically linked states. States are grouped based on emerging economic mega-regions. This is appealing because demand for the large infrastructure projects, that is, where PPP units are most helpful, reflects mega-region economic activity rather than state boundaries. Under our proposal, PPP unit structure reflects the large-scale economic activity that propels demand for major infrastructure projects. Moreover, infrastructure needs would likely vary substantially across US mega-regions. For example, the renovation and maintenance of existing facilities may be more important than new design and construction, depending on economic region. PPP unit mission should vary accordingly.

WHAT ARE PPP UNITS?

PPPs are used increasingly worldwide to deliver critical infrastructure facilities. However, public sector procurement agencies – particularly in countries with little history of PPP use – often lack the expertise or administrative capacity necessary to properly structure, evaluate, negotiate and enforce PPP contracts, which can be complex. Therefore, fully understanding the long-term implications of entering into a PPP arrangement is essential for public officials wishing to use them. PPP units have been established worldwide to help address such challenges (Istrate and Puentes, 2011).

A PPP unit's functions, coverage, governance and funding source may differ across jurisdictions. Although a single, widely accepted definition remains elusive, international organizations have offered viable definitions. The Organisation for Economic Co-operation and Development defines a PPP unit as "any organization set up with full or partial aid of the government to ensure that the necessary capacity to create, support, and evaluate multiple public–private partnership agreements is made available and clustered together within government" (OECD, 2010). The World Bank offers a broader definition. It states that these organizations are granted "a lasting mandate to manage multiple PPP transactions, often in multiple sectors" and are specifically designed to promote and improve

PPPs, managing quantity and quality of PPPs, and "[ensuring] that PPPs meet specific quality criteria such as affordability, value-for-money (VfM), and appropriate risk transfer" (Kim, 2015).

Regarding structure and function, the European PPP Expertise Centre (2014) states:

> PPP Units (sometimes also referred to as "agencies" or "task forces") can serve a wide variety of purposes. In this report, a PPP Unit broadly refers to a unit that operates across sectors and projects at either a national or subnational/state/municipal government level. In this context, such a PPP Unit may be a division within a cross-sectional ministry, established as a separate agency or an incorporated entity that is at least partly publicly owned.

Although PPP units are typically not procuring agencies themselves, these dedicated units frequently assist other government bureaus in procuring multiple projects, either from a single sector or from numerous sectors. More specifically:

> A PPP unit is a public entity (government, public/private corporation, or nonprofit) that supports other government agencies to procure projects through a PPP process; it is not the procuring agency. It is a "dedicated" agency, meaning that it has a permanent structure dealing with multiple projects versus ad-hoc teams put together in ministries and departments to deal with procurement through a specific PPP project. It may support government agencies in procuring PPP projects that span multiple sectors or in just a specific sector, such as transportation. (Istrate and Puentes, 2011)

Carefully considering PPP unit functions helps to illuminate their benefits. The European PPP Expertise Centre divides the main functions of a PPP unit into three areas: (1) PPP policy support and related activities; (2) program and project delivery support; and (3) project approval and quality control. We consider each area in turn.

The first functional area includes crucial tasks such as initial support for the jurisdiction's PPP program. This is particularly important for emerging PPP programs (that is, the development of a series of projects for delivery as PPPs) that are intended to grow over time. Such activities are expansive. In addition to basic PPP education and training, they include raising awareness of the costs and benefits of PPPs as applied in that region, coordinating PPP efforts across governmental units, working to standardize the basic provisions of PPP contracts, interacting with potential private partners, and managing information on PPP projects (European PPP Expertise Centre, 2014).

The second functional area focuses on project-level PPP support. This includes technical support both for longer-term PPP programs and for individual projects. Support at the project level includes technical assistance with project selection, preparation and management. This can be both immediate (as a kind of help desk) and longer term (to structure a viable PPP program). There is typically a focus on offering PPP-related skills that are not readily available from outside consultants, or which require careful interpretation and explanation if they are. Skills include objective value for money (VfM) analysis of projects, in which the expected net present value of costs and benefits of the project delivered as a PPP is compared to a "public sector comparator" (the expected net present value of costs and benefits associated with a traditional design–bid–build and or design–build delivery approach), using a rigorous methodology. Additional tasks include objective assessment of a particular PPP project's impact on the government's longer-term budget situation. Members of PPP units also occasionally serve on project-specific oversight bodies even though the actual procuring authority remains responsible for project oversight. Although PPP units rarely act as explicit transaction advisers, they always strive to ensure that public sector officials are cognizant of what both individual projects and longer-term PPP programs require in terms of public resources, time and expertise.

The third functional area – project approval and quality control – includes whether to offer the project to investors as a PPP and when to commence procurement under a PPP structure. Although units vary widely in their authority to actually approve specific projects as PPPs, they typically provide technical support and expertise to those bodies holding such authority. There are several key functions that PPP units would likely perform in this area. They play a crucial role in helping public agencies prioritize the projects that are tendered as PPPs. They also help public officials to decide, as a matter of policy, whether they will accept unsolicited project proposals. PPP units may also assess any allowed unsolicited proposals that are submitted and whether those must be offered for general bidding. Regarding technical support, PPP units assist public officials if the contract is renegotiated or goes to arbitration after the project has begun.

The PPP unit concept is well grounded in economic theory. Two broad, related economic theories help to explain PPP units. First, PPPs are complex contracts involving sunk, network assets. Those contracts are characterized by high transaction costs, which include the costs of gathering information about potential transactions, actually negotiating the transaction, and then enforcing the contract (Benham and Benham, 2010). Indeed, contracting costs are often posited as the main social cost associated with the PPP approach, against which potential benefits must be weighed. The complexity of projects that bundle together numerous project delivery elements adds to those costs. PPP units can thus be understood as a way of reducing or economizing on transaction costs. Rather than having PPP expertise spread out over many public sector agencies, for example, a PPP unit centralizes and consolidates that expertise so that one team – which may have PPP experience across numerous economic sectors – can help to prepare and negotiate viable PPP contracts. More simply, a PPP unit can be viewed as a fixed social cost. PPP units can lower the transaction costs per PPP by spreading that fixed cost out over more contracts, particularly if they are organized along regional lines, as we propose.

The second economic justification for PPP units relates to the inherent nature of infrastructure investment itself. Infrastructure often requires large amounts of sunk, irreversible investment that is specific to a particular purpose, location or relationship. This creates scope for opportunism, which was defined by Williamson (1985) as "self-interest seeking with guile." That is, once large infrastructure investments are made, both the public sector project sponsor and the private partner have incentives to engage in opportunism by reneging on or renegotiating the original agreement.

Opportunistic incentives are, of course, known by both parties before contract close. This gives rise to the hold-up problem: although both parties know they would likely benefit from the transaction, they may be reluctant to invest for fear that their partner will renege on the agreement. Substantial infrastructure policy research focuses on addressing the problem of opportunism and thus on ways to reduce the hold-up problem. This helps to promote large investment in socially valuable infrastructure.

As our analysis suggests, solutions to the hold-up problem require both parties to credibly precommit to refraining from opportunistic behavior. Both long-term contracts and PPP-enabling laws can be understood as mechanisms aiding credible precommitment. We view PPP units as akin to other mechanisms that help to signal credible precommitment on the part of project sponsors. We consider somewhat less abstract benefits of PPP units below.

BENEFITS OF PPP UNITS

We divide our assessment of benefits created by PPP units into those accruing to any jurisdiction and those specific to the United States. Regarding general benefits, properly structured PPPs can effectively reduce the substantial transaction costs associated with PPP contracts, as noted above. They also enhance credible precommitment by both the public and the private sectors, reducing the hold-up problem. Consolidating the skills and information necessary to undertake PPPs, which may be distributed across many public sector agencies, is a straightforward example of transaction cost reduction.

Additional benefits stem from reducing project risk. By improving public sector expertise and capacity to undertake projects such as PPPs, PPP units help to reduce the risks associated with the contracting approach and with infrastructure project delivery in general. This occurs through several channels. First, PPP units lower risks via improved project prescreening and structure for delivery as a PPP. Similarly, by depoliticizing and prioritizing the projects offered, units help to ensure that the highest-valued opportunities are offered first. These steps reduce the risk that inappropriate or low-value projects are pursued and brought to market, perhaps for political reasons. This, in turn, lowers the risk associated with the jurisdiction's overall PPP portfolio. Finally, by learning from global best practices across sectors, PPP units can help public agencies to create a standardized, generally accepted framework that has been effective in other jurisdictions.

Second, PPP units reduce project risk via enhanced transparency throughout the PPP process. Creating an institutionalized, formal structure and process for project screening and prioritization enhances transparency, as does the adoption of a clear framework for PPP structure within the jurisdiction. Although deviations from the default process are possible, they require added justification and explanation. Careful consideration of deviations from standard contractual structure would also help to build confidence in the PPP process.

Third, PPP units institutionalize the process of discerning and adopting best practices from other jurisdictions. This is particularly important in the United States, which has relatively little experience with this delivery approach. This function helps public sector project sponsors to avoid reliance on PPP contractual provisions that may increase public sector risk, while encouraging adoption of other provisions that help manage risks effectively.

In addition to risk management, PPP units create benefits through interactions with potential private partners. This includes explaining, marketing and providing information on the set of projects planned in the jurisdiction (that is, the PPP program) under that unit's aegis. This lowers the cost to investors, particularly from outside the jurisdiction, of learning about infrastructure investment opportunities. An effective PPP unit thus not only signals that the region is "open for infrastructure business" but also facilitates understanding of the specific opportunities that are available.

Finally, given their role, the unit's senior staff will likely have extensive experience with PPP structure and financing. Indeed, PPP units often attract expertise in PPPs that is normally unavailable to the public sector. This is due to greater flexibility in compensation relative to other government agencies, and a specialized, compelling mission attractive to experienced experts.

We next consider reasons why the United States, more than other jurisdictions, would likely reap benefits from the creation of PPP units. The United States is unusual in not using dedicated PPP units more intensively, despite having the world's largest economy, highly developed network infrastructure across sectors and a pressing need for added investment, and prominent efforts in other countries. PPP units would likely generate substantial value due to the relatively small role that privately provided equity financing has historically played in the United States. This is often combined with limited or no bundling of various project elements. Together, those features constitute what is sometimes termed "traditional delivery" of US infrastructure.

Although the definition varies across countries, traditional infrastructure delivery in the United States refers to procuring unbundled projects using a design–bid–build contracting approach while relying heavily on tax-exempt municipal bond financing. Public sector officials in the United States thus have less experience with private sector financing (and transfer of risk to private sector partners) and with procuring projects when various basic functions are combined. This may also lead to poor coordination across agencies when using PPPs, and limited institutional learning from global PPP experience. Both bundling and risk transfer via PPPs requires that public procurement officials acquire new skill sets. Economically speaking, the current lack of familiarity with innovative project delivery suggests that aspects of PPP-related transaction costs are relatively high in the United States and could be lowered substantially using PPP units.

Another reason the United States lags behind other developed countries in PPP use stems from its highly federalist structure. We refer to this as the 50-plus-two jurisdictional problem. That is, PPP contracts are controlled by the applicable procurement laws in the 50 states, the District of Columbia and Puerto Rico, and in some cases large municipalities. This creates challenges for PPP delivery and for large investors who must contend with differing state-level PPP-enabling laws – if such laws exist at all – combined with idiosyncratic state procurement regulations. Participating in PPPs may have high costs, including understanding state-specific social norms and acquiring state-specific institutional knowledge. Investors may be loath to devote the extensive time and effort required to learn the PPP laws in one state or locality, particularly when the anticipated number of PPPs from that jurisdiction is low. This reluctance reduces competition in bidding for those PPPs that are offered. Conversely, increasing the number of PPP bidders that PPP units can facilitate also increases competition across jurisdictions, which is an important benefit.

On the supply-of-projects side, PPP units would likely increase the number of PPP contracts offered because of improved advising, project screening, project prioritization, and the adoption of a standard-form contract for a particular PPP type (for example, a toll road or bridge). The costs incurred by potential investors in learning the US market would be applicable to more jurisdictions, more infrastructure sectors, and thus more possible contracts. This results in more PPP-viable projects. Moreover, for economic regions containing numerous relatively small states (and thus smaller PPP deal flow), such as the Northeast, there would likely be substantial scale economies in technical assistance and PPP oversight. (Indeed, five large states – California, Florida, Texas, Virginia and North Carolina – account for the vast majority of United States PPP activity.) We next consider the structure of PPP units in Canada, which we view as a leader in this area.

PPP UNITS IN CANADA

Canada's experience with PPP units is instructive for the United States. Canada has relied on PPPs for decades, and is a recognized world leader in their use. Canada shares some of the same infrastructure challenges as the United States, including similar weather, and mature systems across sectors in need of renovation, combined with demand for selected system expansion. It also shares a federalist structure with the United States and has PPP units at both the federal and provincial levels. Canada's reliance on PPP units in public procurement provides government authorities with the necessary capacity to offer, conclude and enforce PPP contracts.

The federal government uses a PPP unit called PPP Canada. Established in 2009 as a federal Crown corporation that reports through the Minister of Finance to Parliament, PPP Canada works to improve Canada's PPP expertise and develop its national PPP market. It also manages Canada's $1.25 billion PPP Canada Fund and part of the $14 billion New Building Canada Fund (Infrastructure Canada Government of Canada, 2014). The latter was created in 2014 to support infrastructure projects having national, regional and local significance. PPP Canada's organizational structure includes a chief executive officer, an independent board of directors and a board chair. It also works with PPP units at the provincial level to help standardize Canada's procurement processes and improve coordination among various government agencies.

Although PPP Canada and the federal government play an important role in influencing PPP procurement procedures and policies, their direct involvement in infrastructure provision is minimal. Similar to US states, Canadian provinces retain responsibility for actual infrastructure provision. They use PPP units extensively to facilitate efficient procurement. Provincial units include Partnerships British Columbia, Infrastructure Ontario, Infrastructure Quebec, Alberta Infrastructure, Partnerships New Brunswick and SaskBuilds. These entities are primarily responsible for advertising PPP projects, conducting PPP project technical assistance and advisory services, instituting standardized procurement best practices, and offering policy guidance to their respective provincial governments.

This two-tier institutional structure is likely a key driver of Canada's effective use of PPPs in infrastructure project delivery. Although US PPP units would be structured differently than some PPP units abroad to account for America's multi-jurisdictional structure, adopting a basic two-tiered institutional framework of PPP units, similar to that employed in Canada, would facilitate private investment in infrastructure at multiple levels. Australia operates a similar PPP structure.

REGIONAL US PPP UNITS

We next examine how PPP units could be productively applied to increase private participation in US infrastructure delivery. Using the Canadian PPP unit structure as a guide, we focus on an appropriate organizational structure given the US multi-jurisdictional setting.

Outside of the federal level, regional – rather than state-specific – PPP units are an appealing structure. First, America's 50-plus-two jurisdictions may constrain infrastructure policy-making to boundaries that are poorly aligned with broader economic activity in the region. Second, greater coordination across states is important for projects with various infrastructure systems that are likely to be increasingly interconnected due to technological advances. The multi-jurisdictional problem will also fail to spread the fixed, institutional cost of creating a PPP unit across numerous projects.

We suggest structuring PPP units to include states in emerging economic mega-regions. Regional units will help member states to develop standard-form PPP contracts applicable to that region, including a core set of contractual clauses and provisions. These provisions would clarify such issues as treatment of non-compete clauses, compensation clauses, revenue-sharing agreements, availability payments, confidentiality agreements and the acceptability of unsolicited proposals, among many other considerations, in PPP agreements (Geddes and Wagner, 2013). Regional units would also help member states to create performance-based PPP contracts. Such contracts include clearly defined key performance indicators (KPIs) with appropriate penalties and rewards depending on observed performance. KPIs may include pavement smoothness, level of service ratings, lane availability, and other observables. Regional PPP units would also provide technical assistance to government agencies regarding best practices throughout the region and to outside groups that may wish to engage the PPP unit.

This concept is not novel. Organizations such as the Western High Speed Rail Alliance and the West Coast Infrastructure Exchange (WCX) focus on regional infrastructure challenges. Moreover, the National Governors Association is coordinating metropolitan planning and infrastructure investment across states. The National Conference of State Legislatures (Rall et al., 2015) has produced a PPP toolkit to help legislators better understand PPPs. Those efforts could be expanded by creating regional PPP units, which would facilitate greater multi-state collaborative PPP efforts.

A regional structure facilitates consideration of the interconnectivity and network characteristics of infrastructure, which often transcends state lines. It also encourages cooperation across state and local boundaries. We consider aligning regional PPP units with seven distinct mega-regions, defined by similar demographics and economic structures, as shown in Figure 11.1. These regional PPP units would facilitate state participation in regional infrastructure partnerships.

The WCX offers an excellent example that could be tailored to regional PPP units throughout the United States. The WCX was created in 2012 by the governors and treasurers of California, Oregon and Washington, in concert with the premier of British Columbia. Headquartered in Portland, Oregon, it was designed to be a regional platform to address critical infrastructure needs along the Pacific Coast. It functions as an independent 501(c)(3) non-profit. Its board of directors consists of two senior officials from each of the three US member states appointed by the governors and treasurers. The board also includes the executive director of Partnerships British Columbia, a PPP unit in British Columbia tasked with bringing private sector financing, alternative procurement structures (for example, PPPs) and operational expertise to infrastructure projects in the province.

In its ideal structure, the board would create direction for the organization by outlining its work platform, providing oversight and approval of its annual budget, and supervising both its exchange manager and an advisory council. While the exchange manager and its staff of industry

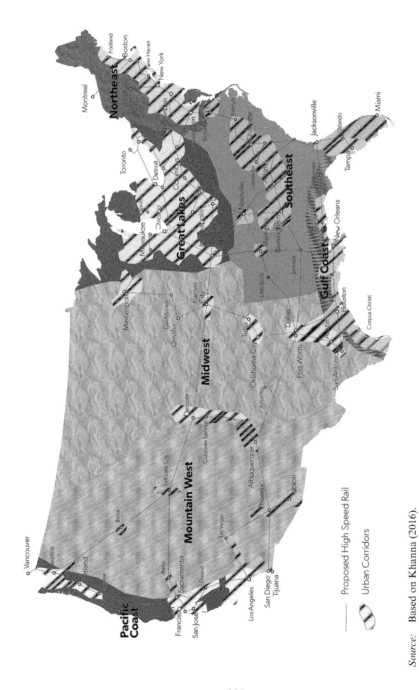

Source: Based on Khanna (2016).

Figure 11.1 Rethinking the map: America's seven mega-regions

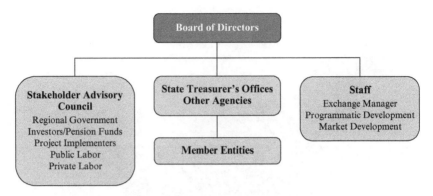

Source: CH2M HILL, West Coast Infrastructure Exchange final report. November 16, 2012. https://www.calpers.ca.gov/docs/forms-publications/wcx-final-report.pdf.

Figure 11.2 Proposed regional PPP unit organizational structure

professionals would lead programmatic and market development, an advisory council would bring together institutional investors, representatives from local and regional governments, project developers, implementation experts and organized labor to address stakeholder concerns while also ensuring protection of the public interest. This framework is well suited for regional PPP units (see Figure 11.2).

The WCX's proposed functions also make it a sound model for US regional PPP units. These key functional categories include: (1) developing standards for private sector participation in infrastructure project delivery; (2) promoting infrastructure development, finance and operations best practices; (3) assessing the full-life cycle and sustainability considerations of infrastructure investment decisions; (4) providing objective expertise, technical assistance and advisory services to the public sector; (5) using the expertise of PPP innovators such as Partnerships British Columbia; (6) evaluating traditional and alternative financing and procurement models for infrastructure projects; and (7) developing an infrastructure pipeline that connects projects with private capital before investment. The WCX model offers an adaptable organizational structure to America's seven economic mega-regions, helping to address the multi-jurisdictional problem. Figure 11.3 illustrates how each state would fit into one of the seven mega-regions.

Although the WCX's current structure offers a model for the US regional PPP unit's organizational framework, these entities must also respect state sovereignty. We do not recommend that states be required to join a regional PPP unit. We instead argue that dedicated PPP units will create such high value for states, at relatively low cost, that they would opt

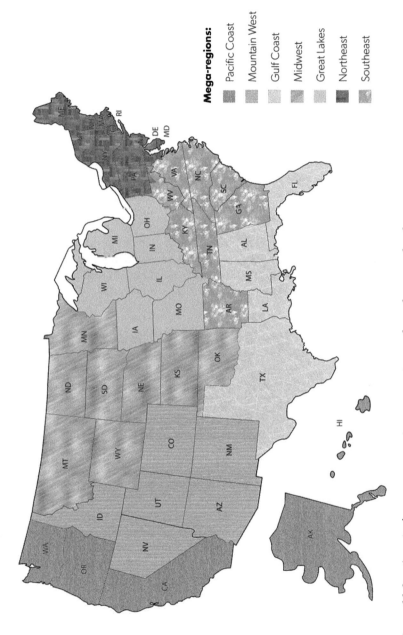

Figure 11.3 America's seven economic mega-regions, adapted to state borders

in voluntarily as regional PPP group members. Consequently, states would be free to leave the group at any time.

Regional PPP units would also remain in a strictly advisory role and would be unable to impose restrictions on PPP structure in non-member states. Member states would remain free to create PPPs outside of the regional PPP unit framework and to modify the basic contractual structure as needed (but again, subject to a greater standard of justification).

We also rely on international experience regarding PPP unit funding. Participating member states would partially fund their regional PPP unit via annual membership fees and modest consulting fees for specific professional advisory and technical services. States may also pay supplemental fees to their respective regional PPP unit for promotion and advertising services (for example, advertising infrastructure in their economic region to global investors). Finally, although regional PPP units may receive some taxpayer support, units could defray their costs by including some of their expenses in the closing costs of PPP projects procured by member states. Under this structure, PPP unit success would depend largely on the performance and quality of services provided to each member state. Member states would exit from regional units that systematically underperform or otherwise fail to create value.

NATIONAL US PPP UNIT: PARTNERSHIPS USA

Regional PPP units raise the question of the appropriate federal role in PPP facilitation. Following Australia and Canada, we suggest a national-level PPP unit (which we call "Partnerships USA"). This unit would be charged with streamlining national PPP procurement guidance, offering PPP training, and promoting global best practices. We suggest forming Partnerships USA by combining several extant entities. Under the Fixing America's Surface Transportation Act of 2015, the Secretary of Transportation has the authority to consolidate USDOT entities. The Secretary could feasibly merge the newly formed Build America Bureau with the recently authorized National Surface Transportation and Innovative Finance Bureau, which is an entity responsible for advising state and local transportation authorities on best practices relating to project procurement, funding, and financing. Together these agencies would constitute Partnerships USA (American Road and Transportation Builders Association, 2015).

Once formed, Partnerships USA would acquire an organizational structure similar to PPP Canada. Remaining within USDOT, Partnerships USA would be restructured as a government-owned corporation subject to private corporate law (that is, "corporatized"). It would be governed by a board of directors with a fiduciary duty to act in the interest of its (sole) shareholder, the Secretary of Transportation. Under this quasi-governmental structure, Partnerships USA would fulfill a variety of infrastructure roles across multiple sectors. One is facilitating cooperation, best practices, global outreach and learning across the seven regional PPP units. Partnerships USA would also facilitate collaboration across regional PPP units, particularly for large projects crossing mega-regions. For example, a PPP project to improve passenger rail service in the Northeast Corridor from Richmond to Boston – perhaps by upgrading rail infrastructure to allow higher speeds – requires coordination among economic regions. Using our definition of a regional PPP unit, such a PPP would require cooperation between the Great Northeast and the Southeast Manufacturing Belt units. Similarly, a PPP rail project from Los Angeles to Las Vegas would require cooperation between the Pacific Coast and the Inland West regional units. Partnerships USA could serve as a platform for facilitating such agreements. Importantly, creating regional PPP units will diminish greatly the number of governmental entities that would need to coordinate to conclude such large multi-state agreements.

Partnerships USA would also obtain funding through a combination of consulting fees for specific professional services, both technical and advisory in nature (such as VfM analysis) and application fees related to the administration of various competitive grant and loan programs (that is, TIFIA, RRIF, Transportation Investment Generating Economic Recovery Discretionary Grants, PABs, Water Infrastructure Finance and Innovation Act, and so on). Partnerships USA may also receive fees from regional US PPP units that heavily use its policy guidance, procurement materials, and other advisory services.

However, to mitigate potential conflicts of interest, we suggest that Partnerships USA, like its sister regional PPP units, receives some taxpayer support. Through this funding approach, Partnerships USA would be held to high standards of performance, accountability and transparency, while limiting its budgetary impact.

Partnerships USA's role would be mainly advisory, however. It would have no authority to impose a PPP contractual structure on any state or regional entity. This allows procuring agencies to tailor their PPP agreements to specific circumstances and project conditions while benefiting from global best practice and regional coordination. Moreover, general recommendations made by Partnerships USA would not impose required standards of PPP management across other levels of government. Alternatively, public agencies, procuring authorities and regional PPP units would be free to adopt procurement guidance, policies and procedures that meet regional, state, municipal and local infrastructure needs. Finally, as with regional units, Partnerships USA would encourage PPP procurement in the United States by promoting US PPPs abroad.

OUR PROPOSAL'S BENEFITS

Based on the Canadian experience, establishing a national PPP unit along with regional entities would help to address barriers hindering US PPP development. By establishing PPP units as quasi-independent entities, these entities would have greater flexibility and ability to adapt to changes in market conditions than under the current approach. PPP units are, by design, vehicles of consistency and transparency that allow for responsive policy change.

In the US context, PPP units would be instrumental in addressing America's multi-jurisdictional challenges. Establishing regional PPP units in the United States would help to avoid duplication of public sector PPP capacity across 52 jurisdictions. Although there is a general consensus that the United States needs to build more public sector capacity in the PPP space, a federalist structure makes it costly for many states to pursue active PPP programs. As a result, some states may be poorly positioned to develop projects as PPPs that cross state lines or are affected by mega-region economic activity. Regional PPP units would help to internalize such state spillovers. Regional PPP units may also have the effect of harmonizing various aspects of PPP laws from state to state, to the extent that they are in conflict, while providing the scale needed to develop PPPs in the United States.

Regional PPP units also provide a level of expertise, transparency and precommitment beyond that offered by a state-level PPP-enabling law. Such units would allow member states to develop a multi-state project protocol that standardizes investment decision-making. This helps states to avoid common, widely recognized problems with PPPs that lead to hold-up problems in infrastructure investment and contractual breakdown later in the process. It also reduces the problem of renegotiation of PPP contracts, allowing states to use more sophisticated PPP bidding structures, while creating infrastructure transactions that are both more predictable and more attractive to private investors.

Finally, regional PPP units would create an institutional structure to facilitate the salutary wrapping of projects across state lines, which conserves on PPP transaction costs. The premier example of multi-project wrapping in the United States is the Pennsylvania Rapid Bridge Replacement PPP. This innovative PPP consolidated the renovation of 558 aging Pennsylvania bridges into one contract, which was awarded to

Plenary Walsh Keystone Partners. Since the launch of the project in 2015, more than 400 bridges have been renovated, and the project is expected to finish around the end of 2018. Upon completion, Walsh Infrastructure Management, a partner within Plenary Walsh Keystone Partners (PWKP), will provide maintenance of the bridges for a 25-year period. The bridges are mostly crossings on smaller state highways in rural areas. They typically do not cross interstate highways or large river crossings. Regional PPP units would be well positioned to facilitate the wrap of similar projects across state lines.

Ultimately, the establishment of a two-tiered system of PPP units would facilitate investment in performance-based infrastructure and create robust, transparent and objective measures that streamline project evaluation, assessment and procurement capacity for state and local governments. It would also enhance their risk management capacity, project screening and project finance capabilities.

SUMMARY AND CONCLUSIONS

US infrastructure faces serious challenges, including years of deferred maintenance, lack of rehabilitation, and inadequate investment. To remain economically competitive in an era of rapid technological change and increasing globalization, new ways to direct capital into reconditioning, replacing and improving physical infrastructure must be explored. PPPs have emerged as a key tool to facilitate greater private participation in infrastructure delivery. Many countries have turned to PPP units to successfully deliver well-structured PPPs.

The United States has been surprisingly slow to create dedicated PPP units to encourage PPP procurement and attract investment dollars to critical US infrastructure projects. We recommend that the US adopts a comprehensive and robust two-tiered system of PPP units to facilitate greater private investment in US infrastructure. We suggest the formation of regional PPP units that correspond with emerging economic mega-regions throughout the country, in addition to the creation of a national PPP unit. The latter could be accomplished via consolidation of USDOT entities such as the Build America Bureau and the National Surface Transportation and Innovative Finance Bureau.

By developing PPP units at the regional level, these entities would benefit from economies of scale and scope in PPP unit design. Using the WCX as a model, each regional entity would include several states that correspond to emerging economic mega-regions. By avoiding replication of public sector capacity across 52 US jurisdictions, regional PPP units enhance the flexibility of procuring authorities looking to adapt to changing PPP market conditions. Additionally, the need for large infrastructure projects is often more appropriately reflected by mega-region economic activity than by state boundaries. Under our proposal, PPP unit structure is tailored to the large-scale economic activity that drives demand for major infrastructure projects.

At the national level, instituting a PPP unit would help to streamline bureaucratic structures, standardize PPP procurement guidance, and promote policies that efficiently and effectively support the management of US PPPs projects. The success of regional PPP units will rely heavily on performance, quality, and the ability to evolve and adapt to the constantly changing needs and conditions of infrastructure investing throughout the country.

Overall, the creation of a two-tiered system of PPP units throughout the US would increase transparency in infrastructure investment, reduce the substantial transaction costs associated with PPP contracts, and enhance credible precommitment by both the public and the private sectors, thereby reducing the hold-up problem. It would help to establish a market for infrastructure investment that is built around asset performance, streamlined project evaluation, robust delivery assessment and improved public sector procurement capacity. In this way, state and local governments throughout the US can improve their project planning, screening, finance and risk management skills while effectively addressing pressing infrastructure needs throughout the country.

NOTE

1. This chapter was first published as a policy brief by the American Enterprise Institute on October 26, 2016 as "Private participation in US infrastructure: the role of PPP units," www.aei.org/publication/private-participation-in-us-infrastructure-the-role-of-ppp-units/. It has been adapted and used with the permission of the American Enterprise Institute.

PART V

Emerging tools for infrastructure project finance and delivery

We have discussed at length some of the governance challenges of recent public–private partnership (PPP) concessions and the approaches that have been used in the last few decades for addressing these governance challenges. This final part of the book describes two innovative approaches for financing infrastructure that are gaining increasing traction: the first, top-down; and the second, bottom-up.

In Chapter 12, Caroline Nowacki describes how Infrastructure New South Wales in Australia has begun to sell concessions to operate, and charge users for, existing infrastructure assets that have been built and operated by the government for long enough to predictably forecast their current and future demand revenue to potential PPP concessionaires. The idea is that the proceeds from selling these operating concessions will be then used by the government agency to finance new infrastructure assets or upgrade existing infrastructure assets and deliver them using traditional design–bid–build or design–build public works construction approaches. The assets will initially be operated by the cognizant public agency, rather than having the infrastructure financed, designed, built and operated under a typical design–build–finance–operate–maintain (DBFOM) PPP concession.

Once the asset has been up and running for long enough to establish a clear demand revenue trajectory – typically, for a few years – an operating concession on the asset can be sold to a concessionaire, and the funds raised from the concession sale will be used to fund the development and initial operation of future infrastructure assets. This coordinated, revolving fund approach has the government agency assuming the regulatory risk, construction risk and demand risk related to a given asset; all major risks that can scare off PPP investors and lenders, especially demand risk. Demand risk, in particular, has historically been misestimated by concessionaires – in some cases, deliberately and strategically underestimated by the concession sponsors in their enthusiasm to win a concession contract – which has subsequently led to concession bankruptcies when the optimistically forecasted regulatory review duration, construction cost or user demand failed to materialize. Having the government agency de-risk the asset by entitling it, developing it and operating it for a revenue ramp-up period allows the award of a pure "operating concession" that has already been built, with any time and cost overruns having been borne by the government. The asset has also been in operation long enough to demonstrate what its current and long-term user demand is likely to be. The operating concession is then less risky and more straightforward for prospective concessionaires to value, so that this approach should result in more realistic and competitive concession bids.

The innovative top-down approach, often termed "asset recycling," is actually just a variant of "infrastructure privatization" that ringfences the funds raised through privatizing operating assets and requires that they can only be used to create new infrastructure assets, not to subsidize underfunded pension obligations, nor for any other government purposes, as has often occurred in countries such as the United States (US).

This independent infrastructure agency in New South Wales (NSW) addresses the prioritization of infrastructure assets, the redirection of the proceeds of privatizations toward new projects, and the effective development of new assets. While the sale of newly built assets with the proceeds from operating concessions is only envisioned at this time and has not yet occurred, the professionalism brought to reinvestment and delivery of new projects by this agency makes it very likely that this will start to occur soon, enabling the government to build a mechanism close to an "evergreen fund."

In Chapter 13, this book's final chapter, Kate E. Gasparro discusses "crowdfunding," a bottom-up approach for catalyzing the development of small, local infrastructure projects. The approach builds on crowdfunding strategies and new, cloud-based software platforms that enable a project sponsor to crowdsource community input from a broad set of local stakeholders about the community's users' needs or desires for a given local infrastructure project, along with other community stakeholders' perceptions about the prospective project's potential positive or negative impacts. In addition, the new infrastructure crowdsourcing platforms enable efficient and transparent crowdfunding of a portion of the costs of delivering the asset.

In this approach, a project sponsor – typically a non-profit or non-governmental organization – acts as an organizing entity to engage a broad spectrum of community members in order to understand and address the need for, and any potential negative impacts of, a small-scale infrastructure asset. During this process, the sponsor engages in extensive community outreach to understand the project's impacts on a broad set of stakeholders, including community members who perceive a need and desire for the asset, local businesses that could be impacted positively or negatively by the new infrastructure asset, and governmental agencies and legislative bodies that will need to approve, co-fund and co-manage the development of the project.

If there is a strong perceived community demand and sufficient stakeholder buy-in or acceptance for a new or renovated infrastructure asset such as a protected bicycle lane or a local park, the sponsor will attempt to raise around five percent of the estimated total project cost from community members in the form of crowdfunded donations. The "crowdfunds" are typically raised using infrastructure-specific crowdfunding platforms that operate similarly to traditional start-up crowdfunding platforms such as Kickstarter.

This final chapter presents the background and history of crowdfunding and describes two matched, in-depth case studies of protected bicycle lane developments in two different US cities in order to begin evaluating a set of propositions about the public benefits and costs of crowdfunding small-scale urban infrastructure assets compared to delivering them conventionally, and to identify causal factors that could impact their success.

12. The financier state: infrastructure planning and asset recycling in New South Wales, Australia

Caroline Nowacki

INTRODUCTION

Can governments make the most of private investors' appetite for existing infrastructure assets? Privatization programs have had mitigated success, notably because of the perception that governments give up value when leasing assets to the private sector, and that the proceeds of the sale/lease seem to disappear as they are used to repay debts and correct an imbalanced budget. This case study of New South Wales (NSW) argues that the state can organize to make the most of private investors' will to buy operating assets to support a strong program of reinvestment in new infrastructure projects, thus not giving up value or expertise in the privatization process. It inspires a new model of the developmental state that gains inspiration from working with the private sector, without necessarily giving up on social and environmental considerations. This chapter describes infrastructure asset recycling as an improved privatization program using sale proceeds to fund an integrated, long-term infrastructure plan, and how a new independent government agency was key to ensure that the reinvestment step was successful.

THE GREENFIELD INFRASTRUCTURE FUNDING GAP

In the aftermath of the global financial crisis (GFC), several trends increased the amount of private investments in infrastructure. First, institutional investors with long-term mandates, such as pension and sovereign funds, started looking for alternatives to bonds in a very low interest-rate environment. Public–private partnerships (PPPs) and privatization of infrastructure assets gave them access to stable, predictable cash flows, and an increasing number of institutional investors started buying equity in brownfield infrastructure. Between 2009 and 2014, 60 percent of the sovereign funds globally invested in infrastructure, and direct infrastructure acquisitions went up four basis points compared to the previous five years, to reach 10 percent of all sovereign funds' deals (Preqin, 2015).

Second, neoliberalist policies in several countries supported free market agreements and opened the market of infrastructure privatization to foreign investors. Third, governments saw their debt levels rise considerably, forcing them to find new sources of cash and to think about how to engage the private sector. The global gross government debt-to-gross domestic product (GDP) ratio grew from 65 percent in 2008 to 79.8 percent in 2014. At the end of 2017, advanced economies' debt-to-GDP ratio was 103.4 percent[1] and 19 countries had debt-to-GDP ratios above the critical level of 90 percent, including Japan, Greece, Italy, the United States, Spain and France.[2] However, if the GFC accentuated public debt, structural changes are likely to make them a new standard. Most notably, the aging of the population will maintain high debt levels for the next decade, which means that governments are likely to have less funds to allocate to infrastructure.

It seems that private investors' growing appetite for infrastructure, and government's need for cash, should solve the infrastructure gap. However, investors' interest in infrastructure is not aligned with the needs identified by international organizations and governments to support economic growth. Investors primarily want to buy existing assets in developed countries, when most of the need is in new assets and developing countries. Even for an existing asset privatization in a developed country, the bidding process used by governments and the terms of the contract will dramatically impact the price investors are willing to pay. Changes requested after the contract is signed will also subsequently change the risk perception of investors and command higher returns for investors, which equates to less funds for the government.

The "infrastructure gap" derives primarily from a perceived lack of "investable projects": a gap between the requirements and expectations of private investors and the characteristics of existing projects, regulations and bidding process. It also highlights how divergent interests and knowledge discrepancies can prevent governments from attracting investors in the first place and be detrimental to them when they close a deal.

This question has led scholars to research the risks of each infrastructure project, and the regulations, governance and project structuration that could reduce these risks and align interests between governments and private investors (Loosemore, 2006; Yescombe, 2014; Déau, 2011; Page et al., 2008). Governments with repeated experience with the private sector also came up with standardized bills and processes such as "value for money" to reduce the knowledge gap. However, the broader questions are: how do governments need to change, and what are some general government characteristics that seem to lead to successful partnerships with the private sector to build infrastructure that is both financially attractive and maximizes regional development?

METHODOLOGY

This chapter describes a case study of an infrastructure program led by NSW to recycle infrastructure assets, with specific attention to the role of Infrastructure New South Wales (InNSW), an independent infrastructure agency in this program. The guiding research question was to understand the key structural and functional characteristics of this independent infrastructure agency and of the infrastructure asset recycling program. This understanding led to questioning the theories of how the state can lead development described in the literature, and to the proposal of an alternative model inspired by this case study.

The description and analysis of InNSW and the Asset Recycling Program is based on a review of government documents[3] as well as expert reviews and reports on both the independent infrastructure agency and the asset recycling program. This document review was completed by informal face-to-face interviews during the three months the author spent in Australia in 2015, phone interviews with employees of Infrastructure NSW in the fall of 2017, and a presentation of the asset recycling program by a member of the NSW government. The purpose of this study is not to assess the success of this agency and program but to describe some of its key features, practices and achievements, and in turn to describe how this example informs our understanding of how the state can lead development and increase investments into new infrastructure projects.

THE TWO LEGS OF INFRASTRUCTURE ASSET RECYCLING

Infrastructure asset recycling consists of two legs: selling or leasing existing assets, and reinvesting the proceeds into new infrastructure assets. In NSW, the first step was handled by the state government, with a strong implication of the newly elected Premier to garner public support for the sale and lease of assets. Private sector experts and consultants, as well as special task forces, helped the government to advertise and handle the bids by private sector consortia, with the goal of maximizing the sale/lease price and protecting the quality of services rendered to citizens. This step resembles other programs of "privatizations" in which states delegate the operation of large infrastructure projects to a private company.

However, asset recycling was unique in the degree of sophistication given to the second step: reinvesting the proceeds from the sale/lease of existing assets. Indeed, this step built on the creation of an independent infrastructure agency to improve the long-term planning and delivery of infrastructure projects. It took away decision power from the political executives to give more leeway to this agency, which was required to follow transparent, rationalized processes to choose projects. This agency worked to increase the stability of infrastructure plans and their transparency to citizens. However, giving such responsibilities to a newly created and small government agency required a set of processes for it to ensure that it could bring the desired innovation, independence and transparency, and still work collaboratively with existing government actors and processes.

Below, I start by discussing the asset recycling program and how its two legs make it different from traditional privatization programs. Next, I focus on the organizational solution that made the second leg possible – having an independent infrastructure agency in charge of reinvestment – and how the innovation it brought to government infrastructure planning was key to the success of the program and more generally for infrastructure planning and delivery in the state.

INFRASTRUCTURE ASSET RECYCLING IN NSW[4]

The NSW State Government launched the Rebuilding NSW program in July 2011 to lease existing assets, capture the money in a fund named Restart NSW, and reinvest it into new infrastructure projects. The process is summarized in Figure 12.1.

Restart NSW is a fund aimed at directing capital toward high-priority future infrastructure projects. This mission is made possible by the work of InNSW to establish a prioritized list of projects and to control that the funds only go to those projects. Between 2011 and June 2017, AU$29.8 billion were deposited in Restart NSW, AU$9.8 billion more than the 2011 government ten-year plan to invest AU$20 billion in new infrastructure through this scheme. The capital come primarily from the sale or lease of existing infrastructure assets. The 99-year lease of the Transgrid electricity distribution network for AU$10.258 billion at the end of 2015 yielded the deposit of AU$6.579 billion to the Restart NSW fund, while the AU$16 billion Ausgrid transaction yielded AU$5.6 billion to the fund. The third-highest contribution came from the privatization of two ports for

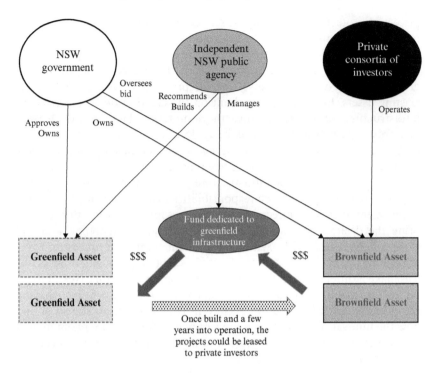

Figure 12.1 The asset recycling mechanism in NSW, Australia

AU$4.3 billion in 2013 (see 2017–18 Budget Paper No. 2 – Infrastructure Statement – Chapter 2: Restart NSW). Waratah Bonds (fixed interest bonds issued by the New South Wales Treasury Corporation), interest income and windfall tax revenue complement the capital coming from the "recycling" of existing infrastructure.

In 2018, about 40 percent of the Restart NSW fund (AU$11.9 billion) had been committed to identified infrastructure projects and programs as part of the government's 20 billion Rebuilding NSW plan, supporting around 400 infrastructure projects, including delivering 80 local infrastructure projects. Sydney Metro City and Southwest Project, a 30 km metro rail line, was allocated AU$7 billion from this program and is currently under construction, with an expected delivery for 2024 (2017–18 Budget Paper No. 2 – Infrastructure Statement – Chapter 2: Restart NSW).

Almost a third of the proceeds of Restart NSW are reserved for projects in regional NSW, with 10 percent of this funding to be spent on the Resources for the Regions program, which aims to ensure a fair share of infrastructure for communities affected by mining activity. In addition, out of the lease of one port, AU$100 million were put into the Restart NSW Illawarra Infrastructure Fund. Funds for regional projects are allocated using a review process that engages local councils, community groups, industry and business groups, and non-government organizations to identify the regions' highest priority infrastructure projects. The mix of tax, bonds and proceeds from privatization into the fund makes the nature of this capital enigmatic. The government describes the mechanism as a funding solution, but it most closely resembles a financing mechanism, which deserves further discussion, as it has been a major critique of the asset recycling program.

Is Asset Recycling a Funding or a Financing Mechanism?

Capital raised through "financing" must be paid back in the future. Sources of financing are equity and debt, both of which expect cash flows in the future to pay back the capital, and interest to compensate for the value of time. The future cash flows needed to pay back creditors come from funding sources. Funding sources can be cash flows created by the project such as user fees, or funds sustainably dedicated to a project as in the case of taxes. Financing can help to create value, when the money borrowed is invested in projects that will create an incremental stream of cash flows worth more than the repayment of the debt and interest. We can analyze asset recycling using this difference between funding and financing.

Potential Profits from the Lease of Assets

With asset recycling, the government obtains funds when leasing an asset, but commits to giving away user fees or giving availability payments to the leaseholder. On its balance sheet, it has also exchanged capital for cash. Theoretically, the government did not create value. In practice, it can make a profit if the bid value is higher than the present value of the future cash flows it would have received from owning and operating the asset. In that case, the value creation is highly dependent on the procurement process, and the ability of the government to attract multiple investors to compete in the bid and package the deal so that, from their point of view, the money it gets is superior to the net present value (NPV) of future cash flows. It is also debatable to decide whether the government made a profit, because the NPV calculation depends on assumptions for the discount rate used to transform future cash flows into a present value. However, comparisons with other deals can provide a good benchmark.

By this standard, the NSW government has been successful at setting up bids for assets and getting high payments for them by industry standards.

Part of the high price can be explained by the fact that many investors are interested in brownfield infrastructure assets, and competition is driving prices up. However, this explanation seems to be insufficient, because other deals for brownfield assets in developed countries did not draw as much interest, or as high prices. The consortium that won the bid for TransGrid paid about 14.7 times the earnings before interest, tax, depreciation and amortization (EBITDA) of the company, less than the 28 times EBITDA some investors paid for a toll road and tunnel in Brisbane, but more than the 8–11 times EBITDA usually paid for regular private companies. For regulated assets, a bid price of between 1.3 and 1.4 times the regulated asset value is considered normal, but TransGrid was sold for 1.65 times its asset value. The asset was highly levered, but after repaying debts the NSW government was estimated to obtain about AU$7.3 billion (Maiden, 2015). The bid also attracted four bidding consortia with institutional investors from all over the world. The winning consortium was composed of the Canadian pension fund Caisse de depot et placement du Quebec (CDCQ) with 24.99 percent, Hastings (20.02 percent), the Abu Dhabi Investment Authority (19.99 percent), Kuwait Investment Authority (19.99 percent), and with the remaining 15.01 percent held by Spark Infrastructure, which will operate the asset (Robins, 2015).

Comparing the Value of Owning an Asset to Using these Funds to Build a New Asset

Another important question to assess whether asset recycling creates value is to compare the projects sold to the new projects being funded. A report from the McKell Institute (Ferrer et al., 2014) supports this comparison. It classifies projects based on their profitability and the value and certainty of the cash flows coming from different infrastructure projects. It underlines that the assets being sold are probably the most profitable. Therefore, from an investor's perspective, for the reinvestment to be worth the sale, the new projects being funded should have a net present value superior to the ones just sold. This would mean that the government must invest in toll roads, for example, and not in hospitals or schools, according to their classification of infrastructure projects by potential to generate future revenues. However, a critical difference is that the government values economic development creation and livability as well as purely financial cash flow generation. In addition, the cash flows for the government need not necessarily come from user fees: they can come from taxation, notably of new businesses and activities born thanks to new infrastructure.

The new projects in which the NSW government invests the Restart NSW's funds show both the desire to invest in projects that make financial and economic sense, as well as in projects that reflect a sense of duty to invest fairly across the territory. Part of Restart NSW was earmarked for community projects, in which communities had a large say about the projects they wanted to see built, demonstrating attention to local social and civic values. On the other hand, the first flagship project being financed and developed by InNSW is the WestConnex road in Sydney. Although this project is attractive for many institutional investors and seems as though it would bring profitable cash flows, the government had enough money to decide whether development would be better handled internally or by using a private consortium. In this case, it judged that it could design and build the project more cost-efficiently itself, mainly because the private sector prices the construction and demand risks higher than the government. The private sector might also pay a premium to buy the asset once it is operating, largely compensating the government for the risk of construction. The government did not originally announce that it would sell the project, but the Restart NSW fund could become a sort of revolving fund in which the government could take on the construction and demand risk for some projects, but sell projects that are less risky, creating steady cash flows that allow investment in new projects that drive economic growth.

In summary, asset recycling makes the government give up future cash flows from existing projects to fund the construction of new projects. However, operation and maintenance costs still need to be covered by other sources of funds, taxes or user fees; and ideally, construction costs would also be recouped through these funding sources if the government does not want to lose capital. In addition, securing future cash flows is essential to continue recycling assets, and to sell these greenfield projects to private investors in the future. Nevertheless, future cash flows do not necessarily need to come from user fees to make the project more valuable to the community and the government. Thus, a transit project not fully funded by user fees might create more economic value and tax revenues, avoid future costs to the government, and be more valuable overall to the government and citizens than a toll road fully funded by user fees.

Restart NSW is therefore not strictly a funding mechanism, as the government gains access to new capital only when it makes a profit on a transaction. Thinking of it as a financing mechanism might be closer, but comparing it to other financing mechanisms does not do justice to the freedom it gives to government, and the potential other benefits brought by privatizing selected projects. When comparing asset recycling to traditional funding and financing sources, one should think in broader terms than comparing the costs and revenues of one project. Indeed, an integrated plan can both reduce the costs of projects and give the government access to indirect revenues created by the economic development made possible by new infrastructure.

Reinvestments are at the heart of the asset recycling program. I have discussed why these are an interesting alternative financing mechanism, giving more freedom and flexibility to the government than traditional loans and budget allocation. I now focus on Infrastructure NSW, the agency in charge of reinvesting the proceeds from the sale/lease of existing assets, as a key component of the success of the asset recycling program.

INFRASTRUCTURE NSW AS AN AGENT OF CHANGE

In 2011, the state of NSW, Australia created by legislative Act a government agency called Infrastructure New South Wales (InNSW) to "secure the efficient, effective, economic and timely planning, co-ordination, selection, funding, implementation, delivery and whole-of-life cycle asset management of infrastructure that is required for the economic and social well-being of the community, and to ensure that decisions about infrastructure projects are informed by expert professional analysis and advice" (Infrastructure NSW Act 2011 No 23).

While subject to the control and direction of the State Premier in the exercise of its functions, this agency was given some independence through a board of directors and a chief executive officer (CEO). Composed of the director-generals of five government departments, and up to five experts from the private sector appointed by the Premier, the board determines the general policies and strategic direction of the agency and advises both the CEO and the Premier. While the Premier retains the final say on the strategies proposed by InNSW, the board may publicly express its disapproval of the Premier's changes.

With about 30 employees and a flat structure, InNSW is quite different from the traditional government agencies that have helped to plan and operate infrastructure projects in the state. Indeed, its structure and governance make it less subject to political negotiations happening inside the government and the bureaucracy. More of its work is also available openly to the public, where the bureaucracy's recommendations are mostly kept as internal documents.

InNSW was created with the key mission of creating an innovative, cross-sector and comprehensive long-term strategic plan over 20 years. This plan innovated by using demographic and economic projections to identify the needs before thinking about the projects. It aimed at disrupting the previous process of each government department proposing projects without an overarching view of the needs of the state, and getting rid of the biases of bureaus for one type of technical solution, such as an opposition between "train enthusiasts" and "car enthusiasts." Its core missions include providing independent, professional policy advice to the government, with the goal of reducing the political biases and inconsistency that had characterized infrastructure planning in the state and had led it to a significant drop in the quality and availability of infrastructure under previous governments.

It also features project management and helping the government with the delivery of new projects, a mission quite different from planning, and potentially difficult to combine in such a small agency. InNSW undertook it step by step, taking on one project first, and increasing its capacity when the project proved successful. With its expertise and track record improving with time, its activities increased to project assurance, review of business cases prepared by the bureaucracy for new projects, and most importantly to overseeing the reinvestment of the proceeds from the state's asset sales, stored in a fund named Restart NSW and part of its asset recycling program.

The capital coming from privatization or lease of existing assets can only go to the projects that InNSW prioritized publicly in the long-term plan, limiting the ability of politicians to privilege pet projects. This mechanism of limiting the power of the executive in using the proceeds from privatizations is a core difference of the asset recycling mechanism compared to other privatization programs. Its success was highly dependent on the ability of InNSW to change government and bureaucratic practices in planning and delivering new infrastructure, previously hampered by political considerations and stiff siloed processes.

A Key Change: Integrated Long-Term Planning

A key role of InNSW is to provide an integrated plan for infrastructure development in NSW, breaking the silos of traditional government departments. According to an interviewee, the way government budgets used to work was that, under each minister and ministry, there was an agency. The agency would make its own list of projects, price them, and then ask the Treasurer (under the Premier) for the amount it wanted. Then the Treasurer would negotiate with each agency under each ministry. The process led to a five-year plan updated every year that would allocate funds to each ministry. This process created two main issues: first, there was virtually no possibility to adopt an integrated plan in which projects across ministries were thought of as complementary to each other, and investment in one was thought of in correlation with investment in others to decrease costs and increase benefits. The budget was negotiated and distributed in a way that hindered holistic, systematic and integrated infrastructure planning. The second issue was that projects would get politicized: a minister might give priority to a project in their constituency, for example.

InNSW proposed a solution to both issues by establishing integrated plans and transparent funding processes. First, InNSW requires that each agency and ministry makes a business case for each project proposed. This role was described as "umbrella oversight" and an "overarching viewpoint" by an interviewee. InNSW does not gather the information about each project; it requires departments to develop a business case, manage external consultants and auditors to check the business case, then recommend to the Treasurer and Premier which projects to fund based on the criteria of "strategic fit" and "economic merit." Second, the Treasurer can only say "yes" or "no" to these recommendations, which avoids "unfair" political pressure for "earmarked" projects. In line with its overarching role, InNSW is meant to stay "small and nimble" and to use the same requirements for itself and the agencies it tries to change.

An Efficient and Effective State

Although privatizations were a key aspect of the asset recycling program, the state continued to build internal expertise through the creation of InNSW. InNSW wishes to build the tools for the government to assess what type of procurement is best for each project, and how to be an effective project manager if the government decides to handle design and construction, which is the case for some of the large greenfield infrastructure projects being developed now in NSW. On one hand, InNSW does follow up on projects approved for funding, doing regular "health checks" on time and cost compliance and on the risks identified during the planning stage. On the other hand, InNSW itself is responsible for the delivery of some important infrastructure projects in Sydney, and created to this end Projects NSW, an internal team of specialists.

Projects NSW mirrors the skills and knowledge that an owner's representative might gather and makes sure that InNSW can effectively monitor its contractors and avoid being a "price taker." With this expertise, Projects NSW could become the internal consultant of all other government departments needing to build infrastructure. Not all projects will be delivered internally, but this team reduces information asymmetry between contractors and the government.

The efforts from InNSW to build capabilities to design and deliver infrastructure projects can be understood through the history of greenfield projects delivered as PPPs in Australia. Private consortia took patronage risks for new toll roads for which the forecast in traffic did not materialize, leading to the bankruptcies of Sydney's Cross City and Lane Cove tunnels, which left their parent companies in the hands of administrators. These experiences led many private investors to rule out considering projects where they had to take on patronage "demand" risk. In a recent enquiry by the Productivity Commission related to private investment into transport infrastructure, the private sector overwhelmingly asked the government to take on a larger proportion of both construction and patronage risk in greenfield projects. As an interviewee puts it: private operators "learned their lessons." After these projects' failures, the government had to offer availability payments if they wanted to attract private money. This did not exclude leasing projects once built and operating, since this stage of the project attracts far more private investors. Competition could then help the government to make profits later. However, this scenario can only happen if the government has the internal capabilities to identify, measure and mitigate risks, as well as to deliver projects on time and on budget. InNSW therefore gives the government the capabilities to build new projects effectively and to reap the benefits of taking construction and demand risks in cases where it decides to lease or sell operating assets to the private sector later.

Practices Used by InNSW Employees to Innovate and Change Government

While bringing a new integrated plan and new methods to monitor the good delivery of projects seem attractive enough to win over other government agencies, this also created tensions, and InNSW must constantly balance finding new tools and visions with convincing other government actors of its usefulness to them and its benefits for the population.

The catchphrase that people see when visiting InNSW's website changes between "We collaborate," "We challenge" and "We transform." As these suggest, InNSW needs to be both innovative and independent enough to challenge, and collaborative enough to influence the decisions and operations of the bureaucracy to transform the government. Bringing this type of innovation can be classified in two steps: ideation and integration (Downs and Mohr, 1976). Interviews revealed that a typical process led by InNSW employees to craft strategic recommendations consists of the following steps:

1. Ideation:
    a. Gather a group of renowned experts on the topic from a broad background in academia, the private sector and civil society, using the help of private sector board members to find these actors.

b. Come up with a detailed paper with evidence on the key problem and a set of proposed solutions, with several options on language and approach, and recommendations on how to go forward.
   c. Present this paper to the board and ensure the infrastructure agency's leadership will back the paper.
2. Integration: Reach out to relevant government departments and agencies with the proposed paper through:
   a. a meeting or workshop to reach consensus on direction;
   b. individually reaching out to leaders of agencies to give an opportunity for feedback and comments, and evaluating their ability to practically implement recommendations; changes following these interactions are minor and mainly linked to language.

This process shows a clear differentiation in time, but also in the actors engaged and the activities performed between innovation through ideation, and influence through integration of the recommendations. Figure 12.2 shows how these actors and practices differ, distinguishing between the stakeholders engaged outside the infrastructure agency, and the persons inside the infrastructure agency overseeing those processes.

Ideation Stage: Collaboration as Co-creation of Knowledge

At the ideation stage, employees of InNSW rely on finding new ideas and perspectives thanks to the practice of co-creating knowledge. This practice

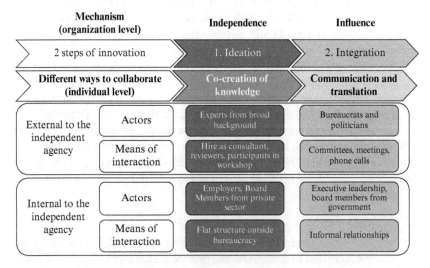

Figure 12.2   A two-step model for state innovation

is supported by formal processes to source ideas from external experts. It is also characterized by the fact that the bureaucracy and political executive do not participate in this practice.

Outside experts are chosen for their subject matter expertise. They are either non-affiliated politically, "honest, independent brokers," or the process deliberately sources ideas from people representing a variety of political views. Experts bring data, experience and different perspectives that help InNSW employees to "kick around ideas." A key difference with the bureaucracy is that InNSW can interact with a wider range of experts, because it can use the network of private sector board members to access high-level experts. However, there is a risk that InNSW might depend too much on consultants and experts or be biased by their contribution. To tackle this challenge, InNSW uses very rigorous processes to source knowledge from external stakeholders. Examples of processes include roundtables of experts led by InNSW employees, use of frameworks to guide experts' analysis, and use of technical reports that are reviewed and incorporated by employees with experience in the field.

InNSW internal characteristics are also essential to ideation. Its flat structure and interactions between internal teams and executives allow for more exchanges of ideas. The small size and senior level of employees make these exchanges possible. Interactions with experts are handled by its employees, while the board of directors and CEO give directions, contribute different perspectives and help to connect with people who can shed new light on government challenges. The cognitive diversity of board members is reflected in InNSW employees, who come from different disciplines and are primarily chosen for their strategic thinking abilities and emotional intelligence.

Integration Stage: Communication to Build Trust and Translation to Facilitate Adoption

At the integration stage, collaboration is mainly with the bureaucracy and political executive. However, the practice is not co-creation of knowledge, but communication to build trust, and "translation" to facilitate the integration of new ideas into existing bureaucratic processes. These practices are supported by informal, ongoing, non-project-specific communication that builds trust. In addition, formal processes of communication, which often occur prior to and after an analysis, enable the translation of new ideas in terms that are acceptable and implementable by the government.

Informal communication with bureaucrats happens mainly at the CEO and senior executive levels. It is frequent, in person or on the phone, and focuses on high-level topics and activities. Its main goal is to strengthen relationships and build trust. It is part of a strategy of being transparent and not taking government by surprise. These practices are in fact used to increase InNSW's ability to disagree with the bureaucracy without being perceived as an enemy. They entertain a sense of collaboration and communicate the expertise of InNSW. These interactions correspond to the practice of communicating to build trust, which is necessary for the second practice, translation, to take place.

There are also formal interactions with bureaucrats and elected officials: at the beginning of an analysis, to share data and ensure the salience of the topics, for example agreeing to share evidence gathered by each agency and agreeing on which metrics to use in an analysis to ensure comparability of advice sent to government. Another important activity is sharing the results of an analysis. The goal is to preserve the content of the analysis, which rests on robust, rational processes, but also to get a sense of the resonance of the advice with decision-makers and people in charge of implementing this advice.

Common issues might be a disbelief in the results if the process is not well understood; or the results differing from the conclusion of the bureaucracy or ideas of the political executive. Then the communication focuses on convincing by showing the steps of the research that led to this conclusion, and how it eventually serves the public good. Another issue might be the difficulty to implement some recommendations, and communicating can help to make the recommendation more feasible. Finally, some opposition arises from differences in vocabulary that make the recommendations foreign to government and can also lead to disbelief. I therefore talk about a practice of "translation," because modifications are often referred to as "language modification," and because it denotes work at the cognitive and cultural level. These processes allow the transfer of ideas from other fields to bureaucrats and elected officials, by being translated into their cultural context.

A NEW MODEL OF DEVELOPMENTAL STATE: THE FINANCIER STATE

The goals of InNSW were to change the existing state bureaucracy process to achieve a more integrated plan in between existing agencies, and to use metrics and processes inspired by the private sector to prioritize projects. In that sense the program used a mix of social and developmental criteria and of financial returns as an indicator of the soundness of projects.

Chibber (2002) already noted the potential problems of divergent short-term interests between government agencies and the necessity to give one agency authority and power over others to use resources efficiently. In the case of NSW, the agency, InNSW, benefited from regulative authority over important planning and financing decisions through its oversight of the Restart NSW fund. This was key to help the agency have a base for its independence and influence over established actors. However, it was not enough, and the independent agency's employees also used practices to foster different types of collaboration with different actors. Collaboration with private sector actors enables the agency to innovate and to bring new visions and processes to government. Collaboration with government actors focuses on finding a common language to adapt the tools to their needs and convince them of their usefulness. This distinction is essential to understand how an independent infrastructure agency can bring innovation to government.

The example also showed that privatization need not mean that the government will lose all capabilities and blindly trust the private sector. Instead, many practices from the private sector are adopted to better monitor the private sectors' activities as an operator and supplier of public services.

The proposed model of the "financier state" emphasizes the state as protecting its difference and capabilities from the private sector, but also understanding private sector actors' interests, culture and practices enough to effectively partner with them. This ideal might not always be possible, but the goal is to build a strong state, able to steer other stakeholders and align interests. The term "financier state" comes from the heavy use of practices and frameworks from the field of investing, rationalizing processes to assess the value of new projects, but also choosing the projects to lease, and managing the bids to maximize the value of sale/lease proceeds while safeguarding the population's interests.

While the term "financier state" is singular, this hides the fact that it relies on a network of government agencies and task forces that are specialized and play the role of a bridge between the operational state bureaucracy, which is still quite insular, hierarchical and rule-based, and private sector actors which can provide expertise in planning, assessing and operating infrastructure projects. A task force in the Ministry of Finance handled the bids and played this role for the first leg of asset recycling. In this chapter, we have focused on the second leg, which was more unique to asset recycling in NSW, and described the role and practices of the independent agency Infrastructure NSW.

In summary, this new model of developmental state emphasizes how the state can devise a program based on making the most of private sector actors' interests to then gain enough capital and knowledge to lead development in a hybrid manner, optimizing financial but also social and environmental factors. Contrary to Evans and Rauch (1999) and Chibber (2002), and with Ó Riain et al. (2000) and Tsui-Auch (2004), this study shows that internal cohesiveness can be an obstacle to the change needed to attract new actors. The example of InNSW shows that strong regulative powers and practices to bridge normative and cultural gaps are essential to overcome the issue of fragmentation brought up by Ó Riain et al. (2000). The key elements of the financier state model are:

- The will to attract private investments, but to serve social good and development goals as well.
- The reliance on independent agencies or government units that play the role of change leader and have the following characteristics:
  - the agency hires people with cultural-cognitive embeddedness in fields that the state want as collaborators, usually a mix from the private sector and the bureaucracy;
  - this embeddedness serves to build insiders' knowledge and a strong state, able to negotiate with private sector counterparties on a more equal footing, and to convince bureaucrats of the value of new ideas;
  - the emphasis is on aligning private interests, and using incentives instead of suppressing or constraining private interests, be this at the individual level in the workforce or with private companies;
  - the agency infuses optimization processes and efficiency values from the private sector – here the infrastructure investing and development sectors – into its practice, and the practices of other government agencies;
  - the agency benefits from regulative powers, and the support of the political leader of the state.

CONCLUSIONS AND FURTHER RESEARCH

Through this case study, I have detailed a model of developmental state that differs from existing theories about the developmental bureaucratic state and the flexible state: the financier state. This model was inspired by how the state of NSW created a new kind of coordinating agency, which was a key element of the program of asset recycling in which the interests and processes of the private sector are indirectly put to serve state developmental goals. Some key elements of the proposed model are that the government tries to instigate change in the state bureaucracy by giving regulatory power to a coordinating agency. This agency adopts processes and knowledge from the private sector to reinforce the power of the state when dealing with private partners, but also to be able to create structures where interests are aligned, and risk is managed by the most capable stakeholder. In this case, the coordinating agency did not have to deal with a large number of diverse stakeholders, which can explain why there might have been less fragmentation than in Ó Riain et al.'s (2000) study of Ireland. I posit that with an increase in complexity (number and diversity of stakeholders), several agencies might be needed to deal with fields that have very little in common.

I also detailed an innovative structure overseen by the coordinating agency, the asset recycling fund Restart NSW. The fund benefited from the isolation from the government's budget. Partitioning the proceeds from privatization from the government's budget gave confidence to voters and ensured the rational use of funds toward the goal of maximizing economic benefits. The mechanism was based on the idea of maximizing profits from the sale, and choosing the correct projects, notably with the capabilities to efficiently procure them internally if necessary. To realize this vision, InNSW had to build capabilities, and not only gather knowledge and communicate it. It also had to create internal capabilities to evaluate and mitigate construction and patronage risk. An underlying assumption supporting the success of this fund is the capacity of the state to handle better construction and demand risks, or to use funds from indirect consequences of a project to fund that same project. Although subsidizing a project with other revenues is often considered bad investment practice in the private sector, it makes more sense from the government's perspective, given the externalities created by infrastructure projects. Indeed, infrastructure projects benefit from being planned consistently with each other, and each project's value can increase by the addition of another project. However, if the state claims to be guided by a sound financial and economic analysis, such a "transfer" still needs to be based on an economic analysis assessing the real costs and revenues of a project over its life cycle. In addition, the asset recycling mechanism in and of itself does not guarantee that a new project will be funded over its entire life cycle. The government still needs to secure long-term funding for the operation and maintenance of new projects, be this through user fees, taxes or other innovative capture of the value created by new projects.

Finally, this single case study could be augmented by comparing the different Australian states (Australian Government et al., 2015) to strengthen the model by getting variation on the proposed explicative factors, and the outcome of developing infrastructure and/or creating asset recycling funds. The model would also benefit from being tested in other settings, notably in developing countries and for development projects that include industries as well as infrastructure. I have also only briefly described the key mechanisms that create the ability to procure projects, and to structure the sale of existing assets. Given the importance of such skills, further research could focus on understanding those mechanisms more fully.

NOTES

1. IMF, https://www.imf.org/external/datamapper/GGXWDG_NGDP@WEO/OEMDC/ADVEC/WEOWORLD.
2. Trading Economics, https://tradingeconomics.com/country-list/government-debt-to-gdp.
3. New South Wales Government website, webpage of the Treasury (available at: http://www.treasury.nsw.gov.au/); Infrastructure New South Wales (InNSW) website (available at: http://www.infrastructure.nsw.gov.au/); New South Wales Government website, webpage on infrastructure strategy and the included documents (available at: http://www.nsw.gov.au/initiative/state-infrastructure-strategy and at: https://www.nsw.gov.au/sites/default/files/miscellaneous/nsw_government_submission_cover_letter.pdf); New South Wales Government submission to the electricity networks leasing inquiry (available at: https://www.parliament.nsw.gov.au/committees/DBAssets/InquiryReport/ReportAcrobat/5402/Report%20-%20Leasing%20of%20electricity%20infrastructure.pdf); New South Wales Government webpage on Rebuilding New South Wales (available at: https://www.nsw.gov.au/rebuilding).
4. Based partially on: New South Wales Government website, webpage of the Treasury (available at: http://www.treasury.nsw.gov.au/); Infrastructure New South Wales (InNSW) website (available at: http://www.infrastructure.nsw.gov.au/); New South Wales Government website, webpage on infrastructure strategy and the included documents (available at: http://www.nsw.gov.au/initiative/state-infrastructure-strategy and at: https://www.nsw.gov.au/sites/default/files/miscellaneous/nsw_government_submission_cover_letter.pdf); New South Wales Government webpage on Rebuilding New South Wales (available at: https://www.nsw.gov.au/rebuilding).

13. Community investment and crowdfunding as partnership strategies for local infrastructure delivery

Kate E. Gasparro

INTRODUCTION

It is the local infrastructure – the roads we drive on to get to the grocery store, the pipes that send us water through our kitchen faucets, the electricity networks that connect us to the elusive "electrical grid" – that make our lives work and have become a more critical part of our existence. Even though the aggregation of local infrastructure projects constructed and maintained in a given year can improve the day-to-day quality of life, much of the research on infrastructure delivery has centered on delivery of large infrastructure projects that bring new acclaim to politicians and supposedly catalyze economic development. Because large infrastructure projects, with their complicated stakeholder networks, critical schedules and high budgets, can easily be derailed by complications and unexpected circumstances, practitioners and academics have turned toward public–private partnerships as a means to mitigate these issues. Private sector partners are invited to participate in infrastructure delivery because they can bring new innovations and efficiencies. But why should these partnerships be limited to large infrastructure projects? As local infrastructure assets start to deteriorate and need rehabilitation and intense maintenance, partnership strategies could aid flailing local governments which are limited by lack of personnel and dwindling budgets. At the same time, as pressure to expand infrastructure services increases, partnership strategies could catalyze new local infrastructure construction. To understand how partnership strategies can be used for local infrastructure projects, I explore a new phenomenon that has been used to realign stakeholder interests and increase resources during infrastructure delivery: crowdfunding.

HISTORY OF PARTNERSHIPS IN INFRASTRUCTURE DELIVERY

Over the last 100 years in the United States (US), infrastructure project stakeholder networks have evolved, introducing new stakeholders and redistributing power among stakeholders. Because infrastructure assets are public goods and susceptible to free-rider and resource management issues (Ostrom and Ostrom, 1977), governments at the local, state and federal levels have historically taken sole responsibility for infrastructure delivery. As government agencies have faced challenges in providing resources and managing stakeholder relationships, US policies have evolved to allow partnership strategies (reflected in procedural, contractual and financial arrangements) to facilitate infrastructure delivery. Similar to the introduction of public–private partnerships, the use of crowdfunding is another effort by local governments to obtain resources and manage stakeholder relationships during local infrastructure delivery. This section provides a brief history of infrastructure delivery and the need for partnership strategies.

During the first half of the twentieth century, US federal policies such as the National Highway System and the Tennessee Valley Authority, gave responsibility to national agencies to deliver large, centralized infrastructure projects. These projects resulted in urban sprawl and industrial development that led to an outcry of concern over environmental degradation. This national response ushered in an era of grassroots environmental and social activism (Tarr, 1984). The conflict between large-scale development and grassroots activism played out in several ways. The National Environmental Policy Act (NEPA) of 1969 tried to address the unintended consequences of large-scale development by requiring external stakeholder engagement (primarily engagement with impacted and beneficiary communities) during project planning phases (Hayes, 2014). Capitalizing on the knowledge base of communities, demand and community-driven strategies were incorporated into infrastructure delivery.

As decentralization trends of the 1990s shifted power away from federal agencies (Oates, 1999), local governments (typically states and municipalities) became more responsible for infrastructure delivery. Unlike their federal counterparts, local governments often lacked (and still lack) the technical know-how and resources for delivering successful infrastructure assets. Therefore, project stakeholder networks expanded beyond state and local agencies (Alm, 2015) to include private sector partners which could provide technical resources. To support this trend, the United States Congress passed the Federal Acquisitions Reform Act in 1996 to allow local governments and government agencies to extend decision-making power to the private sector through innovative contracting arrangements (Ghavamifar and Touran, 2008). But as stakeholder networks expanded to include more private sector providers, external stakeholders such as community members were increasingly excluded from project shaping phases.

Despite the community's role as the beneficiary (and sometimes as the affected party) of infrastructure delivery, community members have a limited role in influencing decisions regarding infrastructure delivery. Even though private sector providers have more technical expertise and capacity for delivering projects efficiently, they are often motivated by profit margins and guided by short-sighted time frames instead of community welfare. The misalignment of priorities between the community and private sector providers has become a growing issue (Forrer et al., 2010), leading to episodes of community resistance and mobilization (Rucht, 2002). Further, local governments often lack the necessary insights and resources to represent the preferences of constituents accurately or to act in the best interest of the wider community (Pratchett, 2004), which can lead to community opposition to local infrastructure delivery.

To counteract these trends, public participation processes, once extolled in policies such as the National Environmental Policy Act (Shepherd and Bowler, 1997) as a means to increase community engagement during project shaping phases, are becoming more formalized during the infrastructure delivery process to mitigate future community backlash. Project partners, local governments and private partners alike are seeing the value of including community feedback throughout the delivery process, and especially during project shaping phases (Miller and Olleros, 2000). With formalization of public participation processes, there have been new trends that are shifting the ways project partners conduct public participation. Recent online crowd technologies, such as Popularise.com and Neighborland.com, are facilitating informal external stakeholder engagement to inform policy-makers about the preferences of residents affected by local urban development (Brabham, 2010).

While these trends help to explain the foundation and impacts of public–private partnerships for large infrastructure projects, they also foreshadow the introduction of crowdfunding in local infrastructure delivery. First, the use of private sector partners and private sector financing to improve efficiencies and capacity opens the door to other innovative funding and financing strategies for infrastructure projects. Second, decentralization trends shift more responsibility to local governments during infrastructure delivery, forcing local governments to build capacity for infrastructure planning, design, construction and maintenance. Third, there is a renewed focus on public participation as a way to re-engage communities and constituents. Last, in the years following the 2009 Recession, local governments have had to become creative with how they deliver and maintain essential public services as funds decline due to lower property values (and subsequent property taxes) (Muro and Hoene, 2009). As such, innovative partnership strategies that could: (1) introduce innovative financing and funding; (2) improve capacity for local governments; and (3) engage communities have become attractive options for motivating infrastructure delivery.

COMMUNITY INVESTMENT AS A PARTNERSHIP TOOL

In 2012, after several years of using donation-based crowdfunding for small projects, the United States Congress passed the JOBS Act to further legitimize innovative strategies, specifically crowdfunding, for infrastructure delivery (Farajian et al., 2015). Even though recent United States legislation highlights crowdfunding as a legitimate partnership tool for infrastructure delivery, older forms (which are referred to as community investment) have been used for infrastructure delivery. Community investment is founded on the concept that substantial financial resources for a specific project can be raised by a large pool of individuals who contribute relatively small amounts of financial resources. Although each community investment model shares this idea, the models range from donation and capital cost sharing processes (where there is no expectation of a financial return on investment) to equity investing opportunities (where investors take on more risk in hopes of receiving an attractive financial return on their investment). Each model meets the characteristics of community investment to varying degrees. In this section, I discuss the landscape of community investment models that have been used to increase resources and manage stakeholder relationships during infrastructure delivery.

Capital Cost Sharing

In developing and emerging market countries, where capital markets are not well developed and donor and multilateral agencies – that is, non-governmental organizations (NGOs), development banks and foundations – are highly involved in public service delivery, capital cost sharing is common practice for infrastructure delivery. As a condition of their involvement in project delivery, donor or lending agencies will often require the benefiting community to contribute to the project's capital costs. The project sponsor that interfaces between the community and donor or lending agency will often procure a specified amount of capital funding from the community through a variety of means. Capital cost sharing is not restricted to household monetary contributions. It may also include labor and material contributions.

Capital cost sharing processes are founded on the principle that initial capital cost sharing increases financial responsibility and project sustainability because of increased community sense of ownership and "buy-in" of the asset. For example, Engineers Without Borders is one such NGO that requires 5 percent of capital costs to be provided by the community prior to constructing an infrastructure project, claiming that "community contributions (cash and in-kind) institute a sense of ownership in the beneficiary community and contribute to ensuring project sustainability" (Knight et al., 2014). Research supports these claims; in Isham and Kähkönen's (1999) work, it was found that individuals who contribute finances at the beginning of a project have a higher likelihood of paying tariffs during the operation and maintenance of the asset. Additional studies have shown that household contributions can result in an elevated sense of ownership (Marks and Davis, 2012) which can potentially increase project sustainability. As part of managing capital cost sharing, communities have created local governance bodies to facilitate resource collection from community members, organize community feedback, consolidate representation and govern community stakeholders (Khwaja, 2009).

Municipal Bonds

Municipal bonds are another form of community investment used for large infrastructure funds or specific revenue-backed infrastructure projects in developed countries. The idea of using municipal bonds for infrastructure delivery dates back to 1812, when New York City issued debt to local constituents for financing a canal project (Cutler and Miller, 2006). Since then, selling bonds has provided a financial lifeline for local governments to finance capital projects and day-to-day operations. Additionally, because of their tax advantages in the United States (including federal income tax exemptions, and potential state and local tax exemptions) and perceived fiscal safety (due to governmental assurance), municipal bonds have become a common way for Americans to invest their money. Despite these benefits, municipal bonds have a lower financial return than other fixed income securities such as corporate bonds. And, recently, municipal bonds have lost some credibility as cities such as Detroit, Michigan and Stockton, California have fallen into bankruptcy and been unable to meet bond obligations.

As public participation practices have become more popular, several cities are restructuring their municipal bond programs to increase community engagement. In Denver, the local government decided to increase community engagement by creating "mini bonds," where a typical $20000 municipal bond was reduced to $500 (Ebi, 2014). The campaign sought to increase community and constituent engagement in infrastructure delivery by allowing only Denver residents (restricted by zip code) to participate in the campaign. Although selling "mini bonds" increased costs to the city because of higher transaction fees and the assurance of an attractive financial return, the "mini bond" campaigns have been very successful at increasing engagement in and around Denver and preventing sales of municipal bonds on secondary markets. During the last campaign round in 2014, $12 million worth of Better Denver Mini Bonds sold out within one hour of opening the funding portal (Murray, 2014). These funds are currently being used to build and renovate public works projects within the city. Building on this concept, neighbor.ly (a crowdfunding platform turned registered broker-dealer) is working with municipalities to restructure bonds and replicate Denver's "mini bonds" program.

Civic Crowdfunding

Traditionally, infrastructure projects were solicited and prioritized by politicians and agencies and paid for via bond measures and taxes. Recently, external stakeholders, both individuals and NGOs, have taken it upon themselves to initiate infrastructure delivery by requesting donations on online platforms. In some cases, these campaigns are initiated to showcase community support for projects and increase political will for moving projects forward (Davies, 2014). Crowdfunding campaigns that support local infrastructure projects are now being hosted on a subset of crowdfunding platforms (such as ioby.com and Spacehive.com) that allow community members to fund and support delivery of public goods and civic infrastructure. Building on this model, forward-thinking state agencies have even sponsored state-level crowdfunding campaigns for civic infrastructure. For example, Michigan began a statewide initiative, Public Spaces, Community Places, through the Patronicity.com civic crowdfunding platform to increase public participation and community leadership, while also increasing support and funding for civic infrastructure. Additionally, the Michigan Economic Development Corporation (MEDC) is providing marketing and financial resources (including matching grants) to projects on Patronicity.com, hoping to spark grassroots infrastructure delivery in cities throughout the state (DeVito, 2014). During the first year of this initiative, Patronicty.com raised $1.7 million through crowdfunding, which spurred nearly $10.9 million in private investment toward civic infrastructure projects in Michigan (Ault, 2015).

Equity Crowdfunding

Equity financing represents the highest level of financial participation for external stakeholders and is the newest form of community investment. It has received impetus from new legislation that legitimizes the use of crowdfunding. The JOBS Act of 2012 was originally passed to regulate the crowdfunding industry and allow external stakeholders, such as community members, to invest in start-up business ventures. Cities and forward-thinking community organizations are beginning to apply the JOBS Act to fund and finance infrastructure delivery (Farajian et al., 2015). And recently, the Securities and Exchange Commission has released rulings related to equity crowdfunding for both accredited and unaccredited investors.

Over the last few years, there have been many policy and business model developments in the real estate and energy sectors to include equity crowdfunding for infrastructure delivery. Equity crowdfunding, also referred to as regulation crowdfunding or crowdfinancing, allows unaccredited investors to invest financially in projects with the expectation of a financial return on investment. Equity crowdfunding exists because of a persistent revenue stream from user fees. For example, equity crowdfunding platforms, such as FundRise.com and Solstice.com, repackage financing deals, allow community members (and others) to invest equity, provide infrastructure services (apartment buildings and solar energy, respectively), and collect user fees to provide financial returns to investors. Although this model has its own limitations, there is a lot of potential for equity crowdfunding to be used for larger, revenue-backed projects.

In each of these models, community investment is a partnership strategy that facilitates infrastructure delivery by increasing resources and contributing to the management of stakeholder relationships. Community investment, as a partnership strategy for infrastructure delivery, rests on a stakeholder structure that bridges the project owner, the project sponsor and the community investors (crowdfunders). The project owner is the stakeholder that owns the infrastructure asset once it is constructed. The project sponsor is a private sector or third-sector partner that initiates the community investment process and takes responsibility for the delivery of the infrastructure asset. The community investors are the community members who will benefit from or be impacted by the project and choose to support the project by contributing financial (and other) resources. Although these stakeholders are not as easily identified in each model, the interplay between the different stakeholders helps to predict potential outcomes for local infrastructure delivery.

PROPOSITIONS FOR USING COMMUNITY INVESTMENT FOR INFRASTRUCTURE

As we have seen, crowdfunding and other community investment models, as partnership strategies, increase resources and manage stakeholder relationships during infrastructure delivery. Partnership strategies such as public–private partnership structures, contracts and financial arrangements have been studied for larger projects. Past research has found that these strategies, in providing resources and managing stakeholder relationships, have impacted project outcomes (see Chapter 1 in this volume). While this research has been useful for practitioners in understanding how to successfully execute partnership strategies for large infrastructure projects, there is very little written about local infrastructure delivery and the potential for partnership strategies. Based on preliminary interviews with industry stakeholders and an expansive literature review, propositions can be formed for how community investment, as a partnership strategy, can influence outcomes for local infrastructure delivery.

Proposition 1: While communicating the project to potential community investors, the project sponsor learns more (than in traditionally funded projects) about the wants and needs of the community, allowing them to improve the project design.

During the process of community investment, local knowledge exchange becomes a critical part of the interaction between the project owners, project sponsors and community investors. Building on the insights of Geertz (1983), Malecki defines local knowledge as the privately held knowledge and shared expertise that transfers only through networks of interactions (Malecki, 2002). Local knowledge exchange between stakeholders allows for user feedback to inform the decision-making process, especially in terms of fee increases, maintenance plans, project updates and crisis planning. This process of knowledge exchange provides more information on and transparency of the project. Project owners, as internal stakeholders, are able to communicate the desired objectives and goals for a project. Project sponsors, who act on behalf of project owners to increase resources for infrastructure delivery, interface with project owners and community members. As project sponsors embark on the community investment process, they must engage with community members and advertise the project details and expectations in the hopes of attracting more community investors. These types of interactions require an intimate exchange of knowledge, where the project sponsor can gain insights about user behaviors as well as potential design and construction conflicts. In traditionally funded projects, formal public participation processes do not allow for meaningful one-on-one conversations between project owners and sponsors and community members. Public meetings can lack the representation that is needed to have true engagement. With the addition of community investment, conversations with affected community members can result in more representation and engagement. And, in return, community members, as external stakeholders, can choose to be community investors and approve or disapprove of the project by contributing money. This knowledge exchange can help the project owner and sponsor to gain local knowledge to make better decisions during the early project planning phases.

Proposition 2: *The project sponsor, as a private sector or third-sector partner, becomes a more powerful stakeholder during community investment because the project sponsor can provide more resources to the project owner and interacts more with the community.*

Community investment processes involve an intermediary, the project sponsor, who organizes the community investment campaign and serves as the connection between traditional internal stakeholders, such as the project owner, and the community investors. The project sponsor dedicates time to disseminating project information, contacting potential investors, and creating the system, process and tools for collecting money. As a result, the project sponsor becomes a key point of contact for community investors. As part of their responsibilities, the project sponsor screens information and reorganizes it in a way that is manageable for community members to understand (Latham, 2003). These stakeholders, as intermediaries, are not only crucial to knowledge dissemination, but they also play a role in mediating resources for the stakeholders they represent (Pajunen, 2006). The intermediary is able to consolidate individual feedback and provide a direct conduit for knowledge exchange, and in doing so can facilitate conflict resolution. For infrastructure projects, in which there are several phases and the potential for changes to fee structures and project scope, the project sponsor serves a crucial role in insuring the inclusion of the community investors throughout a project's life cycle as the project owner takes over more project responsibility. The presence of an intermediary during community investment provides community members with additional legitimacy within the stakeholder network. In turn, the more community members and community investors there are, the more power the project sponsor has within the stakeholder network (Friedman and Miles, 2002).

Proposition 3: The presence of financial contributions via community investment increases accountability for project owners and project sponsors to deliver the proposed project.

Although community investment varies widely, the involvement of financial resources and support is a commonality among all the community investment models. And, regardless of the extent of financial contributions, community investors hold the project owner and sponsor more accountable because they are providing resources to a dedicated project. At one end of the spectrum, equity crowdfunding has specific financial rules that reflect this expectation, such as expected repayment schedules and an expected investment return. Additionally, equity financing comes with other tools for increasing internal stakeholder accountability, including ownership rights in which the community investor has access to financial documentation and voting rights conditional on the terms of the specific equity investment. In general, equity financiers have "skin in the game" because they own a portion of the venture, are in a "first loss" position relative to lenders, and are usually the last to receive a financial return on their initial investment (increasing their level of risk). Municipal bonds, as a form of community investment, also have financial rules that ensure a financial return on investment. And, although there is less risk with this type of investment, collective action clauses formalize the accountability process between internal stakeholders and community investors.

Civic crowdfunding and capital cost sharing do not have a financial return on investment (ROI). Despite the absence of a financial ROI, civic crowdfunding and capital cost sharing have their own expectations. Duncan (2004) argues that the expectation of the donor receiving a good or service promised by a project sponsor is qualitatively similar to an investor's expectation of a financial return. Similar to the expectation of a financial return on investment, donors "invest" in projects because they expect either public service delivery or private consumption satisfaction. Fehr and Hishigsuren (2006) take the donor expectations even further by arguing that donations can be thought of as equity investments because equity investments are not ensured a financial return on investment (unlike debt investments with lower risks and collective action clauses). Thus, both types of investors have similar risk levels and may influence the infrastructure delivery stakeholder network in the same way. The expectation that the proposed project will be delivered means that community investors have an inherent obligation to hold project owners and sponsor accountable.

EXPLORING THE PROPOSITIONS

The three propositions outlined in the previous section were derived from preliminary interviews with practitioners, as well as past empirical and theoretical research. There is still a great need to develop early-stage theoretical frameworks for community investment, as a partnership strategy, in infrastructure delivery. Most early studies have utilized a case study research methodology to describe and explore this new phenomenon. Using Yin's (2013) embedded multiple-case methodology, I conducted an initial matched pairs case study that compared a traditionally funded local infrastructure project with a crowdfunded local infrastructure project.

Among the different types of community investment models, civic crowdfunding has most commonly been used for local infrastructure projects and involves local governments as project owners. My study involved a project owner, a project sponsor, and the community investors (crowdfunders) who worked in concert to deliver a local infrastructure project. Other criteria used to limit the project pool were that the projects occurred within the United States and resulted in the design and construction of a public good with a long life cycle. These case selection criteria removed cases where private developers used crowdfunding to raise funds for private or club goods like real estate. Once the crowdfunded project was selected, the matching (traditionally funded) project was chosen based on the similarity of project scope, proximity to the crowdfunded project, and the time at which the project was constructed.

Yin's embedded multiple-case design allows for multiple units of analysis to understand the process of a phenomenon (Yin, 2013). Therefore, in conducting this matched pairs case study, I studied the political and governance landscapes in which these projects take place, the individual stakeholders, the relationships between stakeholders, and the infrastructure delivery events. As a result, the case study produced a "thick descriptive narrative" of project delivery across the phases of each project. The data collection was comprised of archival research of project and governance documents and interviews with key stakeholders. For each project, I interviewed between eight and 20 individuals using a semi-structured interview style. At the center of these interviews were the project owner and the project sponsor, because of their partnership. The data analysis process included thorough coding of field memos, project documents and interview transcriptions. The first round of coding was used to identify project details and large themes related to project delivery and stakeholder relations. The following sections describe the project delivery process and initial findings from this research in relationship to the three previously discussed propositions.

A Tale of Two Protected Bike Lanes

Between the years 20(XX) and 20(XX+1), Central City[1] constructed two protected bicycle lanes. These were the first two protected bicycle lanes to be constructed in this city and among the first in the country. Unlike other types of infrastructure, protected bike lane projects are complex because they require a behavior shift from everyone who uses transportation infrastructure: drivers must adhere to new signage and cannot drive or park between the barricade and the sidewalk; cyclists can no longer ride among vehicles and have to abide by bicycle-specific signage and lights; and pedestrians must pay attention to cyclists and vehicles that now have two separate systems for signage, route and lighting. Even though these two projects presented new transportation challenges, they brought to light a shift in Central City's approach to infrastructure delivery. Whereas the first project was constructed using traditional methods and funding, the second project was constructed using an entrepreneurial approach and was funded, in part, through a crowdfunding campaign.

At the beginning of the planning phase for the first project (the 1st Street Protected Bicycle Lane), the Project Owner (in this case, the Department of Public Works) only had one person, the Bicycle Manager, who managed bicycle and pedestrian infrastructure. Although this individual was able to champion the 1st Street Protected Bicycle Lane, the Project Owner lacked the resources to adequately manage the project: the Bicycle Manager reviewed the designs and oversaw five different contractors and, in doing so, shepherded the project through the traditional design and construction process. As the first project of its kind in the city, the individuals working on the project were hesitant. Together with a top-down, traditional delivery approach, it took four years for the 1st Street Protected Bike Lane to be delivered.

The earliest documentation of the project indicates that the Project Owner wrote to the Business Improvement District regarding initial assessment of protected bike lane projects. Following this correspondence, the project planning began with preliminary outreach to stakeholder groups and assessment of design alternatives. The initial design alternatives showed that there was a need for a full traffic analysis of the 1st Street corridor. The analysis pushed the project out by a year. Using consultants and designing a delivery process that involved alternative design analysis resulted in a lengthy process that limited involvement from the community. But, as the project was being completed and the city leadership evolved, the Mayor's Office began to dedicate more personnel and resources to pedestrian and bicycle infrastructure. And, seeing the success of the first project, the Business Improvement District decided to take a larger role in the following bicycle infrastructure projects. In the months following the construction of this project, the Project Owner commissioned a report that found a 30 percent increase in the number of cyclists using the 1st Street corridor, a 62 percent reduction of cyclists riding on the sidewalk (reducing the potential for bicycle and pedestrian accidents), and nearly a 100 percent increase in bicycling during peak afternoon times.

Whereas the Project Owner took a top-down approach for delivering the first project, the Project Owner purposefully took on a quick-build mentality with the second project. And, true to form, the 2nd Street Protected Bicycle Lane took less than one year from project planning to ribbon-cutting, an anomaly among public works projects of similar size and scope. Prior to beginning the project, the Business Improvement District was interested in expanding the protected bike lane network in the downtown area and was developing a plan to identify which streets were most conducive to network expansion. During this process, the Business Improvement District, in an effort to increase funding for this project and show support for more protected bicycle facilities, launched a crowdfunding campaign. In doing so, the Business Improvement District became the Project Sponsor for this project. With more resources and the strength of the Business Improvement District's partnership, there was added legitimacy for approaching businesses along the 2nd Street corridor about design elements and the construction process. This was needed because of unique conditions along the corridor: high traffic volumes required special design treatments to protect cyclists among the existing travel lanes. And the surrounding land use meant that the protected bike lane had to be flexible enough to accommodate unique requests. After a rapid design and construction period, a ribbon-cutting ceremony was held at which the Mayor committed to building three more protected bicycle lanes in the following year. And, in the months following the ribbon-cutting, the 2nd Street Protected Bicycle Lane was named one of the top ten best bicycle lanes installed during that year in the United States.

The differences between these two projects highlight a new partnership model (facilitated by the crowdfunding campaign) and a management shift within the city. This matched pairs case study helps to highlight how a third-sector partner, the Business Improvement District, utilized crowdfunding to increase resources for a project and to manage stakeholder relationships. The Project Owner, through this partnership strategy, was able to expedite the delivery of the local infrastructure project. In addition to providing support for the propositions, other findings that emerged during the data analysis process shed light on the intricacies of local infrastructure delivery and relationships between the Project Owner, Project Sponsor and community investors.

ELABORATING THE PROPOSITIONS

Proposition 1: While communicating the project to potential community investors, the Project Sponsor learns more (than in traditionally funded projects) about the wants and needs of the community, allowing them to improve the project design.

Crowdfunding played a significant part of the public participation process for the 2nd Street Protected Bicycle Lane Project. The crowdfunding campaign, as a marketing campaign, opened up new formal and informal channels to engage more community members during the early project shaping phases. The crowdfunding campaign involved a diverse and widespread marketing campaign that sought to inform the community and others about the project. With face-to-face interactions between the Project Sponsor and potential crowdfunders (primarily community members), the public participation process became much more individualized than traditional public meetings. The Business Improvement District, as the Project Sponsor, developed a pop-up event that allowed the community to experience the project in a simulated manner. During this exhibit, the Project Sponsor was able to introduce the new type of infrastructure and get community input. In the process of raising money for the crowdfunding campaign, the Project Sponsor also interacted on an individual basis with community members. A representative from the Project Sponsor and Project Owner approached business owners along the route of the project and spoke with them at length about the project design and potential unintended consequences of constructing a protected bicycle facility along the street.

Proposition 2: The Project Sponsor, as a private sector or third-sector partner, becomes a more powerful stakeholder during community investment because the Project Sponsor can provide more resources to the Project Owner and interacts more with the community.

Crowdfunding acted as a signal of a strong third-sector partner. In the process of developing the crowdfunding campaign and working on the project delivery process, the Project Sponsor became a much more salient stakeholder. The traditionally funded projects were initiated and driven primarily by the Bicycle Manager. As a government employee and part of the Project Owner stakeholder group, the Bicycle Manager was able to direct government resources and work with other government agencies to develop the 1st Street Protected Bicycle Lane. During this project, the

Bicycle Manager (hence, the Project Owner) did not interact with the Business Improvement District or local stakeholders to the same extent. Instead, the Project Owner hosted a public meeting to introduce the project and did not work hand-in-glove with community members and those most impacted by the project, to redesign project components that could negatively impact the project. Instead, the project design process was the primary responsibility of a consulting firm that worked for more than a year to develop project design details and alternatives. During the 2nd Street project, by contrast, the Project Sponsor took it upon itself to launch a robust public participation campaign, in an attempt to raise awareness and funds for the project. As a result of these interactions, the Project Sponsor displaced the Project Owner to some extent. The role of the Project Sponsor was important not only during early project shaping phases, but also in subsequent developments as community investors turned to the Project Sponsor to ascertain the project's status.

Proposition 3:   *The presence of financial contributions via community investment increases accountability for Project Owners and Project Sponsors to deliver the proposed project.*

Within this matched pairs case study, it was difficult to determine the extent to which financial contributions increased accountability for the Project Owner and Project Sponsor during the operations and maintenance of the 2nd Street Project. But the presence of a strong Project Sponsor and additional funding, via the crowdfunding campaign, convinced the Project Owner to reallocate resources to ensure the project was completed in a timely manner. The additional resources for the 2nd Street project also allowed the Project Owner to work on more bicycle infrastructure projects within Central City's downtown area. While the 1st Street project demonstrated the need for protected bicycle infrastructure, the added support from the community and the Project Sponsor helped to expedite the delivery of the 2nd Street project.

New Proposition: *A Project Owner with previous experience with a similar project will be more willing to build partnership capabilities with a Project Sponsor and to allow crowdfunding to happen.*

Planning, designing, and constructing protected bicycle facilities is still a relatively novel process in US cities. Because protected bicycle facilities require a behavioral change from all travelers, regardless of mode, and because protected bicycle facilities are often seen as non-necessary infrastructure projects, there is often a backlash against these types of projects. Therefore, the decision to crowdfund a protected bicycle facility was successful in Central City, in part, because a protected bicycle facility had been constructed previously, removing potential opposition and increasing familiarity with the type of infrastructure. In this case, the Project Owner and the Mayor's Office were more receptive to the crowdfunding and delivery of a second protected bicycle facility. Additionally, the Project Owner, having gone through the process of delivering a similar project, was able to offer resources and lessons learned to improve the outcome of the second project.

IMPLICATIONS

This chapter explores the evolution of partnerships in infrastructure delivery and the use of a partnership strategy, community investment and crowdfunding, in local infrastructure delivery. As cities struggle to continue to provide quality infrastructure assets and services, partnerships will become more prevalent. In agreeing to partnership strategies and structures, such as the one described in Central City, it is important for local governments and other project owners to understand the consequences of working with external partners. Therefore, local governments that are already resource-constrained need to cultivate the involvement of private sector and third-sector partners and work with them to varying degrees to ensure the longevity of projects and adequate public participation.

Currently, this research is in its nascent stage. The case study work that is being developed will build upon the propositions offered in this chapter and seek to uncover others. While this work is reliant on qualitative studies, it is important to recognize its limits. The two projects in Central City are strongly affected by their specific context, making it difficult to extrapolate the findings to other traditionally and crowdfunded local infrastructure projects. Additionally, because of the range of community investment models, it is difficult to apply these findings to projects that use different types of community investment models. Despite these limitations it is becoming more important to understand the capacity of local governments to provide local infrastructure services and the potential for partnership strategies to supplement traditional sources of funding.

While local governments struggle with the pressures associated with urbanization and deteriorating infrastructure assets, partnership strategies that have yielded success for large infrastructure projects should be studied and scaled for smaller projects. We have seen that increasing resources and improved techniques of managing stakeholder relationships for infrastructure delivery remain essential parts of achieving success during infrastructure planning, design, construction and operations. It appears that crowdfunding and community investment, if understood and applied carefully, can increase the potential for successful infrastructure delivery by strengthening partnerships between local governments, private and third-sector partners, and communities.

NOTE

1. Project names, locations, dates and names of organizations have been anonymized or changed to protect confidentiality.

Bibliography

Aaltonen, K., and Kujala, J. (2010). A project lifecycle perspective on stakeholder influence strategies in global projects. Scandinavian Journal of Management, 26(4), 381–397.

AASHTO (2011). South Bay Expressway (SR-125). Washington, DC: American Association of State Highway and Transportation Officials. Accessed at http://www.transportation-finance.org/projects/south_bay_expressway.aspx 2012.

Acerete, B., Gasca, M., Stafford, A., and Stapleton, P. (2015). A comparative policy analysis of healthcare PPPs: examining evidence from two Spanish regions from an international perspective. Journal of Comparative Policy Analysis: Research and Practice, 17(5), 502–518.

Afonso, A., Schuknecht, L., and Tanzi, V. (2005). Public-sector efficiency: an international comparison. Public Choice, 123(3/4), 321–347.

Akintoye, A., Taylor, C., and Fitzgerald, E. (1998). Risk analysis and management of private finance initiative projects. Engineering, Construction and Architectural Management, 5(1), 9–21.

Albalate, D., Bel, G., and Geddes, R.R. (2015). The determinants of contractual choice for private involvement in infrastructure projects. Public Money and Management, 35(1), 87–94.

Albalate, D., Bel, G., and Geddes, R.R. (2017). How much vertical integration? Contractual choice and public–private partnerships in the United States. Review of Industrial Organization, 51(1), 25–42.

Allen, G. (2001). The private finance initiative (PFI). House of Commons Library Research Paper 01/117. House of Commons Library, Economic Policy and Statistics Section. London.

Alm, J. (2015). Financing urban infrastructure: knowns, unknowns, and a way forward. Journal of Economic Surveys, 29(2), 230–262. http://doi.org/10.1111/joes.12045.

Almassi, A., McCabe, B., and Thompson, M. (2012). Real options-based approach for valuation of government guarantees in public–private partnerships. Journal of Infrastructure Systems, 19(2), 196–204.

American Road and Transportation Builders Association (ARTBA) (2015). "2015 'Fixing America's Surface Transportation Act': A Comprehensive Analysis." Washington, DC.

American Road and Transportation Builders Association (ARTBA) (2017). Analysis of the Trump Administration's FY 2018 US Department of Transportation Budget Proposal. Washington, DC.

Anderlini, L., and Felli, L. (1999). Incomplete contracts and complexity costs. Theory and Decision, 46(1), 23–50.

Andonov, A. (2013). Pension fund asset allocation and performance. PhD dissertation. Datawyse. Maastricht University.

Andrews, R., and Entwistle, T. (2010). Does cross-sectoral partnership deliver? An empirical exploration of public service effectiveness, efficiency, and equity. Journal of Public Administration Research and Theory, 20(3), 679–701.

Angola LNG (2006). Angola LNG ESHIA Disclosure Report – Executive Summary: Chevron.

Ansell, C.K. (1998). Symbolic networks: the realignment of the French working class, 1887–1894. American Journal of Sociology, 103(2), 359–390.

Ansoff, H.I. (1980). Strategic issue management. Strategic Management Journal, 1(2), 131–148.

Argyres, N.S., and Liebeskind, J.P. (1999). Contractual commitments, bargaining power, and governance inseparability: incorporating history into transaction cost theory. Academy of Management Review, 24(1), 49–63.

Arnstein, S.R. (1969). A ladder of citizen participation. Journal of the American Institute of Planners, 35(4), 216–224.

Artto, K.A., Lehtonen, J.-M., and Saranen, J. (2001). Managing projects front-end: incorporating a strategic early view to project management with simulation. International Journal of Project Management, 19(5), 255–264.

Artz, K.W., and Brush, T.H. (2000). Asset specificity, uncertainty and relational norms: an examination of coordination costs in collaborative strategic alliances. Journal of Economic Behavior and Organization, 41(4), 337–362.

ARUP PB Joint Venture (2010). Analysis of Delivery Options for the Presidio Parkway Project. CTC Project Proposal Report Submission. San Francisco: ARUP PB.

Ashuri, B., Kashani, H., Molenaar, K., Lee, S., and Lu, J. (2011). Risk-neutral pricing approach for evaluating BOT highway projects with government minimum revenue guarantee options. Journal of Construction Engineering and Management, 138(4), 545–557. https://doi.org/10.1061/(ASCE)CO.1943-7862.0000447.

Athias, L., and Saussier, S. (2007). Contractual flexibility or rigidity for public–private partnerships? Theory and evidence from infrastructure concession contracts. MPRA Paper No. 10541. https://mpra.ub.uni-muenchen.de/10541/.

Ault, I. (2015). The MEDC and Patronicity's Public Spaces, Community Places completes successful first year: Part 2. November 19. Michigan State University Extension. http://msue.anr.msu.edu/news/the_medc_and_patronicitys_public_spaces_community_places_completes_2.

Australian Government, Australian Trade Commission and Unlimited Australia (2015). Investment Opportunities in Australian Infrastructure. https://www.austrade.gov.au/ArticleDocuments/5569/Investment-Opportunities-in-Australian-Infrastructure-brochure.pdf.aspx.

Axelrod, R., and Hamilton, W.D. (1981). The evolution of cooperation. Science, 211(4489), 1390–1396.

Ayres, I., and Gertner, R. (1989). Filling gaps in incomplete contracts: an economic theory of default rules. Yale Law Journal, 99(1), 87–130.

Azevedo, J. (1997). Mapping Reality: An Evolutionary Realist Methodology for the Natural and Social Sciences. Albany, NY: SUNY Press.

Aziz, A.M.A. (2007). Successful delivery of public–private partnerships for infrastructure development. Journal of Construction Engineering and Management, 133(12), 918–931. http://dx.doi.org/10.1061/(ASCE)0733-9364(2007)133:12(918).

Bailey, K., Grossardt, T., Ripy, J., Toole, L., Williams, J., and Dietrick, J. (2007). Structured public involvement in context-sensitive large bridge design using casewise visual evaluation: case study of section 2 of Ohio River bridges project. Transportation Research Record: Journal of the Transportation Research Board, (2028), 19–27.

Bain, R. (2009). Error and optimism bias in toll road traffic forecasts. Transportation, 36(5), 469–482.

Baker, G., Gibbons, R., and Murphy, K.J. (2002). Relational contracts and the theory of the firm. Quarterly Journal of Economics, 117(1), 39–84.

Barlow, J. (2000). Innovation and learning in complex offshore construction projects. Research Policy, 29(7/8), 973–989.

Barnes, J.A. (1972). Social Networks. Reading, MA: Addison-Wesley.

Bastian, M., Heymann, S., and Jacomy, M. (2009). Gephi: an open source software for exploring and manipulating networks. ICWSM, 8, 361–362.

Bayliss, R., Cheung, S.O., Suen, H.C., and Wong, S.P. (2004). Effective partnering tools in construction: a case study on MTRC TKE contract 604 in Hong Kong. International Journal of Project Management, 22(3), 253–263.

Bearman, P. (1997). Generalized exchange. American Journal of Sociology, 102(5), 1383–1415.

Beeferman, L. (2008). Pension fund investment in infrastructure: a resource

paper. Stewardship Project Labor and Worklife Program, Harvard Law School, Occasional Paper Series, 3, 1–78.
Bel, G., and Fageda, X. (2009). Factors explaining local privatization: a meta-regression analysis. Public Choice, 139(1/2), 105–119.
Bell, R. (1985). Professional values and organizational decision making. Administration and Society, 17(1), 21–60.
Benford, R.D., and Snow, D.A. (2000). Framing processes and social movements: an overview and assessment. Annual Review of Sociology, 26(1), 611–639.
Benham, A., and Benham, L. (2010). The costs of exchange. In P.G. Klein and M.E. Sykuta (eds), The Elgar Companion to Transaction Cost Economics. Cheltenham, UK and Northampton, MA, USA: Edward Elgar Publishing. https://ideas.repec.org/h/elg/eechap/4136_11.html.
Bennett, J., and Iossa, E. (2006). Building and managing facilities for public services. Journal of Public Economics, 90(10/11), 2143–2160.
Bennon, M., Kim, M.J., and Levitt, R.E. (2017a). US infrastructure gap(s): federal policy and local public institutions. https://papers.ssrn.com/sol3/papers.cfm?abstract_id=3036650.
Bennon, M., Monk, A.H.B., and Cho, Y.J. (2017b). In-kind infrastructure investments by public pensions: the Queensland motorways case study. Stanford Global Projects Center, June 5. SSRN: https://ssrn.com/abstract=2981707.
Bercovitz, J., Jap, S.D., and Nickerson, J.A. (2006). The antecedents and performance implications of cooperative exchange norms. Organization Science, 17(6), 724–740.
Besley, T., and Ghatak, M. (2005). Competition and incentives with motivated agents. American Economic Review, 95(3), 616–636.
Bhattacharya, C.B., Sen, S., and Korschun, D. (2008). Using corporate social responsibility to win the war for talent. Sloan Management Review. https://sloanreview.mit.edu/article/using-corporate-social-responsibility-to-win-the-war-for-talent/.
Bigelow, B., Fahey, L., and Mahon, J.F. (1991). Political strategy and issues evolution: a framework for analysis and action. In K. Paul (ed.), Contemporary Issues in Business Ethics and Politics (pp. 1–26). Lewiston, NY: Edwin Mellen.
Bigelow, B., Fahey, L., and Mahon, J.F. (1993). A typology of issue evolution. Business and Society, 32(1), 18–29.
Bill, J.A., and Hardgrave Jr, R.L. (1981). Comparative Politics: The Quest for Theory. Washington, DC: Bell & Howell University Press of America.
Bing, L., Akintoye, A., Edwards, P.J., and Hardcastle, C. (2005). The allocation of risk in PPP/PFI construction projects in the UK. International Journal of Project Management, 23(1), 25–35.

Bingham, L.B., and O'Leary, R. (2014). Big Ideas in Collaborative Public Management. Armonk, NY: Routledge.

Bingham, L.B., Nabatchi, T., and O'Leary, R. (2005). The new governance: practices and processes for stakeholder and citizen participation in the work of government. Public Administration Review, 65(5), 547–558.

Blau, P.M. (1964). Justice in social exchange. Sociological Inquiry, 34(2), 193–206.

Blau, P.M. (1994). Structural Contexts of Opportunities. Chicago, IL: University of Chicago Press.

Boardman, A.E., and Vining, A.R. (2012). The political economy of public–private partnerships and analysis of their social value. Annals of Public and Cooperative Economics, 83(2), 117–141.

Boardman, A.E., Greve, C., and Hodge, G.A. (2015). Comparative analyses of infrastructure public–private partnerships. Journal of Comparative Policy Analysis: Research and Practice, 17(5), 441–447.

Boardman, A.E., Poschmann, F., and Vining, A. (2005). North American infrastructure P3s: examples and lessons learned. In G. Hodge and C. Greve (eds), The Challenge of Public–Private Partnerships: Learning from International Experience (pp. 162–189). Cheltenham, UK and Northampton, MA, USA: Edward Elgar Publishing.

Bodie, Z., Marcus, A.J., and Merton, R.C. (1988). Defined benefit versus defined contribution pension plans: what are the real trade-offs? In Z. Bodie, J.B. Shoven and D.A. Wise (eds), Pensions in the US Economy (pp. 139–162). Chicago, IL: University of Chicago Press.

Bolonkin, A., and Cathcart, R.B. (2009). Macro-Projects. New York: NOVA Publishing.

Bonacich, P. (1972). Factoring and weighting approaches to status scores and clique identification. Journal of Mathematical Sociology, 2(1), 113–120.

Bonacich, P. (2007). Some unique properties of eigenvector centrality. Social Networks, 29(4), 555–564.

Borcherding, J.D. (1972). An exploratory study of attitudes that affect human resources in building and industrial construction. PhD Dissertation, Dept. of Civil Engineering, Stanford University, Stanford, CA.

Borgatti, S.P., and Foster, P.C. (2003). The network paradigm in organizational research: a review and typology. Journal of Management, 29(6), 991–1013.

Bovaird, T. (2004). Public–private partnerships: from contested concepts to prevalent practice. International Review of Administrative Sciences, 70(2), 199–215.

Box, G.E., and Draper, N.R. (1987). Empirical Model-Building and Response Surfaces. New York: Wiley.

Boyer, E.J. (2016). Identifying a knowledge management approach for public–private partnerships. Public Performance and Management Review, 40(1), 158–180.

Boyer, E.J., and Scheller, D.S. (2017). An examination of state-level public–private partnership adoption: analyzing economic, political, and demand-related determinants of PPPs. Public Works Management and Policy, 23(1), 5–33.

Brabham, D.C. (2010). Crowdsourcing as a model for problem solving: leveraging the collective intelligence of online communities for public good. Dissertation, University of Utah, December.

Bradach, J.L., and Eccles, R.G. (1989). Price, authority, and trust: From ideal types to plural forms. Annual Review of Sociology, 15(1), 97–118.

Brandão, L.E., Bastian-Pinto, C., Gomes, L.L., and Labes, M. (2012). Government Supports in Public–Private Partnership Contracts: Metro Line 4 of the São Paulo Subway System. Journal of Infrastructure Systems, 18(3), 218–225.

Brandão, L.E.T., and Saraiva, E. (2008). The option value of government guarantees in infrastructure projects. Construction Management and Economics, 26(11), 1171–1180.

Brealey, R., Cooper, I., and Habib, M. (2000). The financing of large engineering projects. In R. Miller and D. Lessard (eds), The Strategic Management of Large Engineering Projects: Shaping Institutions, Risks and Governance (pp. 75–92). Cambridge, MA: MIT Press.

Brekke, K.A., and Nyborg, K. (2008). Moral hazard and moral motivation: corporate social responsibility as labor market screening (No. 2004, 25). Memorandum, Department of Economics, University of Oslo.

Brinkerhoff, D.W., and Brinkerhoff, J.M. (2011). Public–private partnerships: perspectives on purposes, publicness, and good governance. Public Administration and Development, 31(1), 2–14.

Brinkerhoff, J.M. (2002). Assessing and improving partnership relationships and outcomes: a proposed framework. Evaluation and Program Planning, 25(3), 215–231.

Brinkerhoff, J.M. (2007). Partnership as a means to good governance: toward an evaluation framework. In P. Glasbergen, F. Biermann and A.P.J. Mol (eds), Partnerships, Governance and Sustainable Development: Reflections on Theory and Practice (pp. 68–89). Cheltenham, UK and Northampton, MA, USA: Edward Elgar Publishing.

Bruyn, S. (1991). The Field of Social Investment. Cambridge: Cambridge University Press.

Bryson, J.M. (2004). What to do when stakeholders matter: stakeholder identification and analysis techniques. Public Management Review, 6(1), 21–53.

Bryson, J.M., Crosby, B.C., and Stone, M.M. (2006). The design and implementation of cross-sector collaborations: propositions from the literature. Public Administration Review, 66, 44–55.

Build America Bureau (2017). About the Build America Bureau. US Department of Transportation. Accessed November 21, 2017 at https://www.transportation.gov/buildamerica/about.

Burger, P., and Hawkesworth, I. (2011). How to attain value for money: comparing PPP and traditional infrastructure public procurement. OECD Journal on Budgeting, 11(1). http://www.oecd.org/gov/budgeting/49070709.pdf.

Burgess, J.W. (1902). Political Science and Comparative Constitutional Law. Boston, MA: Ginn.

Burt, R.S. (1980). Models of network structure. Annual Review of Sociology, 6(1), 79–141.

Burt, R.S. (1982). Toward a Structural Theory of Action: Network Models of Social Structure, Perception, and Action. New York: Academic Press.

Burton, R.M., and Obel, B. (2004). Strategic Organizational Diagnosis and Design: The Dynamics of Fit, Vol. 4. Berlin: Springer Science and Business Media.

Buxbaum, J.N., and Ortiz, I.N. (2007). Protecting the public interest: the role of long-term concession agreements for providing transportation infrastructure (No. 07-02). Keston Institute for Public Finance Policy and Infrastructure Policy, University of Southern California.

Caldwell, N.D., Roehrich, J.K., and Davies, A.C. (2009). Procuring complex performance in construction: London Heathrow Terminal 5 and a Private Finance Initiative hospital. Journal of Purchasing and Supply Management, 15(3), 178–186.

California (1989). Assembly Bill No. 680 (Baker, Trans.) Streets and Highways Code (Vol. Section 143).

Caltrans (2009). State Route 91 (91 Express Lanes). Corona, CA: California Department of Transportation.

Camerer, C.F., and Fehr, E. (2006). When does "economic man" dominate social behavior? Science, 311(5757), 47–52.

Cameron, B.G. (2007). Value network modeling: a quantitative method for comparing benefit across exploration architectures. Master's Thesis, Department of Aeronautics and Astronautics and Engineering Systems Division, Massachusetts Institute of Technology, Cambridge, MA.

Cameron, B.G., Crawley, E.F., Feng, W., and Lin, M. (2011a). Strategic decisions in complex stakeholder environments: a theory of generalized exchange. Engineering Management Journal, 23(3), 37–45.

Cameron, B.G., Crawley, E.F., Loureiro, G., and Rebentisch, E.S. (2008).

Value flow mapping: using networks to inform stakeholder analysis. Acta Astronautica, 62(4/5), 324–333.
Cameron, B.G., Seher, T., and Crawley, E.F. (2011b). Goals for space exploration based on stakeholder value network considerations. Acta Astronautica, 68(11/12), 2088–2097.
Campbell, D.J. (1988). Task complexity: a review and analysis. Academy of Management Review, 13(1), 40–52.
Carbonara, N., Costantino, N., and Pellegrino, R. (2014). Revenue guarantee in public–private partnerships: a fair risk allocation model. Construction Management and Economics, 32(4), 403–415.
Carpintero, S., Vassallo, J.M., and Soliño, A.S. (2015). Dealing with traffic risk in Latin American toll roads. Journal of Management in Engineering, 31(2), 05014016. https://doi.org/10.1061/(ASCE)ME.1943-5479.0000266.
Casady, C.B., and Geddes, R.R. (2016, reprinted in this volume as Chapter 11). Private Participation in US Infrastructure. Washington, DC: American Enterprise Institute (AEI).
Cawley, K.P. (2013). Testimony on the Status of the Highway Trust Fund (No. 44434). Congressional Budget Office.
Chamberlin, J.R., and Jackson, J.E. (1987). Privatization as institutional choice. Journal of Policy Analysis and Management, 6(4), 586–611.
Chan, A.P., Chan, D.W., Chiang, Y.H., Tang, B.S., Chan, E.H., and Ho, K.S. (2004). Exploring critical success factors for partnering in construction projects. Journal of Construction Engineering and Management, 130(2), 188–198.
Chan, H.F. (2010). To talk or to fight? Collective effects of strategic, cultural, and institutional factors on investors' renegotiation approach in public–private concessions. PhD Dissertation, Dept. of Civil and Environmental Engineering, Stanford University, Stanford, CA.
Chapman, J. (2009). Taxpayers slapped with £4bn bill to bail-out failed PFI projects. Daily Mail, February 17. https://www.dailymail.co.uk/news/article-1147884/Taxpayers-slapped-4bn-bail-failed-PFI-projects.html.
Chappatta, B. (2015). Obama proposes new muni bonds for public–private investments. Bloomberg News, January 16. www.bloomberg.com/news/articles/2015-01-16/obama-proposes-new-muni-bonds-for-public-private-infrastructure.
Charness, G., and Rabin, M. (2002). Understanding social preferences with simple tests. Quarterly Journal of Economics, 117(3), 817–869.
Charoenpornpattana, S., Minato, T., and Nakahama, S. (2002). Government supports as bundle of real options in built–operate–transfer highways projects. Paper presented at the 7th Annual International Conference on Real Options.

Chase, W.H. (1982). Issue Management Conference – A Special Report. Corporate Public Issues and Their Management, 7, 1–2.

Chase, W.H. (1984). Issue Management: Origins of the Future. Stamford, CT: Issue Action Publishers.

Chasey, A., Maddex, W., and Bansal, A. (2012). Comparison of public–private partnerships and traditional procurement methods in North American highway construction. Transportation Research Record: Journal of the Transportation Research Board, 2268, 26–32.

Cheah, C.Y., and Liu, J. (2006). Valuing governmental support in infrastructure projects as real options using Monte Carlo simulation. Construction Management and Economics, 24(5), 545–554.

Cheng, E.W., Li, H., Drew, D.S., and Yeung, N. (2001). Infrastructure of partnering for construction projects. Journal of Management in Engineering, 17(4), 229–237.

Cheung, S.O., Ng, T.S., Wong, S.P., and Suen, H.C. (2003). Behavioral aspects in construction partnering. International Journal of Project Management, 21(5), 333–343.

Chiara, N., Garvin, M.J., and Vecer, J. (2007). Valuing simple multiple-exercise real options in infrastructure projects. Journal of Infrastructure Systems, 13(2), 97–104.

Chibber, V. (2002). Bureaucratic rationality and the developmental state. American Journal of Sociology, 107(4), 951–989. http://doi.org/10.1086/341010.

Chinowsky, P. (2011). Engineering project organization: defining a line of inquiry and a path forward. Engineering Project Organization Journal, 1(1), 3–10.

Choguill, C.L. (1996). Ten steps to sustainable infrastructure. Habitat International, 20(3), 389–404.

Chou, J., and Pramudawardhani, D. (2015). Cross-country comparisons of key drivers, critical success factors and risk allocation for public–private partnership projects. International Journal of Project Management, 33(5), 1136–1150.

Chung, D., and Hensher, D. (2015). Risk management in public–private partnerships. Australian Accounting Review, 25(1), 13–27.

Chung, D., and Hensher, D.A. (2016). Risk-sharing in public–private partnerships: a contractual economics perspective. In M.C.J. Bliemer, C. Mulley and C.J. Moutou (eds), Handbook on Transport and Urban Planning in the Developed World (pp. 254–273). Cheltenham, UK and Northampton, MA, USA: Edward Elgar Publishing.

Chung, D., Hensher, D.A., and Rose, J.M. (2010). Toward the betterment of risk allocation: investigating risk perceptions of Australian

stakeholder groups to public–private-partnership tollroad projects. Research in Transportation Economics, 30(1), 43–58.
Clark, G.L. (2000). Pension Fund Capitalism. Oxford: Oxford University Press.
Clark, G.L., and Evans, J. (1998). The private provision of urban infrastructure: financial intermediation through long-term contracts. Urban Studies, 35(2), 301–319.
Clark, G.L., and Monk, A.H.B. (2013). Principles and policies for in-house asset management. Journal of Financial Perspectives, 1(3), 1–9.
Clark, G.L., and Urwin, R. (2008a). Best-practice pension fund governance. Journal of Asset Management, 9(1), 2–21.
Clark, G.L., and Urwin, R. (2008b). Making pension boards work: the critical role of leadership. Rotman International Journal of Pension Management, 1(1), 38–45.
Clark, G.L., and Urwin, R. (2016). Best-practice pension fund governance. In S. Satchell (ed.), Asset Management (pp. 295–322). Cham: Palgrave Macmillan. https://doi.org/10.1007/978-3-319-30794-7_13.
Clark, G.L., Monk, A.H., Orr, R., and Scott, W. (2011). The new era of infrastructure investing. Pensions: An International Journal, 17(2), 103–111.
Clegg, S., Bjørkeng, K., and Pitsis, T. (2011). Innovating the practice of normative control in project management contractual relations. In P.W.G. Morris, J. Pinto and J. Söderland (eds), The Oxford Handbook of Project Management (pp. 410–437). Oxford: Oxford University Press.
Clemens, E.S. (1997). The People's Lobby: Organizational Innovation and the Rise of Interest Group Politics in the United States, 1890–1925. Chicago, IL: University of Chicago Press.
Coase, R.H. (1937). The nature of the firm. Economica, 4(16), 386–405.
Coleman, J.S. (1990). Foundations of Social Theory. Cambridge, MA: Harvard University Press.
Collier, J., and Esteban, R. (2007). Corporate social responsibility and employee commitment. Business Ethics: A European Review, 16(1), 19–33.
Committee of Public Accounts (2003). Delivering better value for money from the Private Finance Initiative. Twenty-Eighth Report of the 2002–03 Session, House of Commons, London.
Conner, K.R., and Prahalad, C.K. (1996). A resource-based theory of the firm: knowledge versus opportunism. Organization Science, 7(5), 477–501.
Cook, K.S. (2000). Charting futures for sociology: structure and action. Contemporary Sociology, 29, 685–692.
Crane, T.G., Felder, J.P., Thompson, P.J., Thompson, M.G., and Sanders,

S.R. (1997). Partnering process model. Journal of Management in Engineering, 13(3), 57–63.

Crane, T.G., Felder, J.P., Thompson, P.J., Thompson, M.G., and Sanders, S.R. (1999). Partnering measures. Journal of Management in Engineering, 15(2), 37–42.

Crawley, E.F. (2009). Identifying value – reducing ambiguity in the system. Lecture Notes for ESD.34 System Architecture. Massachusetts Institute of Technology, Cambridge, MA.

Crocker, K.J., and Masten, S.E. (1991). Pretia ex machina-prices and process in long-term contracts. Journal of Law and Economics, 34(1), 69–99.

Crocker, K.J., and Reynolds, K.J. (1993). The efficiency of incomplete contracts: an empirical analysis of air force engine procurement. RAND Journal of Economics, 24(1), 126–146.

Crowley, L.G., and Karim, M.A. (1995). Conceptual model of partnering. Journal of Management in Engineering, 11(5), 33–39.

Cruz, C.O., and Marques, R.C. (2012). Risk-sharing in highway concessions: contractual diversity in Portugal. Journal of Professional Issues in Engineering Education and Practice, 139(2), 99–108.

Cruz, C.O., and Marques, R.C. (2013). Flexible contracts to cope with uncertainty in public–private partnerships. International Journal of Project Management, 31(3), 473–483. http://dx.doi.org/10.1016/j.ijproman.2012.09.006.

Cutler, D.M., and Miller, G. (2006). Water, water everywhere: municipal finance and water supply in American cities. In E.L. Glaeser and C. Goldin (eds), Corruption and Reform: Lessons from America's Economic History. Chicago, IL: University of Chicago Press. http://www.nber.org/books/glae06-1.

Daily, C.M., Dalton, D.R., and Cannella Jr, A.A. (2003). Corporate governance: decades of dialogue and data. Academy of Management Review, 28(3), 371–382.

Dal Bó, P., Foster, A., and Putterman, L. (2008). Institutions and behavior: experimental evidence on the effects of democracy. American Economic Review, 100(5), 2205–2229.

Davies, R. (2014). Civic crowdfunding: participatory communities, entrepreneurs and the political economy of place. May 9. https://ssrn.com/abstract=2434615 or http://dx.doi.org/10.2139/ssrn.2434615.

Davis, J.B. (2007). Akerlof and Kranton on identity in economics: inverting the analysis. Cambridge Journal of Economics, 31(3), 349–362.

Davis, J.H., and Kelly, K. (2017). Trump plans to shift infrastructure funding to cities, states and business. New York Times, June 3.

De Schepper, S., Dooms, M., and Haezendonck, E. (2014). Stakeholder dynamics and responsibilities in public–private partnerships: a mixed experience. International Journal of Project Management, 32(7), 1210–1222.

De Tocqueville, A. (1835/2004). Democracy in America. Authus Goldhammer, Trans. New York: Library of America.

De Tocqueville, A. (1856/1998, 2001). The Old Regime and the Revolution, Vols 1–2. A.S. Kahan, Trans. Chicago, IL: University of Chicago Press.

Déau, T. (2011). How to foster investment in long-term assets such as infrastructure? OECD Journal: Financial Market Trends, 2011(1). https://www.oecd.org/finance/financial-markets/48619695.pdf.

DeCorla-Souza, P., Lee, D., Timothy, D., and Mayer, J. (2013). Comparing public–private partnerships with conventional procurement: incorporating considerations from benefit–cost analysis. Transportation Research Record: Journal of the Transportation Research Board, 2346, 32–39.

Della Croce, R. (2012). Trends in large pension fund investment in infrastructure. OECD Working Papers on Finance, Insurance and Private Pensions, No. 29. Paris: OECD Publishing. https://doi.org/10.1787/5k8xd1p1p7r3-en.

DeVito, L. (2014). Patronicity gets crowdfunding dollars with an eye on Detroit. Detroit Metro Times, November 5. http://www.metrotimes.com/detroit/patronicity-gets-crowdfunding-dollars-with-an-eye-on-detroit/Content?oid=2264662.

de Weck, O.L., Roos, D., and Magee, C.L. (2011). Engineering Systems: Meeting Human Needs in a Complex Technological World. Cambridge, MA: MIT Press.

Dewulf, G., Garvin, M.J., and Duffield, C. (2016). Multinational comparison of the tension between standards and context in public–private partnerships. In A. Roumboutsos (ed.), Public–Private Partnerships in Transport: Trends and Theory (pp. 267–291). Abingdon: Routledge.

Dezember, R., and Glazer, E. (2013). Drop in traffic takes toll on investors in private roads. Wall Street Journal, November 20.

DiMaggio, P.J., and Powell, W.W. (1983). The iron cage revisited: institutional isomorphism and collective rationality in organizational fields. American Sociological Review, 48(2), 147–160.

Downs, A. (1967). Inside Bureaucracy. New York: Little, Brown.

Downs, G.W., and Mohr, L.B. (1976). Conceptual issues in the study of innovation. Administrative Science Quarterly, 21, 700–714.

Duncan, B. (2004). A theory of impact philanthropy. Journal of Public Economics, 88(9/10), 2159–2180. http://doi.org/10.1016/S0047-2727(03)00037-9.

Dutton, J.E., Dukerich, J.M., and Harquail, C.V. (1994). Organizational images and member identification. Administrative Science Quarterly, 39(2), 239–263.

Dyer, J.H., and Chu, W. (2000). The determinants of trust in supplier–automaker relationships in the US, Japan and Korea. Journal of International Business Studies, 31(2), 259–285.

Dyer, J.H., and Chu, W. (2003). The role of trustworthiness in reducing transaction costs and improving performance: empirical evidence from the United States, Japan, and Korea. Organization Science, 14(1), 57–68.

Ebi, K. (2014). How crowdfunding and mini-bonds are paying for Better Denver. Accessed November 8, 2016 at http://smartcitiescouncil.com/article/how-crowdfunding-and-mini-bonds-are-paying-better-denver.

Eccles, R.G. (1981). The quasi-firm in the construction industry. Journal of Economic Behavior and Organization, 94(Supplement), s17–s51.

Edkins, A., Geraldi, J., Morris, P., and Smith, A. (2013). Exploring the front-end of project management. Engineering Project Organization Journal, 3(2), 71–85.

Eisenhardt, K.M., and Graebner, M.E. (2007). Theory building from cases: opportunities and challenges. Academy of Management Journal, 50(1), 25–32.

Ekeh, P.P. (1974). Social Exchange Theory: The Two Traditions. Cambridge, MA: Harvard University Press.

El-Gohary, N.M., Osman, H., and El-Diraby, T.E. (2006). Stakeholder management for public–private partnerships. International Journal of Project Management, 24(7), 595–604.

Elsbach, K.D. (1994). Managing organizational legitimacy in the California cattle industry: the construction and effectiveness of verbal accounts. Administrative Science Quarterly, 39(1), 57–88.

Elsbach, K.D., and Glynn, M.A. (1996). Believing your own "PR": embedding identification in strategic reputation. Advances in Strategic Management, 13, 65–90.

Embrechts, P., Klüppelberg, C., and Mikosch, T. (2013). Modelling Extremal Events: For Insurance and Finance. Berlin: Springer.

Emerson, R.M. (1962). Power dependence relations. American Sociological Review, 27, 31–41.

Emerson, R.M. (1964). Power dependence relations: two experiments. Sociometry, 27, 282–298.

Emerson, R.M. (1972a). Exchange theory, part I: a psychological basis for social exchange. In J. Berger, M. Zelditch Jr and B. Anderson (eds), Sociological Theories in Progress. Boston, MA: Houghton-Mifflin.

Emerson, R.M. (1972b). Exchange theory, part II: exchange relations and networks. In J. Berger, M. Zelditch Jr and B. Anderson (eds), Sociological Theories in Progress. Boston, MA: Houghton-Mifflin.

Emerson, R.M. (1976). Social exchange theory. Annual Review in Sociology, 2, 335–362.

Engel, E., Fischer, R., and Galetovic, A. (1997). Highway franchising: pitfalls and opportunities. American Economic Review, 87(2), 68–72.

Engel, E.M., Fischer, R.D., and Galetovic, A. (2001). Least-present-value-of-revenue auctions and highway franchising. Journal of Political Economy, 109(5), 993–1020.

Engel, E., Fischer, R., and Galetovic, A. (2013). The basic public finance of public–private partnerships. Journal of the European Economic Association, 11(1), 83–111.

Engel, E., Fischer, R.D., and Galetovic, A. (2014). The Economics of Public–Private Partnerships: A Basic Guide. Cambridge: Cambridge University Press.

Eppinger, S.D., and Browning, T.R. (2012). Design Structure Matrix Methods and Applications. Cambridge, MA: MIT Press.

Esty, B.C. (2004). Modern Project Finance: A Casebook. New York: John Wiley & Sons.

European PPP Expertise Centre (2014). Establishing and reforming PPP units: analysis of EPEC member PPP units and lessons learnt. August. http://www.eib.org/epec/resources/publications/epec_establishing_and_reforming_ppp_units_en1.

Evans, P., and Rauch, J.E. (1999). Bureaucracy and growth: a cross-national analysis of the effects of Weberian state structures on economic growth. American Sociological Review, 64(5), 748–765.

Fang, L.H., Ivashina, V., and Lerner, J. (2015). The disintermediation of financial markets: direct investing in private equity. Journal of Financial Economics, 116(1), 160–178.

Farajian, M., Lauzon, A., and Cui, Q. (2015). Introduction to a crowd-funded public–private partnership model in the United States: policy review on crowdfund investing. Transportation Research Record: Journal of the Transportation Research Board, 2530, 36–43.

Farquharson, E., Torres de Mästle, C., and Yescombe, E.R. (2011). How to engage with the private sector in public–private partnerships in emerging markets. World Bank.

Farrugia, C., Reynolds, T., and Orr, R.J. (2008). Public–private partnership coordination agencies: a global perspective. Working paper. Collaboratory for Research on Global Projects, Stanford University.

Fassin, Y. (2009). The stakeholder model refined. Journal of Business Ethics, 84(1), 113–135.

FDOT (2009a). Concession Agreement for I-595 Corridor Roadway Improvements Project. Tallahassee, FL.

FDOT (2009b). I-595 Corridor Roadway Improvements: Value for Money Analysis. Tallahassee, FL.

FDOT (2009c). I-595 Corridor history. Accessed July 1, 2009 at http://www.i-595.com/history.aspx.

Federal Highway Administration (FHWA) (2017a). Center for Innovative Finance Support – State P3 Legislation. Office of Innovative Program Delivery (OIPD).

Federal Highway Administration (FHWA) (2017b). Fact Sheet: Public–Private Partnerships. Washington, DC.

Federal Highway Administration (FHWA) (2018a). FHWA P3 Toolkit. Washington, DC. https://www.fhwa.dot.gov/ipd/p3/toolkit/.

Federal Highway Administration (FHWA) (2018b). Project Profile: South Bay Expressway (formerly SR 125 South Toll Road). Office of Innovative Program Delivery, Center for Innovative Finance. https://www.fhwa.dot.gov/ipd/project_profiles/ca_southbay.aspx.

Fehr, D., and Hishigsuren, G. (2006). Raising capital for microfinance: sources of funding and opportunities for equity financing. Journal of Developmental Entrepreneurship, 11(2), 133–143. http://doi.org/10.1142/S1084946706000301.

Fehr, E., and Simon, G. (2000). Fairness and retaliation: the economics of reciprocity. Journal of Economic Perspectives, 14(3), 159–181.

Feng, W. (2013). Strategic management for large engineering projects: the stakeholder value network approach. Doctoral dissertation, Massachusetts Institute of Technology.

Feng, W., Crawley, E.F., de Weck, O.L., Keller, R., Lin, J., and Robinson, B. (2012a). BP stakeholder value network. In S.D. Eppinger and T.R. Browning (eds), Design Structure Matrix Methods and Applications (pp. 122–127). Cambridge, MA: MIT Press.

Feng, W., Crawley, E.F., Lessard, D.R., Cameron, B.G., and de Weck, O.L. (2013a). Moving beyond single relations: a multi-relational network theory of stakeholder power. Strategic Management Society (SMS) 33rd Annual International Conference.

Feng, W., Lessard, D., Cameron, B., and Crawley, E. (2013b). Stakeholders, issues and the shaping of large engineering projects. Engineering Project Organizations Conference, Devil's Thumb Ranch, Colorado, July 9–11.

Feng, W., Lessard, D., Crawley, E., de Weck, O., and Cameron, B. (2012b). Understanding the impacts of indirect stakeholder relationships– stakeholder value network analysis and its application to large engineering projects. MIT Sloan Research Paper No. 4978-12. Cambridge, MA.

Feng, Z., Zhang, S.-B., and Gao, Y. (2015). Modeling the impact of government guarantees on toll charge, road quality and capacity for build– operate–transfer (BOT) road projects. Transportation Research Part A: Policy and Practice, 78, 54–67.

Ferrer, E., Macken, S., and Stewart, S. (2014). Getting us there: funding the transport infrastructure of tomorrow. McKell Institute, November.

Fischer, M., Khanzode, A., Ashcraft, H.W., and Reed, D. (2017). Integrating Project Delivery. New York: John Wiley & Sons.

Fisher, G., and Babbar, S. (1996). Private Financing of Toll Roads. Washington, DC: World Bank.

Fitzgerald, P. (2015). Indiana toll road exits bankruptcy protection. Wall Street Journal. http://www.wsj.com/articles/indiana-toll-road-exits-bankruptcy-protection-1432907793.

Fligstein, N. (1997). Social skill and institutional theory. American Behavioral Scientist, 40(4), 397–405.

Fligstein, N. (2001). Social skill and the theory of fields. Sociological Theory, 19(2), 105–125.

Flyvbjerg, B. (2004). Procedures for dealing with optimism bias in transport planning. Guidance Document. London: British Department for Transport.

Flyvbjerg, B. (2011). Case study. In N.K. Denzin and Y.S. Lincoln (eds), The SAGE Handbook of Qualitative Research (pp. 301–316). Thousand Oaks, CA: SAGE.

Flyvbjerg, B. (ed.) (2017). The Oxford Handbook of Megaproject Management. Oxford: Oxford University Press.

Flyvbjerg, B., Bruzelius, N., and Rothengatter, W. (2003). Megaprojects and Risk: An Anatomy of Ambition. Cambridge: Cambridge University Press.

Flyvbjerg, B., Bruzelius, N., and Rothengatter, W. (2005a). Megaprojects and Risk: An Anatomy of Ambition. Cambridge: Cambridge University Press.

Flyvbjerg, B., Holm, M.S., and Buhl, S. (2002). Underestimating costs in public works projects: error or lie? Journal of the American Planning Association, 68(3), 279–295.

Flyvbjerg, B., Skamris Holm, M.K., and Buhl, S.L. (2005b). How (in)accurate are demand forecasts in public works projects? The case of transportation. Journal of the American Planning Association, 71(2), 131–146.

Forrer, J., Kee, J.E., Newcomer, K.E., and Boyer, E. (2010). Public–private partnerships and the public accountability question. Public Administration Review, 70(3), 475–484.

Freeman, R.E. (1984). Strategic Management: A Stakeholder Approach. Boston, MA: Pitman.

Freeman, R.E., and McVea, J. (2006). A stakeholder approach to strategic management. In M.A. Hitt, R.E. Freeman and J.S. Harrison (eds), The Blackwell Handbook of Strategic Management (pp. 189–207). Hoboken, NJ: Blackwell Publishing.

Freeman, R.E., Harrison, J.S., Wicks, A.C., Parmar, B.L., and De Colle, S. (2010). Stakeholder Theory: The State of the Art. Cambridge: Cambridge University Press.

Friedman, A., and Miles, S. (2002). Developing stakeholder theory. Journal of Management Studies, 39(1), 1–21. http://doi.org/10.1111/1467-6486.00280.

Friedman, M. (1953). Essays in Positive Economics. Chicago, IL: University of Chicago Press.

Friedman, M. (1970). The social responsibility of business is to increase its profits. New York Times Magazine, September 13.

Frooman, J. (2010). The issue network: reshaping the stakeholder model. Canadian Journal of Administrative Sciences, 27(2), 161–173.

Froud, J. (2003). The Private Finance Initiative: risk, uncertainty, and the state. Accounting, Organizations and Society, 28(6), 567–589.

Fu, F., Feng, W., Li, Z., Crawley, E.F., and Ni, W. (2011). A network-based modeling framework for stakeholder analysis of China's energy conservation campaign. Energy, 36(8), 4996–5003.

Gächter, S., and Fehr, E. (1999). Collective action as a social exchange. Journal of Economic Behavior and Organization, 39(4), 341–369.

Galbraith, J.R. (1973). Designing Complex Organizations. Reading, MA: Addison-Wesley.

Gamson, W.A. (1992). The social psychology of collective action. In A.D. Morris and C.M. Mueller (eds), Frontiers in Social Movement Theory (pp. 53–76). New Haven, CT: Yale University Press.

GAO (2006). Military Housing: Management Issues Require Attention as the Privatization Program Matures. Washington, DC: GAO.

GAO (2009). Military Housing Privatization: DOD Faces New Challenges Due to Significant Growth at Some Installations and Recent Turmoil in the Financial Markets. Washington, DC: GAO.

Garvey, M. (1999). 91 express lanes pull in a profit for first time. Los Angeles Times, April 24.

Garvin, M. (2009). Public–Private Partnerships for Highway Infrastructure: Capitalizing on International Experience. Alexandria, VA: FHWA, DOT.

Garvin, M.J. (2007a). America's infrastructure strategy: drawing on history to guide the future. White Paper. Washington, DC: KPMG LLP and Stanford University.

Garvin, M.J. (2007b). Are public–private partnerships effective as infrastructure development strategies? In E. Hughes (ed.), Proceedings of the Construction Management and Economics 25th Anniversary Conference: Past, Present and Future, July 15–17, University of Reading, UK. Taylor & Francis, CD-ROM.

Garvin, M.J. (2010). Enabling development of the transportation public–private partnership market in the United States. Journal of Construction Engineering and Management, 136(4), 402–411.

Garvin, M.J. (2015). Payment structures in public–private partnership projects: contrasting tolls and availability payments. Research Report for Virginia's Office of Public–Private Partnerships (VAP3), Virginia Tech, Blacksburg, VA.

Garvin, M.J., and Bosso, D. (2008). Assessing the effectiveness of infrastructure public–private partnership programs and projects. Public Works Management and Policy, 13(2), 162–178.

Garvin, M.J., and Cheah, Y.J. (2004). Valuation techniques for infrastructure investment decisions. Construction Management and Economics, 22(5), 373–383.

Garvin, M.J., and Gonzalez, E.E. (2013). PPP fiscal support options framework. Arup Global Research Challenge Report, Virginia Tech, Blacksburg, VA.

Geddes, R.R. (2011). The Road to Renewal: Private Investment in United States Transportation Infrastructure. Washington, DC: American Enterprise Institute (AEI) Press.

Geddes, R.R., and Reeves, E. (2017). The favourability of US PPP enabling legislation and private investment in transportation infrastructure. Utilities Policy, 48, 157–165.

Geddes, R.R., and Wagner, B.L. (2013). Why do US states adopt public–private partnership enabling legislation? Journal of Urban Economics, 78, 30–41.

Geertz, C. (1983). Local Knowledge: Further Essays in Interpretive Anthropology. Basic Books.

Ghavamifar, K., and Touran, A. (2008). Alternative project delivery systems: applications and legal limits in transportation projects. Journal of Professional Issues in Engineering Education and Practice, 134(1), 106–111. http://doi.org/10.1061/(ASCE)1052-3928(2008)134:1(106).

Ghoshal, S., and Moran, P. (1996). Bad for practice: a critique of the transaction cost theory. Academy of Management Review, 21(1), 13–47.

Gil, N. (2009). Developing cooperative project client–supplier relationships: how much to expect from relational contracts? California Management Review, 51(2), 144–169.

Goffman, E. (1974). Frame Analysis: An Essay on the Organization of Experience. New York: Harper Colophon.

Gonzalez, E.E., Gross, M.E., and Garvin, M.J. (2015). Use of fiscal support mechanisms in public–private partnerships: an exploration of three international case studies. 2nd International Conference on Public–Private Partnerships, Austin, TX, May 25–29.

Gorst, I. (2006). Mission improbable. Financial Times, London, November 20.
Gouldner, A.W. (1960). The norm of reciprocity: a preliminary statement. American Sociological Review, 25(1), 161–178.
Gramlich, E.M. (1994). Infrastructure investment: a review essay. Journal of Economic Literature, 32(3), 1176–1196.
Granovetter, M. (1985). Economic action and social structure: the problem of embeddedness. American Journal of Sociology, 91(3), 481–510.
Granovetter, M. (1992). Problems of explanation in economic sociology. In N. Nohria and R.G. Eccles (eds), Networks and Organizations: Structure, Form, and Action (pp. 25–56). Boston, MA: Harvard Business School Press.
Gransberg, D.D., Dillon, W.D., Reynolds, L., and Boyd, J. (1999). Quantitative analysis of partnered project performance. Journal of Construction Engineering and Management, 125(3), 161–166.
Greening, D.W., and Turban, D.B. (2000). Corporate social performance as a competitive advantage in attracting a quality workforce. Business and Society, 39(3), 254–280.
Greenwood, R., Oliver, C., Sahlin, K., and Suddaby, R. (eds) (2008). The SAGE Handbook of Organizational Institutionalism. Los Angeles, CA: SAGE.
Greif, A., Milgrom, P., and Weingast, B.R. (1994). Coordination, commitment, and enforcement: the case of the merchant guild. Journal of Political Economy, 102(4), 745–776.
Greve, C., and Hodge, G. (2010). Public–private partnerships and public governance challenges. In S. Osborne (ed.), The New Public Governance? Emerging Perspectives on the Theory and Practice of Public Governance (pp. 149–162). London: Routledge.
Grimsey, D., and Lewis, M.K. (2002). Evaluating the risks of public private partnerships for infrastructure projects. International Journal of Project Management, 20(2), 107–118.
Grimsey, D., and Lewis, M.K. (2005). Are public private partnerships value for money? Evaluating alternative approaches and comparing academic and practitioner views. Accounting Forum, 29(4), 345–378.
Grimsey, D., and Lewis, M. (2007). Public Private Partnerships: The Worldwide Revolution in Infrastructure Provision and Project Finance. Cheltenham, UK and Northampton, MA, USA: Edward Elgar Publishing.
Groat, G. (2004). Loosening the belt. Roads and Bridges, 42, 36–41.
Groat, G. (2006). Network futurevision. Roads and Bridges, 44(9), 32–34.
Gross, C. (2007). Community perspectives of wind energy in Australia: the

application of a justice and community fairness framework to increase social acceptance. Energy Policy, 35(5), 2727–2736.
Gross, M.E., and Garvin, M.J. (2011). Structuring PPP toll-road contracts to achieve public pricing objectives. Engineering Project Organization Journal, 1(2), 143–156.
Grossman, S.J., and Hart, O.D. (1986). The costs and benefits of ownership: a theory of vertical and lateral integration. Journal of Political Economy, 94, 691–719.
Guasch, J.L. (2004). Granting and renegotiating infrastructure concessions: doing it right. World Bank.
Gulati, R., and Nickerson, J.A. (2008). Interorganizational trust, governance choice, and exchange performance. Organization Science, 19(5), 688–708.
Gunnarson, S., and Levitt, R.E. (1982). Is a building construction project a hierarchy or a market? In Proceedings of the Seventh World Congress of Project Management (pp. 521–529). Copenhagen, September.
Halai, I. (2009). Landmark Floridian deal reaches financial close. Infrastructure Journal Online, 4. Accessed March 4, 2009 at www.ijonline.com.
Hall, P.A., and Soskice, D. (eds) (2001). Varieties of Capitalism: The Institutional Foundations of Comparative Advantage. New York: Oxford University Press.
Harback, H.F., Basham, D.L., and Buhts, R.E. (1994). Partnering paradigm. Journal of Management in Engineering, 10(1), 23–27.
Hart, O.D. (1988). Incomplete contracts and the theory of the firm. Journal of Law, Economics, and Organization, 4(1), 119–139.
Hart, O. (1995). Firms, Contracts, and Financial Structure. New York: Oxford University Press.
Hart, O. (2003). Incomplete contracts and public ownership: remarks, and an application to public–private partnerships. Economic Journal, 113(486), C69–76. http://onlinelibrary.wiley.com/journal/10.1111/%28ISSN%291468-0297/issues.
Hart, O. (2009). Hold-up, asset ownership, and reference points. Quarterly Journal of Economics, 124, 267–300.
Hart, O., and Moore, J. (1988). Incomplete contracts and renegotiation. Econometrica: Journal of the Econometric Society, 56(4), 755–785.
Harvey, D. (2003). The New Imperialism. Oxford: Oxford University Press.
Harvey, D. (2005). A Brief History of Neoliberalism. Oxford: Oxford University Press.
Hayes, D.J. (2014). Addressing the environmental impacts of large infrastructure projects: making "mitigation" matter. Environmental Law Reporter, 44, 10016–10021.

Heide, J.B., and Wathne, K.H. (2006). Friends, businesspeople, and relationship roles: a conceptual framework and a research agenda. Journal of Marketing, 70(3), 90–103.

Heilbroner, R.L. (1983). The Worldly Philosophers: The Lives, Times and Ideas of the Great Economic Thinkers. London: Pelican.

Hein, A.M., Jankovic, M., Feng, W., Farel, R., Yune, J.H., and Yannou, B. (2017). Stakeholder power in industrial symbioses: a stakeholder value network approach. Journal of Cleaner Production, 148, 923–933.

Hellowell, M., and Vecchi, V. (2015). The non-incremental road to disaster? A comparative policy analysis of agency problems in the commissioning of infrastructure projects in the UK and Italy. Journal of Comparative Policy Analysis: Research and Practice, 17(5), 519–532.

Helper, S., MacDuffie, J.P., and Sabel, C. (2000). Pragmatic collaborations: advancing knowledge while controlling opportunism. Industrial and Corporate Change, 9(3), 443–488.

Henisz, W.J. (2002). The institutional environment for infrastructure investment. Industrial and Corporate Change, 11(2), 355–389. http://dx.doi.org/10.1093/icc/11.2.355.

Henisz, W.J., and Zelner, B.A. (2005a). Legitimacy, interest group pressures, and change in emergent institutions: the case of foreign investors and host country governments. Academy of Management Review, 30(2), 361–382.

Henisz, W.J., and Zelner, B.A. (2005b). PowerTrip or Powerplay: AES-Telasi. Philadelphia, PA: Wharton School.

Henisz, W.J., Levitt, R.E., and Scott, W.R. (2012). Toward a unified theory of project governance: economic, sociological and psychological supports for relational contracting. Engineering Project Organization Journal, 2(1/2), 37–55.

Hirschman, A.O. (1957). Economic policy in underdeveloped countries. Economic Development and Cultural Change, 5(4), 362–370.

HM Treasury (2012). A New Approach to Public Private Partnerships. London: HM Treasury.

Ho, S.P., and Tsui, C.W. (2009). The transaction costs of public–private partnerships: implications on PPP governance design. In Proceedings of the ASCE LEAD Speciality Conference Global Governance in Project Organizations (pp. 5–7). November.

Ho, S.P., Levitt, R., Tsui, C., and Hsu, Y. (2015). Opportunism-focused transaction cost analysis of public–private partnerships. Journal of Management in Engineering, 31(6), 1–11.

Hochberg, Y.V., Ljungqvist, A., and Lu, Y. (2007). Whom you know matters: venture capital networks and investment performance. Journal of Finance, 62(1), 251–301.

Hodge, G.A. (2013). Keynote presentation to Global Challenges in PPP: Cross-Sectoral and Cross-Disciplinary Solutions? November 6–7, Universiteit Antwerpen, City Campus, Hof Van Liere.
Hodge, G.A., and Greve, C. (eds) (2005). The Challenge of Public–Private Partnerships: Learning from International Experience. Cheltenham, UK and Northampton, MA, USA: Edward Elgar Publishing.
Hodge, G.A., and Greve, C. (2007). Public–private partnerships: an international performance review. Public Administration Review, 67(3), 545–558.
Hodge, G.A., Greve, C., and Boardman, A. (eds) (2010). International Handbook of Public–Private Partnerships. Cheltenham, UK and Northampton, MA, USA: Edward Elgar Publishing.
Hoffman, E., McCabe, K.A., and Smith, V.L. (1998). Behavioral foundations of reciprocity: experimental economics and evolutionary psychology. Economic Inquiry, 36(3), 335–352.
Hofstede, G. (1984). Culture's Consequences: International Differences in Work-Related Values. Beverly Hills, CA: SAGE.
Hofstede, G. (1991). Cultures and Organizations. New York: McGraw-Hill.
Homans, G.C. (1958). Social behavior as exchange. American Journal of Sociology, 63(6), 597–606.
Homans, G.C. (1961). Social Behavior. New York: Harcourt, Brace & World.
Horii, T., Yan, J., and Levitt, R. (2004). Modeling and analyzing cultural influences on team performance through virtual experiment. Proceedings of North America Association for Computational Social and Organizational Science Conference, June, Pittsburgh, PA.
Huang, Y.L., and Chou, S.P. (2006). Valuation of the minimum revenue guarantee and the option to abandon in BOT infrastructure projects. Construction Management and Economics, 24(4), 379–389.
Hult, K.M., and Walcott, C.E. (1990). Governing Public Organizations: Politics, Structures, and Institutional Design. Pacific Grove, CA: Brooks/Cole Pub. Co.
Husted, B.W., and Folger, R. (2004). Fairness and transaction costs: the contribution of organizational justice theory to an integrative model of economic organization. Organization Science, 15(6), 719–729.
Hwang, R. (2008). Social networks and water cooperatives in Argentina. Workshop on Increasing Access to Water by the Poor in Latin America: Institutional Innovations, Networks and Small Scale Providers, Stanford University, January 18–19.
Inderst, G. (2009). Pension fund investment in infrastructure. OECD Working Papers on Insurance and Private Pensions, No. 32. OECD Publishing. https://www.oecd.org/finance/private-pensions/42052208.pdf.

Indiana Department of Transportation (INDOT) (2013). Public–Private Partnership Program: Implementation Guidelines. Indianapolis, IN.

Infrastructure Australia (2008). National Public Private Partnership Policy Framework. Commonwealth of Australia, Canberra, ACT, Australia.

Infrastructure Canada Government of Canada (2014). The 2014 New Building Canada Fund: focusing on economic growth, job creation and productivity. February 13. http://www.infrastructure.gc.ca/plan/nbcf-nfcc-eng.html.

Infrastructure Ontario (2012a). An Introduction to Value for Money. Toronto, Ontario: Infrastructure Ontario.

Infrastructure Ontario (2012b). Welcome to Infrastructure Ontario. Toronto, Ontario: Ontario Infrastructure and Lands Corporation. http://www.infrastructureontario.ca/About-Infrastructure-Ontario/.

Iossa, E., and Martimort, D. (2012). Risk allocation and the costs and benefits of public–private partnerships. RAND Journal of Economics, 43(3), 442–474.

Iossa, E., and Martimort, D. (2015). The simple microeconomics of public–private partnerships. Journal of Public Economic Theory, 17(1), 4–48. http://dx.doi.org/10.1111/jpet.12114.

Irwin, T. (2003). Public Money for Private Infrastructure: Deciding When to Offer Guarantees, Output-based Subsidies, and Other Fiscal Support. Washington, DC: World Bank.

Iseki, H., Eckert, J., Uchida, K., Dunn, R., and Taylor, B.D. (2009). Task B-2: status of legislative settings to facilitate public private partnerships in the US. California PATH Program, Institute of Transportation Studies, University of California at Berkeley.

Isham, J., and Kähkönen, S. (1999). What determines the effectiveness of community-based water projects. Social Capital Initiative Working Paper, 14.

Ismail, S. (2013). Critical success factors of public private partnership (PPP) implementation in Malaysia. Asia-Pacific Journal of Business Administration, 5(1), 6–19.

Istrate, E., and Puentes, R. (2011). Moving Forward on Public Private Partnerships: US and International Experience with PPP Units. Washington, DC: Brookings Institution.

Iyer, K.C., and Sagheer, M. (2011). A real options based traffic risk mitigation model for build–operate–transfer highway projects in India. Construction Management and Economics, 29(8), 771–779.

Jackson, M.O. (2008). Social and Economic Networks, Vol. 3. Princeton, NJ: Princeton University Press.

Jap, S.D. (2001). "Pie sharing" in complex collaboration contexts. Journal of Marketing Research, 38(1), 86–99.

Jap, S.D., and Anderson, E. (2007). Testing a life-cycle theory of cooperative interorganizational relationships: movement across stages and performance. Management Science, 53(2), 260–275.

Jap, S.D., and Ganesan, S. (2000). Control mechanisms and the relationship life cycle: implications for safeguarding specific investments and developing commitment. Journal of Marketing Research, 37(2), 227–245.

Jin, Y., and Levitt, R.E. (1997). The virtual design team: a computational model of project organizations. Journal of Computational and Mathematical Organization Theory, 2(3), 171–195.

Jin, Y., Levitt, R.E., Christiansen, T., and Kunz, J.C. (1995). The virtual design team: a computer simulation framework for studying organizational aspects of concurrent design. Simulation, 64(3), 160–174.

Johnson, S., McMillan, J., and Woodruff, C. (2002). Courts and relational contracts. Journal of Law, Economics, and Organization, 18(1), 221–277.

Johnston, J. (2010). Examining "tunnel vision" in Australian PPPs: rationales, rhetoric, risks and "rogues." Australian Journal of Public Administration, 69, S61–S73. http://dx.doi.org/10.1111/j.1467-8500.2009.00660.x.

Jones, C., Hesterly, W.S., and Borgatti, S.P. (1997). A general theory of network governance: exchange conditions and social mechanisms. Academy of Management Review, 22(4), 911–945.

Jooste, S.F., and Scott, W.R. (2011). Organizations enabling public–private partnerships: an organization field approach. In W.R. Scott, R.E. Levitt and R.J. Orr (eds), Global Projects: Institutional and Political Challenges (pp. 377–402). Cambridge: Cambridge University Press.

Jooste, S.F., and Scott, W.R. (2012). The public–private partnership enabling field: evidence from three cases. Administration and Society, 44(2), 149–182.

Jun, J. (2010). Appraisal of combined agreements in BOT project finance: focused on minimum revenue guarantee and revenue cap agreements. International Journal of Strategic Property Management, 14(2), 139–155. http://dx.doi.org/10.3846/ijspm.2010.11.

Kalb, S. (2015). Sovereign wealth funds in the global capital markets: reintermediation and new collaborative models. CFA Institute Conference Proceedings, 32(4), 18–26.

Kee, J.E., Newcomer, K.E., Trent, D.L., Oster, V., and Rosen, S. (2007). Keeping the public interest in public–private partnerships (No. 5). Working Paper.

Kettl, D.F. (1993). Sharing Power. Washington, DC: Brookings Institution.

Kettl, D.F. (2011). Sharing Power: Public Governance and Private Markets. Washington, DC: Brookings Institution Press.

Khan, M.F.K., and Parra, R.J. (2003). Financing Large Projects: Using Project Finance Techniques and Practices. New York: Pearson Prentice Hall.

Khanna, Parag (2016). A New Map for America. New York Times, April 15. http://www.nytimes.com/2016/04/17/opinion/sunday/a-new-map-for-america.html.

Khanzode, A., Fischer, M., and Reed, D. (2008). Benefits and lessons learned of implementing building virtual design and construction (VDC) technologies for coordination of mechanical, electrical, and plumbing (MEP) systems on a large healthcare project. Stanford, CA: Department of Civil and Environmental Engineering, Stanford University.

Khwaja, A.I. (2009). Can good projects succeed in bad communities? Journal of Public Economics, 93(7/8), 899–916.

Kilduff, M., and Tsai, W. (2003). Social Networks and Organizations. Thousand Oaks, CA: SAGE.

Kim, H.R., Lee, M., Lee, H.T., and Kim, N.M. (2010). Corporate social responsibility and employee–company identification. Journal of Business Ethics, 95(4), 557–569.

Kim, J., and Ryan, J. (2015a). Public-sector deficit risk and infrastructure P3s: a value for funding analytical approach to evaluation. Journal of Structured Finance, 21(2), 63–73.

Kim, J., and Ryan, J. (2015b). Value for funding: expanding the analytical framework for infrastructure P3 evaluation. Journal of Structured Finance, 21(2), 60–62.

Kim, Kang-Soo (2015). How national PPP units can influence regional performance: Korea's experience. Washington, DC: Public–Private Infrastructure Advisory Facility, World Bank. https://blogs.worldbank.org/ppps/how-national-ppp-units-can-influence-regional-performance-korea-s-experience.

Kim, W.C., and Mauborgne, R.A. (1991). Implementing global strategies: the role of procedural justice. Strategic Management Journal, 12(S1), 125–143.

Kim, W.C., and Mauborgne, R.A. (1993a). Effectively conceiving and executing multinationals' worldwide strategies. Journal of International Business Studies, 24(3), 419–448.

Kim, W.C., and Mauborgne, R.A. (1993b). Procedural justice, attitudes, and subsidiary top management compliance with multinationals corporate strategic decisions. Academy of Management Journal, 36(3), 502–526.

Kim, W.C., and Mauborgne, R.A. (1995). A procedural justice model of strategic decision-making – strategy content implications in the multinational. Organization Science, 6(1), 44–61.

Kim, W.C., and Mauborgne, R.A. (1996). Procedural justice and managers' in-role and extra-role behavior: the case of the multinational. Management Science, 42(4), 499–515.

Kim, W.C., and Mauborgne, R.A. (1998). Procedural justice, strategic decision making, and the knowledge economy. Strategic Management Journal, 19(4), 323–338.

Kim, W.C., and Mauborgne, R.A. (2002). The psychology of legitimacy: emerging perspectives on ideology, justice, and intergroup relations. Administrative Science Quarterly, 47(3), 571–575.

Kivleniece, I., and Quelin, B.V. (2012). Creating and capturing value in public–private ties: a private actor's perspective. Academy of Management Review, 37(2), 272–299.

Klein, D.B., and Yin, C. (1996). Use, esteem and profit in voluntary provision: toll roads in California, 1850–1902. Economic Inquiry, 34(4), 678–692.

Knight, J., Smithwick, G., and Templeton Rivas, A. (2014). The importance of cash contributions on sustainability of international development projects. Proceedings of World Environmental and Water Resources Congress, 1647–1660.

Knoke, D., and Yang, S. (2008). Social Network Analysis, Vol. 2. Los Angeles, CA: SAGE.

Kogut, B., and Zander, U. (1992). Knowledge of the firm, combinative capabilities, and the replication of technology. Organization Science, 3(3), 383–397.

Kogut, B., and Zander, U. (1996). What firms do? Coordination, identity and learning. Organization Science, 7(5), 502–518.

Koppenjan, J.F.M., and Enserink, B. (2009). Public–private partnerships in urban infrastructures: reconciling private sector participation and sustainability. Public Administration Review, 69(2), 284–296.

Korsgaard, M.A., Schweiger, D.M., and Sapienza, H.J. (1995). Building commitment, attachment, and trust in strategic decision-making teams: the role of procedural justice. Academy of Management Journal, 38(1), 60–84.

KPMG (2010). Procurement, review of barriers to competition and efficiency in the procurement of PPP projects. KPMG Corporate Finance (Aust).

Krick, T., Forstater, M., Monaghan, P., and Sillanpää, M. (2006). The Stakeholder Engagement Manual: The Practitioners Handbook on Stakeholder Engagement. Accountability, the United Nations Environment Programme, and Stakeholder Research Associates.

Krippendorff, K.H. (2013). Content Analysis: An Introduction to Its Methodology. Thousand Oaks, CA: SAGE.

Kwak, Y.H., Chih, Y., and Ibbs, C.W. (2009). Towards a comprehensive understanding of public private partnerships for infrastructure development. California Management Review, 51(2), 51–78.

Lamb, E. (2018). Michigan Gov. Rick Snyder creates two infrastructure councils. Transport Topics, July 9. http://www.ttnews.com/articles/michigan-gov-rick-snyder-creates-two-infrastructure-councils (accessed July 23, 2018).

Lammam, C., MacIntyre, H., and Berechman, J. (2013). Using Public–Private Partnerships to Improve Transportation Infrastructure in Canada. Vancouver: Fraser Institute.

Landa, J. (1995). Trust, Ethnicity, and Identity: Beyond the New Institutional Economics of Ethnic Trading Networks, Contract Law, and Gift-Exchange. Ann Arbor, MI: University of Michigan Press.

Laplume, A.O., Sonpar, K., and Litz, R.A. (2008). Stakeholder theory: reviewing a theory that moves us. Journal of Management, 34(6), 1152–1189.

Larson, E. (1997). Partnering on construction projects: a study of the relationship between partnering activities and project success. IEEE Transactions on Engineering Management, 44(2), 188–195.

Latham, M. (1994). Constructing the Team. London: HMSO.

Latham, M. (2003). Democracy and infomediaries. Corporate Governance – An International Review, 11(2), 91–101. http://doi.org/10.1111/1467-8683.00010.

Laumann, E.O., Marsden, P.V., and Prensky, D. (1983). The boundary specification problem in network analysis. In R.S. Burt and M.J. Minor (eds), Applied Network Analysis: A Methodological Introduction (pp. 18–34). Beverly Hills, CA: SAGE.

Lawrence, P.R. (1993). The contingency approach to organization design. In R.T. Golembiewski (ed.), Handbook of Organization Behavior (pp. 9–18). New York: Marcel Dekker.

Lawrence, P.R., and Lorsch, J.W. (1967). Organization and Environment: Managing Differentiating and Integration. Cambridge, MA: Graduate School of Business Administration, Harvard University.

Lessard, D., and Miller, R. (2000). Mapping and facing the landscape of risks. In R. Miller and D. Lessard (eds), The Strategic Management of Large Engineering Projects: Shaping Institutions, Risks and Governance (pp. 75–92). Cambridge, MA: MIT Press.

Lessard, D.R., and Miller, R. (2013). The shaping of large engineering projects. In H. Priemus and B. van Wee (eds), International Handbook on Mega Projects (pp. 93–112). Cheltenham, UK and Northampton, MA, USA: Edward Elgar Publishing.

Levin, I.P., Gaeth, G.J., Schreiber, J., and Lauiola, M. (2002). A new look at framing effects: distribution of effect sizes, individual differences and independence of types of effects. Organizational Behavior and Human Decision Processes, 88(1), 411–429.

Levin, I.P., Schneider, S.L., and Gaeth, G.J. (1998). All frames are not created equal: a typology and critical analysis of framing effects. Organizational Behavior and Human Decision Processes, 76, 149–188.

Levine, S., and Shah, S. (2003). Towards a theory of large-scale generalized exchange. Annual Meeting of the American Sociological Association. Atlanta, GA.

Lévi-Strauss, C. (1949/1969). The Elementary Structures of Kinship, rev. edn. Boston, MA: Beacon Press.

Lévi-Strauss, C. (1963). Structural Anthropology. New York: Basic.

Levitt, R.E. (1984). Superprojects and superheadaches: balancing technical economics of scale against management diseconomies of size and complexity. Project Management Journal, 15(4), 82–89.

Levitt, R. (2015). An extended coordination theory for governance of tasks, projects, firms and business ecosystems. GPC Working Paper, Stanford University, Stanford, CA. https://gpc.stanford.edu/sites/default/files/micro-governanceofinterdependenttasks-160113.pdf.

Levitt, R.E., and Eriksson, K. (2016). Developing a governance model for PPP infrastructure service delivery based on lessons from Eastern Australia. Journal of Organization Design, 5(1). https://jorgdesign.springeropen.com/articles/10.1186/s41469-016-0009-3.

Levitt, R., Henisz, W., Scott, W., and Settel, D. (2010). Governance challenges of infrastructure delivery: the case for socio-economic governance approaches. Construction Research Congress 2010 (Vol. May, pp. 757–767).

Levitt, R.E., Logcher, R.D., and Ashley, D.B. (1980). Allocating risk and incentive in construction. Journal of the Construction Division, 106(3), 297–305.

Levitt, R.E., Thomsen, J., Christiansen, T.R., Kunz, J.C., Jin, Y., and Nass, C. (1999). Simulating project work processes and organizations: toward a micro-contingency theory of organizational design. Management Science, 45(11), 1479–1495.

Lew, S., and Porcari, J. (2017). Eight years later: what the recovery act taught us about investing in transportation. The Avenue Blog, Brookings Institution, February 22. https://www.brookings.edu/blog/the-avenue/2017/02/22/eight-years-later-what-the-recovery-act-taught-us/ (accessed June 12, 2018).

Lind, E.A., and Tyler, T.R. (1988). The Social Psychology of Procedural Justice. New York: Plenum Press.

Lindblom, C.E. (1977). Politics and Markets. New York: Basic Books.

Liu, J., Love, P., Davis, P., Smith, J., and Regan, M. (2015). Conceptual framework for the performance measurement of public–private partnerships. Journal of Infrastructure Systems, 21(1), 04014023. http//dx.doi.org/10.1061/(ASCE)IS.1943-555X.0000210.

Liu, J., Love, P.E., Smith, J., Regan, M., and Davis, P.R. (2014). Life cycle critical success factors for public–private partnership infrastructure projects. Journal of Management in Engineering, 31(5), 04014073.

Liu, T., Bennon, M., Garvin, M.J., and Wang, S. (2017). Sharing the big risk: assessment framework for revenue risk sharing mechanisms in transportation public–private partnerships. Journal of Construction Engineering and Management, 143(12), 04017086. https://doi.org/10.1061/(ASCE)CO.1943-7862.0001397.

Liu, T., Wang, Y., and Wilkinson, S. (2016). Identifying critical factors affecting the effectiveness and efficiency of tendering processes in public–private partnerships (PPPs): a comparative analysis of Australia and China. International Journal of Project Management, 34(4), 701–716. http://dx.doi.org/10.1016/j.ijproman.2016.01.004.

Loosemore, M. (2006). Risk allocation in the private provision of infrastructure. International Journal of Project Management, 25(2007), 66–76.

Lubatkin, M., Lane, P.J., Collin, S., and Very, P. (2007). An embeddedness framing of governance and opportunism: towards a cross-nationally accommodating theory of agency. Journal of Organizational Behavior, 28(1), 43–58.

Lucea, R. (2007). Essays on global non-market strategy. Doctoral dissertation, Massachusetts Institute of Technology. http://hdl.handle.net/1721.1/42337.

Mackey, A., Mackey, T.B., and Barney, J. (2007). Corporate social responsibility and firm performance: investor preferences and corporate strategies. Academy of Management Review, 32(3), 817–835.

MacLeod, B.W. (2007). Reputations, relationships, and contract enforcement. Journal of Economic Literature, 45, 595–628.

Macquarie (2009). Infrastructure Sector. Macquarie Equities Research.

Mahalingam, A. (2010). PPP experiences in Indian cities: barriers, enablers, and the way forward. Journal of Construction Engineering and Management, 136(4), 419–429.

Mahalingam, A., and Levitt, R.E. (2007). Institutional theory as a framework for analyzing conflicts on global projects. Journal of Construction Engineering and Management, 133(7), 517–528.

Mahon, J.F., Heugens, P.P., and Lamertz, K. (2004). Social networks and non-market strategy. Journal of Public Affairs: An International Journal, 4(2), 170–189.

Maiden, M. (2015). $10.3 billion NSW power sale a good deal for the Baird government. Sydney Morning Herald, November 25.

Malecki, E.J. (2002). Creating and sustaining competitiveness: local knowledge and economic geography. In J.R. Bryson, P.W. Daniels, N. Henry and J. Pollard (eds), Knowledge, Space, Economy (pp. 112–128). London: Routledge.

Malinowski, B. (1920). Kula, the circulating exchange of valuables in the archipelagoes of Eastern New Guinea. Man, 20, 97–105.

Mallett, W.J. (2014). Indiana toll road bankruptcy chills climate for public–private partnerships. CRS Insights, September 29.

March, J.G., and Simon, H.A. (1958). Organizations. New York: John Wiley & Sons.

Markowitz, H. (1952). Portfolio selection. Journal of Finance, 7(1), 77–91.

Marks, S.J., and Davis, J. (2012). Does user participation lead to sense of ownership for rural water systems? Evidence from Kenya. World Development, 40(8), 1569–1576. http://doi.org/10.1016/j.worlddev.2012.03.011.

Martimort, D., and Pouyet, J. (2008). To build or not to build: normative and positive theories of public–private partnerships. International Journal of Industrial Organization, 26(2), 393–411.

Martin, L., Lawther, W., Hodge, G., and Greve, C. (2013). Internationally recommended best practices in transportation financing public–private partnerships (P3s). Public Administration Research, 2(2). http://www.ccsenet.org/journal/index.php/par/article/view/30857.

Mashaw, J.L. (1985). Bureaucratic Justice: Managing Social Security Disability Claims. New Haven, CT: Yale University Press.

Maskin, E. (2002). On indescribable contingencies and incomplete contracts. European Economic Review, 46(4), 725–733.

Matos-Castaño, J., Mahalingam, A., and Dewulf, G. (2014). Unpacking the path-dependent process of institutional change for PPPs. Australian Journal of Public Administration, 73(1), 47–66. http://dx.doi.org/10.1111/1467-8500.12062.

Mayer, K.J., and Argyres, N.S. (2004). Learning to contract: evidence from the personal computer industry. Organization Science, 15(4), 394–410.

McAdam, D. (2011). Social movements and the growth in opposition to global projects. In W.R. Scott, R.E. Levitt and R.J. Orr (eds), Global Projects: Institutional and Political Challenges (pp. 86–110). Cambridge: Cambridge University Press.

McAdam, D., McCarthy, J.D., and Zald, M.N. (1988). Social movements. In N.J. Smelser (ed.), Handbook of Sociology (pp. 695–737). Newbury Park, CA: SAGE.

McAdam, D., McCarthy, J.D., and Zald, M.N. (1996). Comparative Perspectives on Social Movements: Political Opportunities, Mobilizing Structures and Cultural Framings. New York: Cambridge University Press.

McEvily, B., Perrone, V., and Zaheer, A. (2003). Trust as an organizing principle. Organization Science, 14(1), 91–103.

McMillan, J., and Woodruff, C. (1999a). Dispute prevention without courts in Vietnam. Journal of Law, Economics and Organization, 15(3), 637–658.

McMillan, J., and Woodruff, C. (1999b). Interfirm relationships and informal credit in Vietnam. Quarterly Journal of Economics, 114(4), 1285–1320.

Merrow, E.W. (2011). Industrial Megaprojects: Concepts, Strategies, and Practices for Success. Hoboken, NJ: Wiley.

Mesquita, B.B. de, Morrow, J.D., Siverson, R.M., and Smith, A. (1999). Policy failure and political survival: the contribution of political institutions. Journal of Conflict Resolution, 43(2), 147–161.

Metrick, A., and Yasuda, A. (2010). The economics of private equity funds. Review of Financial Studies, 23(6), 2303–2341.

Meyer, J.W., and Rowan, B. (1977). Institutionalized organizations: formal structure as myth and ceremony. American Journal of Sociology, 83(2), 340–363.

Miller, J.B. (1995). Aligning infrastructure development strategy to meet current public needs. PhD Dissertation, MIT, Cambridge, MA.

Miller, R., and Floricel, S. (2000). Transformations in arrangements for shaping and delivering engineering projects. In R. Miller and D. Lessard (eds), The Strategic Management of Large Engineering Projects: Shaping Institutions, Risks, and Governance (pp. 51–73). Cambridge, MA: MIT Press.

Miller, R., and Lessard, D.R. (2000). The Strategic Management of Large Engineering Projects: Shaping Institutions, Risks, and Governance. Cambridge, MA: MIT Press.

Miller, R., and Olleros, X. (2000). Project shaping as a competitive advantage. In R. Miller and D. Lessard (eds), The Strategic Management of Large Engineering Projects: Shaping Institutions, Risks and Governance (pp. 93–130). Cambridge, MA: MIT Press.

Mitchell, R.K., Agle, B.R., and Wood, D.J. (1997). Toward a theory of stakeholder identification and salience: defining the principle of who and what really counts. Academy of Management Review, 22(4), 853–886.

Modigliani, F., and Miller, M.H. (1958). The cost of capital, corporation finance and the theory of investment. American Economic Review, 48(3), 261–297.

Molm, L. (1990). Structure, action, and outcomes: the dynamics of power in social exchange. American Sociological Review, 55, 427–447.

Monk, A., Sharma, R., and Sinclair, D.L. (2017). Reframing Finance: New Models of Long-Term Investment Management. Stanford, CA: Stanford University Press.

Muralidhar, A.S. (2001). Innovations in Pension Fund Management. Stanford, CA: Stanford University Press.

Muro, M., and Hoene, C.W. (2009). Fiscal challenges facing cities: implications for recovery. Metropolitan Policy Program at Brookings, November. https://www.brookings.edu/wp-content/uploads/2016/06/1118_cities_fiscal_challenges_paper.pdf.

Murray, J. (2014). Denver's $500 "mini-bonds" sell out in first hour, raising $12 million. Denver Post. Accessed November 8, 2016 at http://www.denverpost.com/2014/08/04/denvers-500-mini-bonds-sell-out-in-first-hour-raising-12-million/.

Myers, S.C. (1977). Determinants of corporate borrowing. Journal of Financial Economics, 5(2), 147–175.

Nee, V., and Ingram, P. (2001). Embeddedness and beyond: institutions, exchange and social structure. In M.C. Brinton and V. Nee (eds), New Institutionalism in Sociology (pp. 19–45). Stanford, CA: Stanford University Press.

Newcombe, R. (2003). From client to project stakeholders: a stakeholder mapping approach. Construction Management and Economics, 21(8), 841–848.

Nguyen, D.A., Garvin, M.J., and Gonzalez, E.E. (2018). Risk allocation in US public–private partnership highway project contracts. Journal of Construction Engineering and Management, 144(5), 04018017. https://doi.org/10.1061/(ASCE)CO.1943-7862.0001465.

Nombela, G., and de Rus, G. (2001). Auctions for infrastructure concessions with demand uncertainty and unknown costs. Munich Personal RePEc Archive, Germany.

Nombela, G., and de Rus, G. (2004). Flexible-term contracts for road franchising. Transportation Research Part A: Policy and Practice, 38(3), 163–179.

North, D.C. (1990). Institutions, Institutional Change, and Economic Performance. New York: Cambridge University Press.

North, D. (1991). Institutions. Journal of Economic Perspectives, 5(1), 640–655.

Oates, W.E. (1999). Essay on fiscal federalism. Journal of Economic Literature, 37(3), 1120–1149.

Obermann, G. (2007). The role of the state as guarantor of public services: transaction cost issues and empirical evidence. Annals of Public and Cooperative Economics, 78(3), 475–500.

OCTA (2011). 91 Express Lanes 2010–2011 Annual Report. Orange, CA: OCTA.

OECD (2010). Dedicated Public–Private Partnership Units: A Survey of Institutional and Governance Structures. Paris: OECD Publishing. https://dx.doi.org/10.1787/9789264064843-en.

OECD (2012). Recommendation of the Council on Principles for Public Governance of Public–Private Partnerships. Paris: Organisation for Economic Co-operation and Development (OECD).

Officer, R.R. (2008). The respective roles of government and the private sector and private/public partnerships. Paper presented at CP2 Club Conference, April 29–30, Boston, MA.

Oliver, C. (1991). Strategic responses to institutional processes. Academy of Management Review, 16(1), 145–179.

Olson, M. (1965). The Logic of Collective Action: Public Goods and the Theory of Group. Cambridge, MA: Harvard University Press.

O'Neill, P.M. (2009). Privatization. In P.J. Atkins (ed.), International Encyclopedia of Human Geography (pp. 442–447). Oxford: Elsevier.

Opara, M., Elloumi, F., Okafor, O., and Warsame, H. (2017). Effects of the institutional environment on public–private partnership (P3) projects: evidence from Canada. Accounting Forum, 41(2), 77–95.

Ó Riain, S., Autler, G., Egan, T., Burawoy, M., Evans, P., Grimes, S., and Zook, M. (2000). The flexible developmental state: globalization, information technology, and the "Celtic Tiger." Politics and Society, 28(2), 157–193. http://doi.org/10.1177/0032329200028002002.

Orr, R.J. (2005). Unforeseen conditions and costs on global projects: learning to cope with unfamiliar institutions, embeddedness and emergent uncertainty. Doctoral dissertation, Stanford University.

Osei-Kyei, R., and Chan, A.P.C. (2015). Review of studies on the critical success factors for public–private partnership (PPP) projects from 1990 to 2013. International Journal of Project Management, 33(6), 1335–1346. http://dx.doi.org/10.1016/j.ijproman.2015.02.008.

Ostrom, E. (1990). Governing the Commons: The Evolution of Institutions for Collective Action. Cambridge: Cambridge University Press.

Ostrom, E. (2005). Understanding Institutional Diversity. Princeton, NJ: Princeton University Press.

Ostrom, V., and Ostrom, E. (1977). Public Goods and Public Choices. Workshop in Political Theory and Policy Analysis, Indiana University, Bloomington, IN. https://ostromworkshop.indiana.edu/library/node/64009.

Ouchi, W.G. (1980). Markets, bureaucracies and clans. Administrative Science Quarterly, 25, 129–141.

Outlaw, B. (2003). Transportation Secretary Mineta announces $140 million loan for SR 125 South Toll Road, salutes California public–private partnership. Washington, DC: US Department of Transportation. https://www.fhwa.dot.gov/pressroom/fhwa0318.cfm.

Padgett, J.F., and Powell, W.W. (2012). The Emergence of Organizations and Markets. Princeton, NJ: Princeton University Press.

Page, S.N., Ankner, D.W., Jones, C., and Fetterman, R. (2008). The risks and rewards of private equity in infrastructure. Public Works Management and Policy, 13(2), 100–113.

Pajunen, K. (2006). Stakeholder influences in organizational survival. Journal of Management Studies, 43(6), 1261–1288. http://doi.org/10.1111/j.1467-6486.2006.00624.x.

Parker, M. (2011). Availability payments and other forms of P3s for surface transportation. Forum on Funding and Financing Solutions for Surface Transportation in the Coming Decade. Conference Report, AASHTO Center for Excellence in Project Finance, Washington, DC.

Peck, J., and Tickell, A. (2002). Neoliberalizing space. Antipode, 34(3), 380–404.

Pegg, S. (2009). Chronicle of a death foretold: the collapse of the Chad–Cameroon pipeline project. African Affairs, 108, 311–320.

PEI Media (2010). The Infrastructure Investor 30. Infrastructure Investor.

Perkins, J. (2004). Confessions of an Economic Hitman. San Francisco, CA: Berrett-Koehler Publishers.

Peter, A.H. (1989). The Political Power of Economic Ideas: Keynesianism across Nations. Princeton, NJ: Princeton University Press.

Peter, S. (2011). San Diego metro association hopes buy of 125/SBX tollroad will avert need for upgrade of I-805. Frederick, MD: Toll Road News. Available at: http://www.tollroadsnews.com/node/56412012.

Polletta, F. (1998). Contending stories: narrative in social movements. Qualitative Sociology, 21, 419–446.

Pongsiri, N. (2002). Regulation and public–private partnerships. International Journal of Public-Sector Management, 15(6), 487–495. http://dx.doi.org/10.1108/09513550210439634.

Poole Jr, R.W. (1988a). In a pinch, turn partly to toll roads, private sector. Los Angeles Times, July 7.

Poole, R.W. (1988b). Private Tollways: Resolving Gridlock in Southern California. Policy Insight No. 111. Los Angeles, CA: Reason Foundation.

Poole, R.W. (2017). How asset recycling could solve Trump's infrastructure problem. Public Works Financing, 325, 20–21.

Poppo, L., and Zenger, T. (2002). Do formal contracts and relational governance function as substitutes or complements? Strategic Management Journal, 23, 707–725.

Porter, M., and Kramer, M. (2006). Strategy and society. Harvard Business Review, 84(12), 78–92.
Powell, W.W. (1990a). Neither market nor hierarchy – network forms of organization. Research in Organizational Behavior, 12, 295–336.
Powell, W.W. (1990b). Neither market nor hierarchy: network forms of organization. In M.B. Staw and L.L. Cummings (eds), Research in Organizational Behavior (pp. 295–336). Greenwich, CT: JAI.
Pratchett, L. (2004). Local autonomy, local democracy and the "new localism." Political Studies, 52(2), 358–375. http://doi.org/10.1111/j.1467-9248.2004.00484.x.
Preqin (2009). Preqin Online Infrastructure Database.
Preqin (2010). Infrastructure Spotlight. June.
Preqin (2015). 2015 Preqin Global Infrastructure Report. Preqin.
Preston, A.E. (1989). The nonprofit worker in a for-profit world. Journal of Labor Economics, 7(4), 438–463.
Probitas Partners (2010). Infrastructure Market Review and Institutional Investor Survey. http://probitaspartners.com/pdfs/probitas_partners_2011_infra_investor_survey_112010.pdf.
Public Works Financing (PWF) (2017a). Public Works Financing Major Projects Database. http://pwfinance.net/projects-database/.
Public Works Financing (PWF) (2017b). The Journal of Record for Public–Private Partnerships, Vol. 324 (March).
Public Works Financing (PWF) (2017c). The Journal of Record for Public–Private Partnerships, Vol. 331 (November).
Pula, K. (2016). Public–private partnerships for transportation: categorization and analysis of state statutes. National Conference of State Legislatures, Washington, DC.
Queiroz, C., and Lopez Martinez, A. (2013). Legal frameworks for successful public–private partnerships. In P. De Vries and E.B. Yehoue (eds), The Routledge Companion to Public–Private Partnerships (pp. 75–94). Abingdon: Routledge.
Ragin, C.C. (1987). The Comparative Method: Moving Beyond Qualitative and Quantitative Strategies. Berkeley, CA: University of California Press.
Ragin, C.C. (2000). Fuzzy-Set Social Science. Chicago, IL: University of Chicago Press.
Rainey, H.G. (1991). Understanding and Managing Public Organizations. San Francisco, CA: Jossey-Bass.
Raisbeck, P., Duffield, C., and Xu, M. (2010). Comparative performance of PPPs and traditional procurement in Australia. Construction Management and Economics, 28(4), 345–359.
Rall, J., Reed, R.B., and Farber, N.J. (2015). Public–private partnerships

for transportation: a toolkit for legislators. National Conference of State Legislatures (NCSL).
Rauch, J.E. (1995). Bureaucracy, infrastructure, and economic growth: evidence from US cities during the Progressive Era. American Economic Review, 85(4), 968–979.
Rausser, G., and Stevens, R. (2009). Public–private partnerships: goods and the structure of contracts. Annual Review of Resource Economics, 1(1), 75–98.
Recovery (2009). Where is your money going? http://www.recovery.gov/?q=content/investments (accessed June 3, 2009).
Reed, A.M., and Reed, D. (2009). Partnerships for development: four models of business involvement. Journal of Business Ethics, 90, 3–37.
Reeves, E., Palcic, D., Flannery, D., and Geddes, R.R. (2017). The determinants of tendering periods for PPP procurement in the UK: an empirical analysis. Applied Economics, 49(11), 1071–1082.
Reinhardt, W. (2011). The case for public–private partnerships in the US. Public Works Financing, 265(11), 87–102.
Reinhardt, W. (2017a). Confusion reigns over Trump infrastructure plan. Public Works Financing, 326, 1–2.
Reinhardt, W. (2017b). SH 130 refinancing leaves TIFIA with $600m equity stake. Public Works Financing, 328, 9–111.
Richman, B.D. (2005). How community institutions create economic advantage: Jewish diamond merchants in New York. Paper presented at American Law and Economics Association Annual Meeting.
Ring, P.S., and Van de Ven, A.H. (1992). Structuring cooperative relationships between organizations. Strategic Management Journal, 13, 483–498.
Ring, P.S., and Van de Ven, A.H. (1994). Developmental processes of cooperative interorganizational relationships. Academy of Management Review, 19(1), 90–118.
Roberts, M.R. (2015). The role of dynamic renegotiation and asymmetric information in financial contracting. Journal of Financial Economics, 116(1), 61–81. https://doi.org/10.1016/j.jfineco.2014.11.013.
Robins, B. (2015). Transgrid deal: NSW power network asset sale proceeds set to top $20b. Sydney Morning Herald, November 26.
Rocha Armada, M.J., Pereira, P.J., and Rodrigues, A. (2012). Optimal subsidies and guarantees in public–private partnerships. European Journal of Finance, 18(5), 469–495. https://doi.org/10.1080/1351847X.2011.639789.
Roloff, J. (2008). Learning from multi-stakeholder networks: issue-focussed stakeholder management. Journal of Business Ethics, 82(1), 233–250.
Ross, T.W., and Yan, J. (2015). Comparing public–private partnerships and traditional public procurement: efficiency vs. flexibility. Journal of Comparative Policy Analysis: Research and Practice, 17(5), 448–466.

Rousseau, D.M. (1995). Psychological Contract in Organizations: Understanding Written and Unwritten Agreements. Newbury Park, CA: SAGE.

Rowley, T.J. (1997). Moving beyond dyadic ties: a network theory of stakeholder influences. Academy of Management Review, 22(4), 887–910.

Rucht, D. (2002). Mobilization against large techno-industrial projects: a comparative perspective. Mobilization: An International Journal, 7(1), 79–95. http://doi.org/10.1017/CBO9781107415324.004.

Rufin, C., and Rivera-Santos, M. (2010). Between commonweal and competition: understanding the governance of public–private partnerships. Journal of Management, 38(5), 1634–1654. https://doi.org/10.1177/0149206310373948.

Ruster, J. (1997). A retrospective on the Mexican toll road program (1989–94). Public policy for the private sector, Note no. 125, World Bank, Washington, DC.

Sahlins, M. (1965). Essays in Economic Anthropology. Seattle, WA: University of Washington Press.

Sahlman, W.A. (1990). The structure and governance of venture-capital organizations. Journal of Financial Economics, 27(2), 473–521.

Sakhrani, V., Chinowsky, P.S., and Taylor, J.E. (2017). Grand challenges in engineering project organization. Engineering Project Organization Journal, 7, 4–20.

Salamon, L.M., and Elliott, O.V. (2002). The Tools of Government: A Guide to the New Governance. Oxford: Oxford University Press.

Samuel, P. (2010). South Bay Expressway company files for bankruptcy in San Diego. tollroadnews.com.

Samuelson, P.A. (1948). Economics: An Introductory Analysis. New York: McGraw-Hill.

SANDAG (2012). SANDAG Board approves purchase of SR 125. San Diego, CA: San Diego Association of Governments (SANDAG). https://www.sandag.org/index.asp?newsid=731&fuseaction=news.detail.

Sarkar, M., Aulakh, P.S., and Cavusgil, S.T. (1998). The strategic role of relational bonding in interorganization collaborations: an empirical study of the global construction industry. Journal of International Management, 4(2), 85–107.

Savas, E.S. (2000). Privatization and Public–Private Partnerships. New York: Seven Bridges Press.

Saz-Carranza, A., and Longo, F. (2012). Managing competing institutional logics in public–private joint ventures. Public Management Review, 14(3), 331–357.

Schank, R.C., and Abelson, R.P. (1977). Scripts, Plans, Goals, and

Understanding: An Inquiry into Human Knowledge Structures. Hillsdale, NJ: Lawrence Erlbaum.
Schumpeter, J.A. (1954). History of Economic Analysis. New York: Oxford University Press.
Scott, J. (2000). Social Network Analysis: A Handbook. Thousand Oaks, CA: SAGE.
Scott, S.G., and Lane, V.R. (2000). A stakeholder approach to organizational identity. Academy of Management Review, 25(1), 43–62.
Scott, W.R. (1995). Institutions and Organizations, 1st edn. Los Angeles, CA: SAGE.
Scott, W.R. (2008). Institutions and Organizations: Ideas and Interests, 3rd edn. Thousand Oaks, CA: SAGE Publications.
Scott, W.R. (2014). Institutions and Organizations: Ideas, Interests, and Identities, 4th edn. Los Angeles, CA: SAGE.
Scott, W.R., and Davis, G.F. (2007). Organizations and Organizing: Rational, Natural and Open System Perspectives. Upper Saddle River, NJ: Pearson/Prentice Hall.
Scott, W.R., and Meyer, J.W. (1994). Institutional Environments and Organizations: Structural Complexity and Individualism. Thousand Oaks, CA: SAGE.
Scott, W.R., Levitt, R.E., and Orr, R.J. (eds) (2011). Global Projects: Institutional and Political Challenges. Cambridge, MA: Cambridge University Press.
Shan, L., Garvin, M.J., and Kumar, R. (2010). Collar options to manage revenue risks in real toll public–private partnership transportation projects. Construction Management and Economics, 28(10), 1057–1069.
Sharma, D., and Cui, Q. (2012). Design of concession and annual payments for availability payment public private partnership (PPP) projects. Construction Research Congress 2012: Construction Challenges in a Flat World (pp. 2290–2299).
Sheffer, D.A., and Levitt, R.E. (2010). How industry structure retards diffusion of innovations in construction: challenges and opportunities. Collaboratory for Research on Global Projects Working Paper, 59.
Shepherd, A., and Bowler, C. (1997). Beyond the requirements: improving public participation in EIA. Journal of Environmental Planning and Management, 40(6), 725–738. http://doi.org/10.1080/09640569711877.
Shrage, M. (2000). Serious Play: How the World's Best Companies Simulate to Innovate. Boston, MA: Harvard Business School Press.
Siemiatycki, M. (2013). Is there a distinctive Canadian PPP model? Reflections on twenty years of practice. In Second CBS–Sauder–Monash PPP Conference, Vancouver, BC, June (pp. 13–14).
Simon, H.A. (1945/1997). Administrative Behavior: A Study of

Decision-Making Processes in Administrative Organizations. New York: Macmillan, Free Press.

Skelcher, Chris (2010). Governing partnerships. In G. Hodge, C. Greve and A. Boardman (eds), International Handbook on Public–Private Partnerships (pp. 292–304). Cheltenham, UK and Northampton, MA, USA: Edward Elgar Publishing.

Skocpol, T., and Fiorina, M.P. (2004). Civic Engagement in American Democracy. Washington, DC: Brookings Institution Press.

Smith-Doerr, L., and Powell, W.W. (2005). Networks and economic life. In N.J. Smleser and R. Swedberg (eds), The Handbook of Economic Sociology, 2nd edn (pp. 379–402). Princeton, NJ and New York: Princeton University Press and Russell Sage Foundation.

Snow, D., and McAdam, D. (2000). Identity work processes in the context of social movements: clarifying the identity/movement nexus. In S. Stryker, T. Owens and R. White (eds), Self, Identity, and Social Movements (pp. 41–67). Minneapolis, MN: University of Minnesota Press.

South, A.J., Levitt, R.E., and Dewulf, G.P.M.R. (2015). Dynamic stakeholder networks and the governance of PPPs. In Proceedings of the 2nd International Conference on Public–Private Partnerships (pp. 26–29), May.

Sparkes, R., and Cowton, C. (2004). The maturing of socially responsible investment: a review of the developing link with corporate social responsibility. Journal of Business Ethics, 52(1), 45–57.

Spiller, P. (2011). Basic economic principles of infrastructure liberalization: a transaction cost perspective. In M. Finger and R.W. Künneke (eds), International Handbook of Network Industries: The Liberalization of Infrastructure (pp. 11–25). Cheltenham, UK and Northampton, MA, USA: Edward Edgar Publishing.

Stinchcombe, A.L. (1965). Social structure and organizations. In J.G. March (ed.), Handbook of Organizations (pp. 142–193). Chicago, IL: Rand McNally & Company.

Stinchcombe, A.L. (1985). Contracts as hierarchical documents. In A.L. Stinchcombe and C.A. Heimer (eds), Organization Theory and Project Management: Administering Uncertainty in Norwegian Offshore Oil. Oslo: Norwegian University Press, distributed by Oxford University Press.

Stinchcombe, A.L., and Heimer, C. (1985). Organization Theory and Project Management. Bergen: Universitetsforlaget.

Suchman, M.C. (1995). Managing legitimacy: strategic and institutional approaches. Academy of Management Review, 20, 571–610.

Sullivan, E.C. (1998). Evaluating the impacts of the SR 91 variable-toll express lane facility – final report. San Luis Obispo: Applied Research and Development Facility, California Polytechnic State University.

Sun, Y., and Zhang, L. (2014). Balancing public and private stakeholder interests in BOT concessions: minimum revenue guarantee and royalty scheme applied to a water treatment project in China. Journal of Construction Engineering and Management, 141(2), 04014070. https://doi.org/10.1061/(ASCE)CO.1943-7862.0000930.

Sutherland, T.A. (2009). Stakeholder value network analysis for space-based Earth observation. Master's thesis, Department of Aeronautics and Astronautics and Engineering Systems Division, Massachusetts Institute of Technology, Cambridge, MA.

Tang, L., Shen, Q., and Cheng, E.W.L. (2010). A review of studies on public–private partnership projects in the construction industry. International Journal of Project Management, 28(7), 683–694. http://dx.doi.org/10.1016/j.ijproman.2009.11.009.

Tarr, J.A. (1984). The evolution of the urban infrastructure in the nineteenth and twentieth centuries. In Division of Behavioral and Social Sciences and Education, Commission on Behavioral and Social Sciences and Education, and Committee on National Urban Policy (eds), Perspectives on Urban Infrastructure (pp. 4–66). Retrieved from https://www.nap.edu/read/561/chapter/3.

Tarrow, S. (1992). Mentalities, political cultures and collective action frames. In A.D. Morris and C.M. Mueller (eds), Frontiers in Social Movement Research (pp. 174–202). New Haven, CT: Yale University Press.

Taylor, J.E., and Levitt, R. (2007). Innovation alignment and project network dynamics: an integrative model for change. Project Management Journal, 38(3), 22–35.

Taylor, V., and Whittier, N.E. (1992). Collective identity in social movement communities: lesbian feminist mobilization. In Aldon Morris and Carol Mueller (eds), Frontiers of Social Movement Theory (pp. 104–130). New Haven, CT: Yale University Press.

Thibaut, J., and Walker, L. (1975). Procedural Justice: A Psychological Analysis. Hillsdale, NJ: L. Erlbaum Associates.

Thompson, J.D. (1967). Organizations in Action: Social Science Bases of Administration. New York: McGraw-Hill.

Thornton, E. (2007). Roads to riches: why investors are clamoring to take over America's highways, bridges, and airports – and why the public should be nervous. BusinessWeek, May 7, 4033, 50–57.

Thornton, P.H., and Ocasio, W. (2008). Institutional logics. In R. Greenwood, C. Oliver, R. Suddaby and K. Sahlin (eds), The SAGE Handbook of Organizational Institutionalism (pp. 99–128). London: SAGE Publications. http://dx.doi.org/10.4135/9781849200387.

Tirole, J. (1999). Incomplete contracts: where do we stand? Econometrica, 67(4), 741–781.

Tooby, J., Cosmides, L., and Price, M.E. (2006). Cognitive adaptations for n-person exchange: the evolutionary roots of organizational behavior. Managerial and Decision Economics, 27(2/3), 103–129.

Towers Watson (2009). Global Pension Assets Study, February. Accessed April 14, 2011 at http://www.towerswatson.com/united-kingdom/research/3761.

Trigeorgis, L. (1999). Real Options: Managerial Flexibility and Strategy in Resource Allocation. Cambridge, MA: MIT Press.

Tsui-Auch, L.S. (2004). Bureaucratic rationality and nodal agency in a developmental state – the case of state-led biotechnology development in Singapore. International Sociology, 19(4), 451–477. http://doi.org/10.1177/0268580904047367.

Turban, D., and Greening, D. (1997). Corporate social performance and organizational attractiveness to prospective employees. Academy of Management Journal, 40(3), 658–672.

Turner, J.H. (1987). Towards a sociological theory of motivation. American Sociological Review, 52, 15–27.

Tversky, A., and Kahneman, D. (1981a). The framing of decisions and the psychology of choice. Science, 211(1), 453–458.

Tversky, A., and Kahneman, D. (1981b). Prospect Theory. Econometrica, 47(2), 263–291.

US Department of Transportation (USDOT) (2009). DOT and Recovery Act. https://www.transportation.gov/recovery.

US Department of Transportation (USDOT) (2016). About the Build American Bureau. August 30. Accessed at https://cms.dot.gov/policy-initiatives/build-america/about.

US Department of the Treasury (2014). Expanding our nation's infrastructure through innovative financing. https://www.treasury.gov/resource-center/economic-policy/Documents/3_Expanding%20our%20Nation's%20Infrastructure%20through%20Innovative%20Financing.pdf.

US Department of Treasury (2015). Expanding the market for infrastructure public–private partnerships: alternative risk and profit sharing approaches to align sponsor and investor interests. Office of Economic Policy, US Department of Treasury. https://www.treasury.gov/resource-center/economic-policy/Documents/2_Treasury%20Infrastructure%20White%20Paper%20042215.pdf.

Van de Ven, A.H. (1976). On the nature, formation, and maintenance of relations among organizations. Academy of Management Review, 1(4), 24–36.

Van den Hurk, M., Brogaard, L., Lember, V., Helby Petersen, O., and Witz, P. (2016). National varieties of public–private partnerships (PPPs): a comparative analysis of PPP-supporting units in 19 European countries.

Journal of Comparative Policy Analysis: Research and Practice, 18(1), 1–20.

Vassallo, J.M. (2004). Short-term infrastructure concessions: conceptual approach and recent applications in Spain. Public Works Management and Policy, 8(4), 261–270.

Vassallo, J.M. (2006). Traffic risk mitigation in highway concession projects: the experience of Chile. Journal of Transport Economics and Policy (JTEP), 40(3), 359–381.

Vassallo, J., and Gallego, J. (2005). Risk sharing in the new public works concession law in Spain. Transportation Research Record: Journal of the Transportation Research Board, 1932, 1–8.

Vassallo, J., and Soliño, A. (2006). Minimum income guarantee in transportation infrastructure concessions in Chile. Transportation Research Record: Journal of the Transportation Research Board, 1960, 15–22.

Ventresca, M.J., and Mohr, J.W. (2005). Archival research methods. In J.A.C. Baum (ed.), The Blackwell Companion to Organizations (pp. 805–828). Malden, MA: Blackwell Publishing.

Vernon, R. (1980). The obsolescing bargain: a key factor in political risk. In Mark B. Winchester (ed.), The International Essays for Business Decision Makers (pp. 281–286). Houston: Center for International Business.

Vernon, R., and Vernon, H. (1977). Storm over the Multinationals: The Real Issues. Cambridge, MA: Harvard University Press.

Vigoda, E. (2002). From responsiveness to collaboration: governance, citizens, and the next generation of public administration. Public Administration Review, 62(5), 527–540. http://dx.doi.org/10.1111/1540-6210.00235.

Vining, A.R., Boardman, A.E., and Poschmann, F. (2005). Public–private partnerships in the US and Canada: "There are no free lunches." Journal of Comparative Policy Analysis: Research and Practice, 7(3), 199–220.

Virginia Department of Transportation (VDOT) (2017). PPTA Implementation Manual and Guidelines, Richmond, VA.

Vives, A. (1999). Pension funds in infrastructure project finance regulations and instrument design. Journal of Structured Finance, 5(2), 37–52.

Vives, A. (2008). Adapting PPP structures to local conditions. Keynote Address, 2008 Specialty Conference on Leadership and Management in Construction, October 17, South Lake Tahoe, CA.

Waddock, S. (2000). The multiple bottom lines of corporate citizenship: social investing, reputation, and responsibility audits. Business and Society Review, 105(3), 323–345.

Wang, H., Xiong, W., Wu, G., and Zhu, D. (2018). Public–private partnership in public administration discipline: a literature review. Public Management Review, 20(2), 293–316.

Wang, Y. (2015). Evolution of public–private partnership models in American toll road development: learning based on public institutions' risk management. International Journal of Project Management, 33(3), 684–696.

Wang, Y., and Liu, J. (2015). Evaluation of the excess revenue sharing ratio in PPP projects using principal–agent models. International Journal of Project Management, 33(6), 1317–1324.

Wasserman, S., and Faust, K. (1994). Social Network Analysis: Methods and Applications. New York: Cambridge University Press.

Wathne, K.H., and Heide, J.B. (2000). Opportunism in interfirm relationships: forms, outcomes, and solutions. Journal of Marketing, 64(4), 36–51.

Weber, R.P. (1990). Basic Content Analysis. Newbury Park, CA, USA and London, UK: SAGE.

Weigelt, K., and Camerer, C. (1988). Reputation and corporate strategy. Strategic Management Journal, 9, 443–454.

Wells, L.T., and Ahmed, R. (2007). Making Foreign Investment Safe. New York: Oxford University Press.

Weston, D.C., and Gibson, E. (1993). Partnering-project performance in US Army Corps of Engineers. Journal of Management in Engineering, 9(4), 410–425.

Westphal, J.D., and Zajac, E.J. (1997). Defections from the inner circle: social exchange, reciprocity, and the diffusion of board independence in US corporations. Administrative Science Quarterly, 42(1), 161–183.

Wettenhall, R. (2003). The rhetoric and reality of public–private partnerships. Public Organization Review, 3(1), 77–107.

Wettenhall, R. (2005). The public–private interface: surveying the history. In G.A. Hodge (ed.), The Challenge of Public–Private Partnerships: Learning from International Experience (pp. 22–43). Cheltenham, UK and Northampton, MA, USA: Edward Elgar Publishing.

White House (2017). Fact Sheet – 2018 Budget: Infrastructure Initiative. Washington, DC.

Wibowo, A. (2004). Valuing guarantees in a BOT infrastructure project. Engineering, Construction and Architectural Management, 11(6), 395–403.

Wibowo, A., and Kochendoerfer, B. (2010). Selecting BOT/PPP infrastructure projects for government guarantee portfolio under conditions of budget and risk in the Indonesian context. Journal of Construction Engineering and Management, 137(7), 512–522.

Wibowo, A., Permana, A., Kochendörfer, B., Kiong, R.T.L., Jacob, D., and Neunzehn, D. (2012). Modeling contingent liabilities arising from government guarantees in Indonesian BOT/PPP toll roads. Journal of Construction Engineering and Management, 138(12), 1403–1410. http://dx.doi.org/10.1061/(ASCE)CO.1943-7862.0000555.

Williamson, O.E. (1975). Markets and Hierarchies, Analysis and Antitrust Implications: A Study in the Economics of Internal Organization. New York: Free Press.

Williamson, O.E. (1979). Transaction-cost economics: the governance of contractual relations. Journal of Law and Economics, 22(2), 233–261.

Williamson, O.E. (1981). The economics of organization: the transaction cost approach. American Journal of Sociology, 87(3), 548–577.

Williamson, O.E. (1985). The Economic Institutions of Capitalism: Firms, Markets and Relational Contracting. New York: Free Press.

Williamson, O.E. (1996). The Mechanisms of Governance. New York: Oxford University Press.

Williamson, O.E. (1999). Public and private bureaus: a transaction cost perspective. Journal of Law, Economics and Organization, 15(1), 306–342.

Wilson, J.Q. (1989). Bureaucracy: What Government Agencies Do and Why They Do It. New York: Basic Books.

Wilson, R.A., Songer, A.D., and Diekmann, J. (1995). Partnering: more than a workshop, a catalyst for change. Journal of Management in Engineering, 11(5), 40–45.

Wolfe, R.A., and Putler, D.S. (2002). How tight are the ties that bind stakeholder groups? Organization Science, 13(1), 64–80.

Woodhouse, E.J. (2006). The obsolescing bargain redux? Foreign investment in the electric power sector in developing countries. New York University Journal of International Law and Politics, 38, 121–219.

World Bank (2014). Public–private partnerships reference guide 2.0. World Bank. https://ppp.worldbank.org/public-private-partnership/library/public-private-partnerships-reference-guide-version-20.

World Bank and DFID (2009). Good Governance In Public–Private Partnerships: A Resource Guide for Practitioners. Washington, DC, USA and London, UK: World Bank and Department for International Development of the United Kingdom (DFID).

World Economic Forum (2016). Innovations in Long-Term Capital Management: The Practitioner's Perspective. World Economic Forum White Paper. http://www3.weforum.org/docs/WEF_GAC_Future_of_Investing_Executive_Summary.pdf.

Xu, Y., Yeung, J.F., and Jiang, S. (2014). Determining appropriate government guarantees for concession contract: lessons learned from 10 PPP projects in China. International Journal of Strategic Property Management, 18(4), 356–367.

Yang, Y., Hou, Y., and Wang, Y. (2013). On the development of public–private partnerships in transitional economies: an explanatory framework. Public Administration Review, 73(2), 301–310.

Yescombe, E.R. (2011). Public–Private Partnerships: Principles of Policy and Finance. Boston, MA and New York, USA; Oxford and London, UK: Butterworth-Heinemann.

Yescombe, E.R. (2014). Principles of Project Finance, 2nd edn. Boston, MA and New York, USA; Oxford and London, UK: Academic Press, Elsevier.

Yin, R.K. (2013). Case Study Research: Design and Methods. SAGE Publications. Accessed at http://search.ebscohost.com/login.aspx?direct =trueanddb=cin20andAN=2001030774andsite=ehost-live.

Zaheer, A., and Venkatraman, N. (1995). Relational governance as an interorganizational strategy: an empirical test of the role of trust in economic exchange. Strategic Management Journal, 16(5), 373–392.

Zhang, X. (2005). Critical success factors for public–private partnerships in infrastructure development. Journal of Construction Engineering and Management, 131(1), 3–14.

Zheng, J., Roehrich, J.K., and Lewis, M.A. (2008). The dynamics of contractual and relational governance: evidence from long-term public–private procurement arrangements. Journal of Purchasing and Supply Management, 14(1), 43–54.

Zsidisin, G.A., Panelli, A., and Upton, R. (2000). Purchasing organization involvement in risk assessments, contingency plans, and risk management: an exploratory study. Supply Chain Management, 5(4), 187–198.

Index

AASHTO *see* American Association for State Highway and Transportation Officials (AASHTO)
Abu Dhabi Investment Authority 252
accountability 10, 191, 195, 201, 222, 239, 274, 279
AIAI *see* Association for the Improvement of American Infrastructure (AIAI)
Alberta Infrastructure 233
amateur-like organizations 155
American Association for State Highway and Transportation Officials (AASHTO) 221
American Recovery and Reinvestment Act (2009) 205
American Road and Transportation Builders Association (ARTBA) 221, 238
anchor-tenant concept 37, 52, 54, 57, 58
AP *see* availability payments (AP)
Argentina 73
Ashuri, B. 175
asset recycling 116–17, 207, 244, 248–9, 253–5, 262–3
  cash flows and 253
  creating value 252
  as financing mechanism 251
  infrastructure 248–51
  InNSW *see* Infrastructure New South Wales (InNSW)
  privatizations and 256
  profit from lease of assets 251–2
  reinvestments and 254
Asset Recycling Program 116–7, 248–9, 255, 256
  reinvestments 254
asset sale 144, 209, 255
Association for the Improvement of American Infrastructure (AIAI) 221
Athias, L. 125, 137
Australia 31, 105, 107, 109, 110, 116
  EastLink PPP 215
  government agencies 114
  Infrastructure New South Wales in 243
  pension funds 118
  PPP model 118–19
  SPV concession agreements 114
Australian PPP governance
  government agency and SPV 113–17
  internal governance issues 117–18
  national infrastructure needs, prioritization of 110
  PPP *vs.* traditional delivery approaches 111–13
  state-level governance issues 110–11
availability payments (AP) 22, 34, 111, 113, 141, 171, 172, 175, 210, 233, 251, 257
Ayres, I. 124

Babbar, S. 176
Baker, G. 70
BaR–BC comparative framework 178–80
BATIC *see* Build America Transportation Investment Center (BATIC)
Better Utilizing Investments to Leverage Development (BUILD) Transportation Discretionary Grants program 205
Borcherding, J.D. 78
Borgatti, S.P. 91
borrowing capacity (BC) 141, 177, 179, 182
Brandão, L.E. 175, 176

Brealey, R. 12
Brown (Governor of California) 32
budget resiliency 113
Build America Bureau 198, 199, 206, 225, 238, 241
Build America Transportation Investment Center (BATIC) 198, 220, 221, 225
Burgess, J.W. 9
Business Improvement District 276–9

Caisse de Depot et Placement du Quebec (CDPQ) 165, 168, 252
California Department of Transportation 31, 44
California I-Bank 32
California
  PPP 27, 31–4
  SR91X see SR91X
  SR125 33
California Private Transportation Company (CPTC) 44, 53, 58
California State Route 91 Express Lanes see SR91X
California Transportation Commission 32
Caltrans (California Department of Transportation) 31, 32, 44–6, 52–4, 58
Campbell, D.J. 3
Canada
  pension funds 117, 252
  public–private partnerships units in 232–3
Capital Beltway Express 210, 217
capital cost sharing 268–9, 274
Carbonara, N. 175
Carpintero, S. 175
cash flows 12, 140, 142, 146, 147, 177, 246, 252
  asset recycling and 253
  net present value of 251
cash flows available for debt service (CFADS) 177
CDPQ see Caisse de Depot et Placement du Quebec (CDPQ)
Center for Innovative Finance Support 206, 215
CFADS see cash flows available for debt service (CFADS)

Chan, H.F. 71
Channel Tunnel project 68, 115
Cheah, C.Y. 175
Chiara, N. 175
Chibber, V. 260, 262
Chou, S.P. 175
Chung, D. 125
civic crowdfunding 270, 274, 275
civic sector 17, 36, 37, 40, 58
  stakeholders 39, 57, 59
Clark, G.L. 70, 145, 155
Clegg, S. 65
Coase, R.H. 8, 122, 123
cognitive frames 76–8
cognitive governance 65, 71, 72, 78–9, 81–6
cognitive institutions see cognitive governance
co-investment arrangement 151
co-investment platforms 164
co-investments 149, 152
collaborative governance, institutional and organizational challenges in 190–92
collaborative model infrastructure investment vehicles 164
collective norms 64, 74, 76, 77, 79, 81, 82, 84
community investment 280–81
  financial contributions 274, 279
  as partnership tool 268–71
    capital cost sharing 268–9, 274
    civic crowdfunding 270, 274
    equity crowdfunding 271, 274
    municipal bonds 269–70, 274
  propositions for
    bike lane projects 276–7
    elaborating 278–80
    exploring 275–7
    project owner 272–4, 276–80
    project sponsors 272–5, 277–9
  see also crowdfunding
compensation event mechanism 132
concession agreement 30–31, 33, 114
  infrastructure PPPs 42
conflict-of-interest problem 68
ConnectEast 215
construction costs 45, 69, 163, 166, 253
construction risk 22, 33, 68, 243
contentious interdependence 4, 8

contract analysis approach 127
contract design 121, 137
contracting costs 228
contract management process 125
contractors 21, 28, 33, 53, 66–8, 84, 85, 103, 108, 117, 189
  design–construct 114, 115
  short-term 161
contract theory 161
contractual disputes 69
contractual hazards 66, 71, 72, 80, 85
  of displaced agency 60, 79, 83, 86
contractually guaranteed maintenance 25
conventional design–bid–build approach 113
counterparties 60–64, 66, 67, 69–72, 74, 76, 79–85, 262
  mutual economic dependence 81
  shared identity 72
creditors 28
Crocker, K.J. 124
crowdfinancing *see* equity crowdfunding
crowdfunding 244–5, 265, 280, 281
  campaigns 270, 276–9
  civic 270, 274, 275
  equity 271, 274
  infrastructure delivery and 266, 267
  legitimate partnership tool 268
crowdsourcing 244
crowd technologies 267
Cui, Q. 175
cultural-cognitive institutions 65, 83
cultural norms 73

data collection and analysis, SR91X case 46
DB *see* design–build (DB)
DBB *see* design–bid–build (DBB)
DBFOM *see* design–build–finance–operate–maintain (DBFOM)
debt service coverage ratio (DSCR) 173, 177
debt-to-gross domestic product (GDP) ratio 247
decision-making process 74, 85, 159, 162, 168, 191, 272
defined benefit (DB) plans 146, 166
defined contribution (DC) plans 146

demand risk 213–14, 219, 243–4, 253, 257, 263
de Rus, G. 174, 175
design–bid–build (DBB) 21, 67, 111–13, 119, 209, 228, 231, 243
  public procurement approach 25
design–build (DB) 22, 28, 111–13, 209, 243
  construction contractor 67
  contracts 67, 192
  delivery approach 113
  projects 198
design–build–finance–operate–maintain (DBFOM) 22, 102, 165, 173, 198, 210, 243
  agreements 174, 192
  model 165
design–build–finance (DBF) 58, 209
design–build–operate–maintain (DBOM) 22
design–construction contractors 114, 115
design/construction phase 36, 38, 53
De Tocqueville, A. 9
developer ratio adjustment mechanism (DRAM) 173, 219
direct infrastructure investors 160
direct investments 149, 151, 152, 158, 159
displaced agency 17, 62–4, 66, 67, 71, 79, 81, 85
  contractual hazard of 60, 79, 83, 86
  costs 80, 85
  and relational contracting 80–81, 85
dominant institutional logics 38, 41–3, 57–8
Downs, A. 10
due diligence process 117, 158, 166
Duncan, B. 274

earnings before interest, tax, depreciation and amortization (EBITDA) 252
EastLink PPP 210, 215
economic exchange 91, 92
economic governance 63–4
economic theories, PPP units and 228–9
economic theorists 144
egocentric distortion 101

Elizabeth River Tunnels project 220
Emerson, R.M. 96
Engel, E. 172, 174, 175
engineering project organization (EPO) 188
engineering systems 88–9
engineer, procure and construct (EPC) contractor 67
Engineers Without Borders 269
EPO *see* engineering project organization (EPO)
equity crowdfunding 271, 274
equity financing 231, 274
equity investors 28, 29, 115, 117, 118, 152
equity stakes 29, 31, 68, 115
Eriksson, Kent 120
European PPP Expertise Centre 227
Evans, P. 262
ex ante
　contingent situations 122
　drafting costs 123, 125
　effort 127
　governance mechanisms 64, 79
　transaction costs 127, 137
　treatment *vs. ex post* resolution 122, 126, 133–6, 138
excess revenue sharing (ERS) 173, 175, 180, 181
exchange patterns 93
exchange relationships 96
exchange strategies 101
ex post
　governance mechanisms 79
　transaction costs 137
external stakeholders 3, 6, 78, 259, 267, 270, 271, 273

FASTLANE grant program 225
Federal Acquisitions Reform Act (1996) 266
federal credit enhancement 199
Federal Highway Administration (FHWA) 206, 208, 209, 215, 220, 221
Fehr, D. 274
Feng, W. 96, 98, 101
Feng, Z. 175
FHWA *see* Federal Highway Administration (FHWA)

50-plus-two jurisdictional problem 231, 233
finance theory 12–13
financial incentives 63, 64
financial return on investment (ROI) 274
financier state model 261–2
financing
　alternative sources of 25
　of infrastructure projects 5–6
fiscal support assessment framework 178
fiscal support mechanisms, framework to assess 170
　ability to raise financing 177
　BaR–BC comparative framework 178–80
　conception 176
　government financial risk exposure 177–8
　governmental support mechanisms 171–6
　illustration 180–82
Fisher, G. 176
Fixing America's Surface Transportation Act of 2015 198, 238
flexible contract 125
flexible-term contract 172, 175, 180
Floricel, S. 5
Folger, R. 82
formal contracting 83
formal institutional logics 37
formal relationships 50
　in stakeholders networks 54–6
formal sub-network change 54
Foster, P.C. 91
Foxx, Anthony 225
Freeman, R.E. 39, 99
Friedman, M. 11, 12, 143
Frooman, J. 94
Froud, J. 212
FundRise.com 271
funds
　Infrastructure New South Wales 256
　large 159–60
　medium–large 157–9
　Partnerships USA 239
　pension *see* pension funds

PPP Canada Fund 232
private 23
regional US PPP units 238
Restart NSW *see* Restart NSW fund
small–medium 155–7
sovereign 3, 147
spending 26

Gallego, J. 214
game theory 63–4
Gasparro, Kate 244
Geertz 272
General Services Administration 31
Gertner, R. 124
GFC *see* global financial crisis (GFC)
Gibson, E. 75
Global Alternatives Survey 152
global financial crisis (GFC) 246, 247
global issue space 94
golden handshake, examples of 165–7
governance 202
    challenges 3–7
        economic factors 7
        financing of infrastructure projects 5–6
        pension funds 154–5
        infrastructure PPP investors 154–5
        institutional and organizational 190–92
        project complexity 3–4
        technical uncertainty 4–5
        United States, institutional maturity assessment 196–201
    choice variable 71
    cognitive 65, 71, 72, 78–9, 81–6
    collaborative 190–96
    economic and legal 63–4
    equity PPP investors 161–4
    infrastructure PPP 35, 38–9, 43, 104–10, 202–4, 226
    integrated theory 78–83
    issues
        in government agency and SPV 113–17
        institutional investors 117–118
        pension fund 141
        SPV design and construction agreement 117
        state-level 110–11
    network 69–71

normative 65, 71, 72, 78–9, 81–6
"people" 156, 160
regulative 65–7, 70–71, 78–80, 82–6
sociological and psychological 64–5
trilateral 69
unified 66–9, 84, 85
government agencies 6, 31, 108, 191, 234, 260, 261, 266
    governance issues in 113–17
governmental fiscal support 171
government budget at risk indicator 182
government financial risk exposure 177–8
government infrastructure agencies 113
Granovetter, M. 91
Great Depression 145
greenfield infrastructure funding gap 246–8

Harback, H.F. 75
Hart, O. 122, 124
Hastings 252
Hayek, Frederick 143
Hensher, D. 125
highway projects 4
Hishigsuren, G. 274
homo economicus 143, 168
homogeneous utility 101
Ho, S.P. 123
Huang, Y.L. 175
hub-and-spoke (H&S) model 90, 99
Hult, K.M. 10
Husted, B.W. 82
Hwang, R. 73

I-4 Ultimate project 210
I-77 HOT Lanes project 173, 219
identification phase 36–8, 41, 48, 52, 54
implicit flexibility 137
incomplete contracts 109, 124–5
Indiana Toll Road 170, 207, 210–11
indirect investment method 150
informal institutional logics 37–8
informal institutional relationships 50
    in stakeholder networks 54–6
informal network change 54
infrastructure 104–6
    advisory agencies 111
    agencies 109

asset recycling 248
  in New South Wales 249–51
  reinvesting 249
  selling or leasing existing assets 248–9
assets 116, 243, 244, 252, 266
  privatization of 246–7
defined 1
delivery 265
  in Australia 118–19
  capital cost sharing for 268–9, 274
  civic crowdfunding 270, 274
  community investment *see* community investment
  community member's role in 267
  crowdfunding 265
  equity crowdfunding 271, 274
  history of partnerships in 266–8
  implications 280–81
  innovative partnership strategies 268
  local governments and 266, 267–8, 280
  municipal bonds for 269–70, 274
  private sector partners in 265
  public participation processes 267
  stakeholders 266–7, 270, 271–3, 275
development 21, 108, 114
finance 115
gap 247
investment 28–9, 107, 147, 205, 207, 225, 229, 230, 234, 240, 242
  team 159
  units 29
  vehicles 144, 147–9, 152–4, 164, 168
maintenance 25
need for 2–3
needs, prioritization of national 110
PPPs *see* infrastructure PPPs
privatization 244
procurement policy 26–7
project 113, 118
proposals 111
public financing of 112
service 106
see also Infrastructure New South Wales (InNSW)
Infrastructure America 221, 222

infrastructure asset recycling 248–51
Infrastructure Australia 110, 112, 187, 221
Infrastructure Initiative 206, 220, 222
Infrastructure New South Wales (InNSW) 116, 243, 248
  as agent of change 254–5
  collaboration
    as co-creation of knowledge 258–9
    with different actors 261
  communication to build trust 259–60
  employees to innovate and change government 257–8
  ideation stage 257–9
  integration stage 258, 259–60
  "financier state" model 261–2
  funding processes 256
  goals of 260
  infrastructure development 255, 256
  integrated long-term planning 255–6
  mission of 254–5
  private consortia and 256–7
  Projects NSW 256
  State Premier 254
  website 257, 264
Infrastructure Ontario 30, 233
infrastructure PPPs
  concession agreement 42
  development phases 36–8, 41–3, 48–51, 56–7
    change over 54–6
  governance 35, 38–9, 43
  and institutional theory 40–41
  life cycles 35, 37, 38, 43, 52–4, 57
  social network analysis *see* social network analysis (SNA)
  SR91X *see* SR91X
  stakeholders networks 40–41, 48–9, 54–7
  stakeholder theory and 39–40
Infrastructure Quebec 233
initial public offerings (IPOs) 114, 144
Innovative Finance Bureau 238, 241
InNSW *see* Infrastructure New South Wales (InNSW)
institutional capacity 196, 199, 203, 221
institutional infrastructure investment 149, 150

institutional investors, role of
  accessing infrastructure 147–51
  characteristics of 143
  data on infrastructure PPP equity
    152–60
  financial intermediaries 142
  golden handshake, examples of
    165–7
  private investment in infrastructure
    143–5
  re-intermediation, collaboration and
    insourcing 161–4
  rise of pensions and their suitability
    145–7
institutional logics 37–8, 57, 58
  dominant 41–3
institutional maturity 188, 202
  assessment 196–201
institutional reform in US PPP market
  203–4
institutional risks 7
institutional theory 40–41, 43, 62, 64–5
  see also governance
integrated project delivery (IPD) 84
integrated theory, governance 78–83
interdependence 4
interdisciplinary governance 86
internal governance issues 117–18
internal stakeholders 6, 272–4
Interstate Highway System 26
investment arms 28–9, 114–16
investment banking industry 151
investment consultants 140, 150, 154,
  156, 158
investment vehicles 144, 147–9, 152–4,
  164, 168
investor–manager contracts 163
IPOs *see* initial public offerings (IPOs)
Irwin, T. 176
Isham 269
issue-based stakeholder value network
  (SVN)
  connections between stakeholders
    and issues 93–4
  insights from 97–8
  integration of issues and 94–5
  motivations of proposal 94–5
  network density of 96
  normative power 98
  Project Phoenix 97–8
  reduced complexity 98
  relative density 95
  simpler analysis 98
  three propositions for 95–6
issue-focused stakeholder management
  94
issue network 94
Iyer, K.C. 175

JOBS Act of 2012 268, 271
Jooste, S.F. 186
Jun, J. 175

Kahkonen 269
Kettl, D.F. 192
Keynesian model 143, 144
Keynes, John Maynard 143
key performance indicators (KPIs)
  214–15, 220, 234
Kochendoerfer, B. 175
KPIs *see* key performance indicators
  (KPIs)
Kuwait Investment Authority 252

laissez-faire economics 143
large engineering projects (LEPs) 87–9
  engineering systems 88–9
  issue-based SVN *see* issue-based
    stakeholder value network
    (SVN)
  organizational sociology 89
  shaping of 88
  strategic management 89
  SVN *see* stakeholder value network
    (SVN)
large pension funds 159–60
Laumann, E.O. 93
least present value of net revenue
  (LPVNR) 175
legal governance 63–4
legal sanction 64
legitimacy 11, 191
LEPs *see* large engineering projects
  (LEPs)
Lessard, D.R. 88
Levitt, R. 4, 8, 80
liberal market economies 80
life cycle sustainability 25
limited partner–general partner
  (LP–GP) contract 163

Liu, J. 175
Liu, T. 180, 182
loan life coverage ratio (LLCR) 177
local knowledge exchange 272–3
Long Beach Courthouse 27
long-term risks 68
Lucea, R. 91, 94

Mahon, J.F. 91, 94
Malecki, E.J. 272
"Managers' Mental Model" 97
managers, social skills 76
Manila Water 73
March, J.G. 9
market-driven PPP proposals 110
market economies 1, 3, 80
market risk 213–14
Markowitz, H. 12
Masten, S.E. 124
McKell Institute 252
MEDC *see* Michigan Economic Development Corporation (MEDC)
medium to large funds 157–9
meso-level networks 100
Michigan Economic Development Corporation (MEDC) 270
Michigan Infrastructure Council 221
Miller, J.B. 209
Miller, M.H. 12
Miller, R. 1, 88
mini bond campaigns 270
minimum revenue guarantee (MRG) 171, 173, 175, 176, 179–82
misconceptions about PPPs 25–6
Mission Toll Road 27
Modigliani, F. 12
Monte Carlo simulations 112
motivation 78
MRG *see* minimum revenue guarantee (MRG)
multi-attribute utility theory (MAUT) 101
municipal bonds 269–70, 274
mutual economic dependence 81
myths about PPPs 23–30

National Conference of State Legislatures 234

National Environmental Policy Act (NEPA) of 1969 266, 267
National Governors Association 234
National Highway System 266
national infrastructure needs, prioritization of 110
National PPP Policy and Guidelines 221
National PPP Working Group 221
National Surface Transportation 238, 241
National US PPP unit 238–40, 242
natural monopolies 20–21
negative net present values (NPVs) 176
Neighborland.com 267
neoliberalism 144
NEPA *see* National Environmental Policy Act (NEPA) of 1969
network
  analysis 93–4
  density 96
network governance 69–71
  by reputational capital 70–71
  by shared ownership 69–70
New Building Canada Fund 232
new economic sociology (NES) 91
New South Wales (NSW) 116, 214, 220–21, 246, 261, 262
  asset recycling mechanism 250
  infrastructure agency in 244
  infrastructure asset recycling in 248–51
  see also Infrastructure New South Wales (InNSW)
Nombela, G. 174, 175
non-cooperation 82
normalization 220–21
normative governance 65, 71, 72, 78–9, 81–6
normative institutions *see* normative governance
normative justification 99–100
normative power 97, 98
Nowacki, Caroline 243
NSW *see* New South Wales (NSW)

obsolescing bargain 68
OCTA 53
Office of Innovative Program Delivery 206, 215, 220

OM phase *see* operate/maintain (OM) phase
one-off organizations 185
operate/maintain (OM) phase 37–8, 41, 53, 54, 58
opportunism 8–9
opportunistic behavior 74, 77, 82
opportunistic incentives 229
Organisation for Economic Co-operation and Development PPP unit 226
organizational coherence 155
organizational complexity 8
organizational sociology 89
organization of infrastructure PPP 35
organization theory and design 7–8
Ó Riain, S. 262, 263

PABs *see* private activity bonds (PABs)
Padgett, J.F. 37
partnering 75–6, 165, 168
partnership agreement 75, 226
Partnerships British Columbia 233, 234, 236
Partnerships New Brunswick 233
Partnerships UK 185
Partnerships USA 238–40
 advisory role 239–40
 funding 239
 organizational structure 238–9
pathfinder projects 197
Patronicity.com 270
pay-offs 71, 81–5
PDAs *see* predevelopment agreements (PDAs)
Pennsylvania Rapid Bridge Replacement PPP 240–41
pension fund investments 33, 70, 146
pension funds 3, 29, 116, 145–7, 150, 165–7
 analysis of 152–4
 Australian aggregators of 118
 Canadian 117, 252
 clients, distribution of 154
 governance challenges of 154–5
 governance issues 141
 industry 145
 investments 70
 investor 150–51
 large funds 159–160
 United States 117
performance measures 214–15, 220
PFI *see* Private Finance Initiative (PFI)
Philippines 73
Plenary Walsh Keystone Partners (PWKP) 241
Poole, Robert Jr. 45
Popularise.com 267
Portugal, VfM methods 212
Powell, W.W. 37
power balance 97, 99
power-dependency theory 96
power of stakeholders 89, 93, 96
PPB *see* provisional preferred bidder (PPB)
PPP Canada 232–3
 Fund 232
PPP development road map 43
PPPs *see* public–private partnerships (PPPs)
predevelopment agreements (PDAs) 217
Preqin 149
 database 152
Presidio Parkway project 27, 30, 31, 34, 215
private activity bonds (PABs) 24, 199, 225, 239
private actors 108, 109, 118–9, 144, 191, 195, 203
private domain 36
Private Finance Initiative (PFI) 192, 211–3
private financing 112
 benefit 25–6
 cost 34
 public and 23–4
private funds 23, 206
private investment 33, 143–5, 197, 224, 225, 233, 241, 246, 257, 262, 270
private sector
 actors 261
 companies 108
 financing 231, 234, 267
 participation 38, 45, 107, 220, 222, 224–6, 233, 236, 241
 partners 265–7
 PPPs as 27–30
 profit 30

project sponsor as 271, 273, 278–9
revenue risk or share 172
role 20, 28
stakeholders 39, 57
privatizations 27–30, 142, 144, 168, 209, 249, 256, 261
   capital from 255
   infrastructure 244, 246–7
   programs 246
Probitas Partners 152
probity auditors 29, 116
procurement 138, 171, 197
   competitive 217
   phase 49, 52–3, 58
   processes 213, 217–19
   regulations 212–13
project analysis and selection 211–12
project identification 211
   and analysis 215
project life cycles 60, 61, 67, 114, 138, 188, 192, 194, 202
project partnership model 75
Project Phoenix (PP), issues 97–8
Projects New South Wales (Projects NSW) 256
property rights theory 124
provisional preferred bidder (PPB) 213
PSC *see* Public Sector Comparator (PSC)
psychological governance 64–5, 79
P3-SCREEN analytical tool 215, 221
P3-VALUE analytical tool 215, 221
Public Activity Bonds (PABS) 24, 199, 225, 239
public administration 9–11, 106
public choice models 107
public infrastructure 30, 45, 112
   assets 194
   delivery 30, 32, 108
   financing 31–2
   private funds for 23
   projects 185
   risk in developing 29
public organizations 13, 38, 68, 122, 186, 190–91
public–private hybrids 20–21
public–private partnerships (PPPs) 205, 216, 224
   characteristics of 22, 218–19
   highway (1993–2017) 218–19

concession agreement 30, 31, 33
defining 208–11
from design–bid–build to custom-designed 21
educational programs 221
enabling legislation 216
governance challenges in projects 3–7
infrastructure *see* infrastructure PPPs
Infrastructure Oversight Commission 216
life cycles 35, 37, 38, 43, 52–4, 57
myths and misconceptions
   benefit of PPP 25–6
   infrastructure procurement policy 26–7
   private funds for public infrastructure 23
   private sector's profit and public sector's expense 30
   privatizations 27–30
   public and private financing 23–4
   tolls 26, 30
participating in 231
prior research on 105–9
project/service delivery systems 209–10
selecting and implementing, recommendations for 30–34
for social infrastructure 31
transaction 68
in United States 224–5
units
   benefits of 229–32, 240–41
   in Canada 232–3
   contracting costs 228
   definition 226–7
   economic theories and 228
   50-plus-two jurisdictional problem 231
   functional area 227–8
   infrastructure investment 225, 229
   interactions with private partners 230
   laws 231–2
   national US 238–40, 242
   policy support and related activities 227

program and project delivery support 227–8
project approval and quality control 228
as quasi-independent entities 240
reducing project risk 230
regional US 233–240
two-tiered system of 241, 242
see also Partnerships USA
Public Sector Comparator (PSC) 211, 212, 228
public sectors 28, 68, 104
agencies 171
California 32
entities 190
expense 30
institutions 202
stakeholders 39, 59
public sponsor 41–2, 52–4, 57, 58
Pula, K. 216
PWKP *see* Plenary Walsh Keystone Partners (PWKP)

Qualified Public Infrastructure Bonds (QPIBs) 225
Queensland Investment Corporation (QIC) 166–8
Queensland Motorways (QML) 166–7

Rail Alliance 234
Railroad Rehabilitation and Improvement Financing (RRIF) 199, 225, 239
Rainey, H.G. 10
rational cooperation 83
Rauch, J.E. 262
Reagan, Ronald 27
reciprocal interdependence 4, 8
regional US PPP units 233–9
benefits of 240
functional categories 236
funding 238
infrastructure challenges 234
mega-regions 234, 235, 237
organizational structure 236
structuring 233–4
West Coast Infrastructure Exchange 234, 236, 241
regulative governance 65–7, 70–71, 78–80, 82–6

regulative institutions *see* regulative governance
regulatory frameworks 215–17
regulatory risk 243
re-intermediation 162, 163, 168
relational contracting 9, 60, 68, 79
cognitive frames 76–8
costs and competences 80, 81
displaced agency costs 80–81, 85
efficacy 62–3
game theory 63–4
governance
cognitive 65, 71, 72, 78–9, 81–6
economic and legal 63–4
integrated theory 78–83
network 69–71
normative 65, 71, 72, 78–9, 81–6
regulative 65–7, 70–71, 78–80, 82–6
sociological and psychological 64–5
trilateral 69
unified 66–9, 84, 85
norms 162–3
partnering 75–6
procedural justice, power of 73–4
social exchange in pre-existing communities 72–3
transaction cost economics 63–4
relational infrastructure contracts 163
relational instability 80
relationships
exchange 96
formal and informal 50, 54–6
stakeholders 90–91
representativeness 10, 191
reputational capital 63, 67, 70–72
request for information (RFI) process 158
request for proposal (RFP) 36, 42, 158
Restart NSW fund 116, 252–3, 255, 261, 263
capital for 249–50
for community projects 253
for infrastructure projects 250
for regional projects 251
Resources for the Regions program 250
revenue bonds 21, 24
Reynolds, K.J. 124

RFP *see* request for proposal (RFP)
Ricardo, David 143
Ring, P.S. 82
risk allocation 121, 138, 220, 222
risk management 125, 177, 192, 224, 230, 241, 242
risk-sharing mechanisms 127, 138
  classification of 136
  frequency of 136, 137
  and usage 127–32
risk transfer 24–6, 112, 212, 227, 231
  revenue 141, 171
Rocha Armada, M.J. 175
Roloff, J. 91, 94
RRIF *see* Railroad Rehabilitation and Improvement Financing (RRIF)

Sagheer, M. 175
SaskBuilds 233
Saussier, S. 125, 137
Savas, E.S. 209
Schwarzenegger administration (2003–2011) 27
Scott, W.R. 17, 64–6, 184, 186
Securities and Exchange Commission 271
Shan, L. 175
shared identity 72, 76, 77, 82–4
Sharma, D. 175
"shovel-ready" projects 205
Simon, H.A. 10
Smith, Adam 143
social capital 73, 162, 168
social embeddedness 91
social exchange theory (SET) 89, 91–3
social network analysis (SNA) 17, 56, 91, 94
  development phases of PPPs 48–51
  informal and formal sub-network changes over 54
  total network change over 52–4
  SR91X case 48–51
social network theory 162
social norms 74, 76, 203, 231
social sanctions 65, 72–3, 80
  leveraging of 74
social skills 76
sociological perspectives on governance 64–5, 79
Solstice.com 271

sovereign wealth funds (SWFs) 33, 114, 140, 142, 147, 149, 168
Spain
  key performance indicators 215
  open competition model 213
  VfM methods 212
Spark Infrastructure 252
special purpose vehicles (SPVs) 5, 22, 28, 29, 44, 53–4, 58, 68, 105, 108–10, 118–19, 184
  design and construction agreement 117
  government agency and 113–17
  organization of 108
SPVs *see* special purpose vehicles (SPVs)
SR91X 43, 44, 58
  background 45–6
  data collection and analysis 46
  social network analysis 48–51
stakeholder-based SVN model 90, 95, 97
stakeholder involvement 39, 41, 42, 57, 75, 185
stakeholders 6, 36–8
  approaches 11–12
  dependency 96
  institutional logics 37
  issues and large engineering projects 87–9
  networks 40–41, 48–9, 57, 266–7
    formal relationships 54–6
    informal institutional relationships 54–6
  power of 89, 93, 96
  relationships 90–91
  second-order coding 48, 56
  theory 39–40, 43
  see also infrastructure PPPs
stakeholder value network (SVN)
  concepts and definitions 90
  issue-based *see* issue-based stakeholder value network (SVN)
  key assumptions for 92–3
  limitations of 99–101
  normative justification 99–100
  relationships mapping 90–91
  strategy implementation 101
  theoretical development of 91–2

Index

state-level governance issues 110–11
static characteristics 100
strategic implications 87, 89, 91, 93, 95, 97, 98
strategic management 39, 89, 93
strategy implementation 101
structured rationality 10, 191
Sun, Y. 175
sustainability 25, 269
SVN *see* stakeholder value network (SVN)
SWFs *see* sovereign wealth funds (SWFs)

tax-exempt bonds 5, 23–4
Taylor, J.E. 80
TCEs *see* transaction cost economics (TCEs)
Tennessee Valley Authority 266
Thompson, J.D. 4, 7
TIFIA *see* Transportation Infrastructure Financing and Innovation Act (TIFIA)
traditional indirect fund model 162
traditional infrastructure procurement 111–13, 189, 195
transaction cost 77
transaction cost economics (TCEs) 8–9, 60–61, 63–4, 66, 69, 77, 122–4
TransGrid 249, 252
Transmanche Link (TML) 68–9
Transportation Infrastructure Financing and Innovation Act (TIFIA) 24, 173, 199, 205–6, 219, 225, 239
Transportation Investment Generating Economic Recovery (TIGER) Discretionary Grants program 205
transportation public–private partnership market 205
  background 207–8
  Infrastructure Initiative 206, 220, 222
  international practice 211
    demand or market risk 213–14
    performance measures 214–15
    procurement processes 213
    procurement regulations 212–13
    project analysis and selection 211–12
    project identification 211
    project/service delivery systems 209–10
  public–private partnerships, defining 208–11
  recommendations for 220
    normalization 220–21
    training 221–2
  US state of practice
    demand risk 219
    performance measures 220
    procurement processes 217–19
    project identification and analysis 215
    regulatory frameworks 215–17
Transurban 111
Trump infrastructure plan 206, 220
Tsui-Auch, L.S. 262

unbalanced funding model 197
unified governance 66–9, 84, 85
United Kingdom 31, 75, 102
  Private Finance Initiative (PFI) strategy 211, 213
United States
  governance challenges in 196–201
  pension funds 117
  public–private partnerships 224–5, 231, 241
  recommendations for PPP market
    normalization 220–21
    training 221–2
  state of practice
    demand risk 219
    performance measures 220
    procurement processes 217–19
    project identification and analysis 215
    regulatory frameworks 215–17
  traditional infrastructure delivery in 231
urban infrastructures 145
  networks 144
  property rights of 144
Urwin, R. 155
US Department of Transportation (USDOT) 225, 238, 241
US highway PPP projects 126

contract analysis approach 127
ex ante treatment vs. ex post resolution 122, 133–6
incomplete contracts 124–5
risks and contracts 121
risk sharing mechanisms and usage 127–32
transaction cost economics 122–4
US PPP market, institutional reform in 203–4
US Transportation Infrastructure Finance and Innovation Act (TIFIA) 24, 173, 199, 205–6, 219, 225, 239
value at risk (VaR) 177, 178, 180
value cycle 90, 92, 93, 96, 101
value exchange 90–93, 97, 100
relationships 96
value flow 90, 92, 97, 101
value for funding (VfF) 113
value-for-money (VfM) 194, 227
analysis 30–31, 112, 118, 211–12, 215, 228, 239
value path 90, 92
Van de Ven, A.H. 82, 91
Vassallo, J.M. 173, 175, 214

VfM see value-for-money (VfM)
Vives, A. 70, 208–9

Walcott, C.E. 10
Walk the Line Policy 73
Walsh Infrastructure Management 241
Wang, Y. 175
Water Infrastructure Council 221
WCX see West Coast Infrastructure Exchange (WCX)
weighted average cost of capital (WACC) 177
West Coast Infrastructure Exchange (WCX) 234, 236, 241
Western High Speed Rail Alliance 234
Weston, D.C. 75
Wibowo, A. 175, 176
Williamson, O.E. 8, 9, 17, 66, 123, 229
Wilson, J.Q. 10
World Bank 226

Yescombe, E.R. 209
Yin, R.K. 275

Zhang, L. 175